A

# TREATISE

ON THE

# LAW OF HIGHWAYS,

BY

JOSEPH K. ANGELL, AND THOMAS DURFEE.

BOSTON:
LITTLE, BROWN AND COMPANY.
1857.

RIVERSIDE, CAMBRIDGE:
PRINTED BY H. O. HOUGHTON AND COMPANY.

# PREFACE.

I owe it to the Public to state by what chance it happened that the completion of the following work, commenced and partly written by one of the most celebrated of American law-writers, fell into the hands of one so unknown to the Profession as myself. For some time previous to the decease of the late Joseph K. Angell, this book had been advertised as in preparation; but the more pressing demand for new editions of his former works continually retarded its appearance. In order that its publication might not be unreasonably delayed, he procured my assistance; and, at the time of his death, had already obtained from me the chapter entitled "Highways by Prescription and Dedication," and the chapter entitled "Nuisances and their Remedies." He had also frequently conversed with me about the plan of the work, and, with the frankness and the candor which formed so amiable a trait of his character, had, I am inclined to believe, fully acquainted me with his ideas upon the subject in so far as they had then become matured. When, therefore, by his sudden and lamented death, it became necessary to find some one to carry forward to its completion the work which he had begun, a knowledge of these facts led, not unnaturally perhaps, to my selection for that service. In the performance of it, my aim has been to embody the design which I received from his own lips.

Besides the plan, Mr. Angell's share of this book embraces the first two chapters, already in print at the time of his decease, and much the larger portion of the fourth chapter. For the remainder I am responsible. And, though I cannot flatter myself, that I have preserved the symmetry in its parts and the correspondence in the views presented, which would have characterized it, had it been the product of a single mind, I trust, nevertheless, that the few blemishes of this kind, which the reader may detect, will not materially detract from its utility.

Another apparent deficiency may seem to call for explanation. The Reports abound with decisions upon English and American statutes, which are omitted. On this point it might be sufficient to say that I was expressly informed by Mr. Angell, that the compilation of these decisions formed no part of his design. I have, however, examined them myself, with the hope of discovering some principle of classification by which they could be pressed into service; but have found, that they relate to statutory provisions, so local and so heterogeneous in their character, that their introduction would only add to the bulk of the volume, without, in any corresponding degree, enhancing its usefulness.

THOMAS DURFEE.

PROVIDENCE, October 1, 1857.

# CONTENTS.

## CHAPTER I.

MEANING OF HIGHWAYS. DIFFERENT KINDS OF, AND DISTINCTIVE QUALITIES OF EACH.



## CHAPTER II.

OF THE LAYING OUT AND THE CONSTRUCTION OF HIGHWAYS BY LEGISLATIVE AUTHORITY.

## CHAPTER III.

### HIGHWAYS BY PRESCRIPTION AND DEDICATION.



## CHAPTER IV.

### ASSESSMENT OF ESTATES BENEFITED BY THE OPENING, WIDENING, OR IMPROVING STREETS.

## CHAPTER V.

### DAMNUM ABSQUE INJURIA.



## CHAPTER VI.

### NUISANCES AND THEIR REMEDIES.



## CHAPTER VII.

### THE FEE IN HIGHWAYS.

## CHAPTER VIII.

### TRAVEL UPON HIGHWAYS.

# TABLE OF CASES.

THE FIGURES REFER TO THE SECTIONS.

D.



E.



F.

I.



J.



K.

N.

## Q.



## R.

# LAW OF HIGHWAYS.

# TREATISE

ON THE

# LAW OF HIGHWAYS.

## CHAPTER I.

MEANING OF HIGHWAYS. DIFFERENT KINDS OF, AND DISTINCTIVE QUALITIES OF EACH.

1. Way.
2. Highways.
3. Turnpike Roads.
4. Plank Roads.
5. Railroads.
6. Street and Cul-de-Sac.
7. Railways in Streets.
8. Bridges.
9. Ferries.
10. Canals.
11. Navigable Rivers.
12. Tow Paths on Navigable Rivers.

### 1. *Way.*

§ 1. The word "way" is derived from the Saxon, and means a right of use for passengers.[1] It may be private or public. The title of this work imposes but little obligation to offer much as to private ways; no more than enough to render the distinction between private and public ways clearly understood. By the term "right of way," is generally meant a private way, which is an incorporeal hereditament of

[1] Sax. *waeg*, *weigh*. Dut. *vig*. or *wig*, M. Goth. See Whart. Law Lex. tit. "Way."

that class of easements,[1] in which a particular person, or particular description of persons, have an interest and a right, though another person is the owner of the fee of the land, in which it is claimed. An individual may claim a right of way by an express grant, or by long user, *(prescription,)* also by *necessity*, originating thus: If a man grant a piece of ground in the middle of his field, he, at the same time, tacitly and impliedly, gives a way to go to it and from it. So the inhabitants of the village of A, or the owners or occupiers of the village of B, may have a prescriptive right of going over another individual's land. If it be a right of way in gross, or a mere personal right, it cannot be assigned to any other person, nor transmitted by descent, it dying with the person; and it is so exclusively personal, that the owner of the right cannot take another in company with him. But when a right of way is appendant or annexed to an estate, it may pass by assignment when the land is sold to which it was appurtenent.[2] If a right of way be from close A to close B, and both closes be united in the same person, the right of way, by grant or prescription, as well as other subordinate rights, is extinguished by *unity of possession*.[3]

---

[1] 2 Bla. Comm. 35; 3 Kent, Comm. 419; Woolrych on Ways, 2. Easement is from the French word *aise*, and is defined to be a privilege or convenience (see the above authorities) which one neighbor has of another, as a *right of way*, a right to bring water through another's land, &c. Easements are treated of by the civilians, under the name of *services*, some of which they call *real*, and some *personal;* the former being a service which *one estate* owes to another, for the advantage and convenience of the owner of another estate. But by a *personal* service, is understood such as has not been constituted for the benefit of the estate, but which has been created for the use of the person merely; and differs from an easement which is imposed on corporeal property only. The service of a private right of way, *(iter,)* belongs to the most familiar and important class of private easements. Ayl. Civil Law, tit. 5, of Services; 1 Bla. Comm. 20; Domat, Civil Law, [1 tit. 12]; 1 Kauf. Mack. 339.

[2] See the authorities above referred to, and Pierce *v.* Selleck, 18 Conn. R. 39; McDonald *v.* Lindell, 3 Rawle, (Penn.) R. 492.

[3] 3 Kent, Comm. 420.

## 2. *Highways.*

§ 2. Highways are public roads, which every citizen has a right to use.[1] One of the proper and important aims of civil policy has been the establishment of towns, market-places, and cities, and a connection with each other by thoroughfares, in order that a mutual intercourse may be promoted and kept up between them.[2] In the statute law of the State of New York, the word "road" is used synonymously with highway,[3] in which all obstructions, not warranted, may be removed by any individual. We perceive, then, the striking distinction between a private right of way and one that is public and common; the former belonging only to the particular *parties* by whom it has been acquired, while the latter is for the free use of every member of the community.

§ 3. Highways are of various kinds, according to the state of civilization and wealth of the country through which they are constructed, and according to the nature and extent of the traffic to be carried on upon them—from the rude paths of the aboriginal people, carried in direct lines over the natural surface of the country, passable only by passengers or pack-horses, to the comparatively perfect modern thoroughfare.[4] Lord Coke, adopting the Civil Law, states that there are three kinds of highways; 1, a footway, called *iter;* 2, a footway and horseway, called *actus;* 3, a cartway, called *via.*[5] A

---

1 3 Kent, Comm. 32; Sutcliffe *v.* Greenwood, 8 Price, R. 535; Rex *v.* Camberworth, 3 B. & Adol. R. 108; and for other English authorities, see Shelford on Highways, and Woolrych on Ways; and see American authorities—Makepeace *v.* Worden, 1 N. Hamp. R. 10; Peck *v.* Smith, 1 Conn. R. 103; Robins *v.* Borman, 1 Pick. (Mass.) R. 122; Jackson *v.* Hathaway, 15 Johns. (N. Y.) R. 447; Stackpole *v.* Healy, 16 Mass. R. 33, and many cases therein cited; Cool *v.* Crommet, 1 Shep. (Me.) R. 250.

2 2 Domat, 280.

3 Fowler *v.* Lansing, 9 Johns. (N. Y.) R. 349; Griffin *v.* Martins, 7 Barb. (N. Y.) Co. R. 297.

4 Brande, Dict. of Science, Literature and Art, tit. "Roads."

5 Coke, Litt. 56 a; 1 Brown, Civil Law, 177.

carriage-way will comprehend a horseway, and always includes a footway.[1] A *drift-way* is a road over which cattle are driven; and Lord Mansfield has laid down, that "In general, a public highway is open to cattle, though it may be so unfrequented that no one has seen an instance of their going there; but the presumption would be for cattle, as well as carriages, otherwise cattle could not be driven from one part of the kingdom to another."[2] The public have not, at common law, any right of passing over private property for sea-bathing.[3]

§ 4. It is said by an English author, in treating of the qualities of a highway, that footway and *bridle-way* appear to be used almost in contradistinction; whereas, he adds, the latter term being of itself sufficient to comprehend all public ways whatsoever, ought to have been allowed its full legal force, instead of being used in the more confined and vulgar meaning of a turnpike, or great carriage road. He then shows, from authorities, that the term "highway" is applicable to all public ways for horse and foot passengers.[4]

§ 5. Another point of law presents itself, which has regard to the respective rights and duties of the public and the owners of land adjacent to a highway. If a common highway is so

---

1 Per Heath, J., in Ballard *v.* Dyson, 1 Taunt. R. 285; and see Poole *v.* Hawkins, 11 M. & Welsb. R. 827.

2 Ballard *v.* Dyson, *ub. sup.*

3 Blundell *v.* Catterall, 5 B. & Ald. R. 268. See Benest *v.* Pipon, 1 Knapp, (Privy Council) R. p. 67.

4 Wellbeloved on Highways, 3, citing Regina *v.* Faintiff, 6 Mod. R. 255, and Madox's case, Cro. Eliz. 63; Rex *v.* Inhabitants of Limehouse, 2 Show. 455, pl. 412. From all the decisions, it may be pretty clearly deduced, that the term "highway," in England, extends to all public ways; and, for which, see Allen *v.* Ormond, 8 East, R. 4, and Logan *v.* Burton, 5 B. & Cress. R. 513; and see, also, 13 East, R. 95, in which Lord Ellenborough observes: "There is no doubt that a public footway or *bridle-way* is a highway; it is a highway for foot passengers, or for horse passengers; and the parish is bound to repair it, till they can throw the *onus* upon others. So all public bridges are *primâ facie* repairable by the inhabitants of the county, without distinction of foot, horse, or carriage bridges, unless they can show that others are bound to repair particular bridges."

*founderous* and out of repair as to become impassable, or even dangerous to be travelled over, or incommodious, the public have a right to go upon the adjacent ground; and it makes no difference whether it be sown with grain, or not.[1] And indeed it has been holden, that if there be an highway in an open field, and the people have used, time out of mind, when the way was bad, to go by outlets on the land adjoining, such outlets are parcel of the way; for the king's subjects ought to have a good passage, and the good passage is the way, and not only the beaten tract; from whence it follows, that if such outlets be sown with corn, and the beaten tract be founderous, the king's subjects may justify going upon the corn.[2] And in one case it was held, that where a man incloseth, and doth not make a good way, (as in such a case he is bound to do by reason of the inclosure,) it is lawful for passengers to make gaps in his hedges to avoid the ill way; so that they do not go further into his inclosed grounds, than is needful for avoiding the bad way. This, it may be observed, was the case of a footpath.[3]

§ 6. But this privilege of going over the adjoining land, if the way be impassable or founderous is confined to highways; and the grantee of a private way cannot take advantage of any such liberty. This was decided by the case of Taylor *v.* Whitehead.[4] And that decision is confirmed by the later case of Bullard *v.* Harrison,[5] in which the *locus in quo* was a private way; and it was endeavored, but without success, to establish this right of traversing the adjoining land, upon the plea of necessity. Lord Ellenborough, in delivering the judgment of the Court, said: The question intended to be agitated upon this

---

1 See 1 Roll. Ab. 390, A., pl. 1, and B. pl. 1.

2 1 Hawk. P. C. c. 76, s. 2.

3 Henn's case, Sir W. Jones, 296. See also, Absor *v.* French, 2 Show. 28, pl. 19; 2 Lev. 234, S. C.; and Young *v.* ———, 1 Ld. Raym. 725.

4 Doug. R. 745.

5 4 M. & S. R. 387.

record is, whether, in the case of a private way, the grantee may break out and go *extra viam*, if it be impassable, as in the case of a public way. As to that I consider Taylor *v.* Whitehead[1] has settled the distinction, that the right of going on the adjoining land extends not to private, as well as to public ways.

§ 7. Again, public highways, in reference to position or *locality*, may be called urban, suburban, and rural, although the same principles of law apply to each. Where a private act of Parliament empowered a water company to "break up the soil and pavement of roads, highways, *footways*, &c., and 'public places,'" it was held, that the word "footway," as there used, meant those footways in large towns which are too narrow to admit of carriages and horses, and not a path over a private ground. "Looking," says Burrough, J., "at the general purview of the act, and the context, it is clear that the word *footway* means one of those paved ways running by adjacent buildings, and not a path over a private ground."[2]

### 3. *Turnpike Roads.*

§ 8. A distinct class of highways has been created under the appellation of *turnpike roads*, which are, in general, constructed by incorporated companies with provisions in the act of incorporation for their management. And the legislature has power to authorize a turnpike company to lay out their road upon a common public highway.[3] The same diligence, it may be stated, is required of turnpike companies, which is demanded by towns, to insure safety to travellers, upon other highways, and they, as well as towns, are primarily

---

1 Taylor *v.* Whitehead, Doug. R. 745; and see Pomfret *v.* Rycroft, Saunders, 323, note b; Williams *v.* Safford, 7 Barb. (N. Y.) Sup. Ct. R. 309; Holmes *v.* Seeley, 19 Wend. (N. Y.) R. 518.

2 Scales *v.* Pickering, 4 Bing. R. 448.

3 State *v.* Hampton, 2 N. Hamp. R. 22.

liable to the traveller.[1] And if the corporate franchise of a turnpike company extends to the building of *toll-houses* within the corporate limits, they would be forfeited, if turned to uses foreign to the original purpose.[2]

§ 9. A turnpike road is distinguishable from highways in general, by the manner in which the expense attending the construction and maintenance of it is defrayed, viz., by *tolls collected from the passengers*.[3] The principal question in Commonwealth *v.* Wilkinson, in the Supreme Court of Massachusetts,[4] was whether a turnpike road, in that State, was a highway, and whether an action would lie against any person for an obstruction thereon as a public nuisance; and, by Shaw, C. J.: "We think, that a turnpike road is a public highway, established by public authority for public use, and is to be regarded as a public easement. The only difference between this and a common highway is, that instead of being made at the public expense in the first instance, it is authorized and laid out by public authority, and made at the expense of individuals in the first instance, and the cost of construction and maintenance, is reimbursed by a toll, levied by public authority, for the purpose. Every traveller has the same right to use it, paying the toll established by law, as he would have to use any other public highway."[5]

---

1 Mathews *v.* Winooski Turnpike Co. 24 Vt. R. 480.

2 Fisher *v.* Coyle, 3 Watts, (Penn.) R. 407.

3 3 Stephens, Comm. 259; Northern Bridge and Road Co. *v.* London and Southampton Railway Co. 6 M. & Welsb. R. 428.

4 Commonwealth *v.* Wilkinson, 16 Pick. (Mass.) R. 175.

5 And see Buncombe Turnp. Co. *v.* Baxter, 10 Ired. (N. C.) R. 222. And see Clarkville, &c. Turnp. Co. *v.* Atkinson, 1 Sneed, (Tenn.) R. 426; Louisville and Nashville Turnp. Co. *v.* Nashville and Kentucky Turnp. Co. 2 Swan, (Tenn.) R. 282; Turnp. Road *v.* Brosi, 10 Harris, (Penn.) R. 29; Sturtevant *v.* County of Plymouth, 12 Met. (Mass.) R. 7; Stormfeltz *v.* Turnp. Co. 1 Harris, (Penn.) R. 555; and see 2 Ibid. 152. Under the provisions of the charter of a turnpike company, which gives the right to recover damages for an injury occasioned by the insufficiency only to those from whom toll is demandable, the person injured may sustain an action, if toll were demanded of him at any gate upon the road, although he was not, at the time of the injury, passing, or intending to pass,

§ 10. The penalty of the payment of a sum of money, imposed by statute upon any person who shall "forcibly or fraudulently pass any gate on any turnpike or plank road, without having paid the legal toll, is not incurred by an individual who merely passes through a gate with his team, and offers a bank-bill in payment of the toll, and refuses to pay in any other way." To make the passage fraudulent, some artifice must be employed, or some deception practised on the toll-gatherer.[1] In the absence of a toll-gatherer, his wife will be deemed to be his agent, for the purpose of demanding and receiving toll.[2]

§ 11. As to *exemption* from tolls. Under the Act of the State of New York of 1849, in relation to turnpike roads, all persons travelling over a turnpike road in going to a religious society of any sect, creed or denomination, having for their professed object the worship of God, and which are tolerated by the Constitution of that State, whether such persons go for the pure purpose of conducting, or of uniting in the exercises of devotion, are equally exempt from the payment of toll. And persons thus exempt from the payment of toll, may, if compelled to pay it, maintain an action against the toll-gatherer for the penalty imposed by the statute for demanding and receiving more toll than by law he is authorized to collect.[3]

---

through or near any gate. Brown *v.* Winooski Turnp. Co. 23 Vt. R. 104; 22 Ibid. 14. Where a turnpike company have established its toll-gates within the distance authorized by law, and have fixed the rates of toll at the several gates, so as not to exceed the legal rates of toll for the entire distance, and for the distance between the several gates, they may lawfully exact the full toll at a particular gate; though the traveller may not have travelled upon the road a distance which, at the legal rate per mile, would amount to such toll. Mallory *v.* Austin, 7 Barb. (N. Y.) Sup. Ct. R. 626.

1 Monterey and Plank-road Co. *v.* Faulkner, 21 Barb. (N. Y.) Sup. Ct. R. 212.

2 Marselis *v.* Seaman, 21 Barb. (N. Y.) Sup. Ct. R. 319.

3 Skinner *v.* Anderson, 12 Barb. (N. Y.) Sup. Ct. R. 648. Conkling *v.* Elting, 2 Johns. (N. Y.) R. 410; and Norvall *v.* Cornell, 16 Ibid. 73, were decided under the provisions of the Act of 1813, which differed essentially in its terms. And see Chetney *v.* Coon, 8 Johns. (N. Y.) R. 150.

§ 12. Erecting a *toll-board*, with rates of toll, written chiefly in the small Roman letter, though but of a size to be legible at a distance of three roods, is a compliance with the statute requiring them to be in "large capital letters."[1]

§ 13. It is not a ground of forfeiture of the charter of a company, that they do not, in all cases, charge the full tolls authorized by the charter; and, unless forbidden by the charter, they may commute tolls for an annual sum.[2]

### 4. *Plank Roads.*

§ 14. What are called *plank roads*, (the name of which indicates the material used in their construction,) now extensively used in different portions of the United States, are public highways when established by law. They are established, like common turnpike roads, and like them public, in the sense that every citizen has the right to travel on them, either on foot, on horseback, in his carriage, or with his team, subject to the payment of legal tolls.[3]

§ 15. A common public highway, taken by a plank road corporation, by virtue of the statute and of its act of incorporation, in New York, does not cease to be a public highway; and on

---

1 Nichols *v.* Bertram, 3 Pick. (Mass.) R. 342.

2 Commonwealth *v.* Alleghany Bridge Co. 8 Harris, (Penn.) R. 185; and so of a canal company, Delaware and Hudson Canal Co. *v.* Pennsylvania Canal Co. 9 Harris, (Penn.) R. 131.

3 Fort Edward and Fort Miller Plank-road Co. *v.* Payne, 17 Barb. (N. Y.) Sup. Ct. R. 567; Rensaeller *v.* Plank-road Co. 21 Barb. (N. Y.) Sup. Ct. R. 56; Plank-road Co. *v.* Husted, 3 W. & Smith, Ohio R. 697; Benedict *v.* Goit, 3 Barb. (N. Y.) Sup. Ct. R. 459; Commissioners of Highways, (matter of,) 15 Barb. (N. Y.) Sup. Ct. R. 136; McAllister *v.* Albion Plank-road Co. 11 Barb. (N. Y.) Sup. Ct. R. 610; 1 Kern, N. Y. (Court of Appeals,) 102; Plank-road Co. *v.* Thomas, 8 Harris, (Penn.) R. 91; Same *v.* Ramage, Ib. 95; Same *v.* Rineman, Ib. 99; Mallory *v.* Austin, 7 Barb. (N. Y.) Sup. Ct. R. 626. See "Practical Compend of the Powers and Duties of the Commissioners and Overseers of Highways, in the State of New York," Auburn, 1851, 19–54; and "General Railroad Law of the State of New York," in reference to the crossing by a railroad over a plank road, p. 93, Rochester, 1853.

a compliance with the requisitions of the law, the corporation succeeds to the rights of the town commissioners to make the repairs and alterations of grade which the public interest requires; and a person suffering damage from reasonable and proper repairs and grading, so made, cannot recover in an action therefor; although for any unreasonable use of its powers the corporation is responsible.[1]

§ 16. In the State of New York, the inhabitants residing in any road district, may grade, gravel, or *plank* the road in such district, by anticipating the highway labor of such road district, for one or more years, and by applying it to the immediate construction of such plank or gravel road; and they will thereupon be exempt from the labor so anticipated and applied, except so far as their labor may be necessary to keep such road in repair. Any road so constructed or improved, will be a free road.[2]

### 5. *Railroads.*

§ 17. Railroads are distinguishable into two classes. 1st, railroads at common law; 2dly, railroads constructed under the authority of the legislature. The former species of railroad again subdivides itself into two, viz: 1, a simple rail or tramway, made by the owner of property on his own land for its more convenient use and occupation, or by several owners of co-terminus property, in pursuance of some mutual arrangement for that purpose between themselves; and, 2, a tram or railway constructed under a way leave, or grant, or right of way.[3]

§ 18. A railroad established and existing under an act or charter of incorporation, like a turnpike or a plank road, is a

---

1 Benedict *v.* Goit, 3 Barb. (N. Y.) Sup. Ct. R. 459.

2 Laws of New York of 1849, chap. 250.

3 Keppel *v.* Bailey, 1 My. & Keen, R. 547; Hemmingway *v.* Fernanden, 21 English Law Journ. Chan. 130; and S. C. 13 Sim. Chan. R. 228; and see Walford on Railways, 1.

public highway; but only to be used in a different mode.[1] In Beekman *v.* Saratoga and Schenectady Railroad Company,[2] Chancellor Walworth thus expresses himself: "It is objected, however, that a railroad differs from other public improvements, and particularly from turnpikes and canals, because travellers cannot use it with their own carriages, and farmers cannot transport their produce in their own vehicles; that the company are under no obligation to accommodate the public with transportation, and that they are unlimited in the amount of tolls which they are authorized to take. If the making of a railroad will enable the traveller to go from one place to another, without the expense of a carriage and horses, he derives a greater benefit from the improvement than if he was compelled to travel with his own conveyance over a turnpike road at the same expense. And if a mode of conveyance has been discovered by which the farmer can procure his produce to be transported to market at half the expense which it would cost him to carry it there with his own wagon and horses, there is no reason why the public should not enjoy the benefit of the discovery. And, if any individual is so unreasonable as to refuse to have the railroad made through his land, for a fair compensation, the legislature may lawfully appropriate a portion of his property, or may authorize an individual or a corporation thus to appropriate it, upon paying a just compensation to the owner of the land, for the damage sustained."[3]

---

1 Per Holroyd, J., in Rex *v.* Severn and Wye Railway Co. 2 B. & Ald. R. 646; and see Walf. on Railways, 151, 152.

2 Beekman *v.* S. & S. Railroad Co. 3 Paige, (N. Y.) Cha. R. 74.

3 And see Inhabitants of Springfield *v.* Connecticut River Railroad Co. 4 Cush. (Mass.) R. 572. The following are American cases of interest in relation to Railroads:—March *v.* Concord Railroad Co. (New Hamp.) reported in Law Rep. for Feb. 1856, p. 570; Taylor *v.* County Commissioners, 13 Met. (Mass.) R. 449; Porter *v.* Same, Ibid. 479; Wyman *v.* Lexington and West Cambridge Railroad Co. Ibid. 316; Bradley *v.* Boston and Maine Railroad Co. 2 Cush. (Mass.) R. 539; Same *v.* Same, 3 Cush. (Mass.) R. 91; Pennsylvania Railroad, 10 Harris, (Penn.) R. 356; Hudson River Railroad Co. *v.* Outwater, 3 Sand

§ 19. In one case[1] a railroad was made under authority of Act of Parliament, by which the proprietors were incorporated, and by which it was provided that the public should have the beneficial enjoyment of the same. The company having determined to render one branch of the railroad impassable, caused the iron tram-plates, for the space of several hundred yards, to be taken up, and thereby destroyed that branch. An application was thereupon made to the proper Court for a *mandamus* to compel the company to reinstate the railroad. Holroyd, J., said: "*It is a public highway, to be used in a particular mode.*" And all the Judges agreed, that for the offence complained of, the company had rendered themselves liable to an *indictment*. But because that remedy was not so effectual, as the one by *mandamus*, and as the Court were of opinion, that the circumstance of the corporation being liable to an *indictment*, was no objection to the granting of a *mandamus*, the rule to that effect was made absolute. And Abbott, C. J., said: "The writ should be to reinstate and lay down again, but not to maintain the tram-road."[2]

§ 20. Although an act of the legislature which authorizes the construction of a railroad between certain *termini* without prescribing its precise course and direction, does not, *primâ facie*,

(N. Y.) Sup. Ct. R. 689; Northern Railroad Co. 7 Fost. (N. Hamp.) R. 183; Mason *v.* Kennebec and Portland Railroad Co. 1 Red. (Me.) R. 215; Haswell *v.* Vermont Central Railroad Co. 23 Vt. R. 228; Field *v.* Vermont and Massachusetts Railroad Co. 4 Cush. (Mass.) R. 150; Meacham *v.* Fitchburg Railroad Co. 4 Cush. (Mass.) R. 291, and Ib. 440 and 467; Polly *v.* Saratoga and Washington Railroad Co. 9 Barb. (N. Y.) Sup. Ct. R. 449; Hamilton *v.* Annapolis, &c. Railroad Co. 1 Md. Ch. R. 107; Metherell, *ex parte*, Eng. Law and Eq. R. 139; Salisbury *v.* Great Northern Railway Co. 10 Eng. Law and Eq. R. 8; Powvey *v.* Calais Railroad Co. 17 Shep. (Me.) R. 498; Vermont Central Railroad Co. *v.* Baxter, 22 Vt. R. 365; Willard *v.* Newbury, 27 Vt. R. 458; Hart *v.* Western Railroad Corp. 13 Met. (Mass.) R. 99. And see the "General Railroad Laws of the State of New York, with Notes and References," by William S. Bishop, Rochester, N. Y. 1853.

1 Rex *v.* Severn and Wye Railway Co. 613.

2 A ———, R. 646.

confer power to lay out the road on and along an existing highway; yet it is competent to the legislature to grant such authority even by implication; and such implication may result either from the language of the act, or from its being shown, by an application of the act to the subject-matter, that the railroad cannot, by reasonable intendment, be laid in any other line.[1] Take, for example, the familiar case of the Notch in the White Mountains, a very narrow gorge, which affords the only practicable passage, for many miles, through that mountain range. A turnpike road through it has already been granted. Suppose the gorge not wide enough to accommodate another road, but the legislature of New Hampshire, in order to accommodate a great line of public travel, should grant power to lay a railroad on that line; they would, by necessary implication, grant a power to take some portion of the road-bed of the turnpike.[2] The case referred to was a bill in equity, brought to enjoin a railroad company from maintaining a railroad, and running cars thereon, upon and over a public highway in Springfield, Massachusetts, on the ground, that such maintenance of the railroad was unauthorized, and constituted a nuisance.

§ 21. In the absence of any action of the legislature, a railroad company is under no obligation to inclose their road against the entrance upon it of cattle from the adjacent grounds, so that the company is not answerable, without gross negligence, in running an engine upon, and killing cattle, which escape from the owner's inclosure and stray upon the track.[3] But in the charters to some companies of this kind, it is made

---

1 Springfield *v.* Connecticut Railroad Co. 4 Cush. (Mass.) R. 63.

2 Ibid. Per Shaw, C. J. — As to the right of appropriating a corporate franchise, for the public benefit, see *post*, Chap. II.

3 The cattle are to be regarded as trespassers, and the law charges their owners with negligence. Munger *v.* Tonawanda Railroad Co. 5 Denio, (N. Y.) R. 255; and 4 Comst. (N. Y.) R. 349; Waldron *v.* Rensellaer Railroad Co. 8 Barb. (N. Y.) Sup. Ct. R. 390; Clark *v.* Syracuse and Utica Railroad Co. 11 Barb. (N. Y.) Sup. Ct. R. 112.

obligatory to fence in the line of their road against the inroad of cattle, and then, if the railroad company do not observe the directions of the act, the company is chargeable in such case, and responsible for injury. The general railroad act of the State of New York, contains the following: "Every corporation formed under this act, shall erect and maintain fences on the sides of their road, of the height and strength of a division fence required by law, with openings, or gates, or bars therein, and farm-crossings of the road for the use of the proprietors of lands adjoining such railroad; and also construct and maintain cattle-guards at all road-crossings, suitable and sufficient to prevent cattle and animals from getting on to the railroad. Until such fences and cattle-guards shall be duly made, the corporation and its agents shall be liable for all damages which shall be done by their agents or engines, to cattle, horses, or other animals thereon; and after such fences and guards shall be duly made and maintained, the corporation shall not be liable for any such damages, unless negligently or wilfully done; and if any person shall ride, lead or drive any horse or other animal upon such road, and within such fences and guards, other than at farm-crossings, without the consent of the corporation, he shall for every such offence forfeit a sum not exceeding ten dollars, and shall also pay all damages which shall be sustained thereby to the party aggrieved. It shall not be lawful for any person, other than those connected with or employed upon the railroad, to walk along the track or tracks of any railroad, except where the same shall be laid along public roads or streets." Since the above enactment, it has been decided in Suydam *v.* Moore,[1] that if a railroad company neglects to erect fences on the sides of the railroad, and construct and maintain cattle-guards at road-crossings, as required by the above statute, and a cow comes upon the track, and is run

[1] Suydam *v.* Moore, 8 Barb. (N. Y.) Sup. Ct. R. 358.

over by the engine and killed, the company is liable to the owner of the cow; for although the accident in this case appears by the evidence to have been clearly, if not quite inevitable, yet no man can shelter himself from responsibility for an act brought upon him by his own violation of duty. Had the fences been erected and the cattle-guards constructed, as by statute required, the injury to the plaintiff's property would not have been occasioned. The legislative action above does not apply to *streets* in cities and villages, in which cattle-guards would be a nuisance.[1]

§ 22. A railroad company, by giving permission to another railroad company to use a part of their track, do not bind themselves to make their track safe, nor to put it in repair, nor to make any change in its existing state.[2] And if a company construct a railroad for its own profit, and open it to the public upon payment of tolls, all who choose to use it, may do so, without danger to lives or property.[3]

§ 23. Under the Revised Statutes of Massachusetts, providing that every railroad corporation may raise or lower any turnpike or way for the purpose of having their railroad *pass over or under* the same, a railroad corporation may raise a turnpike road for the purpose of constructing the railroad across it *upon the same level.*[4]

## 6. *Street and Cul-de-Sac.*

§ 24. The word "highway" is considered as the *genus* of all public ways,[5] so that a common *street* in any city or town,

---

1 Vandekar *v.* Rensellaer and Saratoga Railroad Co. 13 Barb. (N. Y.) Sup. Ct. R. 390; and see New York and Erie Railroad Co. 1 Am. Law Reg. 97.

2 March *v.* Railroad Co. in N. Hampshire, reported in Law Rep. for February, 1856, on p. 570.

3 Lancaster Canal Navigation Co. *v.* Parmely, 5 Adol. & Ell. R. 223.

4 Newbery Turnpike Co. *v.* Eastern Railroad Co. 23 Pick. (Mass.) R. 326.

5 Per Holt, Ch. J., in Regina *v.* Saintiff, 6 Mod. R. 255.

being common to all people, is a public highway.[1] Exceptions were taken in a case in the Supreme Court of Pennsylvania, which related to an act of the legislature respecting roads, and to the proceedings under it, that an application was not for a highway, but for a *street*. But Judge Gibson, in giving the opinion of the Court, said: "In common parlance, the word 'street' is equivalent to 'highway,' and the very words of the act need not be pursued; a substantial compliance with its provisions is all that is required. Few records of proceedings of this nature, would stand the test of a construction so severe as that contended for." [2]

§ 25. A correct distinction has been suggested between a highway in the country, and a street in a populous commercial city; and it has been considered, that the restricted use of highways in the country, has been, that they have been needed for no other purposes; but such is not the case with the streets of a city. There are certain uses to which, in modern times, the latter have generally been applied,—uses not merely conducive to, but almost necessary for, the comfort, health, and prosperity of the public; and they have been both sanctioned by custom and approved by experience.[3] It may be taken for granted, that one of certain uses here referred to, is the use of *water pipes* beneath the surface of a street. A water company having observed the directions of the act of the legislature in laying down their pipes, is not responsible for an escape of water from them, not caused by their own negligence.[4]

---

1 State *v.* Wilkinson, 2 Vt. R. 480; Benedict *v.* Goit, 3 Barb. (N. Y.) Sup. Ct. R. 459; Adams *v.* Rivers, 11 Barb. Sup. Ct. R. 399; City of Cincinnati *v.* White, 8 Peters, (U. S.) R. 431; Livingston *v.* Mayor of New York, 8 Wend. (N. Y.) R. 85; Wyman *v.* Same, 11 Ibid. 486.

2 Case of the Road from Fitzwater-street to Shippen-street, in Moyamensing, 4 S. & Rawle, (Penn.) R. 106; and see Hobbs *v.* Lowell, 19 Pick. (Mass.) R. 405.

3 Per Edwards, J., in Milhau *v.* Sharp, 15 Barb. (N. Y.) Sup. Ct. R. 210.

4 Blyth *v.* Birmingham Water Works Co. 4 Exch. (Hurlston & Gord.) R. 781.

§ 26. Streets in a city sometimes have their original termination at a river or an arm of the sea. It has been held, that where an act of the legislature authorized a proprietor of lands lying on the East River, upon which the city of New York is bounded, which is an arm of the sea, to construct wharves and bulkheads in the river, in front of his land, and there was, at that time, a public highway through said land, terminating at the river; such proprietor could not, by filling up the land between the shore and the bulkhead, obstruct the public right of passage from the land to the water; but that the street was, by operation of law, extended from the former terminus, over the newly-made land, to the water. The design of the act was to confer privileges on the owners of land adjoining the East River, but not to destroy the right of the public to reach its waters through Warren, or any other street, which then led to its shore; nor should the act be so construed as to work a public mischief, unless required by words of the most explicit and unequivocal import.[1] By the *extension* of a *straight* street is to be understood its continuance in a straight line.[2]

§ 27. It has in England been a matter of considerable discussion by the judicial tribunals, whether a passage-way, leading from a street in a town or city, and which is entirely obstructed by buildings at its extreme end, so that there is no communication with any thoroughfare beyond it, is a public highway. Such a passage is termed a *Cul-de-Sac*, a French phrase, signifying literally the *bottom of a bag*, and figuratively, a street not open at both ends.[3] It was expressly decided by Lord Ellen-

1 People *v.* Lambier, 5 Denio, (N. Y.) R. 9.

2 Charlotte-street, 11 Harris, (Penn.) R. 286; Cole *v.* Canaan, 9 Fost. (N. H.) R. 88.

3 2 Bouv. Law Dict. 357; Woodyer *v.* Hadden, 5 Taunt. R. 125. *Cul-de-Sac:* "A blind alley," Spier's Dict. Lord Hale, in Austin's case, (1 Ventr. R. 189,) observed: "If a way lead to a market, and *were a way for all travellers*, and did communicate with a great road, it is an highway; but if it lead *only* to a church, to a private house or village, or to fields, there 'tis a private way. But it is matter of fact, and much depends upon common reputation."

borough, in a case at Nisi Prius,[1] that any way which is open to the public to pass *through* it, or, in other words, a *thoroughfare*,[2] is a highway. In this case, an indictment was brought for obstructing a passage which led from part of a street (circuitous route,) to another point in the same street, and which had been open to the public as far back as could be remembered; and though it could, in general, be of no use to those walking up and down the street, being a most indirect route, which no one would willingly take, yet it was convenient for the public when the street was blocked up by a crowd. The learned Judge held, that this was a highway, for removing the obstructions of which it was proper to proceed by indictment.

§ 28. In the above case, there is this *dictum* of Lord Ellenborough: "I think, that if places are lighted by public bodies, this is strong evidence of the public having a right of way over them; and to say that this right cannot exist because a particular place does not lead conveniently from one street to another, would go to extinguish all highways, where there is no thoroughfare." But this is a mere *dictum*, the point in issue being taken for granted.

---

The observations of the same learned Judge, in Thrower's case, (1 Ventr. R. 208,) are more clear upon this point. The defendant in that case was indicted for stopping *communem viam pedestrem ad ecclesiam*. It was objected, that an indictment could not lie for a church-path; besides, the damage, it was said, is private, and concerns only the parishioners. Hale said: "If this were alleged to be *communis via pedestris ad ecclesiam pro parochiansis*, the indictment would not be good; for then the nuisance would extend no farther than the parishioners, for which they have their particular suits; but, for aught that appears, this is a common footway, and the church is only the *terminus ad quem*, and it may lead *farther*, the church being expressed only to ascertain it; it is laid *ad commune nocumentum*." The reason here given is, that the way in question was a common footpath, which *might lead farther;* that is, that it must be presumed to be a *thoroughfare*, and, *therefore*, a highway. See Wellbeloved on the Law of Highways, 7.

[1] Rex *v.* Lloyd, 1 Campb. R. 260.

[2] "Thorough" and "Thoroughfare." "The first is evidently from the root *door*, which signifies a passage, and the radix of the word signifies *to pass*."—Webster, Dict. The second is defined, "A passage *through ;* a passage from one *street to another ; power of passing*."—Ibid.; and see Ibid. "Door."

§ 29. The cases in the old books certainly do not favor such a position as that of Lord Ellenborough, as above stated.[1] There is one modern decision which, however, supports it, viz., the case of Rugby Charity *v.* Merryweather.[2] It appeared in evidence in this case, that the right of soil was clearly in the plaintiffs; but there had been a common street there, though no *thoroughfare*, by reason of houses at the end,[3] for above fifty years. Lord Kenyon, in addressing the jury, said: "If this rested solely on the ground of a question of right between the plaintiffs and the Foundling Hospital, the former certainly would not have been barred by the time which elapsed from 1780 till the obstruction was put up, pending the treaty between them; but during all that time they permitted the public at large to have the free use of this way, without any impediment whatever, and, therefore, it is now too late to assert the right, for this is quite a sufficient time for presuming a dereliction of the way to the public. '*And as to this not being a thoroughfare, that can make no difference.*'" The jury found a verdict for the defendant upon the issue, on the plea of a common highway.[4]

---

1 See *ante*, § 27, note.

2 Rugby Charity *v.* Merryweather, 11 East, 375, (note.)

3 In Woodyer *v.* Hadden, (5 Taunt. R. 138,) Chambre, J., observed, "That there is a slight error in this report, in stating that it was no thoroughfare, by reason that houses were built across at the end. I have the briefs on both sides, and was in the cause." "But, at any rate," says Wellbeloved on Highways, (p. 10, note *a*,) "There was no thoroughfare, on account of the land at the end of the *locus in quo* being private property."

4 Wellbeloved, in his work on the Law of Highways, (p. 11,) remarks, "It is evident that Lord Kenyon, in the above observations, and also Lord Ellenborough, in Rex *v.* Lloyd, were misled by paying too much attention to the particular instance of the streets in so large a town as London, and overlooking the requisites and legal distinctions attached to highways in general. The parishes in London are, I believe, without exception, paved, lighted, and watched, under the regulation of divers acts of Parliament; and are thereby *completely withdrawn from the rules of the common law;* it is, therefore, incorrect, and contrary to all sound reasoning, to extract the qualities of highways in general from the partial instance of the streets of the metropolis; yet, with all deference to these great Judges, this is the source from whence their arguments are derived."

§ 30. Upon this subject, the interest of the tenants residing in the passage, it seems, should be regarded. Lord C. J. Mansfield, in Woodyer *v.* Hadden,[1] observed: "It is intimated that this was an attempt of the plaintiffs to extort a sum of money for passing over this way; but I think the plaintiffs would not act handsomely, if legally, if, for any price, *without the consent of the tenants*—the inhabitants of these houses—they should agree to its becoming a public way; for there are many conveniences attending a private *Cul-de-Sac*, of which, having so let it to them, the lessors have no right to deprive them." The decision in this case, it will be seen, by an attentive examination of it, is opposed to the one in the case of the Rugby Charity.

§ 31. In the still later case of Wood *v.* Veal,[2] Abbott, C. J., in referring to Lord Kenyon's decision, which had been urged in the argument, said: "I have great difficulty in conceiving that there can be a public highway, which is not a thoroughfare, because the *public at large cannot be in the use of it.*" And Holroyd, J., said: "The opinion of Lord Kenyon, in Rugby Charity *v.* Merryweather, is somewhat shaken by the observations of Lord C. J. Mansfield, in Woodyer *v.* Hadden." So, also, Best, J.: "No man has a greater respect for Lord Kenyon than I have, but I think that decision was a departure from the principles usually received in law. If a road be for the accommodation of particular persons only, it is not a public road; and, therefore, I see no reason why the inhabitants of a street, which is not a thoroughfare, should not put up a fence at the end of it, and exclude the public." Undoubtedly, if a lot of land bounded in front upon a *Cul-de-Sac*, and upon a common street in the rear, the grantee is entitled to have the latter kept open for a necessary passage to the rear of his building.[3]

---

1 Woodyer *v.* Hadden, 5 Taunt. R. 125.

2 Wood *v.* Veal, 5 Barn. & Ald. R. 454.

3 Livingston *v.* New York, 8 Wend. (N. Y.) R. 99. Lord C. J. Denman has

## 7. *Railways in Streets.*

§ 32. The introduction and use of railways in the streets of a city have existed in the city of New York for a number of years, and the question as to the *general* power of the city corporation to authorize the laying of a railway track in that city, was well-settled in 1849, in the case of Drake *v.* The Hudson River Railroad Company.[1] It appeared in the case, that by an act of the legislature, the company was authorized to construct a railway between the cities of New York and Albany, commencing in the city of New York, with the consent of the city corporation, and the directors were authorized to locate such railway on any of the streets or avenues of the city, westerly of, and including the Eighth Avenue, on, or westerly of, Hudson Street; provided, that the consent of the mayor and common council should be first obtained. Two questions in the case were distinctly passed upon, and decided by the Court: First, that a railway in a city is not *per se* a nuisance or a purpresture; and, second, that the corporation of the city has the power and the right to authorize the use of its streets for that purpose.

§ 33. It was contended in Milhau *v.* Sharp,[2] upon the argument, that the case noticed above was distinguishable from this case, because in the former, the legislature had, by its *charter* to the company, authorized it to carry the road into the city. But it will be observed, that this authority is made to *depend* entirely upon the assent of the mayor, aldermen, and commonalty of the city. In the present case, it was held, that the power in question existed as one of the general *municipal powers* of the corporation, that body being invested with the largest discretion; so that, whether its laws are wise or un-

---

said: "I never remember a way being claimed, without stating to what place, or from whence it leads." Davies *v.* Stephens, 7 C. & Paine, R. 570.

1 Drake *v.* Hudson River Railroad Co. 7 Barb. (N. Y.) Sup. Ct. R. 508.

2 Milhau *v.* Sharp, 15 Barb. (N. Y.) Sup. Ct. R. 193.

wise, it is not the province of the courts to inquire; and the same has also been held, in several other cases in the State of New York; for, as civilization advances, new uses of streets are found expedient.[1] Where the charter of a company author-

[1] Milhau *v.* Sharp, 15 Barb. (N. Y.) Sup. Ct. R. 193. So in the case of Plant *v.* The Long Island Railroad Co. 10 Barb. (N. Y.) Sup. Ct. R. 26, it was held, that the corporation of the city of Brooklyn had the right to authorize a railroad company to tunnel a public street for the purpose of laying a railway track. And in the case of Adams *v.* S. & W. Railroad Company, 11 Barb. (N. Y.) Sup. Ct. R. 414, a similar power was recognized in the Village of Whitehall. See also, Chapman *v.* A. & S. Railroad Company, 10 Barb. (N. Y.) Sup. Ct. R. 360. In each of these cases, the recipient of the right or thing granted was a body corporate, created by an act of the legislature, but, in every case, the right, or thing granted, was given by the city or village corporation, by virtue of its general powers over its streets. See also, Hentz *v.* Long Island Railroad Co. 13 Barb. (N. Y.) Sup. Ct. R. 646. In relation to the proper authority to confer the power of laying railways in streets, in the city of New York, we subjoin the following account of a later action by the Courts of the State of New York, which we take from the *New York Daily Times* of January 10, 1857, in regard to the grant by the Common Council of the city, of the right to construct a railroad in Broadway. The decision of the Court was embodied in an opinion written by the chief justice, Denio. Justice Comstock, however, while concurring in the decision, dissents from some of the views set forth by the chief justice.

"Soon after this grant was made, it will be remembered, application was made to the Superior Court, at General Term, for an injunction, which was granted. From this judgment the grantees appealed, and the Court of Appeals have now *reversed* it and awarded a new trial.

"The ground upon which this decision is made, it will be seen, however, is purely technical. It was not proved that the parties who applied for the injunction were the owners of lots on Broadway, or that they would be specially injured by the construction of a railroad on Broadway. The Court hold, therefore, that the action cannot be sustained on their behalf.

"But the Court lay down certain principles in regard to the general subject, which are of the utmost importance with regard not only to the future legislation of the city, but to its past action concerning railroads in the public streets. The Court holds, that the establishment of a railroad is not within the jurisdiction conferred upon the Common Council over the roads and streets of the city; — because it is not an object of the same public nature with those which roads and streets are designed to serve. Besides this, it is held, that the grant was a franchise, conferred upon the grantees in perpetuity, and, therefore, beyond the power of the Common Council. The right of making such a grant, and of authorizing the construction of a railroad in any of the public streets of the city, rests, according to this decision, with the legislature. And if the road had

izes it to establish a railway along a public street to a particular point, and to run a locomotive on a turn-out from the main

---

been constructed, under the grant of the Common Council, it would have been a public nuisance.

"Judge Comstock holds, that a railroad may be built, which shall not necessarily be a franchise or monopoly, — provided it is left open to the general use of the public; — and that a highway and a railroad-track may coëxist and constitute one public easement. He holds that the Common Council has power to authorize *such* a railroad; but whether the Broadway Railroad would or would not have been such a one, is a matter of fact which has not been determined. This particular grant, however, was clearly made as a franchise. The effect of the ordinance was no less than an abrogation by the Common Council of their powers and duties over and concerning the public streets, and a surrender of a considerable portion of those powers and duties into the hands of private individuals, or of a private corporation. This, Judge Comstock says, the corporations of New York cannot do; — and he therefore regards the ordinance as null and void.

"The case must now go back to the Superior Court for a new trial. It is clear, however, from the general tenor of this decision, that the Court of Appeals would never sustain the validity of a grant by the Common Council for a Broadway Railroad. Such a grant must come from the legislature."

From the *Law Reporter* for October, 1856, p. 382. Notes of Cases in New York, Wetmore *v.* Story. "Roosevelt, J.—Messrs. Wetmore, Hoppoch and Stuart, of this city, and also owners of property on Greenwich and Washington streets, complain that the defendants, under the name of the Ninth Avenue Railroad Company, and under color of a pretended grant from the city authorities, are about extending their rails through those streets, in front of the plaintiffs premises, to their great injury and annoyance, and in violation of their rights. An injunction granted in the first instance, on their application to restrain the proceeding, was subsequently, at Special Term, dissolved, and the complaint dismissed. From that judgment the plaintiffs have appealed, insisting that the injunction originally issued, instead of being dissolved, should be made perpetual.

"On the part of the defendants, it is not pretended that every citizen has a right to lay a rail-track in the streets of the city. The corporation, however, it is claimed, may do it; or, in their discretion, by a resolution of the Common Council, may grant the privilege, as a franchise, to a particular individual or association of individuals. Such a grant, it is alleged, has been made in this instance. The Judge so held at Special Term. He placed his final decision on that ground. And the question, therefore, is, can a resolution, adopted by the Board of Assistants in one year, be concurred in by the Board of Aldermen in another year, so as to make it, without consulting the existing Board of Assistants, an ordinance of the Common Council? Or must it, as in the case of unfinished business in other legislative bodies, be taken up *de novo?*

"When the charter of 1830 declared that 'the legislative power of the Cor-

track to communicate with a depot erected by them near the terminus of the road, containing the machinery necessary for

---

poration of the City of New York, should be vested in a Board of Aldermen and a Board of Assistants, who together should form the Common Council of the city,' it must be considered as having adopted by implication, so far as applicable, the universally recognized principles of *legislative* bodies, constituted of two independent branches.

"The settled practice and understanding, — indeed, we may say, the common law, — of such bodies, as illustrated in the Congress of the United States, the Legislature of this State, and, it is believed, in the Legislatures of every State in the Union, as well as in the Parliament of Great Britain, repudiates the idea that the Board of Aldermen of 1853, could take up and pass the resolution of the politically deceased Board of Assistants of 1852, and give it effect as law, without consulting the newly-elected body. It might have been, although not so in the present instance, on the express ground of opposition to the particular act of their predecessors, and for the express purpose of preventing its consummation.

"No case has been cited in which the Senate of a State, or of the United States, or of the Upper House of Canada, or of Great Britain and Ireland, has attempted to give effect to the inchoate action of a previous Assembly, House of Representatives, or House of Commons, whose term had expired, and whose places were filled by others newly chosen in their stead.

"To allow an opposite practice in the legislation of the City Common Council, since its new organization, would be at times to defeat the will of the constituents, clearly expressed through the regular channel of the ballot-box, and to render the elective franchise a nullity. Although the corporation of the city is a continuous body, the Common Council, since its division into two branches, is not. Its legal term, like that of the State Legislature, upon whose model it was formed, is one year, and no longer. The Common Council of 1852, is not the Common Council of 1853.

"The primary object of that act, was to prevent the Common Councils of cities from permitting the construction of railroads in the streets of cities without the consent of a majority of property-owners immediately interested; and when it excepted from its operation railroads already 'constructed in part,' it meant those constructed under lawful authority, and not under 'grants, licenses, resolutions or contracts,' which had never been made, given, passed or entered into according to the charter; and which, therefore, having, in judgment of law, no existence, could not be 'confirmed.'

"The confirmation intended, was a confirmation as against the State, and not against the Common Council itself. An opposite construction of the act, instead of restraining the Common Council from permitting injurious railroads, would go to sanction roads commenced in violation of law, and which had never been permitted at all.

"Having had, therefore, no warrant for its commencement, and none for its

reversing the engine, &c., where no objection exists as to the construction of a turn-out at that particular point; such liberty is subject to the police power of the municipal authority, and must be so constructed as not unnecessarily to interfere with the free use of a street.[1] The Philadelphia, Wilmington and Baltimore Railroad Company made a railroad, under authority of law, through the city of Wilmington, in the State of Delaware, by virtue of which the company had power to use locomotive engines propelled by *steam*, with all the incidents of that mode of conveyance; the company being responsible, as individuals would be, for the exercise of due care and prudence. In an action on the case, against the company, for negligently running over the plaintiff's not well-broke-horse, the Court held—"Being authorized to use steam as the propelling power of these engines, the smoke and noise of steam escaping are indispensable, as well as the noise occasioned by the cars, and the usual notice bells; and the company would not be liable from mere accidents arising from fright to horses occasioned by these noises. In the exercise, however, of the right to use this steam-power in passing through a populous town, the company are bound to use all due precaution to avoid danger to others, and to travel at a

---

continuance, the road in question, under the evidence, is not only a public nuisance, of which the plaintiffs have a legal right to complain, as specially injurious to them in their ingress and egress to and from their place of business on the street.

"Such a nuisance, it is well established by numerous decisions, can and ought to be restrained by injunction, if demanded, as in this case, by the parties specially aggrieved.

"The judgment, therefore, of the Special Term, we all agree, should be reversed, and a perpetual injunction awarded.

"*Clerke*, J. — For the reasons above expressed in Judge Roosevelt's opinion, I concur in the conclusion at which both my associates arrived. See 18 Barb. Sup. Ct. R. 222.

1 New Orleans, &c. Railroad Co. *v.* 2d Municipailty, 1 Louis. Annual R. 128; and see March *v.* Concord Railroad Co. (New Hamp.) reported in Law Rep. for February 7, 1856, p. 570; in which case it was held, that the owners of a railroad company are liable, like towns, for all injuries sustained from defects in their road, by persons travelling either on foot or in their own carriages, or in those of other persons.

rate of speed prudent under the circumstances. This prudent and proper rate of speed is either regulated by law, or by the usual and customary speed. It will be for the jury to say, if, on the evidence, the defendants were going on their train at the usual and proper rate of speed, or if they abused, in any manner, their lawful right."[1]

§ 34. In the city of New York, and also in other cities, it is believed that *horse*-power is generally used for railways in streets. The charter of the Cambridge Railroad Company, (the railroad from Boston to Cambridge,) after incorporating certain individuals, their associates and successors, thus provides: "Said tracks or roads shall be operated and used by said corporation with *horse-power only*, and it shall not connect its track with any other railroad on which other power is used. The mayor and aldermen of said cities respectively shall have power at all times to make all such regulations as to the rate of speed and mode of use of said tracks as the public convenience and safety may require. Said corporation shall maintain and keep in repair such portion of the streets and bridges respectively as shall be occupied by their tracks, and shall be liable for any loss or injury that any person may sustain by reason of any carelessness, neglect or misconduct of its agents and servants in the management, construction, or use of said tracks, roads or bridges; and in case any recovery shall be had against either of said cities or said bridge corporation by reason of such defect or want of repair, said corporation shall be liable to pay the said cities and said bridge corporation respectively, any sums thus recovered against them, together with all costs and reasonable expenditures incurred by said cities or said bridge corporation, or either of them, in the defence of any such suit or suits in which recovery shall be had, and shall not encumber any portion of the streets or bridges not occupied by the road or track."

---

1 Burton *v.* Philadelphia, Wilmington and Baltimore Railroad Co. 4 Harring. (Del.) R. 252. See 18 Barb. (N. Y.) Sup. Ct. R. 222.

## 8. *Bridges.*

§ 35. A *bridge* has been defined "a building of brick, wood or iron, erected across a river, ditch, valley, or other place otherwise impassable, for the convenience and benefit of travellers."[1] Again, "a building constructed over a river, creek or other stream, or over a ditch or other place, in order to facilitate the passage over the same."[2] The term "bridge," is a comprehensive one, and embraces every structure in the nature of a bridge, whether over a large stream or a mere culvert or sluiceway.[3] There are, as is generally well known, bridges of a different character. A *private* bridge is one erected for the use of one or more private persons, although it may *occasionally* be used by the public.[4]

§ 36. "How far," says a late writer on Criminal Law,[5] "it is essential to the legal character of a bridge, that water should flow under it, may not be entirely clear; but it need not flow at all seasons of the year; especially if there is one structure, having several arches, the whole may be deemed in law a bridge, though the water pass under some of the arches only at flood times."[6]

§ 37. A bridge with lateral embankments, erected by a railroad corporation for the purpose of raising a highway, and

---

1 Whart. Lexicon, 114.

2 1 Bouv. Law Dict. 224.

3 See pamphlet entitled "A Practical Compend of the Powers and Duties of Commissioners and Overseers of Highways in the State of New York, p. 12. In that State, whenever new roads are laid out in such direction as cross the line of any canal, and in such manner as to require the construction of a new bridge, such bridge must be constructed and forever maintained at the expense of the town in which it may be situate. Ibid., and 1 N. Y. Rev. Sts. 247, 248, § 174, 175, (3d ed.) 279, §§ 220, 221.

4 See *ante*, § 1.

5 1 Bishop on Criminal Law, § 183.

6 And he refers to Rex *v.* Derbyshire, 22 B. 145; 2 Gale & Dav. R. 97; 6 Jur. 438, and cases there cited.

carrying over their roads, is as much a part of the structure authorized by the charter, as the railroad itself.[1]

§ 38. *Public* bridges may be divided into three classes; first, those which belong to the public, as state, county or township-bridges, over which all people have a right to pass, without or with paying toll; these are built by public authority at the public expense, either of the State itself, or of a district or portion of the State; secondly, those which have been built by companies, (like turnpike and railroad companies,)[2] or at the expense of private individuals, and over which all persons have a right to pass, on the payment of a toll fixed by law; thirdly, those which have been built by private individuals, and which have been surrendered or dedicated to the use of the public.[3] And a bridge may be a public bridge which is used by the public at all such times as are dangerous to pass through the river.[4]

§ 39. A causeway and bridge were only used by the public in time of floods, and in the time of very high floods the bridge itself was impassable, but they were at all times open to the public; and this, it was held, was a public bridge.[5]

§ 40. A public bridge being a highway, it follows, that those principles of the common law which relate to highways in general, are alike applicable to public bridges; but although the principles are the same, yet from a difference in the nature of the respective objects of their operation, their reduction to practice in the one case varies from that of the other. A

---

1 Parker *v.* Boston and Maine Railroad, 3 Cush. (Mass.) R. 107; Sussex *v.* Strader, 3 Harrison, (N. J.) R. 168.

2 See *ante*, § 8 and 14.

3 Rex *v.* Inhabitants of Bucks, 12 East, R. 200; Rex *v.* Inhabitants of Northampton, 2 M. & Sel. R. 262; Piscataqua Bridge Co. *v.* N. Hamp. Bridge Co. 7 N. Hamp. R. 59; Callender *v.* Marsh, 1 Pick. (Mass.) R. 432; Charles River Bridge *v.* Warren Bridge, 7 Pick. (Mass.) R. 344, and S. C. 11 Peters, (U. S.) R. 539; and see 1 Campb. R. 26, *n.*

4 Rex *v.* Inhabitants of Northampton, 2 M. & Sel. R. 262. And see *post*, Ch. III.

5 Rex *v.* Inhabitants of Devon, 2 Ry. & Mood. R. 144.

common way may, with the consent of the proprietor, be at once subject to general *user*, without any antecedent act to bring it into existence; but a bridge must have been erected before it can be traversed, and this distinction is the foundation of all the difference between the two cases.[1] The term "highway," does not import a bridge; and in any case where there is occasion to notice any of the differences which exist between highways generally, and bridges, it is indispensable that the difference should be marked by the use of the terms appropriated to each. So that if a party is to be charged with neglect to build or repair a bridge, it must be by the term "bridge," which alone describes such a structure.[2]

§ 41. No State constitution, it is believed, gives the legislature, in terms, a right to make bridges, but such power has always been exercised, and no one doubts the legislative power to make such grants.[3] An act of the legislature authorizing the erection of a bridge over *navigable* water, within the limits of the State, is clearly constitutional.[4] It was said by the counsel, in the case just referred to at the bottom, that the grant of a right to build a bridge, was upon the petition, and for the

---

1 Wellbeloved on Law of Highways, 4, 324; Shelford on Highways, 34. Woolrych says: "The principal circumstance necessary to constitute a public bridge, is, that the people at large may have a free and uninterrupted use of it, not upon sufferance, but as a matter of right." Woolrych, Law of Ways, 196.

2 State *v.* Canterbury, 8 Foster, N. Hamp. R. 195.

3 Piscataqua Bridge Co. *v.* New Hamp. Bridge Co. 7 N. Hamp. R. 35; and see Fletcher *v.* Peck, 6 Cranch, (U. S.) R. 128; Central Bridge Corp. *v.* Bailey, 8 Cush. (Mass.) R. 389; Ib. *v.* Sleeper, 8 Cush. (Mass.) R. 324; South Carolina Railroad Co. *v.* Jones, 4 Rich. (S. C.) Eq. R. 459; Hall *v.* Boyd, 14 Georgia R. 1; Towles *v.* Justices, &c. 14 Georgia R. 301; Erie City *v.* Schwingle, 10 Harris, (Penn.) R. 384; Indianapolis *v.* McClure, 2 Cart. (Ind.) R. 147; Meadville *v.* Erie Canal Co. 6 Harris, (Penn.) R. 66; Harrell *v.* Ellsworth, 17 Ala. R. 576; Damariscota Toll-bridge Co. *v.* Cutter, 1 Red. (Me.) R. 357; State *v.* Milo, 2 Red. (Me.) R. 57; Mayor, &c. *v.* Macon and Western Railroad Co. 7 Geo. R. 221; Strong *v.* Dunlap, 10 Humph. (Tenn.) R. 423; State *v.* Gilmanton, 14 N. Hamp. R. 467; Schuylkill Bridge *v.* Frailey, 13 S. & R. (Penn.) R. 422; Chambersburg, &c. Co. *v.* Commissioners, 6 S. & Rawle, R. 229.

4 Commonwealth *v.* Breed, 4 Pick. (Mass.) R. 460.

especial benefit, of a single individual; this, said the Court, was doubtless true; and that it was also true, that many other enterprises had originated in motives of private gain, which had resulted in great public improvements.[1]

§ 42. Where a bridge corporation erected a bridge, a part of which extended beyond the limits of the State, it was held, the corporation could not enforce the payment of a *toll* against a person passing over that portion only of the bridge which is without the limits of the State, the legislature having no power to give such authority.[2]

§ 43. A toll-bridge, made by two men across a stream, between their lands, by authority of the legislature, is real estate, and on sale thereof by the sheriff, the proceeds of the sale are to be distributed accordingly.[3]

§ 44. By a statute of Connecticut, a turnpike company are bound to repair all bridges which they shall build, if their charter do not designate what bridges they shall build. But if, when erecting them, they insist that the town ought to build and support them, they are not bound to repair them.[4]

§ 45. A vote by the proprietors of a bridge, that "all the present proprietors of stock therein, shall have the right to pass free of toll, with their horses and carriages," is confined to the then proprietors, and does not extend to those who subsequently become the purchasers of the stock then existing.[5]

---

1 And see Austin *v.* Carter, 1 Mass. R. 231; Commonwealth *v.* County Commissioners, 3 Met. (Mass.) R. 202; Parker *v.* Cutler Milldam Corp. 2 App. (Me.) R. 353.

2 Middle Bridge Corp. *v.* Marks, 13 Shep. (Me.) R. 326.

3 Meason's Estate, 4 Watts, (Penn.) R. 341.

4 Canaan *v.* Greenwood's Turnpike Co. 1 Conn. R. 1. Towns, in Vermont, are bound to repair injuries to bridges. Briggs *v.* Guilford, 8 Verm. R. 267. So, in Massachusetts and Connecticut. Lobdell *v.* New Bedford, 1 Mass. R. 153; Lewis *v.* Richfield, 2 Root, (Conn.) R. 436; Eldrige *v.* Pomfret, 1 Ib. 153. So it is presumed in other States.

5 The Central Bridge Corporation *v.* Abbott, 4 Cush. (Mass.) R. 473.

## 9. *Ferries.*

§ 46. The right to a ferry, it is said, must have originally belonged to the owner of the land, and must still be derived through him.[1] But it does not follow, that this is a franchise inseparable from the soil, and that the lord would have no power to grant it to another. Holroyd, J., calls it an incorporeal hereditament; it being such, it may certainly be the subject of a grant.[2] It was in one case said *arguendo*, that a ferry is real property,—an incorporeal hereditament within the parish—that it is demandable in a *precipe quod reddat*—that an *assize* clearly lies for it—that the owner may have a seisin in fee of it. It owes its birth to the land over which it is exercised; but it by no means follows that it cannot have an independent existence. Though in its nature *sui generis*, the same principle which authorizes calling a bridge a public highway, is applicable to the *transverse* navigation by a ferry; and it is not inconsistent with the general principles of law regarding highways.[3] In England, a number of statutes have been passed, regulating the prices of carriage by ferrymen,[4] but then these acts do not vary their liability at common law, as carriers. The duty of a ferryman is to have the *landing* in a proper state for the reception of travellers, and to be provided with proper easements for entering the boat, &c.[5]

§ 47. The right to keep a ferry is, in England, an incorporeal hereditament, being a franchise granted by the crown or de-

---

[1] Wellbeloved on Highways, 33, *et seq.*

[2] Peter *v.* Kendal, 6 B. & Cressw. R. 703.

[3] Rex *v.* Nicholson, 12 East, R. 334; Walker *v.* Jackson, 10 M. & Welsb. R. 161; Smith *v.* Seward, 3 Barr, (Penn.) R. 342; Pomeroy *v.* Donaldson, 5 Missouri R. 30; Cohen *v.* Hume, 1 N. & McCord, (S. C.) R. 19; Gardner *v.* Greene, 8 Ala. R. 96; Trent *v.* Cartersville Bridge Co. 11 Leigh, (Va.) R. 521; Spivy *v.* Farmer's Admr. 1 Murph. (N. C.) R. 339.

[4] 1 Bac. Abr. "Ferry," and see Cohen *v.* Hume, 1 McCord, (S. C.) R. 439.

[5] Pate *v.* Henry, 2 Stew. & Port. (Ala.) R. 101.

pending upon prescription, which supposes a grant. The party entitled to the franchise, has imposed upon him by law, certain duties, incurs certain liabilities, and has a remedy against any one who, without right, interferes with his profits, or disturbs him in the enjoyment of his property.[1] Ferries received the attention of the colonial government of Massachusetts, soon after its first settlement; but how granted, for what periods, for what purpose, or by what tenures, does not appear. All ferries in Massachusetts and in Maine depend upon the general law, except such as were stated and settled as early as 1695.[2] The judicial authorities, in the State of New York, have power to grant licenses to keep ferries on the river Niagara, for the purpose of transporting across persons or goods for profit.[3]

§ 48. A ferry should be regularly established by law; for the owner of a private ferry is not authorized to land passengers on the opposite side of the stream, without the consent of the opposite riparian proprietor.[4] In a petition to establish a ferry in Virginia, it must state, that the applicant owns the land on both sides, or on one side of the stream, and that a public road has been established through the land, to the place where the ferry is sought to be established.[5] To justify the establishment of a ferry across the Ohio River, the applicant must own the land on the Kentucky shore.[6]

---

[1] Blisset *v.* Hart, Willes, R. 508; 5 Com. Dig. 291.

[2] Day *v.* Steson, 8 Greenl. (Me.) R. 365.

[3] People *v.* Babcock, 11 Wend. (N. Y.) R. 584.

[4] Chess *v.* Manown, 3 Watts, (Penn.) R. 219; Chambers *v.* Furey, 1 Yeates, (Penn.) R. 167; Bird *v.* Smith, 9 S. & Rawle, (Penn.) R. 26; Mills County *v.* St. Clair, 2 Gillm. (Ill.) R. 197; Lombard *v.* Cheever, 3 Ibid. 469; and see the doctrine of riparian ownership fully considered by the Judges of the King's Bench, in the important case of Blundell *v.* Catterall, 5 B. & Ald. R. 91; and Gould *v.* Hudson Railroad Co. 12 Barb. (N. Y.) Sup. Ct. R. 616.

[5] Zane *v.* Zane, Virg. Cases, 63.

[6] Jefferson Seminary *v.* Wagnor, 2 A. K. Marsh. (Ken.) R. 379.

## 10. *Canals.*

§ 49. It is almost superfluous to represent that the importance of canals, as a means of inland navigation, attracted attention even in the earliest ages. The Egyptians, who were justly renowned for science and the arts, completed the character of high civilization by an assiduous attention to their internal trade; and the intercourse necessary to conduct it, was facilitated by the same canals, which were constructed by the provident labor of that people, to distribute the capacious bounty of the Nile.[1] Modern nations have respected their example; and in the United States, while nature has greatly assisted the internal trade of the country, it is a just tribute to the enterprising genius of the people, to admire the extent to which that advantage has been augmented by the means of boatable canals,[2] which are *highways* of a particular kind. Their peculiar importance is attested by the fact, that upon their banks one horse will draw as much as thirty horses do on the ordinary turnpike, or on which one man alone will transport as many goods as three men and eighteen horses usually do on common roads.[3] When made by public authority, they are in law public highways, with the right of *tolls* attached.[4]

---

1 See Balmano's Intr. to Sir William Jones on Bailments, 16, 17.

2 See, in regard to the importance of canals to the commercial interest of a country, "Smith's Wealth of Nations," Vol. 1, p. 28, 228.

3 See Phillips' History of Inland Navigation, Preface, p. 9.

4 Rex *v.* Kent, 13 East, R. 220; Rex *v.* Lindsley, 14 East, R. 317; Rex *v.* St. Mary's, Leicester, 6 M. & Sel. R. 400; Rex *v.* Trent and Mersey Canal Co. 2 D. & Ry. R. 752; and S. C. in 1 B. & Cressw. R. 545; Rex *v.* Woking, 5 Adol. & Ell. R. 50; Rex *v.* Oxford Canal Co. 6 D. & Ry. R. 86; Rex *v.* Aire and Calder Navigation, 4 Man. & Ry. R. 84; and S. C. 9 B. & Cressw. R. 95; Rex *v.* Chelsea Waterworks, 5 B. & Ald. R. 156; Rogers *v.* Bradshaw, 20 Johns. (N. Y.) R. 735; and see also, 7 Johns. (N. Y.) R. 326; Cooper *v.* Williams, 4 Ham. (Ohio) R. 391; Commonwealth *v.* Fisher, 1 Penn. R. 462; Rogers's case, 7 Cow. (N. Y.) R. 526; Farnum *v.* Blackstone Canal Corp. 1 Sumn. (Cir. Ct.) R. 46; Riddle *v.* Proprietors of Locks, &c. 7 Mass. R. 169;

§ 50. Canal boats do not come within the description of "vessels of the United States," mortgages of which are declared by act of congress to be void, unless recorded in the office of the collector of customs, where such vessels are registered or enrolled. And there is no law now in force, requiring canal boats to be registered in the collector's office of the United States.[1]

§ 51. A canal company is not bound by the principles of the common law, independent of its charter, to erect and maintain a bridge over the canal where a highway may be laid over the same, after its construction;[2] and the authority conferred by canal commissioners in the State of New York, to take possession of lands of individuals for the use of the canal, can only be executed by them, or under their express direction, in each instance.[3]

§ 52. Freight boats passing on the Erie and Champlain Canal, are bound to give every facility for the passage of packet boats, as well through the locks as elsewhere; and where a freight boat, passing west on the Erie Canal, was waiting for the emptying of a lock, when a packet boat overtook her, the latter was held entitled to pass first.[4]

### 11. *Navigable Rivers.*

§ 53. "God," says Domat, "has given us the use of the seas and rivers which opens the communication with all the

---

City of Lowell *v.* Proprietors of Locks and Canals, 7 Met. (Mass.) R. 1. And see the authorities referred to in the different vols. of the United States Digest, tit. "Canal." Also, "A Practical Compend of the Powers and Duties of Commissioners and Overseers of Highways, in the State of New York," Auburn, 1851.

[1] Hicks *v.* Williams, 17 Barb. (N. Y.) Sup. Ct. R. 523.

[2] Morris Canal and Banking Co. *v.* State, 4 Zabriskie, (N. J.) R. 62; and see King *v.* Kerrison, 3 Maule & Sel. R. 526.

[3] Lyon *v.* Jeremy, 2 Wend. (N. Y.) R. 485.

[4] Farnsworth *v.* Groot, 6 Cow. (N. Y.) R. 608. In respect to collision of canal boats, see Dygent *v.* Bradley, 8 Wend. (N. Y.) R. 469.

world to use, and makes us acquainted with our fellow-men in distant countries."[1] The public right to the use of tide-waters for navigable purposes, has never been called in question; it is said to exist of *common right*, which is but another epithet for *common law;* and a right to which the public right of fishery must always yield, whenever the two rights come in conflict.[2]

§ 54. All rivers, above the flow of tide-water, are, by the common law, *primâ facie* private; but when they are naturally of sufficient depth for valuable *flotage*, the public have an *easement* therein for the purposes of transportation and commercial intercourse; and, in fact, they are *public highways* by water. Such is the common law, as laid down in the excellent treatise of Sir Matthew Hale,[3] which in England has ever commanded profound respect. It certainly has the merit of defining, with much precision, what constitutes a public highway by water, and of illustrating, with an equal degree of perspicuity, the distinction between such rivers as are exclusively private, and those in which the community may assert an interest. *Fresh* rivers, of what kind soever, says he, do, of common right, belong to the owners of the adjacent soil; but that such rivers, as well as those which ebb and flow, may be under the servitude of the public interest; that is to say, they may be of public use for the carriage of boats. As instances, he mentions the Wye, the Severn, and the Thames, which, he says, are public rivers, *juris publici*, as well above as below the flowing of the tide, and as well in the parts where they are of private as of public (as in the case of tide rivers) property;

---

1 1 Domat, Civ. Law, 280.

2 2 Inst. 56; Callis on Sewers, 25; Anonymous, Durham Assizes, Campb. R. 516, note; Mayor of Colchester *v.* Brook, 2 Jur. 290, and 5 Harr. Dig. 781; Hart *v.* Hill, 1 Whart. (Penn.) R. 136; Post *v.* Mann, 1 South. (N. Jersey) R. 61; Wilson *v.* Blackbird Creek Co. 2 Peters, (U. S.) R. 245; Gould *v.* Hudson River Railroad Co. 12 Barb. (N. Y.) Sup. Ct. R. 616.

3 Harg. Tracts, De Jure Maris, &c.

and nuisances and impediments therein are liable to be punished by indictment. They are called public rivers, not in reference to the *property* of the river, for that is in the individuals who own the land,[1] but in reference only to the public use.[2]

§ 55. The territory of the United States is distinguished, especially, for such rivers as come within the above description of public highways by water; and to them has the public at large been extensively indebted for the easy and convenient communication by them afforded, between the maritime cities and the rapidly growing and productive regions of the interior. They have imparted energy to the enterprising genius of the people, and been the means of transforming deserts and forests into cultivated and fruitful fields, flourishing settlements, and opulent cities. That portion of the river Connecticut, which is as high up from tide-water as the State of New Hampshire—it there affording *flotage*—is, by the common law, a public highway.[3] The Potomac is part of the *jus publicum*, and any obstruction to its navigation would, upon the most established principles, be a public nuisance.[4] This river, above tide-water, was not originally navigable; but it has been made so, in a qualified manner, by law in Maryland, to which State it entirely belongs.[5] The river Mississippi is preëminently an open highway, and upon principles of international law, the right of passage in it, by a citizen of one State, within the jurisdiction of another, is classed among imperfect rights; but the right was made perfect by the Constitution of the United States, which provides that the citizens of each State shall be entitled to the

---

1 See *ante*, Chap. I. § 2.

2 Royal Fishery in the River Banne, Davis, R. 152; Carter *v.* Murcot, 4 Burr. R. 2162; Callis on Sewers, 78.

3 Scott *v.* Wilson, 3 N. Hamp. R. 321; and see Moffett *v.* Brewer, 1 Greene, (Iowa) R. 348; Moore *v.* Veazie, 2 Red. (Me.) R. 343.

4 Georgetown *v.* Alexandria Canal Co. 12 Peters, (U. S.) R. 91.

5 Binney's case, 2 Bland, (Md.) Ch. R. 99.

privileges of the several States.[1] Under the ordinance of 1787, stipulating that "the navigable waters leading into the Mississippi and St. Lawrence, shall be common highways, and forever free," he who owns the lands on both banks, owns the entire river, subject only to the easement of navigation; and he who owns the land upon one bank only, owns to the middle of the river, subject to the same easement.[2] The river Muskingum is a common highway under the ordinance above mentioned, and the legislature cannot authorize a dam to be built across which obstructs its navigation.[3]

§ 56. If a stream is naturally of sufficient size to float boats or *mill-logs*, the public have a right to its free use for those *two* purposes, unincumbered with dams, &c.[4] In Varick *v.* Smith, in New York,[5] the Vice-Chancellor held, that the doctrine that fresh water rivers, above tide-water, belong to the owners of the soil adjacent, though capable of being used for the purposes of navigation, had been sanctioned and confirmed by repeated decisions in that State, and applied to streams which were navigable for boats and *rafts*, which had been declared to be public highways by statute. In Scott *v.* Wilson, in New Hampshire,[6] it was held, that the river Connecticut, above the ebb and flow of the tide, had been so long used for the purposes of boating and *rafting*, that it must be considered a high-

---

1 Per Catron, C. J., in Corporation of Memphis *v.* Overton, 3 Yerg. (Tenn.) R. 389.

2 Gavit *v.* Chambers, 3 Ohio R. 495; Cowper *v.* Hall, 5 Ohio R. 320.

3 Hogg *v.* Zanesville Canal Co. 5 Ohio R. 410.

4 Wadsworth *v.* Smith, 2 Fairf. (Me.) R. 278.

5 Varick *v.* Smith, 9 Paige, (N. Y.) Ch. R. 547.

6 Scott *v.* Wilson, 3 N. Hamp. R. 321. When timber is forfeited under the act regulating the mode of putting pine timber into the Connecticut River, the title of the former owner is wholly lost, and a contract with the person who has taken it up, to pay him for his trouble, and take it away, does not revest the title until the contract is executed. Ib. Pine timber put into the Connecticut River, and which may have been liable to forfeiture, cannot be seized as forfeited, after the owner has regained the possession of it, and has it in his custody. Barron *v.* Davis, 4 N. Hamp. R. 338.

way. If a stream has a broad and deep channel, calculated for the purposes of commerce, it would be natural to conclude that it has been a public navigation; but if it is a petty stream, navigable only at certain periods, and then only for a short time, and by very small boats, it is difficult to suppose, that it ever has been a public channel.[1] Upon this it has been remarked: "It might as well be said, that it is difficult to suppose a footpath can be a highway, because horses and carts cannot traverse it. It is a new distinction that the size of a carriage is to determine the nature of the way. It may be evidence to go to a jury, as to the actual public use thereof; but can have nothing to do with the abstract principle."[2]

§ 57. The public likewise have a right to travel on a public river upon the *ice;* and, therefore, if any one cuts holes through the ice upon or near the place where there has been a *winter-way* for twenty years, he is liable to the payment of all damages sustained thereby by those travelling upon such way, without carelessness or fault on their part. The waters of the river Penobscot are, of common right, a public highway, and though the right so to use it by all the citizens, is generally exercised when its waters are in a fluid state, yet when they are congealed, the citizens have still a right to traverse their surface at pleasure. Assuming that the riparian owners have as good a right to the use of the water as the public generally have to the right of passage, the use of the privilege should be such as may be most beneficial and least injurious to all who have occasion to avail themselves of it.[3]

§ 58. A riparian proprietor does not, in England, make his watercourse a public one, or one subject to public use, by making it at his own expense boatable by artificial means, as by locks, or by uniting other waters, unless the improvement be made

---

[1] Rex *v.* Montague, 4 Barn. & Cress. R. 596. Mr. J. Bailey.

[2] Wellbeloved on Highways, 21, *note.*

[3] French *v.* Camp, 6 Shepl. (Me.) R. 438.

by public authority, or for a long continuance of time it has been used by the public.[1] In this country, likewise, such little streams as are not boatable, that is, as cannot, in their natural state, be used for the carriage of boats, rafts, or other property, are wholly and absolutely private; not subject to the public interest, nor to be regarded as public highways by water.[2] If a person be the owner on both sides of such a watercourse, and at his own expense makes it boatable by artificial means, it does not thereby become public; it is still private property, and cannot be infringed, even by the legislature, without a satisfaction being made.[3]

§ 59. But should a person obstruct the flow of the waters of a stream over their accustomed bed, so that it could not be used as formerly for the purpose of boating or floating rafts or logs, and should turn them into a new channel, he would thereby authorize the public to make use of them in the new channel, as they had been accustomed to use them in their former channel. But on the same principle that a riparian owner may improve his watercourse, by locks or otherwise, he may make a new watercourse upon his own land, and withhold its use from all who will not make compensation, and authorize its use by those who will. Nevertheless, those who have been injured by the opening of such new watercourse, may abate it as a nuisance, or recover damages for the injury in an action at law.[4]

§ 60. The legislature of a State cannot, by declaring a river navigable, which is not so in fact, deprive the riparian owners

---

1 Harg. Tracts, Hale's Treatise, De Jure Maris, &c. In England, a person, by license from the crown, may make locks upon a public river flowing through his land for the advantage of the navigation; and the owners of barges passing through the same, are under obligation to pay such tolls as the Privy Council shall appoint. Cro. Car. 132; Cowp. R. 47.

2 Cates *v.* Wadlington, 1 McCord, (S. C.) R. 580.

3 Wadsworth *v.* Smith, 2 Fairf. (Me.) R. 278.

4 Divinel *v.* Barnard, Sup. Jud. Ct. of Maine, Penobscot County, June Term, 1849, reported in Law Rep. for November, 1849, p. 339.

of their rights to the use of the water for hydraulic and other purposes, without rendering them compensation;[1] and the provisions of the legislative resolutions of Ohio, providing for the assessment of damages to the riparian owners upon navigable streams, are construed to extend to all streams, which have been by the legislature declared navigable.[2] Indeed, it has been shown that, by the law of *eminent* domain,[3] a State has not the right, without making compensation, to destroy the property of individuals situated upon a watercourse, in making it navigable, when it is not so by nature; or in appropriating such watercourse to the public use, by artificial erections and improvements.[4] A company incorporated for the purposes of lock-navigation, cannot claim the privileges of a riparian owner; and, therefore, it has no right to increase the water beyond what it derives from the act of incorporation; and being by this required to make compensation "for any damage done to lands or property," must do so under all circumstances, when its works are the cause of the injury; and is answerable for injury even in times of flood, from the forcing back of the water by its dam, upon its neighbors.[5] A stream in Pennsylvania, which has been declared by the legislature to be a public highway, is a "navigable" stream in the sense in which all boatable rivers are viewed by the Courts of that State;[6] but such declaration will not devest property previously acquired to the middle of the stream by a grant from the State.[7] At the same

---

1 Walker *v.* Board of Public Works, 16 Ohio R. 540; Moore *v.* Veazie, 2 Red. (Me.) R. 343.

2 Walker, &c., *ub. sup.* See State *v.* Callum, 2 Speers, (S. C.) R. 581.

3 *Post*, Chap. II.

4 See the opinion of Chancellor Bland, in Binney's case, 2 Bland, (Md.) Ch. R. 158.

5 Monongahela Nav. Co. *v.* Coons, 6 Barr. (Penn.) R. 379.

6 See *post*, Pt. II. of this chapter.

7 Coovert *v.* O'Connor, 8 Watts, (Penn.) R. 447. And see Monongahela Nav. Co. *v.* Coons, 6 Watts & S. (Penn.) R. 101; Susquehanna Canal Co. *v.* Wright, 9 Watts & S. (Penn.) R. 9.

time an act of a State legislature imposing reasonable tolls, as a compensation for *improving* the navigation of a *public* river, is constitutional and valid, unless it conflicts with the power of congress in its actual exercise.[1]

§ 61. It was not the intention of the ordinance of 1787, in declaring the navigable streams of the Northwestern Territory public highways, to prohibit the making of such improvements as might be demanded by the public interests or convenience of the people of the States through which they flow, though some inconvenience might arise to those who were in the habit of using them in a particular manner, before such improvements were authorized.[2]

§ 62. It has appeared, that the line of demarcation of the common law, between such streams of water as are private, and such as are altogether public, is that at which they begin to partake of the sea. Below this point, the water is not only public for all floatable uses, but the *bed* or *soil* over which the water runs, is also public; both the use and the property, in other words, are public. The river Hudson, for example, is entirely private property, in one part; is subject as such to public use in another part; and is wholly and entirely public property from its mouth to as high up therefrom as the tide flows. In that part of the stream wherein the entire right of property is in the public, it is called by the law "navigable," which, in the technical sense, and different from the common acceptation of that word, is confined in its application to fresh water rivers only to the extent to which they are propelled backward by the ingress and pressure of the ocean tides.

§ 63. To determine whether a river is "navigable" in the admiralty acceptation of that term, regard must be had to the

---

1 Thames Bank *v.* Lovell, 18 Conn. R. 566. And see Spring *v.* Russell, 7 Greenl. (Me.) R. 273; Shrunk *v.* Schuylkill Nav. Co. 14 S. & Rawle, (Penn.) R. 71; Hart *v.* Hill, 1 Whart. (Penn.) R. 136.

2 Williams *v.* Beardsley, 2 Cart. (Ind.) R. 591; and see Board of Commissioners, &c. Ibid. 162.

ebbing and flowing of the tide.[1] In the Supreme Court of the United States, in a case which came up from the District Court of the eastern district of Louisiana, the question was presented of admiralty jurisdiction, in the river Mississippi, which the Court considered was to be determined by the ebbing and flowing of the tide; and in determining the question, the ordinary state of the water, uninfluenced by any extraordinary freshets, was to be regarded.[2]

§ 64. It was urged in Rex *v.* Smith,[3] that the river Thames, above London Bridge, was not "navigable," although it was flowing and reflowing, inasmuch as the tide beyond that limit was occasioned by the pressure and accumulation backward of fresh water. But the distinction attempted was, by Lord Mansfield, pronounced new and inadmissible. In a case in the British House of Lords, where the question was, what was to be considered "river" and what "sea;" and where the direction was, that the thing to be looked to is the fact of the absence or prevalence of the fresh water, though strongly impregnated with salt; the direction was held to be erroneous.[4] The Supreme Court of the United States, referring to the above case of Rex *v.* Smith, have decided, that although the current in the river Mississippi, at New Orleans, may be so strong, as not to be turned backwards by the tide; yet, if the effect of the tide upon the current is so great as to occasion a regular rise and fall of the water, it might properly be said to be within the ebb and flow of the tide.[5]

§ 65. This distinction as it regards the law of *meum* and *tuum* between the term "navigable," in its technical sense, when applied to a river, and in the common acceptation of it,

1 Sir Henry Constable's case, 5 Ca. R. 107.
2 Peyroux *v.* Howard, 7 Peters, (U. S.) R. 324.
3 Rex *v.* Smith, 2 Doug. R. 441.
4 Horne *v.* Mackenzie, 6 Clark & Fin. R. 628.
5 Peyroux *v.* Howard, 7 Peters, (U. S.) 324.

when so applied, is important. In the case of the Royal Fishery of the river Banne, in Ireland, it was resolved, "that there are two kinds of rivers, navigable and not navigable; that every navigable river so high as the sea ebbs and flows in it, is a royal river, and belongs to the king, by virtue of his prerogative; but in *every other* river, and in the fishery of such other river, the *ter-tenants* on each side have an interest of common right; the reason for which is, that so high as the sea ebbs and flows, it participates of the nature of the sea, and is said to be a branch of the sea so far as it flows."[1] But all rivers entirely above the influence of the tide, if they are so large as to admit of navigation, and to be of public use for the passage of vessels, boats, &c., may, as well as those which ebb and flow, be under the servitude of the public interest, and be used as "public highways" by water. They are regarded as public, not in reference to the *property* in the soil or bed of the river, for that is in the riparian proprietors; but only in reference to public *use*. The doctrine of the common law as to this distinction, we have seen, is clearly and explicitly laid down by Lord Hale.[2] The right of property in the soil and bed of "navigable" rivers being thus vested in the sovereign, and that in the soil and bed of rivers which are only "public highways," being in the riparian proprietors, in adjusting controversies arising between the public and individuals, as to the right of soil covered by water, and the consequent rights of *fishery*, it may be necessary to ascertain the extent of the flowing of the tide.

§ 66. But the Courts of some of the States in this country have adjudged, that the common law, so far as it recognizes the above distinction, does not apply to our large fresh water rivers, and that these rivers, without reference to the flow and ebb of the tide, do not belong to the owners of the land adja-

---

[1] Royal Fishery, in the river Banne, (case of,) Davies, R. 149.
[2] De Jure Maris, &c.

cent, and that they have not the property in the soil under the water, and the consequent exclusive right of fishing *usque ad filum aquæ*, or, to the middle of the river; or, in other words, these rivers are to be deemed not merely "highways" but "navigable." Learned Judges in New York, have been inclined, on some occasions, to doubt the propriety of applying the rule of the common law to the extensive boatable rivers of this country, which are capable of being used as public highways far above where they are affected by tidal influence. Still, however, the rule remains unaltered in that State.[1] The question was directly passed upon in the Court of Chancery of New York, in Varick *v.* Smith,[2] whether the complainant, in the character of riparian proprietor, was to be regarded as the owner of the bed of the river Oswego, to the middle of the stream, adjacent to his possessions described in the bill; and Williams, V. C., considered it as settled in that State, that grants of land bounded on rivers above tide-water extend *usque ad filum aquæ*, and if the stream is in point of fact navigable for boats or other craft, the public have the easement of a right of passage, and nothing more. Upon an appeal of this case, in 1842,[3] it was, however, contended, that the decision of the Court of Errors, in the case of Canal Appraisers *v.* The People, on the relation of Tibbetts,[4] and certain remarks of the Chancellor himself, made in the course of his opinion in that case, and some few facts given in evidence by the defendants, threw a doubt upon the point. V. C. Gridley, in delivering his opinion upon making the decree appealed from, said it was true, that the counsel in the case just mentioned, contended that

---

1 See Palmer *v.* Mulligan, 3 Caines, (N. Y.) R. 307; Shaw *v.* Crawford, 10 Johns. (N. Y.) R. 236; People *v.* Platt, 17 Ib. 15; Hooker *v.* Cummings, 20 Ib. 90; Jennings, *ex parte*, 6 Cow. (N. Y.) R. 518; Canal Commissioners *v.* The People, 5 Wend. (N. Y.) R. 423; People *v.* Canal Appraisers, 13 Ib. 355.

2 Varick *v.* Smith, 5 Paige, (N. Y.) Ch. R. 137.

3 9 Paige, Ch. R. 547.

4 Canal Appraisers *v.* The People, *ex rel.* Tibbetts, 17 Wend. (N. Y.) R. 574, (in 1836.)

the common-law doctrine was not at all applicable in New York; but, said he, "it would seem to be enough that the most strenuous advocates for the right of the State to the bed of navigable rivers—Senators Beardsley and Tracy—with this very evidence before them, took the precaution to repel, by unequivocal language, the application of the principle contended for in the case before cited, to any other river than that of the Mohawk; and expressly reserving their judgments as to all other cases." An opinion seems to have been entertained, that the various *acts of the legislature* in relation to the river Mohawk, were evidence that the State was the owner of the bed of that river. But all of doubt or uncertainty upon the subject in New York, if any remained, were removed by the decision in the Court of Errors in that State, in the case of the Commissioners of the Canal Fund *v.* Kempshall,[1] in which the judgment of the Supreme Court, in favor of the riparian owners, was unanimously affirmed.

§ 67. This rule of the common law has also been recognized in the States of Massachusetts and New Hampshire, and has been applied by the Courts of both to the river Connecticut, at a point far above that to which the water is propelled backwards by the ingress and force of water from the sea.[2] It has been recognized also as law in the States of Connecticut,[3] Maine,[4] Maryland,[5] Virginia,[6] Ohio,[7] and Indiana.[8] In Illinois

---

1 Commissioners of Canal Fund *v.* Kempshall, 26 Wend. (N. Y.) R. 404.

2 Commonwealth *v.* Chapin, 5 Pick. (Mass.) R. 190; Scott *v.* Wilson, 3 N. Hamp. R. 321; State *v.* Gilmanton, 9 Ib. 461; Gray *v.* Bartlett, 20 Pick. (Mass.) R. 186.

3 Adams *v.* Pease, 2 Conn. R. 48; Chapman *v.* Kimball, 9 Ib. 38; East Haven *v.* Hemingway, 7 Ib. 186; Middletown *v.* Page, 8 Ib. 231.

4 Berry *v.* Carle, 3 Greenl. (Me.) R. 269; Spring *v.* Russell, 7 Ib. 273; Spring *v.* Seavey, 8 Ib. 138; Wadsworth *v.* Smith, 2 Fairf. (Me.) R. 278.

5 Brown *v.* Kennedy, 5 H. & Johns. (Md.) R. 195.

6 Hays *v.* Bowman, 1 Rand. (Va.) R. 417; Mead *v.* Haynes, 3 Ib. 33.

7 Gavitt *v.* Chambers, 3 Ohio R. 495; Lamb *v.* Ricketts, 11 Ib. 311; Walker *v.* Board of Public Works, 16 Ib. 540.

8 Cox *v.* The State, 3 Blackf. (Ind.) R. 193.

it is held, that the portion of the river Mississippi, upon which that State is bounded, is not a "navigable" stream at common law, and that, therefore, the riparian ownership extends to the middle of the stream.[1]

§ 68. On the other hand, the doctrine of the common law, on this subject, has been held to be inapplicable in Pennsylvania to the great rivers of that State, which are boatable far above tide-water, or where they are technically "navigable." It was settled in Carson *v.* Blazer,[2] that such rivers are "navigable;" although there is no flow and reflow of the tide, and that they belong to the State in the same manner, and to the same extent, as an arm of the sea; and that, therefore, the riparian owners have not an exclusive right to fish therein immediately in front of their lands, but the right of fishery in them is open to all. "The qualities," said Mr. J. Yeates, (in giving his opinion in this ably argued case,) "of *fresh* or *salt* water, cannot, amongst us, determine whether a river shall be deemed navigable or not; neither can the flux or reflux of the tides ascertain its character. Pursuing such a rule would, in fact, in the first case, render the river Delaware an unnavigable stream throughout the confines of the State; and in the second, would confine its navigable quality to its several courses south from Trenton. To assert that in either instance the proprietors of lands on the margin of that river have the sole right of fishery to the middle of its bed, corresponding to their title in front of it, is, I presume, a doctrine which the warmest advocates for the right of exclusive fisheries would scarcely contend for." The decision in this case was recognized and established, with much deliberation, in Shrunk *v.* Schuylkill Navigation Company,[3] in which Tilghman, C. J., in giving the judgment of the Court, said: "Many of our rivers, such as the

---

1 Middletown *v.* Pritchard, 3 Scamm. (Ill.) R. 500.

2 Carson *v.* Blazer, 2 Binn. (Penn.) R. 475.

3 Shrunk *v.* Schuylkill Nav. Co. 14 S. & Rawle, (Penn.) R. 71.

Mississippi, Ohio, Alleghany, and Susquehanna, are navigable, even in their natural state, by vessels of considerable burden, and whether if such rivers existed in England, the rule of the common law might not have been different, may certainly admit of a question."[1]

§ 69. Mr. J. McLean apprehended, that the common law doctrine, as to the "navigableness" of streams, could have no application in this country, and that the fact of navigableness did, in no respect, depend on the flowing of the tide;[2] and to that effect it has been held in South Carolina[3] and Tennessee.[4] In Alabama, every stream of water suited to the ordinary purposes of navigation, whether it ebbs and flows or not, (where the government has not expressly granted any part of the bed thereof,) is not only a public highway, but the owners of land bounded upon it, can assert no private right of soil to the bed of the river.[5] It has been held by the Supreme Court of North Carolina, too, that what is a "navigable" river in that State, does not depend upon the rule of the common law; but that waters which are sufficient in fact, to afford a common passage for people in vessels, are to be taken as "navigable."[6] In commenting upon the inapplicability of the common law on the subject, one of the Judges, in one case, in that State, pronounced it entirely inapplicable, and remarked, that by the rule of the common law, Albemarle and Pimlico Sounds, which are inland seas, would not be deemed "navigable" waters, and would be the subject of private property; it makes no difference whether there is, or ever was, any tide in Albemarle Sound.[7] There is much force in the following reasoning of

---

1 See also, Union Canal Co. *v.* Landis, 9 Watts, (Penn.) R. 228; Coovert *v.* O'Connor, 8 Watts, (Penn.) R. 447.

2 Bowman's Devisees *v.* Wathen, 2 McLean, (Cir. Ct.) R. 376.

3 Cates *v.* Waddington, 1 McCord, (S. C.) R. 580.

4 Elder *v.* Burrus, 6 Humph. (Tenn.) R. 358.

5 Bullock *v.* Wilson, 2 Port. (Ala.) R. 436.

6 Wilson *v.* Forbes, 2 Dev. (N. C.) R. 30.

7 Collins *v.* Benbury, 3 Ired. (N. C.) R. 277; and see Ingraham *v.* Threadgill, 3 Dev. (N. C.) R. 59; and 1 Jones, (N. C.) R. 299.

Judge Turley, of Tennessee, upon this subject, in delivering the opinion of the Supreme Court of that State: "All laws are, or ought to be, an adaptation of principles of action to the state and condition of a country, and to its moral and social position. There are many rules of action recognized in England as suitable, which it would be folly in the extreme, in countries differently located, to recognize as law; and, in our opinion, this distinction between rivers "navigable" and not "navigable," causing it to depend upon the ebbing and flowing of the tide, is one of them. The insular position of Great Britain, the short courses of her rivers, and the well-known fact that there are none of them navigable above tidewater but for very small craft, well warrants the distinction there drawn by the common law. But very different is the situation of the continental powers of Europe in this particular. Their streams are many of them large and long, and navigable to a great extent above tide-water; and accordingly we find that the civil law, which regulates and governs those countries, has adopted a very different rule."[1]

§ 70. The decisions cited in the above two sections, conform to the civil law, by which all rivers in which the flow of water is perennial, belong wholly to the public, and the public right extends to the use of the banks as well as to fishing.[2] *Navigable* rivers, in the language of the civil law, are not merely rivers in which the tide flows and reflows, but rivers capable of being navigated, that is, navigable in the *common sense* of the term. In the words of the Digest, a navigable river is "*statio iturve navigio*." In the Code Napoleon, navigable rivers are spoken of as "*flottables*," that is, rivers admitting floats.[3]

§ 71. A collision took place in the river Mississippi, near the Bay of Goulah, and there was much doubt in Waring

1 Elder *v.* Burrus, 6 Humph. (Tenn.) R. 366.

2 Dig. 43, 12, 13, 14; Inst. 212; 2 Domat, Civ. Law, 382, b. 1, t. 8, s. 1, 2.

3 Dig. 43, 12, 13, 14, 15; Zouch, El. Jur. Descriptio Juris et Indicii Maritimi, part 1, s. 5; Code Napoleon, b. 2, t. 2, c. 2, art. 556, 560–563; B. 2, t. 1, c. 3; Ord. Louis. 14, s. 3, art. 5.

*v.* Clarke,[1] whether the tide flowed so high, the evidence being conflicting; but the majority of the Court thought there was sufficient proof of tide there, and consequently, it was not necessary to consider whether the admiralty power extended higher. But this case shows the unreasonableness of giving a construction to the Constitution which would measure the jurisdiction of the admiralty by the tide. By an act of congress, passed the 26th of February, 1845,[2] the admiralty jurisdiction is made to depend upon the navigable character of the water, and not upon the ebb and flow of the tide. This act extended the jurisdiction of the district courts to certain cases upon the lakes and navigable waters connecting the same, and it has been held to be consistent with the Constitution of the United States. The ground upon which the act rests, is not the power granted to congress to regulate commerce, but the lakes and navigable waters connecting them were within the scope of admiralty and maritime jurisdiction as known and understood, in the United States, when the Constitution was adopted. The admiralty jurisdiction granted to the federal government by the Constitution, is not limited to tide-waters, but extends to all the public navigable lakes and rivers where commerce is carried on between different States, or with a foreign nation.[3] Over the *commercial* waters of a State, congress can exercise no commercial power, except as it regards an intercourse with other States of the Union, or foreign countries.[4]

§ 72. A stream nearly two hundred miles above tide-water, which has never been declared a public highway by statute, which is not capable of being used at any time for the passage of vessels or boats, or of floating rafts or logs, except when

---

1 Waring *v.* Clarke, 5 How. (U. S.) R. 441.

2 5 Stat. at Large, 726.

3 Case of the Propeller Genesee Chief, 12 How. (U. S.) R. 443.

4 Per McLean, J., in the Passenger Cases, 7 How. (U. S.) R. 283.

swelled by rains, or the melting of snow, is not, in any legal sense, navigable, but is private property, not subject to the servitude of the public interest by a passage upon it; unless the use of it had been dedicated to the public, by the owners. And where the owner of land on both sides of such a stream, has erected a dam across the same, to supply his mills, which would be injured by the floating of logs down the stream, over such dam, he is entitled to an injunction.[1]

### 12. *Towing on the Banks of Public Rivers.*

§ 73. By the civil law, which prevails in the greatest part of Europe and in Louisiana, the privilege of *towing* on the banks of navigable rivers is embraced in the public right of navigation.[2] In this respect, it is at variance with the common law. Bracton, it is true, has adopted the doctrine of the civilians, and his passage—*Riparum etiam usus publicus gentium sicut ipsius fluminis*—is plainly taken from Justinian; and though the same doctrine is quoted by Callis, in his work on Sewers, it is impeached by the otherwise unanimous current of authority. The little to be found in the books upon the subject, prior to the time of Lord Hale, he has collected, and, after commenting upon it, he very evidently concludes, that no such right as the one in question existed, inasmuch as he says, that where private interests are involved, they shall not be infringed without satisfaction being made to the party injured.[3] The doctrine, therefore, of the civil law on this subject, conflicts with the principle of the common law, and with one of the characteristics of the express written American constitutional law, that public convenience is to be viewed with a due regard to private property. The statute of 19 Hen. VII. c. 18, rel-

---

[1] Curtis *v.* Keesler, 14 Barb. (N. Y.) Sup. Ct. R. 511.

[2] Just. Inst. L. 2, tit. 1, s. 4; Coop. Just. tit. De Usu et Proprietate Riparum. The Civil Code of Louisiana follows the Roman Civil Law.

[3] De Jure Maris et Portibus.

ative to the navigation of the river Severn, allows a towing-path to the navigators, upon making reasonable compensation for the inconvenience they may thereby afford; and it thereby distinctly affords a negative to the idea of a common-law right without compensation. In a modern case, by an act of parliament, authorizing certain persons to make a certain part of the river Avon navigable, and to set out and appoint towing-paths, it was required that satisfaction should first be given to the owners of the land, and commissioners were appointed to settle by inquisition, what satisfaction every person, having a particular estate or interest therein, should receive for his respective interest.[1] But the question was brought directly before the King's Bench, in Ball *v.* Herbert,[2] whether, at common law, the public have the right of towing on navigable rivers, and it was expressly decided that they had not. Lord C. J. Kenyon said, he remembered when the case of Peirse *v.* Lord Fauconberg was sent to that Court from the Court of Chancery; and it was then the current opinion in Westminster Hall, that the right of towing depended on *usage*, without which it could not exist. Some of the passages, he said, in Lord Hale, which seem to favor the common-law right, are rather applicable to banks of the sea, and to ports.[3]

§ 74. The Supreme Court of Illinois, and that of Tennessee, have, however, decided, agreeably to the civil law, that the right of navigators was not limited to the bare privilege of floating upon the river Mississippi, but included a right to land, to fasten to the shore, as the exigencies of the navigation may require; and that such was a burden upon the owner of the land, which he must bear as a part of the public ease-

---

1 Bath River Navigation Co. *v.* Willis, 2 Cases relating to Railways and Canals, 7.

2 Ball *v.* Herbert, 3 T. R. 253.

3 See this case cited and approved by the Judges, in Blundell *v.* Catterall, 5 B. & Ald. R. 91.

ment.[1] Such, doubtless, had become established *usage* in respect to the great river in question, and if so, the decision is in accordance with the opinion of the Court in Ball *v.* Herbert. It was observed by Lord C. J. Kenyon, in that case, that "perhaps small evidence of usage before a jury would establish a right by custom, on the ground of public convenience."

§ 75. In Mississippi, the banks of a river, which is a public highway, are private property, subject to the exclusive appropriation of the owner, and are not subject to the use of the public, although the river itself may be a public highway.[2] The banks of navigable rivers, in Missouri, are public highways, and, though owned by private individuals, fishermen and navigators are entitled to a *temporary* use of them in landing, fastening, and repairing their vessels, and exposing their goods or merchandise; yet this right has its reasonable qualifications and restrictions, and will not allow a navigator to land for an unreasonable length of time, and, under pretence of repairing, employ teams, &c., thereby unreasonably obstructing the owner's enjoyment of his property.[3]

---

1 Middletown *v.* Pritchard, 3 Scam. (Ill.) R. 520; Godfrey *v.* Alton, 12 Ill. R. 29; Alton *v.* Illinois Transp. Co. Ibid. 38; Corp. of Memphis *v.* Overton, 3 Yerg. (Tenn.) R. 390. That the right of the public to tow vessels and boats upon the banks of navigable rivers, may be acquired by usage, see Kinlock *v.* Nevile, 6 Mees. & Welsb. (Eng. Exchr.) R. 794.

2 Morgan *v.* Reading, 3 Smedes & Marsh. (Mississip.) R. 366.

3 O'Fallan *v.* Daggett, 4 Missou. R. 343. The waters of the Albany Basin, as well as the navigable waters of the river, are a public highway. Hart *v.* Mayor, &c. of Albany, 3 Paige, (N. Y.) Ch. R. 213; and see State *v.* Wilkinson, 2 Vt. R. 480; Gould *v.* Hudson River Railroad Co. 12 Barb. (N. Y.) Sup. Ct. R. 616.

# CHAPTER II.

## OF THE LAYING OUT AND THE CONSTRUCTION OF HIGHWAYS BY LEGISLATIVE AUTHORITY.

1. Eminent Domain.
2. Practice in England.
3. Practice in the United States.
4. Of the Public Use.
5. Corporate Franchises.
6. Provision for Mode of Indemnity and the Proceedings under it.
7. Of the Kind and Mode of Compensation.

### 1. *Eminent Domain.*

§ 76. It has ever been the persuasion of mankind, that one of the principal powers, and one of the imperative duties of the sovereign power of a State is to provide for the wants of the community, as well for its own immediate emergencies, means of facilitating communication between distinct localities, both rural and urban. This, it is apparent, cannot be accomplished, (at least to the extent demanded, and in the manner the most desirable and satisfactory to all concerned,) without resort to an appropriation of *private property*. Hence, the power of making this appropriation is included in the general prerogatives which the government of every country retains over the estates of its subjects, a power that has been known and exercised under the appellation of "The Right of Eminent Domain." Persons who have made but partial inquiry into the theory of social organization must perceive that the right which every individual, as one of that organization, has over his own property, must, to a certain degree, ever be subordinate to the right which the

5*

community has over all; for without it there would be no compactness in the social union, nor any really effective force in the sovereign power.[1]

§ 77. Between this right of "Eminent Domain" and the governmental prerogative of "Taxation," the difference is very considerable. Taxation exacts money from individuals as their share of the public burden, and the tax-payer is supposed to receive a just compensation in the benefits conferred by the government, and in the proper application of the tax. It deals, as has been justly remarked[2] with the whole community, or with a special class of persons in the community, on some rule of apportionment. But what is taken under the right of eminent domain, is separate or aside from the owner's share of the common expenses, and to be compelled to contribute more than his share, he must be *reimbursed*.[3]

§ 78. It is indeed a rule insisted on by Pufendorf, Grotius, Vattel, and all eminent publicists as a rule founded in equity, that a provision for COMPENSATION is a necessary attendant on the due exercise of the power of the lawgiver to deprive an

---

[1] That private inconvenience and even injury, is to be endured rather than public inconvenience or injury, is a right of *public necessity*. 2 Kent, Comm. 337, 338. It is justifiable, in case of *fire*, for example, to raze houses to the ground to prevent the spreading of conflagration. Ibid. and the authorities there cited; Peckham *v.* Justices, &c. 9 Geo. R. 391; Taylor *v.* Inhabitants of Plymouth, 8 Met. (Mass.) R. 462. Congress, in 1777, lawfully directed the removal from Philadelphia of articles that were necessary to the maintenance of the continental army, or useful to the enemy, and in danger of falling into his hands; and an individual, whose property was lost in consequence of such removal, had no legal claim to compensation. Respublica *v.* Sparhawk, 1 Dall. R. 357; and see Dorsey's Ex'tor *v.* State, 4 H. & M'Hen. (Md.) R. 165. In regard to *highways*, there can be no destruction of the *public right*, at common law. According to Fowler *v.* Saunders, (Cro. Jac. 446,) a highway must always continue a highway, and can neither be narrowed nor inclosed, except by the agency of the representatives of the people in Parliament.

[2] See the judgment of the New York Court of Appeals in the case of the People *v.* Mayor of Brooklyn, 4 Comst. (N. Y.) R. 419.

[3] See *post*, Chap. IV.

individual of his property without his consent.[1] The law is universally recognized as laid down by Bynkershoek, that "this *eminent domain* may be lawfully exercised whenever public necessity or *public utility* requires it," and that "the sovereign power may take from proprietors those things without which *highroads* cannot be made;" and that "this right may be imparted to others occasionally, as to the chief magistrates of towns, cities," &c. But then he annexes the qualification, that "if houses and lands be taken from individuals, *adequate compensation* should be made."

## 2. *Practice in England.*

§ 79. In England, notwithstanding the transcendent power of parliament, the law on the subject of the construction of highways, under the direction of the sovereign power, has been ad-

---

1 Vattel, ch. 20, § 34, and see 2 Kent, Comm. 339. The greatest despots have not always felt themselves at liberty to take private property for a public purpose without compensation. One of the Judges, in the case of Lindsay *v.* Commissioners, in the Superior Court of South Carolina, 2 Bay, (S. C.) R. 58, has quoted from De Tott's Memoirs of the Turkish government, the following: "The Sultan Mustapha, being desirous of building and endowing a new mosque, fixed upon a spot in the city of Constantinople, which belonged to a number of individuals. He treated with all of them for the purchase of their parts, and they all willingly complied with his wishes, except a *Jew*, who owned a small house on the place, and who refused to give it up. A considerable price was offered to him, but he resisted the most tempting offers; his partiality for the spot, or his obstinacy resisted the most tempting offers. What was the conduct of the Sultan? He consulted his *Mufti*, who answered, that private property was sacred, that the laws of the *Prophet* forbade his taking it absolutely, but he might compel the Jew to lease it to him, as long as he pleased, at a *full rent;* and the Sultan submitted to the law." This is evidence, that the principle of *indemnification* is founded in natural justice. See also, People *v.* White, 19 Barb. (N. Y.) Sup. Co. R. 26; Hamilton *v.* Annapolis and Elk River Railroad Co. 1 Maryland Chancery Decisions, 107; Cooper *v.* Williams, 7 Greenl. (Me.) R. 273; Spring *v.* Russel, 3 Watts, (Penn.) R. 294; Henry *v.* Underwood, 1 Dana, (Ken.) R. 247; O'Hara *v.* Lexington, &c. Railroad Co. 1 Ibid. 232; Perry *v.* Wilson, 7 Mass. R. 395; Chesnut *v.* Shane's Lessee, 16 Ohio R. 599; Greenville and Columbia Railroad Co. *v.* Partlow, 6 Rich. (S. C.) Law 2, 286; County of Sangamon *v.* Brown, 14 Ill. R. 163.

ministered on the above-mentioned just and equitable principles. "If a new road," says Blackstone, "were to be made through the grounds of a private person, it might, perhaps, be extensively beneficial to the public; but the law permits no man, or set of men, to do this without consent of the owner of the land. In vain may it be urged that the good of the individual ought to yield to that of the community; for it would be dangerous to allow any private man, or even public tribunal, to be the judge of this common good, and to decide whether it be expedient, or no. Besides, the public good is in nothing more essentially interested, than in the protection of every individual's private rights, as modelled by the municipal law. In this, and in similar cases, the *legislature alone* can, and indeed frequently does interpose, and compel the individual to acquiesce. But how does it interpose and compel? Not by absolutely stripping the subject of his property in an arbitrary manner; but by giving him a full indemnification and equivalent for the injury thereby sustained. The public is considered as an individual, treating with an individual for exchange. All that the legislature does, is to oblige the owner to alienate his possessions for a reasonable price; and even this is an extension of power which the legislature indulges with caution."[1]

---

[1] 1 Bla. Com. 139. That a "full indemnification" is the condition, by the law of England, on which the valid exercise of the power of laying out highways depends, is evident from the act of parliament for making a new road in London, from Black Friar's Bridge, across St. George's Fields, (Anno. 1756.) The Corporation of London is thereby authorized and directed, to treat with the owners of lands that might be taken away by the road, for the purchase of the same; and in case of refusal to treat for the value of the lands taken, the same to be assessed by a jury. Cited by Waties, J., in Lindsay *v.* Commissioners, 2 Bay, (S. C.) R. p. 58. And see Sutcliffe *v.* Greenwood, 8 Price, Exch'r R. 535. Trespass for entering and breaking plaintiff's close. New assignment, setting out abuttals, to which the defendant pleaded a public highway. The plaintiff replied, that a new road had been made, by virtue of an act of parliament, and traversed the highway. By the act it was enacted, that the new road should be completed, and that the lands constituting the former road, (unless leading over some moor or waste ground, or to some village, town, or place to

§ 80. At this day, it is considered in England, that the true principle applicable to all such cases, is, that the private interest of the individual is never to be sacrificed to a greater extent than is necessary to secure a *public object* of adequate importance, and that the interference is one of an extraordinary character.[1] The English Courts will not, therefore, so construe an act of parliament as to deprive persons of their estates, and transfer them to other parties without compensation, in the absence of any manifest or obvious reasons of policy for so doing, unless they are so fettered by the express words of the statute as to be unable to extricate themselves;[2] for they will not suppose the legislature had such an intention.[3] As it was observed in a recent case, where large powers are intrusted to a company to carry their works through a great extent of country, without the consent of the owners and occupiers of the land through which they are to pass, it is reasonable and just, that any injury to property which can be shown to arise from the prosecution of those works should be fairly compensated to the party sustaining it.[4] The extraordinary powers with which railways and other similar companies in England are invested by parliament,

---

which the new road did not lead, should be vested in trustees and sold. It was held, that the trustees could not make a partial destruction of the road, and that, if the old road lead to a single house, the same remained subject to the public right. Wilkinson *v.* Bagshaw, Peake's Add. Cases, 165. Establishment of Highways by Parliament, see Rex *v.* Lyon, 5 Dowl. & Ry. R. 497; Rex *v.* Miller, 1 B. & Adol. R. 32; Rex *v.* Camberworth, 3 B. & Adol. R. 108; 4 Ibid. 731; Rex *v.* Yorkshire, 5 B. & Adol. R. 1013; Rex *v.* Edge Lane, 6 Nev. & Mann. R. 81; Wilkinson *v.* Bagshaw, Peake's Add. Cases, 165.

1 See, per Lord Eldon, 1 Mylne & Keen, Ch. R. 162; Webb *v.* Manchester and Leeds Railway Co. 4 Mylne & Cr. Ch. R. 116, in which the principles on which equity will exercise its jurisdiction over companies invested with compulsory powers are considered. See also Simpson *v.* Lord Howden, 1 Keen, Ch. R. 598; Lister *v.* Lobley, 7 Adol. & Ell. R. 124.

2 See Broom, Legal Max. 4.

3 Stracey *v.* Nelson, 12 M. & Welsb. R. 540; Hutchinson *v.* Manchester and Rossendale Railway Co. 14 M. & Welsb. R. 694.

4 Regina *v.* East Counties Railway Co. 2 Q. B., cited in Broom, Legal Max. 4; Blakemore *v.* Glamorganshire Canal Co. 1 Mylne & Keen, Ch. R. 162.

are given to them "in consideration of a benefit, which notwithstanding all other sacrifices, is, on the whole, hoped to be obtained by the public;" and that since the public interest is to protect the private rights of all individuals, and to save them from liabilities beyond those which the powers given by such acts necessarily occasion, they must always be carefully looked to, and must not be extended further than the legislature provided, or than is necessarily and properly required for the purposes which it has sanctioned.[1] Walford, in his "Summary of the Law of Railways,"[2] says, in reference to the rules of construction applicable to some of the more important provisions usually found in railway acts of parliament: "A power of this nature, calculated to operate in a manner so highly derogatory to private property must receive a strict interpretation. If, in the supposed exercise of such a power, the company enter upon, or take, any man's land, they must clearly establish their authority to do so; and if the words of the statute on which they rely are ambiguous, every presumption is to be made *against* the company, and *in favor of private property*."[3]

### 3. *Practice in the United States.*

§ 81. Still, it is true, that in England, where the power of parliament is often said to be *omnipotent* (meaning, of course, so far only as *human* agency is implicated,) there may be an abuse of the power of appropriating private property, where the act of appropriation is the concurrent act of the three estates of the realm; but in a State, governed by a *written Constitution*, as each State in this country is, if the legislature should so far forget its duty and the natural rights of an individual,

---

[1] Per Lord Langdale, in Coleman *v.* East Counties Railway Co. 1 Law Journal, (Chan.) 78.

[2] Walford on Railways, 63, (2d ed.) London, 1850.

[3] And see Scales *v.* Pickering, 4 Bing. R. 448; Webb *v.* Manchester and Leeds Railway Co. 4 Mylne & Craig, R. 120; and S. C. 1 Railway Cases, 599, per Lord Cottenham, Ld. Chan.; Selway *v.* Railway Co. 6 M. & Welsb. R. 699.

as to take his private property, and transfer it to another, when there is no foundation for a pretence that the public is to be benefited thereby, such an abuse of the law of eminent domain would be an infringement of the *letter*, as well as the spirit, of the constitutional law, and, therefore, is not within the general powers delegated to the legislature.[1] By the Constitution of the United States, too, "Private property shall not be taken for public use, without just compensation." This particular provision in this instrument, it is true, only restrains the power of the general government, and has no application to the several States;[2] but a prohibition to the same extent is to be found in the constitutions and bills of right of each of the States. Upon the admission of a State, as one of the United States, formed from territory of the latter, the right of eminent domain passes to the State, and nothing remains in the United States but the public lands.[3] Besides, it considered that the constitutional provisions on this subject, both of the United States, and of the several independent States, are only declaratory of the previously existing *universal* law which has been hinted.[4]

1 Varick *v.* Smith, 5 Paige, (N. Y.) Ch. R. 137.

2 Barron *v.* Mayor, &c. of Baltimore, 7 Peters, (U. S.) R. 243; State *v.* Dawson, 3 Hill, (S. C.) R. 100.

3 Pollard *v.* Hagan, 3 How. (U. S.) R. 212.

4 Per Spencer, C. J., in Bradshaw *v.* Hodges, 20 Johns. (N. Y.) R. 106; Wheelock *v.* Pratt, 4 Wend. (N. Y.) R. 647; Bougher *v.* Nelson, 9 G. & Johns. (Md.) R. 299; People *v.* White, 11 Barb. (N. Y.) Sup. Ct. R. 26; Harness *v.* Chesapeake and Ohio Canal Co. 1 Johns. (Md.) Ch. R. 248; Regents of the University of Maryland *v.* Williams, 9 G. & Johns. (Md.) R. 409; Bristol *v.* New Chester, 3 N. Hamp. R. 535; Embury *v.* Connor, 2 Sand. (N. Y.) Sup. Ct. R. 98; Young *v.* Harrison, 6 Georgia R. 131. See the Law of "Eminent Domain" reviewed by Chan. Walworth, in 3 Paige, (N. Y.) Chanc. R. 45. And see Flatbush Avenue, (Matter of,) 1 Barb. (N. Y.) R. 286; Toledo Bank *v.* Bond, 1 Ohio R. (N. S.) 686; Bradshaw *v.* Rogers, 2 Johns. R. 103; Furman, (Matter of,) 17 Wend. 659. The State of New York possesses the power to appropriate to public use the lands of the Indians, within their territory, upon making compensation therefor; notwithstanding the grant of the right of preëmption in such lands to Massachusetts. Wadsworth *v.* Buffalo Hydaulic Association, 15 Barb. (N. Y.) Sup. Co. R. 88.

§ 82. The legislative power of taking private property for public use by providing for adequate compensation, may be exercised directly by the employees of the government,[1] or, as has been long customary, through the medium of *incorporated companies*, or by means of individual enterprise. In Wilson *v.* Blackbird Creek Marsh Company, it is laid down by Chief Justice Marshall, that measures calculated to produce benefits to the public, though effected through the medium of a *private* corporation, are clearly within the powers reserved to the States, provided they do not come in collision with those of the federal government.[2] It appears by the cases referred to in subsequent pages of this work, that charters to private corporations have been repeatedly granted in this country for the reason that they have been necessary for the promotion of enterprises of public utility, and, in very many instances, they have been of essential service in contributing to the convenience of the community as the means of accomplishing public improvements which otherwise would not have been so seasonably undertaken, if at all.

§ 83. It is very obvious, that in taking private property, under the express authority of government, for public use, no more should be taken than is demandable by the exigencies of the community, and the least possible private injury in so doing, should be committed.[3] If the charter of a navigation

---

1 See *ante*, § 78. Power may be delegated to the magistrates of a county, to determine when it is expedient that a bridge should be thrown over a creek or cove. Commonwealth *v.* Charlestown, 1 Pick. (Mass.) R. 180. See Beekman *v.* Saratoga and Schenectady Railroad Co. 3 Paige, (N. Y.) Chan. R. 45.

2 Wilson *v.* Blackbird Creek Marsh Co. 2 Peters, (U. S.) R. 251, and see West River Bridge Co. *v.* Dix, 6 How. (U. S.) R. 183.

3 See Wallace's Appeal, 5 Barr, (Penn.) R. 101; Schaeffer's Road, *in re*, Ibid. 515; Pitt Township, *in re*, 1 Ibid. 356. And see Hooker *v.* Railroad Co. 15 Conn. R. 318; 2 Kent, Comm. 339, n.; Wheeler *v.* Rochester and Syracuse Railroad Co. 12 Barb. (N. Y.) Sup. Ct. R. 227; Hill, &c. *v.* Mohawk and Hudson Railroad Co. 3 Seld. (N. Y.) 152,—Ct. of Appeals.

company authorize the entering upon lands adjoining the works to be constructed, and taking materials therefrom, no more can be taken than as an *incident* to the promotion of what is intended by the charter.[1] So, the presumption is, in laying out a common highway, over the soil owned by an individual, such individual retains every right except the public easement; and hence, a railroad company cannot lay their track upon such highway, if any thing be done unnecessarily injurious to his right of soil.[2]

### 4. *Of the Public Use.*

§ 84. The power of determining upon what occasions, and under what circumstances, public uses of private property afford a sufficient pretension to its appropriation, is a *discretionary legislative* power. Although it must be conceded that the subject is one not without embarrassment, inasmuch as the line of demarcation between a use that is public, and one that is private, is not to be drawn without much consideration, yet the two branches of the legislature, subject only to the qualified veto of the executive, are the sole judges as to the expediency of making police regulations interfering with the natural rights of the citizen, or with the regulations which are conformable to the Constitution, and especially so, as to the expediency of exercising the right of *eminent domain* for the purpose of accomplishing public improvements by constraint, either for the benefit of the inhabitants of the State generally, or of any particular section thereof.[3]

---

1 Hind *v.* Wabash Navigation Co. 15 Ill. R. 72.

2 Trustees, &c. *v.* Auburn and Rochester Railroad Co. 3 Hill, (N. Y.) R. 567.

3 Varick *v.* Smith, 3 Paige, (N. Y.) Ch. R. 137; 2 Kent, Comm. 339; Smith, Comm. on Stat. and Const. Law, § 325; Beekman *v.* Schenectady and Saratoga Railroad Co. 3 Paige, (N. Y.) Ch. R. 45; Harris *v.* Thompson, 9 Barb. (N. Y.) Sup. Ct. 350; Hooker *v.* New Haven, &c. Co. 14 Conn. R. 146; Binney's Case, 2 Bland. (Md.) Ch. R. 99; Pittsburgh *v.* Scott, 1 Barr, (Penn.) R. 309;

§ 85. Although it is difficult, and perhaps not possible to lay down any general rule, that will precisely define the extent of the power of the government, in the exercise of the right of eminent domain; yet it appears from the authorities and the adjudged cases, referred to in the note to the preceding section, that it must be large and liberal enough to meet the public exigencies, and at the same time be so limited and restrained as to secure effectually the rights of the citizen;[1] it is manifestly a high exercise of the sovereign right.[2] One thing is, however, incontrovertible, which is, that the necessities of the public to the use to which the property is appropriated must exist as the *basis* upon which the right is founded.[3] Hence where private property is wanted merely for *ornamental* purposes, this right cannot be exercised; the purpose must be *useful*,[4] unless there is obtained the consent of the proprietor.[5]

§ 86. The doctrine that the right of eminent domain exists for every kind of public use, or for such a use when merely *convenient*, though not *necessary*, does not seem to be clearly maintainable, it being too open to abuse. A road, if really demanded in particular forms and places, to keep up with the wants and improvements of the age—such as its pressing demands for easier social intercourse, quicker political communication, or better internal trade—and advancing with the pub-

---

Commonwealth *v.* Breed, 4 Pick. (Mass.) R. 460; Inhabitants of Springfield *v.* Connecticut Railroad Co. 4 Cush. (Mass.) R. 63; City Waterworks, 27 Ala. R. 104; Dyer *v.* Tuscaloosa Bridge Co. 2 Port, (Ala.) R. 296; Cotrill *v.* Myrick, 2 Fairf. (Me.) R. 222; L. C. & C. Railroad Co. *v.* Chappell, 1 Rice, (S. C.) R. 383; Norman *v.* Heist, 5 Watts & S. (Penn.) R. 171.

1 Water Power Co. *v.* Boston and Worcester Railroad Co. 23 Pick. (Mass.) R. 360.

2 Inhabitants of Springfield *v.* Connecticut Railroad Co. 4 Cush. (Mass.) R. 63.

3 Smith, Comm. on Stat. and Const. Law, § 325; Wilkinson *v.* Leland, 2 Peters, (U. S.) R. 653.

4 See Boston and Roxbury Mill Corp. *v.* Newman, 12 Pick. (Mass.) R. 476; Dunn *v.* Council, &c. Harp. (S. C.) R. 180.

5 Embury *v.* Connor, 3 Comst. (N. Y.) R. 511.

lic necessities, from blazed trees to bridle paths, and thence to wheel roads, turnpikes and railroads. But when we go to other public uses, not so urgent, nor difficult to be provided for, without this power of eminent domain, and in places where it would be only *convenient* but not *necessary*, strong doubts may be entertained of its applicability. The user must be for the people at large—for travellers—for all—must be a right by the people, must be under public regulations as to tolls, or owned or subject to be owned by the State.[1]

---

[1] See opinion of Woodbury, J., in West River Bridge Co. *v.* Dix, 6 How. (U. S.) R. 545, 546; who cites 3 Kent, Comm. 276; Railroad Co. *v.* Chappell, 1 Rice, (S. C.) R. 383; Memphis *v.* Overton, 3 Yerg. (Tenn.) R. 53; King *v.* Russell, 6 B. & Cress. R. 566; King *v.* Ward, 1 Adol. & Ell. R. 384. Mr. Justice Woodbury, in his opinion just above referred to, says: "When we go to other public uses, not so urgent, not connected with precise localities, not difficult to be provided for without the power of eminent domain, and in places where it would be only convenient, but not necessary, I entertain strong doubts of its applicability. Who ever heard of laws to condemn private property for public use, for a marine hospital or State prison?

So a custom-house is a public use for the general government, and a court-house or jail for a State. But it would be difficult to find precedent or argument to justify taking private property, without consent, to erect them on, though appropriate for the purpose. No necessity seems to exist, which is sufficient to justify so strong a measure. A particular locality as to a few rods in respect to their site is usually of no consequence; while as to a light-house, or fort, or wharf, or highway between certain termini, it may be very important and imperative. I am aware of no precedents, also, for such seizures of private property abroad, for objects like the former, though some such doctrines appear to have been advanced in this country. 3 Paige, 45. Again, many things belonging to bridges, turnpikes, and railroads, where public corporations for some purposes, are not, like the land on which they rest, local and peculiar and public, in the necessity to obtain them by the power of the eminent domain. Such seem to be cars, engines, &c., if not the timber for rails, and the rails themselves. Gordon *v.* C. & J. Railway Co. 2 Railway Cases, 809.

Such things do not seem to come within the public exigency connected with the roads which justifies the application of the principle of the eminent domain. Nor does even the path for the road, the easement itself, if the use of it be not public, but merely for particular individuals, and merely in some degree beneficial to the public. On the contrary, the user must be for the people at large,—for travellers—for all,—must also be compulsory by them, and not optional with the owners,—must be a right by the people, not a favor,—must be under public regulations as to tolls, or owned, or subject to be owned, by the State, in order to

§ 87. Very clearly, then, the right of eminent domain does not authorize the government, even for a full compensa-

---

make the corporation and object public, for a purpose like this. 3 Kent, Comm. 270; Railroad Co. *v.* Chappell, 1 Rice, 383; Memphis *v.* Overton, 3 Yerger, 53; King *v.* Russell, 6 Barn. & Cres. 566; King *v.* Ward, 4 Adol. & Ellis, 384.

It is not enough that there is an act of incorporation for a bridge, or turnpike, or railroad, to make them public, so as to be able to take private property constitutionally, without the owner's consent; but their uses, and object, or interests, must be what has just been indicated,—must in their essence, and character, and liabilities, be public within the meaning of the term "public use." There may be a private bridge, as well as private road or private railroad, and this with or without an act of incorporation.

In the present instance, however, the use was to be for the whole community, and not a corporation of any kind. The property was taken to make a free road for the people of the State to use, and was thus eminently for a public use, and where there had before been tolls imposed for private profit and by a private corporation so far as regards the interest in its tolls and property.

And the only ground on which that corporation, private in interest, was entitled in any view originally to condemn land or collect tolls was, that the use of its bridge was public,—was open to all and at rates of fare fixed by the legislature and not by itself, and subjected to the revision and reduction of the public authorities.

It may be, and truly is, that individuals and the public are often extensively benefited by private roads, as they are by mills, and manufactories, and private bridges. But such a benefit is not technically nor substantially a public use, unless the public has rights. 1 Rice, 388. And in point of law it seems very questionable as to the power to call such a corporation a public one, and arm it with authority to seize on private property without the consent of its owners.

I exclude, therefore, all conclusions as to my opinions here being otherwise than in conformity to these suggestions; though when as in the present case, a free public use in a highway and bridge is substituted for a toll-bridge, and on a long or great and increasing line of public travel, and thus vests both a new benefit and use, and a more enlarged one, in the public, and not in any few stockholders, I have no doubt that these entitle that public for such a use to condemn private property, whether owned by an individual or a corporation. Boston W. P. Co. *v.* B. & W. Railroad Corp. 23 Pick. 360. And it is manifest that unless such a course can be pursued, the means of social and commercial intercourse might be petrified, and remain for ages, like the fossil remains in sandstone, unaltered, and the government, the organ of a progressive community, be paralyzed in every important public improvement. 2 Dev. & Bat. 456; 1 Rice, 395; 8 Dana, 309.

tion, *to take the property of one citizen and transfer it to another*, when the public is not beneficially interested in the transfer.[1] The possession and exertion of such a power would be incompatible with the nature and very object of all government; for, it being admitted, that a chief end for which government is instituted, is, that every man may enjoy his own; it follows, necessarily, that the rightful exercise of a power by the government of taking arbitrarily from any man what is his own, for the purpose of giving it to another, would subvert the very foundation-principle upon which the government was organized, and resolve the political community into its original chaotic elements.[2] In the matter of Albany Street, Chief Justice Savage, (in commenting on the section of the law under which the corporation of the city of New York had proceeded in widening a street,) says, that, "the Constitution, by authorizing appropriation of private property to public use, impliedly declares, that for any other use, private property shall not be taken from one and applied to the private use of another." It is in violation, he says, of natural right; and if it is not in violation of the *letter* of the Constitution, it is of its spirit.[3] In Bloodgood *v.* Railroad Company, Mr. Senator Tracy says: "These words of the Constitution should be construed as equivalent to a constitutional declaration, that private property, without the consent of the owner, shall be taken *only* for the public use, and then only upon a just compensation."[4] Chancellor Bland, of Maryland, in giving his opinion in an important case,

---

1 Pittsburgh *v.* Scott, 1 Barr, (Penn.) R. 139; Beekman *v.* Schenectady and Saratoga Railroad Co. 3 Paige, (N. Y.) Ch. R. 45; Varick *v.* Smith, 5 Paige, (N. Y.) Ch. R. 159; Taylor *v.* Porter, 4 Hill, (N. Y.) R. 140.

2 Bloodgood *v.* Mohawk and Hudson Railroad Co. 18 Wend. (N. Y.) R. 56; Hamilton *v.* Annapolis and Elkbridge Railroad Co. 1 Johns. (Md.) Ch. R. 107; Day *v.* Stetson, 8 Greenl. (Me.) R. 365.

3 Albany Street (in the Matter of,) 11 Wend. (N. Y.) R. 149.

4 Bloodgood *v.* Railroad Co. 18 Wend. (N. Y.) R. 59; see Embury *v.* Connor, 2 Sand. (N. Y.) Sup. Ct. R. 98.

says: "The government of this Republic, by virtue of that *eminent domain*, which, for public purposes is intrusted to all governments, may take the property of any individual and cause it to be applied to the use of the public, on making him a reasonable compensation. But," says he, "it cannot arbitrarily take property from one citizen and bestow it on another; because such an act, although not specially prohibited by the Constitution, would be contrary to the fundamental principles of the government itself."[1] As has been declared by a learned Judge in Virginia, "Liberty itself consists essentially, as well in the security of private property, as of the persons of individuals; and this security of private property is one of the primary objects of civil government, which our ancestors, in framing our Constitution, intended to secure to themselves and their posterity, effectually, and forever."[2]

§ 88. There are no instances in which private property of any denomination can be taken by State authority for the mere purpose of raising a revenue (unless in the regular mode of taxation);[3] and an assumption of power to that extent would be entirely destructive of individual right, and annihilate, at the pleasure of the State, all distinctions between *meum* and *tuum*. Therefore, canal commissioners, who are authorized by the legislature to take water enough from a *watercourse* for canal navigation, have no authority, for the purpose of creating hydraulic power, to sell or lease the surplus water for the benefit of the public revenue. Although, in conducting the water to the canal through a feeder, the State agents must necessarily exercise a discretionary power, yet the water can only be taken by them for canal purposes; and if taken and rented to an in-

---

1 Hepburn's case, 3 Bland, (Md.) Ch. R. 98. And the Chancellor refers to Campbell's case, 2 Bland, (Md.) Ch. R. 230; and Partridge *v.* Dorsey, 3 H. & Johns. (Md.) R. 302; Harness *v.* Chesapeake and Ohio Canal Co. 1 Johns. (Md.) Ch. R. 248.

2 Per Mr. J. Green, in Crenshaw *v.* Slate River Co. 6 Rand. (Va.) R. 245.

3 See *ante*, as to taxation, § 77.

dividual, no title would pass against the riparian owners entitled to it by law.[1]

§ 89. Lots bounding upon a river, and immediately below a State dam erected for the use of a canal, were sold by the New York commissioners of the land-office as water lots bounding upon the river; and it was held, that the purchaser of such water lots was entitled to the water privileges connected with such lots at the time of the sale, by *the natural flow of the surplus water* over the State dam, so far as they could be used without interfering with the right of navigation; and that the State officers could not afterwards lease such surplus waters, and authorize the lessee to prevent them from flowing over the dam, to the injury of the water privileges connected with the water lots thus sold. The language of the Court, in the appeal of this case, was: "The government has the power, under the Constitution, to appropriate the private property of its citizens, just so far, and no further, than is necessary for the purpose and object of the appropriation; and that may be an absolute and exclusive right to land or water, or it may be a partial or common or usufructuary right, according to the nature of the property or the circumstances of the case. But when such purpose is accomplished, the right of the State is exhausted, and the whole of the residue of the property, whatever it may be, belongs to the citizen."[2]

§ 90. So, canal commissioners are not authorized to dispose of the water power of a stream to persons who have been injured by the canal, to pay them for their damages;[3] and where the mill of a person is likely to be injured by a dam erected

---

1 Buckingham *v.* Smith, 10 Ohio R. 288.

2 Varick *v.* Smith, 5 Paige, (N. Y.) Ch. R. 137, and on appeal, 9 Paige, (N. Y.) Ch. R. 547. And see Harris *v.* Thompson, 9 Barb. (N. Y.) Sup. Ct. R. 350.

3 M'Arthur *v.* Kelley, 5 Ohio R. 84.

above it to supply a canal feeder, the canal commissioners have no power to dig a race across another person's land, without consent, to conduct the water from the feeder to the mill-owner, and so compensate him for his loss; and, if a threat is made to dig such a race, an injunction will lie.[1]

§ 91. Although, in Ohio, the law authorizes canal commissioners to dispose of the water for hydraulic purposes, with a view to raise a revenue to aid in defraying the expense of the canal, still this relates only to the water which is necessary for the navigation of the canal and which can be used for no other purposes, without interfering with the navigation. It does not authorize them to receive a surplus quantity of water into the canal, that they may dispose of it; for the reason that private property can only be taken by the legislature or its agents when necessary for the promotion of the public welfare, it being in that case necessary to make compensation.[2]

### 5. *Corporate Franchises.*

§ 92. A portion of, or even the whole of, a *corporate franchise*, may be condemned and taken for public use; for although the charter creating it is a contract between the State and the persons or company to whom it is granted, yet, like all private rights, it is subject to the right of eminent domain in the State. This was the doctrine established by the Supreme Court of the United States, in the case of West River Bridge Company *v.* Dix,[3] in which a distinction is made between the power of a State to resume a charter under the power of appropriation, and the peculiar privilege *bonâ fide* exercised by the State to apply it to the benefit of the community. The plaintiffs in error were made a corporation by the legislature of Vermont, and, by the act of incorporation, had granted to them the exclusive

---

1 M'Arthur *v.* Kelley, 5 Ohio R. 84.

2 Cooper *v.* Williams, 3 Ohio R. 244.

3 West River Bridge Co. *v.* Dix, 6 How. (U. S.) R. 507.

privilege of erecting and maintaining a *bridge*[1] over West River, with the right of taking tolls; and the franchise, which was to continue one hundred years, had not yet expired. The property of the plaintiffs, both realty and franchise, was appraised, and due provision made for compensation to the full value of the same; and the decision of the Court was in accordance with the maxim—*Salus populi suprema lex.* It has been held in New Hampshire, that in the exercise of the power of eminent domain, the track and property of one *railroad*[2] may be taken for the use of another, provided the public interests demand it.[3] The act of the legislature of Vermont, passed in 1839, authorizing the Supreme and County Courts to take the franchise of a *turnpike* corporation[4] for a public highway, has been held to be constitutional, provided, of course, compensation be made to the turnpike company.[5] The doctrine, indeed, has widely prevailed in this country.[6]

§ 93. An exclusive franchise may be said to be *taken*, within the meaning of the prohibition to take private property for public use, without compensation, when the owner is deprived of

---

1 See *ante*, § 35.

2 See *ante*, § 17.

3 Northern Railroad *v.* Concord and Claremont Railroad, 7 Fost. (N. H.) R. 183.

4 See *ante*, § 8.

5 Armington *v.* Barnet, 15 Vt. R. 745; White River Turnp. Co. 21 Vt. R. 590.

6 Boston Water Power Co. *v.* Railroad Co. 23 Pick. (Mass.) R. 360; and see 16 Ib. 512; White River Co. *v.* Vermont Central Railroad Co. 21 Vt. R. 598; Miller *v.* New York and Erie Railroad Co. 21 Barb. (N. Y.) 513; Bonaparte, Camden and Amboy Railroad Co. 1 Bald. (Cir. Ct.) R. 222; Tuckahoe Canal Co. *v.* T. and J. River Railroad Co. 11 Leigh, (Va.) R. 42; Enfield Bridge Co. *v.* Hartford and New Haven Railroad Co. 17 Conn. R. 40; Armington *v.* Barnet, 15 Vt. R. 745; Ib. 446; Lexington and Ohio Railroad case, 8 Dana, (Ken.) R. 289; Pierce *v.* Somersworth, 10 N. H. R. 370; 11 Ib. 20; Piscataqua Bridge Co. *v.* New Hampshire Bridge Co. 7 N. Hamp. R. 35, 66; Barber *v.* Andover, 8 N. Hamp. R. 398; White River Railroad Co. *v.* Vermont and Central Railroad Co. 21 Vt. R. 590, and 1 Am. Railway Cases, 233.

the power of exercising it; and it is immaterial how the State deprives him of it, whether directly, or indirectly, or *consequentially*.[1] Any serious interruption to its common and necessary use, is equivalent to the taking of it; as if a corporation is created by the legislature for the purpose of constructing a canal, if there be no compensation provided for the discharge of the water upon the lands of others, they are entitled, in an action on the case, to recover damages for an injury sustained by such discharge.[2] In the Court of Errors of New York, it was distinctly laid down, that the State had not the right, without making or providing for compensation, to damage the property of riparian owners upon rivers above tide-water, by making waters navigable which were not so by nature; or in appropriating the water of such rivers to the public use by artificial erections.[3] By the spirit and meaning of both the constitution and the canal acts of that State, if an individual be *consequentially* injured by the erection of a dam under the authority of the legislature, with a view to afford water to a canal, he is entitled to compensation for the injury sustained equally as though his property is *directly* taken.[4] An action lies by the owner of land against a railroad company, if, in the construction of their road upon, or across a public highway, they raise an embankment, by which the owner of the land is obstructed in passing to and from the road, and his property is rendered otherwise less valuable; notwithstanding the charter of the company authorizes the entry upon, and use

---

1 Hamilton Avenue, (Matter of,) 14 Barb. (N. Y.) Sup. Ct. R. 405; Hooker *v.* Railroad Co. 15 Conn. R. 318.

2 Hooker, &c., *ub. sup.;* Rowe *v.* Granite Bridge Co. 21 Pick. (Mass.) R. 348.

3 Canal Commissioners *v.* People, 5 Wend. (N. Y.) R. 423; and see People *v.* Platt, 17 Johns. (N. Y.) R. 135; Hudson and Delaware Canal Co. *v.* New York and Erie Railroad Co. 9 Paige, (N. Y.) Ch. R. 323.

4 People *v.* Canal Appraisers, 13 Wend. (N. Y.) R. 355.

of, such public highway, the license relates only to the road, and leaves the company liable to consequential damages sustained by individuals.[1]

§ 94. But it has been, on some occasions, a question of very considerable nicety, as to what has amounted to a legal infringement of privileges granted to incorporated companies. The proprietors of a toll-bridge applied for an injunction to restrain the construction of another bridge over the same arm of the sea, as it would injuriously affect the tolls of the first bridge; and the Court, after hearing elaborate arguments of counsel, and upon very great deliberation, dismissed the bill, the Judges being equally divided.[2] The case was then brought to the Supreme Court of the United States,[3] where the decree of the State Court was affirmed, Mr. Justice Story and Mr. Justice Thompson, dissenting. The opinion of the Court, delivered by Taney, C. J., was grounded upon the consideration, that the end of all government is to promote the prosperity of the community by which it is established, and that it should never be assumed to be the intent of government to diminish its power of accomplishing the end for which it was created; this was peculiarly so in this country, free, active and enterprising, and in which new channels of communication were daily found necessary, both for travel and trade, and for the essential welfare of the community at large. The learned Judge pronounced, that the continued existence of government would be of no great value, if, by implications and presumptions, it was to be disarmed of the powers requisite to accomplish the ends of its creation, and if the functions it was designed to perform, were to be transferred to the hands of corporations; while the rights of private property were to be regarded, those of the community should not be disregarded.[4] The statute of the State

[1] Fletcher *v.* Auburn and Syracuse Railroad Co. 25 Wend. (N. Y.) R. 462.

[2] Charles River Bridge *v.* Warren Bridge, 7 Pick. (Mass.) R. 344.

[3] 11 Peters, (U. S.) R. 420.

[4] The same view of the law governed the decision of the Court in Mohawk

of Massachusetts of 1786, as to the selectmen assigning limits to the surveyors respectively, is not contrary to the bill of rights of that commonwealth; which has never been construed to give a right to compensation for an indirect or consequential damage, or expense, resulting from the right use of property, already belonging to the public.[1]

§ 95. The bridge case above referred to, establishes the doctrine, that a State law creating a franchise which may rival and diminish the profits of a preëxisting one, established under a prior law, which does not grant an exclusive privilege, does not violate the *obligation* of any *contract*. So, too, in Lansing *v.* Smith,[2] it was decided, that the grant of a wharf, under an act of the legislature, which conveys a franchise, does not impair the power of the legislature to make a second grant to construct a wharf in the same vicinity, which shall essentially diminish the profits and impair the privileges of the prior one; and that the loss sustained by the proprietor of the wharf first constructed, is *damnum absque injuria*, for which no action lies. Whether a second grant for the same object is in violation of the first grant or not, must depend upon circumstances. If the sole object of the second grant is to promote individual interests, or if it is not called for by the public wants, it would be unjustifiable, and ought not to be made. But it is otherwise where the public good calls for new grants. This was

---

Bridge Co. *v.* Utica and Schenectady Railroad Co. 6 Paige, (N. Y.) R. 554; and see Dyer *v.* Tuscaloosa Bridge Co. 2 Port. (Ala.) R. 296; Hartford Bridge Co. *v.* East Hartford, 16 Conn. R. 150.

1 Callender *v.* Marsh, 1 Pick. (Mass.) R. 417. In 1838, the legislature of the territory of Iowa, authorized one F., his heirs and assigns, to establish and keep a ferry across the Mississippi River, at the town of Dubuque, for the term of twenty years; and the act of the legislature declared, that no Court, or Board of County Commissioners, should authorize any person, unless upon F.'s failure to comply with certain requirements, to keep a ferry within the town of Dubuque; the act did not give an exclusive right to a ferry within the limits of that place. Fanning *v.* Gregoire, 16 How. (U. S.) R. 524.

2 Lansing *v.* Smith, 4 Wend. (N. Y.) R. 3.

the general doctrine laid down by the Court, in the matter of Hamilton Avenue,[1] in which it was held, that the legislative authority conferred to grant one bridge over a certain creek, did not warrant the presumption that the legislature intended that there should be no other over a stream of considerable extent, and passing through a region of country soon to become a part of a crowded city; though a grant may be exclusive, when it is *expressly declared* to be so, or where some general term is used which comprehends the entire privilege. It may, indeed, be considered as entirely settled in the State of New York, that the apprehended damage which a toll-bridge may sustain, in a diminution of their tolls, by a diversion of the travel from their bridge to a public avenue authorized to be opened, is not a grievance that is entitled to redress, if the statute creating the franchise does not confer an exclusive right.[2]

§ 96. In relation to a corporate franchise, the distinction is between a grant that is clearly intended to be of an entire and exclusive privilege, and an implied grant of such privilege, or one sought to be implied.[3] Terms may undoubtedly be used in a grant sufficiently comprehensive, and in reference to the object of it, to embrace an exclusive privilege which cannot be invaded without compensation. If the legislature should grant an exclusive right to erect a toll-bridge *within certain limits*, it cannot authorize, without provision for compensation to the grantees, the erection of another bridge within those limits.[4]

---

[1] Hamilton Avenue, (Matter of,) 14 Barb. (N. Y.) Sup. Ct. R. 405.

[2] Thompson *et al.* *v.* New York and Harlem Railroad Co. 3 Sand. (N. Y.) Ch. R. 625; Mohawk Bridge Co. *v.* Utica and Schenectady Railroad Co. 6 Paige, (N. Y.) Ch. R. 554; Oswego Falls Bridge Co. *v.* Fish *et al.* 1 Barb. (N. Y.) Sup. Ct. R. 547.

[3] Furman Street, (Matter of,) 17 Wend. (N. Y.) R. 649; White River Turnpike Co. *v.* Vermont Central Railroad Co. 21 Vt. 590; and 1 Am. Railway Cases, 233; Hooker *v.* New Haven and Northampton Co. 14 Conn. R. 146; Enfield Toll-Bridge Co. *v.* Hartford and New Haven Railroad Co. 17 Conn. R. 454; Hatch *v.* Central Railroad Co. 25 Vt. R. 49; Lynch *v.* Mallory, 4 Denio, (N. Y.) R. 356; and see Stourbridge *v.* Canal Co. 2 Barn. & Adol. R. 792.

[4] Piscataqua Bridge Co. *v.* New Hampshire Bridge Co. 7 N. Hamp. R. 35.

In New Hampshire, an action will lie against the selectmen of a town, for laying out a highway merely for the purpose of enabling travellers to evade the payment of toll at a turnpike gate.[1] But still, if the public convenience should require that a road be laid out to a turnpike, it can lawfully be done, although it may enable passengers to evade the payment of toll.[2]

§ 97. In the matter of the Flatbush Avenue, in the city of Brooklyn,[3] it appeared, from the report of commissioners respecting the opening of an avenue, that such avenue crossed a public turnpike road at two distinct points, and thus opened a road whereby travellers could avoid the toll-gate of the company, and thereby materially injured the value of the franchise. For this injury the commissioners had awarded to the company no damages, and had awarded only two small sums for the damage arising from taking the road for the avenue, and had assessed them an equal amount for the expense of opening the avenue. The Court refused to confirm the report; and it was adjudged, that the franchise which a turnpike company obtains from the legislature, by its act of incorporation, is as much the subject of value to the company, as the private property of any individual; and that such company have as clear a right as any person owning land, to be indemnified for an injury sustained by them in consequence of the appropriation of their property to the public use. The case of Charles River Bridge was cited by counsel to the contrary; but Edmonds, J., in giving judgment, said: "If this avenue had been *merely a parallel road with the turnpike*, perhaps the doctrine of the Charles River Bridge case might have been applicable. But such is not the case. At two points this avenue invades and takes the

---

1 Proprietors of Third Turnp. *v.* Champney, 2 N. Hamp. R. 199; Cheshire Turnpike *v.* Stevens, 10 N. Hamp. R. 133.

2 By Richardson, Ch. J., in Proprietors of Third Turnp. Co., *ub. sup.*

3 Flatbush Avenue, (in the Matter of,) 1 Barb. (N. Y.) Sup. Ct. R. 286.

land which the company had obtained under their act of incorporation; and thereby the company is brought directly within the statute under which the commissioners have proceeded, and which directs them to estimate the damage to be sustained by the owners of such lands and buildings as may be affected by the improvement." The learned Judge considered, that the case of the Seneca Road Company *v.* The Auburn and Rochester Railroad Company,[1] was decisive of the point, that the turnpike company in question was entitled to recover the damage which it had actually sustained.

§ 98. If a turnpike company complete their road, and put the same in use, and erect a toll-gate thereon opposite the land of A, and A opens a road on his own land parallel to, and adjoining the turnpike road, so that the same is passable for travellers, and is used by them to avoid the toll-gate, a court of equity has power to order A's road to be closed.[2]

§ 99. A case of claim for damages, for remotely consequential damage, is that of Gould *v.* Hudson River Railroad Company.[3] The defendants, in this case, it appeared, (under, and in pursuance of, their charter, authorizing them to construct their railroad from New York to Albany,) entered upon the Hudson River, in front of the plaintiff's farm, and between the ordinary high and the ordinary low water mark, raised a line of solid embankment across the whole river, in front of said farm, about five feet in height above the ordinary high-water mark, and formed a barrier to the passage of vessels, boats, &c. through the same, and laid a railroad track upon such embankment, and ran their cars thereon; and this without the consent of the plaintiff, and without making or tendering any

---

1 Seneca Road Co. *v.* Auburn and Rochester Railroad Co. 5 Hill, (N. Y.) R. 170.

2 Auburn, &c. Plank-road *v.* Douglass, 12 Barb. (N. Y.) Sup. Ct. R. 553.

3 Gould *v.* Hudson River Railroad Co. 12 Barb. (N. Y.) Sup. Ct. R. 616; 2 Selden, (N. Y.) R. 522.

compensation for damage sustained thereby. It was held, that the legislature had not transcended their authority in making the grant, (the State owning to high-water mark); and that the defendants were authorized to do the acts complained of, the plaintiff not having sustained any injury which was actionable.

§ 100. Again, where a municipal corporation, under an authority contained in its charter, grades and levels a street, an action will not lie by an adjoining owner, whose lands are not actually taken, for consequential damages to his premises, there being no want of care or skill in the execution of the work, and no provision in the charter for damages of that sort; because an act done by lawful authority, if done in a proper manner, will not subject the party doing it to an action for the consequences. The corporation of the city of Brooklyn regularly laid out and opened a street, and afterwards proceeded to grade the street for public use, and in thus doing, removed a high bank which constituted a natural support to the premises of an adjoining owner, so that a portion of his land fell. It was held, that the adjoining owner could not maintain an action on the case for the damage sustained by him.[1]

---

[1] Radcliff's Ex'rs *v.* Mayor, &c. of Brooklyn, 4 Comst. (N. Y.) R. 195. In Thurston *v.* Hancock, (12 Mass. R. 220,) the plaintiff had built a valuable house on Beacon Hill, in Boston, one side of the house being within two feet of the side of his land, and had taken the precaution to sink his foundation fifteen feet below the ancient surface of the ground. Seven years afterwards, the defendant commenced digging and carrying away the earth from his adjoining land, and dug to the depth of from thirty to forty-five feet below the natural surface of the ground; by reason of which the foundation of the plaintiff's was rendered insecure, and he was obliged to take his house down; yet it was held, that no action lay for the injury to the house. A similar decision was made in Lasala *v.* Hobrok, 4 Paige, (N. Y.) Ch. R. 169. For a valuable collection of the authorities as to what a man may and may not do in the enjoyment of his own property, assuming that he acts with due care and proper skill, see the opinion of Ch. J. Bronson, in Radcliff's Ex'rs, &c. *ub. sup.*

## 6. *Provision for Mode of Indemnity, and Proceedings under it.*

§ 101. The legislature, in the exercise of its authority of taking private property, is not solely, by itself, to fix the amount of compensation to be awarded to the owner. This can constitutionally be ascertained, fixed and awarded only in three modes; first, by a mutual stipulation between the legislature or its agents, and the proprietor; secondly, by commissions mutually agreed on; and, thirdly, by the intervention of a jury, or other mode equally equitable, as by commissioners or appraisers appointed by law. The government is clearly bound to provide *some* tribunal for indemnity, before which each party may meet and discuss their claims on equal terms;[1] and herein is the important constitutional guard, and the proper degree of restraint upon the exercise of legislative authority on such occasions.[2] The damages, of course, are to be estimated by persons who have previously expressed no opinion.[3]

---

1 2 Kent, Comm. 339, *note.*

2 Van Horne's Lessee *v.* Dorrence, 2 Dallas, (Penn.) R. 313; Beekman *v.* Saratoga and Schenectady Railroad Co. 3 Paige, (N. Y.) Ch. R. 45; Pennsylvania Railroad Co. *v.* Heister, 8 Barr, (Penn.) R. 445; Wyman *v.* Lexington and West Cambridge Railroad Co. 13 Met. (Mass.) R. 316; Morse *v.* Boston and Maine Railroad Co. 2 Cush. (Mass.) R. 536; Walker *v.* Boston and Maine Railroad Co. 3 Cush. (Mass.) R. 91; Fitchburg Railroad Co. *v.* Boston and Maine Railroad Co. 3 Cush. (Mass.) R. 58; Field *v.* Vermont and Massachusetts Railroad Co. 4 Cush. (Mass.) R. 450; Vermont Central Railroad Co. *v.* Baxter, 22 Vt. R. 365; Nashville, &c. Railroad Co. *v.* Concordia, 11 Humph. (Tenn.) R. 449; Baltimore Turnpike case, 5 Binn. (Penn.) R. 481; Armstrong *v.* Jackson, 1 Blackf. (Ind.) R. 374; Haight *v.* Morris Aqueduct, 4 Wash. (Cir. Ct.) R. 601; Vischer *v.* Hudson River Railroad Co. 15 Barb. (N. Y.) Sup. Ct. R. 37. "Liberties," says Guizot, "are nothing unless they have become rights—positive rights formally recognized and consecrated. Rights, even when recognized, are nothing so long as they are not intrenched within guarantees. And lastly, guarantees are nothing so long as they are not maintained by forces independent of them in the limit of their rights. Convert liberties into rights, surround rights by guarantees, intrust the keeping of these guarantees to forces capable of maintaining—such are the successive steps in the progress towards a free government." Guizot, on Rep. Gov. 302.

3 Redding *v.* Dilley, 4 Zabrisk. (N. J.) R. 209.

§ 102. The *trial by jury*, as generally secured by a State constitution, is applicable to trials of issues of fact in civil and criminal cases in courts of justice, and has no relation to assessments of damages sustained by owners of property taken for public uses.[1] Accordingly, the legislature of a State may (as has long been the practice) direct the mode of ascertaining damages, either by a jury or by commissioners.[2] The Constitution of the State of New York provides that assessments for damages for property taken for public uses shall be made by a jury or commissioners, "as shall be prescribed by law;" and the Courts of the State, hold, that no law prescribing such method having been passed since the Constitution, the board of supervisors should proceed to assess such damages according to the law previously in existence, until the legislature should prescribe a different mode under the Constitution; and that a *mandamus* would lie, on the relation of the owner of the land so taken.[3] An act of the State of New Jersey, incorporating a

---

1 Livingston *v.* Mayor of Brooklyn, 8 Wend. (N. Y.) R. 85.

2 Ibid. Bonaparte *v.* Camden and Amboy Railroad Co. 1 Bald. (Cir. Ct.) R. 222; Willyard *v.* Hamilton, 7 Ham. (Ohio R. part 2d.) 112; M'Masters *v.* Commonwealth, 3 Watts, (Penn.) R. 292; Bloodgood *v.* Mohawk, &c. Railroad Co. 14 Wend. (N. Y.) R. 51; S. C. 18 Wend. (N. Y.) R. 9.

3 People *v.* Supervisors, 3 Barb. (N. Y.) Sup. Ct. R. 332. Duty of Commissioners, by the General Railroad Law of New York: mode, proceedings, and compensation to be awarded—their report. § 16. The commissioners shall take and subscribe the oath prescribed by the twelfth article of the Constitution. Any one of them may issue subpœnas, administer oaths to witnesses, and any three of them may adjourn the proceedings before them from time to time, in their discretion. Whenever they meet, except by the appointment of the Court or pursuant to adjournment, they shall cause reasonable notice of such meetings to be given to the parties who are to be affected by their proceedings, or their attorney or agent. They shall view the premises described in the petition and hear the proofs and allegations of the parties, and reduce the testimony, if any is taken by them, to writing; and after the testimony is closed in each case, and without any unnecessary delay, and before proceeding to the examination of any other claim, a majority of them, all being present and acting, shall ascertain and determine the compensation, which ought justly to be made by the company to the party or parties owning or interested in the real estate appraised by them; and in determining the amount of such compensation, they shall not make an

railroad company, providing for the assessment of damages to the owners of land through which it passes, and appointing commissioners, instead of a jury, to estimate the damages, was held to be constitutional.[1] By a long course of legislation in the State of New Hampshire, the damages occasioned by the laying out of highways were to be assessed by the Court, or by a committee; and no provision is found for the intervention of a jury in cases of this character.[2] In Massachusetts, where proceedings for the assessment of damages by a jury for land taken by a railroad company, are conducted in part by a coroner, under the Revised Statutes, section .23, and in part by the sheriff, it is the duty of each of those officers to certify proceedings.[3]

---

allowance or deduction on account of any real or supposed benefits which the parties in interest may derive from the construction of the proposed railroad. They, or a majority of them, shall also determine and certify what sum ought to be paid to a general or special guardian or committee of an infant, idiot or person of unsound mind, or to an attorney appointed by the Court to attend to the interest of any unknown owner or party in interest, not personally served with notice of the proceedings, and who has not appeared, for costs, expenses and counsel fees. They shall make a report to the Supreme Court, signed by them or a majority of them, of the proceedings before them, with the minutes of the testimony taken by them, if any. Said commissioners shall be entitled to three dollars for their expenses and services for each day they are engaged in the performance of their duties, to be paid by the company.

1 Bonaparte *v.* Camden and Amboy Railroad Co., Bald. (Cir. Ct.) R. 205. A charter of a railroad company, giving them authority to enter upon lands, &c., for their road, provided for the appointment of commissioners "to examine and appraise the said land and to assess damages." The order of the Court, appointing the commissioners directed them "to examine and appraise the said lands and to assess the damages to be paid by the said company for the said lands, so required as aforesaid, pursuant to the provisions of the above recited act." Held, that the order was sufficient. Doughty *v.* Somerville, &c. Railroad Co. 1 New Jer. R. 442.

2 Breck *v.* Lebanon, 11 N. Hamp. R. 19. And see Baltimore Turnpike case, 5 Binn. (Penn.) R. 481; Armstrong *v.* Jackson, 1 Blackf. (Ind.) R. 374; Haight *v.* Morris Aqueduct, 4 Wash. (Cir. Ct.) R. 601.

3 Pittsfield, &c. Railroad Co. *v.* Foster, 1 Cush. (Mass.) R. 480. Where a jury summoned to reassess damages for land taken by a railroad, rendered a verdict in which they assessed the damages at a certain sum, "with interest thereon

§ 103. A statute to promote any work for public use, which makes *no* provision for indemnifying the owner of the property proposed to be taken, is entirely void, as being unconstitutional,[1] and an injunction may be obtained to *prevent* the taking.[2] So, an action at law may be maintained, after the damage has been committed.[3] In Jennings, *ex parte*,[4] the water of a certain river was diverted from certain hydraulic works by a dam, the right to erect which was claimed under a legislative grant; and the appraisers, having refused to act, a *mandamus* was directed to be issued. The assessment of damages by commissioners is not, it is held in New Hampshire, a cumulative remedy, but is a substitution of one mode for another, and their decision is final on the merits, subject only to the right of appeal.[5]

§ 104. Commissioners are selected with a cautious regard to their fitness to judge, (after qualifying themselves in the manner prescribed,) of the compensation which ought justly to

---

from the time when the said railroad company took possession of the land," it was held, that the verdict was void for uncertainty, and that the Court could not alter the same. Connecticut River Railroad Co. *v.* Clapp, 1 Cush. (Mass.) R. 550; and see Walker *v.* Boston and Maine Railroad, 3 Cush. (Mass.) R. 1.

1 Thatcher *v.* Dartmouth Bridge Co. 18 Pick. (Mass.) R. 501.

2 Gardner *v.* Newburgh, 2 Johns. (N. Y.) Ch. R. 162; Beekman *v.* Syracuse and Schenectady Railroad Co. 3 Paige, (N. Y.) Ch. R. 45; Wheeler *v.* Rochester and Syracuse Railroad Co. 12 Barb. (N. Y.) Sup. Ct. 227.

3 Stevens *v.* Proprietors of Middlesex Canal, 12 Mass. R. 466; Sinnickson *v.* Jackson, 4 Harris, (N. J.) R. 129; Crittenden *v.* Wilson, 5 Cowen, (N. Y.) R. 165; Denslow *v.* New Haven and Northampton Co. 16 Conn. R. 98; Fletcher *v.* Auburn and Syracuse Railroad Co. 25 Wend. (N. Y.) R. 462; Bloodgood *v.* Mohawk and Hudson Railroad Co. 14 Wend. (N. Y.) R. 51; Aldrich *v.* Cheshire Railroad Co. 1 Fost. (N. Hamp.) R. 359.

4 Jennings, *ex parte*, 6 Cowen, (N. Y.) R. 518; and see People *v.* Supervisors of Westchester, 12 Barb. (N. Y.) Sup. Ct. R. 466. It seems to have been very well settled by decisions in the State of New York, that *Chancery* has no power to review, upon the merits, the proceedings of the commissioners of estimate and assessment in opening streets in the city of New York. Whitney *v.* Mayor, &c. of New York, 1 Paige, (N. Y.) Ch. R. 548, citing 2 Caines, R. 179; 16 Johns. R. 50; 1 Wend. R. 288; 20 Johns. R. 430; and see Wiggin *v.* Mayor, &c. of New York, 9 Paige, (N. Y.) Ch. R. 16; 6 Paige, 76; 8 Ib. 655; 26 Wend. R. 132.

5 Aldrich *v.* Cheshire Railroad Co. 1 Fost. (N. Hamp.) R. 359.

be made for the land to be taken. They are not, like other tribunals, to be governed exclusively by evidence, but their duty is to view the premises, as well as to hear the proofs and allegations of the parties. The one duty is not less imperative or important than the other. If, upon appeal, the Court are satisfied that they have not erred in the principles, upon which they have made their appraisal, no other error will be sufficient to send the report back for review. Any technical departure from established rules in the admission or rejection of evidence cannot be allowed to affect the appraisal, unless it appear that the party appealing has been injuriously affected.[1]

§ 105. Where the owner of the land and the company cannot agree upon the location of the crossing, it is the right of such owner to determine where he will have it, and the duty of the company to make it at the place he selects. Such company, if it should select a different location, must make compensation for the difference between the two, to the owner. The owner must exercise his right of selection reasonably, with a view to his own benefit and convenience, and not capriciously, to injure the company.[2]

§ 106. The value of the land taken for public use, is not restricted to its agricultural or productive qualities, but inquiry should be made as to all other legitimate purposes to which the property could be appropriated;[3] and a just compensation cannot be less than the owner of the property taken has sustained.[4] It was decided in New Jersey, that in the assessment of damages for crossing land by a railroad, the jury must take into consideration the deterioration in value of the adjacent portions of the same tract, by the proximity of the railroad, either for agricultural purposes, or for sale as building lots,

---

1 Troy and Boston Railroad Co. *v.* Lee, 13 Barb. (N. Y.) Sup. Ct. R. 169.

2 Wheeler *v.* Rochester and Syracuse Railroad Co. 12 Barb. (N. Y.) Sup. Ct. R. 227; Wiggin *v.* Mayor, &c. of New York, 9 Paige, (N. Y.) Ch. R. 16.

3 Harrison *v.* Young, 9 Geo. R. 359.

4 Hamilton Avenue, (Matter of,) 14 Barb. (N. Y.) Sup. Ct. R. 415.

increased risk of an increased care required for family and stock, the risk of fire, the inconvenience caused by embankments and excavations, and the obstruction to the free use of buildings.[1] In White *v.* Railroad Company, in the Court of Appeals of South Carolina,[2] it was held, that in estimating "loss or damage" by the right of way taken by the Charlotte and South Carolina Railroad Company, the jury may estimate the value of the land occupied by the company; the deterioration of parcels isolated; the alterations of arrangement required about the homestead; the loss of time and expenditure caused by any increase of care or distance which had been occasioned; and the injury to the value of the place as a stand for a public house.

§ 107. In Troy and Boston Railroad Company *v.* Lee, in the Supreme Court of New York,[3] which was an appeal in pursuance of the general railroad act of the State, (sect. 18,) Harris, J., in delivering the opinion of the Court, says: "It appears from the minutes of testimony taken by the commissioners, that the defendant's farm contains about fifty acres, and that the railroad so divides it, as to leave about thirty-five acres on one side, and fifteen acres on the other. Witnesses were called by the defendant to give their opinion as to the amount of damage he would sustain. This kind of testimony was objected to, but received. One witness testified that he would not give so much for the farm by $1,000 as he would if it had not been interfered with. Another estimated the farm to be worth $50 an acre, without the railroad, and $20 an acre less, with the railroad in operation. A third witness thought the farm as it would be, with the railroad running through it, not worth $20 an acre; and a fourth thought the farm would

---

[1] Somerville and Eastern Railroad *v.* Doughty, 2 Zabriskie, (N. J.) R. 495.—Ogden, J., dissenting, as to risk to family, stock, and by fire. See Yeiser *v.* Railroad Co. 8 Barr, (Penn.) R. 366.

[2] White *v.* Railroad Co. 6 Rich. (S. C.) Law R. 47.

[3] Troy and Boston Railroad Co. *v.* Lee, 16 Barb. (N. Y.) Sup. Ct. R. 169.

be comparatively valueless for farming purposes. These opinions constitute the chief part of the testimony taken. Such testimony, although admissible, is not entitled to great weight. Indeed, it is a departure from a general rule of evidence, to receive it at all. 'The whole history of this kind of evidence,' says a distinguished Judge, 'shows that it is separated from incompetency by a very thin partition.'[1] The opinions of witnesses, at the best, are to be received as 'persuasive evidence,' and never *controlling*. In making appraisals of this kind, the true rule, the only rule which will do equal justice to all parties, is to determine what will be the effect of the proposed change upon the market value of the property. The proper inquiry is, what is it now fairly worth in the market, and what will it be worth, after the improvement is made? 'All classes and conditions of men,' says Bronson, J., in the Matter of Firman Street,[2] 'hold their property subject to the paramount claims of the State, and when it is taken for public purposes, and the question of compensation is presented, the only proper inquiry is, what is its value? The question is not what estimate does the owner place upon it, but what is its real worth, in the judgment of honest, competent, and disinterested men?' And again, he says: 'The proper mode of adjusting the question of damages, is to inquire, what is the present value of the land, and what will it be worth when the contemplated work is completed?' The verdict of a jury is determined by the testimony submitted to their consideration. It is, therefore, the subject of review. It may be presented to the consideration of the Court upon paper. But it is not so in relation to these commissioners of appraisal. The very first thing they are required to do is, to view the premises. Thus, their own senses are made to testify. The information thus acquired, it is impossible to bring before a Court of Review. The commission-

---

1 In the Matter of Pearl Street, 19 Wend. 651. Per Cowen, J.

2 17 Wend. 649.

ers, too, are selected with reference to their general knowledge, qualifying them to judge discreetly upon the matters submitted to them. Unlike a jury, they are restricted to no peculiar species of evidence, or any peculiar sources of information. They may collect information in all the ways which a prudent man usually takes to satisfy his own mind concerning matters of the like kind, where his own interests are involved in the inquiry. They may seek light from other minds, that they may be the better able to arrive at just conclusions, but, at the last, they must be governed by their own judgment. That judgment is not to be controlled or outweighed by the opinions of any number of witnesses. The commissioners have no right to take such opinions, nor indeed any other evidence, as the basis of their appraisal, without exercising their own judgment. They are to hear all the proofs and allegations of the parties, as well as to view the premises, as a means of enlightening their judgment, and having done all, they are then to determine, in the free and uncontrolled exercise of that judgment, thus enlightened and thus informed, what award will best dispense equal justice to all the parties. When the original jurisdiction is to be exercised in this manner, it is impossible, from the very nature of the case, that there should be any thing like a regular judicial review.[1] Regarding the market value of the property, as furnishing the true principle by which the commissioners are to be governed, and the independent exercise of their intelligent judgment, as the true mode of applying that principle to the appraisal, it is scarcely possible for a Court to say upon review, that the commissioners have erred. Indeed, this can never be said, unless it can be made to appear, that they have adopted an erroneous principle in making their appraisal, or have erred in the application of the true principle. Neither can be said to appear in this case. There is nothing

---

[1] See the opinion of Bronson, J., in the Matter of William and Anthony Streets, 19 Wend. 678.

here to show that the appraisal is not the result of the free exercise of the judgment of the majority of the commissioners who signed the report, in reference to the market value of the property, as it was before the railroad was constructed, and as it will be afterwards. If it is, the report ought not to be disturbed. And, perhaps, in strictness, this should be sufficient to justify the Court in denying the application to send it back for review. But from the amount of the award, taken in connection with the character of the testimony submitted to the commissioners, and the further fact, that two very intelligent commissioners have omitted to unite in the appraisal, the Court are apprehensive that the majority of the commissioners may possibly have felt themselves overruled by the opinions of others, and have made those opinions, rather than their own judgment, the basis of their appraisal. For this reason, and not so much for the purpose of correcting any error as to enable the commissioners to review their own decision, and see whether, upon the principles now stated, they have committed any error, we have thought it a discreet exercise to the power which the legislature has thought fit to vest in this Court, to send the proceedings back to the same commissioners for review. The second report will, of course, be final."

§ 108. Where a railroad corporation was authorized to acquire lands, upon an appraisement by appraisers, who were to assess the value of the land, *without any deduction on account of benefits*, an appraisement of them, with a condition, that certain easements are to be reserved to the owner, is unauthorized, and no title will be acquired by the proceeding. In this case, according to the section of the act under which the proceedings were taken, the corporation were entitled to the fee.[1]

§ 109. As to *future* and *remote* damages. In a case de-

[1] Hill, &c. *v.* Mohawk and Hudson Railroad Co. 3 Seld. (N. Y.) R. 152; Court of Appeals; S. C. 5 Denio, (N. Y.) R. 206.

cided by the Supreme Court of Pennsylvania, as lately as January, 1857,[1] Lowrie, J., in giving the opinion of the Court, asks: "Is it reasonable to infer, that remote and contingent future damages, such as accidental fire from locomotives, was intended to be estimated and paid for? We think," he continues, "it is not; we find no act of assembly that indicates that such a thing was ever thought of. The legislature never had any thing like it in its mind when providing for public improvements. The law proclaims its general rule, that it has no remedy for mere accidental injuries; and when providing for the construction of internal improvements, it has uttered no new one. It has given no compensation for the risk of bridges burning or falling back; or toll-houses taking and communicating fire; stationary engines exploding; locomotives running off the track into a man's house; dams and locks giving way and inundating his land, or any thing of that kind. And why should it? If it take a man's land, or injuriously affects his property by the improvement, it gives him full compensation according to the best estimate that it is competent to obtain; and why should he have more? True, his risks may be increased by the improvement, but so is it with every man along the road, even though his land be passed without touching it, and why should he be paid for the risk, and the other not? In going along streets, the locomotives may pass under the very eaves of a thousand houses, without paying in advance for the risk. The improvement increases the risk, but so does improvement by the erection of mansions, and especially of all sorts of steam-works, but no one gets compensation for such risks. It is a simple law of nature, that he who lives in society, must take the risk of those social accidents, which society knows not how to prevent. The incidental hazards

---

[1] Sunbury and Erie Railroad Co. *v.* Hummel, reported in the American Law Register, for February, 1857, p. 244. And see Lee *v.* Milner, 2 M. & Welsb. R. 824.

must stand as balanced by the incidental benefit of the social state. It is also relevant to this question of reasonableness to ask, how the risk is to be measured? There may be but a single shanty on the land of the claimant, and if we are to provide for future risks, the duty is not satisfied by merely ascertaining the risk of the shanty, for there may yet be a hundred houses there; how can it be told how many, or what kind, or value? And who can calculate the chances of accidental fire? We know not yet the kind of fire that may be used; nor the improvements to be made for preventing the emission of sparks, nor how soon there will be another element than fire and steam for locomotive power, nor whether there will be one or one hundred locomotives daily along the road. These considerations show, that an estimate of such a risk for all future time, can be founded on no rational principles, and can be formed only by an average of unintelligent guesses. The present case is an illustration of their uncertainty; for the risk of this barn is estimated at half its value, when most likely it could be shown by experience, that not one erection in a thousand along a railroad is burnt in a year. If all houses near to the track of proposed railroads had to be paid for at this rate, no railroads could be made. It is unreasonable to ask intelligent men to make a sworn estimate of a mere risk which can be founded on no present data, but only on an imaginary future state of things which may never exist, or which may become complicated with other things which may totally change their character, and we are convinced that this law does not intend such an estimate."

## 7. *Of the Kind and Mode of Compensation.*

§ 110. Compensation means amends, recompense, remuneration; so that there must be not only some person to make or render, but another person to accept and receive.[1] The objec-

---

1 Per Brown, J., in People *v.* Mayor, &c. of Brooklyn, 9 Barb. (N. Y.) Sup. Ct. R. 535.

tion to appropriating public property to private use, rests upon the same principle as the objection to appropriating, without a just compensation, private property to public use.[1]

§ 111. The corporate body of the State itself, can claim amends for its private property when taken for public use. Thus, suppose an act of the legislature, by which a railroad corporation is established in the usual manner, and with the ordinary powers and privileges of such corporations, authorizes the corporation to locate their road so that the same may pass over certain land, which belongs to, and is held by, the State, as a body politic, for a particular purpose, but without any expression in the act of a design on the part of the legislature, to aid the corporation in their undertaking. In such case, it cannot be considered to be the intention of the legislature, to grant the land of the State, or any easement therein without compensation, and the State, accordingly, may institute proceedings and prosecute a claim for damages before the appropriate tribunal, in the same manner as an ordinary individual proprietor.[2] In either case, whenever land is taken for a perpetual use, and *paid for*, the former owner is not entitled to further compensation, if it be afterwards appropriated to another public use of no greater injury to the former owner.[3]

§ 112. When private property is taken for public use, the compensation need not precede, nor be contemporaneous with, the taking; the right to it may be ascertained and declared afterwards. But there is imposed upon the legislature an obligation to *provide* for compensation in a *reasonable time*, and also for undoubted security and efficient means for its prompt collection, so that its payment may be made certain.[4] The spirit of the Constitution is complied with if such provisions

---

1 Town of Guilford *v.* Cornell, 18 Barb. (N. Y.) Sup. Ct. R. 615.

2 Commonwealth *v.* Boston and Maine Railroad Co. 3 Cush. (Mass.) R. 25.

3 Chase *v.* Sutton Manufacturing Co. 4 Cush. (Mass.) R. 152.

4 Boynton *v.* Peterborough and Shirley Railroad Co. 4 Cush. (Mass.) R. 469; Bradshaw *v.* Rogers, 20 Johns. (N. Y.) R. 108, 735; Day *v.* Stetson, 8 Greenl. R. 365.

are made,[1] but is not if they are not made.[2] On one occasion, it was observed by Lord Ch. J. Denman, "frequently compensation cannot be ascertained *till the work is done*,"[3] but an act of the legislature must, in New York, make suitable provision for compensation, in case the land be subsequently taken;[4] and thus is the construction in Pennsylvania.[5]

§ 113. The obligation imposed by constitutional law upon a State government to make, or provide for, compensation, when appropriating private property to public use, is, as it were a *debt*, and as such should be paid in *money;* and the inhibition imposed upon the States, by the Federal Constitution, that they shall not make any thing but gold and silver a lawful tender for a debt should be, it has been considered, extended to *such* a debt.[6] A learned Judge, it is true, has seemingly expressed a

1 By the Court, by Sutherland, J., in Bloodgood *v.* Mohawk and Hudson River Railroad Co. 14 Wend. (N. Y.) R. 51.

2 Bonaparte *v.* Amboy Railroad Co. 1 Bald. (Cir. Ct.) R. 228; Parks *v.* Boston, 15 Pick. (Mass.) R. 198; 2 Kent, Comm. 339, *note.*

3 Lisley *v.* Lobley, 7 Adol. & Ell. R. 124.

4 Polly *v.* Saratoga and Washington Railroad Co. 9 Barb. (N. Y.) Sup. Ct. R. 449. It appears to be the settled construction of the Constitution of the State of New York, which prohibits private property to be taken for public use without just compensation, that actual compensation need not precede the appropriation; and the law of the State authorizing the reconstruction and alteration of a road, providing for compensation, and without making it a condition precedent to the entry upon and appropriation of premises, is valid. Smith *v.* Helmert, 7 Barb. (N. Y.) Sup. Ct. R. 416; Bloodgood *v.* Mohawk and Hudson Railroad Co. 18 Wend. (N. Y.) R. 9; and S. C. 14 Ibid. 51; Calking *v.* Baldwin, 4 Wend. (N. Y.) R. 667; Cole *v.* Trustees of Williamsburgh, 10 Wend. (N. Y.) R. 659; People *v.* Hayden, 6 Hill, (N. Y.) R. 359; Smith *v.* Helmer, 7 Barb. (N. Y.) Sup. Ct. R. 416.

5 Pittsburgh *v.* Scott, 1 Barr, (Penn.) R. 309; and see, in Mississippi, Thompson *v.* Grand Gulf Railroad Co. 3 How. (Miss.) R. 240. The Civil Code of Louisiana requires the previous indemnity, (art. 589,) and see the Code Napoleon, (art. 545.)

6 See Smith on Statute and Constitutional Law, 471; Seymour *v.* Carter, 2 Met. (Mass.) 520; Rochester and Syracuse Railroad Co. *v.* Budlong, 6 How. (N. Y.) Pr. R. 467; Jacob *v.* Louisville, 9 Dana, (Ken.) R. 114. By the terms of the Constitution of Vermont the owner ought to receive an equivalent in

different opinion, and after admitting that there is a primary convenience in money, as a medium of commercial exchange, expresses the opinion, that it rests with the legislature to determine the kind of compensation to be made.[1] The learned Judge, on the occasion referred to, was commenting on the case of Van Horne's Lessee *v.* Dorrance,[2] in which it was considered, that no just compensation could be made except in money, that being a common *standard*, by comparison with which, the value of any thing can be ascertained; money being not only a sign which represents the respective value of commodities, but a universal medium, easily portable, liable but to little variation, and readily exchanged for any kind. Compensation is a *quid pro quo*, and must be, (unless otherwise by the election of the parties,) in money.

§ 114. It has been affirmed of the opinion expressed in the above case of Van Horne's Lessee *v.* Dorrance, that its accuracy had been questioned, and been asserted also that if it be a correct exposition of constitutional law, the legislature had violated the provision in question in more instances than one.[3] This remark may have been made in reference to the practice of estimating *the benefits that accrue* to the owner of the property, and taken, in that light, it conflicted with the interpretation in Van Horne's Lessee *v.* Dorrance. But looking at the matter attentively, there appears nothing contradictory, because by the decisions in that State, compensation may be made in *benefits* to the remaining part of the property. In almost every turnpike act in Pennsylvania, in the estimation of damages, the viewers or appraisers are required to take into consideration the advantages accruing, as well as the injury done to the land.

---

money. Armington *v.* Barnet, 15 Vt. R. 475; People *v.* Mayor, &c. of Brooklyn, 9 Barb. (N. Y.) Sup. Ct. R. 546.

[1] Mr. J. Rogers, in M'Masters *v.* Commonwealth, 3 Watts, (Penn.) R. 291.

[2] Van Horne's Lessee *v.* Dorrance, 2 Dallas, R. 313, (Cir. Ct. of U. S. Penn. Dist. 1795.)

[3] Mr. J. Huston, in Satterlee *v.* Mathewson, 16 S. & Rawle, (Penn.) R. 179.

The same principle is engrafted into the canal system of the State, without any objection being made; it being obvious that the equity of the principle must strike the sense of justice of every one.[1] That a *just* and *full* compensation must, in such cases be made in money, is unquestionable; but if, in appropriating land of the value of *four thousand* dollars, when by the same appropriation, the value of what remains is increased *two thousand* dollars, and the value of the property taken be the rule of damages, the owner actually takes *two thousand*, without the least consideration, and thus receives more than the Constitution enjoins to be allowed, because it is *more* than a compensation.[2] If any thing is due the land-owner, after a *set-off* of the benefit derived, the balance must be paid in *money*. The material inquiry is, is the property injured or benefited.[3]

§ 115. In the State of New York, (long well known for its public enterprises,) Bronson, J., in giving the judgment of the Court, in the matter of Furman Street,[4] held that there was nothing in natural equity or justice which forbade the compensation should be made in property instead of money, or in any other form that would secure to the owner a fair equivalent for the land of which he is deprived; and it was upon this principle, he considered, that benefits were set off against damages under the canal laws of the State of New York; and if the land of a farmer worth one hundred dollars, was taken for the construction of a canal, and the canal, when completed, would advance the value of his remaining property to an equal amount, no

---

1 Per Rogers, J., in giving the judgment of the Court in M'Masters *v.* Commonwealth, 3 Watts, (Penn.) R. 292, 295. The rule of assessing damages in Pennsylvania, is a fair and just compensation of the value of the whole tract through which the road passes before and after the improvement is made. Pennsylvania Railroad Co. *v.* Heister, 8 Barr, (Penn.) R. 445.

2 Opinion of Wood, C. J., in Symonds *v.* City of Cincinnati, 11 Ohio R. 174.

3 Pennsylvania Railroad Co. *v.* Heister, 8 Barr, (Penn.) R. 445.

4 Furman Street, (Matter of,) 17 Wend. (N. Y.) 649.

other compensation was made to him. The learned Judge maintained that this was the only just and reasonable rule on the subject, and that a different rule would tax the public for the benefit of individuals. The decision in the case was, that the loss of the privilege of building on the land which formed the streets in Brooklyn, as they were designated on a map by the corporation of that place, under an act of the legislature, had been greatly overbalanced by the benefits resulting from the permanent and uniform plan which was adopted for the future enlargement of the town. In respect to the *test of value*, Bronson, J., remarked: "There is one test which the appellants might have given if they thought proper: What was the value of their land before this provision was made? Would that value, with compound interest from 1819, to the present time be equal to the sum which had been awarded to them by the commissioners for the present value of the land? If not, then what injury have they sustained by this measure, even on the supposition that the land had been actually taken in 1819? If their damages had been estimated according to the former value, they might have had some ground of complaint; but on the facts which they have submitted, it is impossible to say that any injustice has resulted from the practical operation of the statute.[1]" This case, with the cases of the People *v.* Mayor, &c. of Brooklyn,[2] and of Rexford *v.* Knight, in New York,[3] place the constitutionality of setting off benefits derived against damages upon an impregnable basis.

§ 116. In Massachusetts, the general doctrine on this subject is broadly advanced in the case of the Commonwealth *v.* Coombs,[4] that the benefit derived by laying out a highway to the other property of the party seeking to re-

---

1 See Lynch *v.* Mallory, 4 Denio, (N. Y.) R. 356.

2 People *v.* Mayor, &c. of Brooklyn, 4 Comst. (N. Y.) R. 419, Ct. of Appeals.

3 Rexford *v.* Knight, 15 Barb. (N. Y.) Sup. Ct. R. 627.

4 Commonwealth *v.* Coombs, 2 Mass. R. 492.

cover damages for his land taken, should be considered in reduction of the damages for the land taken. The language of the Court in another case in that State is: "The jury might and ought to have returned that the party sustained no damages, if such was their conviction; the benefit the owner of the land derives from the laying out a way over it, may often exceed the value of the land covered by the way."[1] This doctrine has been since expressly recognized in that State.[2] The Revised Statutes of the State, (c. 24, § 31,) in like manner provide, generally, for an allowance by way of deduction for the advancement in value of other property. The statute of the State of Vermont, which provides for estimating the damages which may be sustained by any person interested in lands, by reason of laying out or altering any highway, the benefit which such may receive thereby shall be taken into consideration, is not repugnant to that article in the State Constitution which provides, that, whenever any person's property is taken for the

---

1 Commonwealth *v.* Sessions of Middlesex, 9 Mass. R. 31.

2 Methuen *v.* Fitchburg Railroad Co. 4 Cush. (Mass.) R. 291; Upton *v.* South Reading Branch Railroad Co. 8 Cush. (Mass.) R. 600. In an action for the damage occasioned by the filling up by the defendants of their land lying adjacent to that of the plaintiff, whereby the free flow of water off the plaintiff's land, as formerly existing, had been obstructed; instructions to the jury, that "they should take into consideration the evidence on both sides bearing on this point, and, if they were satisfied that the filling up had actually benefited the plaintiff's estate in any particular, they would, in assessing the damages, make allowance for such benefit, and give the plaintiff such sum in damages as they found upon the evidence would fully indemnify and compensate him for all the damage he had actually sustained," was held to be correct. Luther *v.* Winnisimmit Co. 9 Cush. (Mass.) R. 171. Again: In Meacham *v.* Fitchburg Railroad Company, 4 Cush. (Mass.) R. 201; it was held, that in estimating damages for a highway or railroad, any direct and peculiar benefit or increase of value accruing therefrom to land of the same owner adjoining or connected with the land taken, and forming a part of the same parcel, is to be considered by the jury and allowed by the way of set-off; but not for any general benefit or increase of value received by such land in common with other lands in the neighborhood; nor any benefit to other land of the same owner though in the same town.

use of the public, the owner ought to receive an equivalent in money.[1]

§ 117. It is somewhat important and difficult, in respect to benefit derived, to determine in reduction of money damages any collateral benefit which the person whose land has been appropriated, has received in his other property. Unquestionably, there must be some limitation to the rule. It is not to be extended to contingent, indirect and remote benefit in settling the question of damages for taking a particular parcel of land. In a case in Massachusetts, the jury were instructed, that if the construction of a railroad, by increasing the convenience of the people of a town generally, as a place of residence, and by its anticipated and probable effect in increasing the population, business, and general prosperity of the place, had been the occasion of an increase in the salable value of the real estate generally, near the station, it was too remote a benefit to be brought into consideration in determining the question of damages.[2]

§ 118. In Virginia, the advantages to be derived to the owner of land condemned for the use of a river company for the improvement of the river, for which the charter required the appraisers to have regard, are such advantages as particularly and exclusively affect the identical parcel of land whereof a portion is condemned, but not advantages of a general character which may be derived to the owner in common with the country at large.[3]

§ 119. The Constitution of Pennsylvania, art. 7, sect. 4, (1838,) forbids the legislature to authorize any corporate body or individual to take private property for public use, without compensation to be made, or adequate security to be given, before the taking. Yet the fee in land may be taken for high-

---

[1] Pennsylvania Railroad Co. *v.* Fisher, 8 Barr, (Penn.) R. 445.

[2] Methuen *v.* South Branch Reading Railroad Co. 4 Cush. (Mass.) R. 291.

[3] James River and Kanawha Co. *v.* Turner, 9 Leigh, (Va.) R. 413, Ct. of Appeals.

ways without compensation, as the soil of the State was originally granted in reference to the opening of highways. Under the "concessions agreed upon by William Penn, and the adventurers and purchasers" of lands in Pennsylvania, and the early laws of the province which sanctioned an agreement that an additional quantity of land should be granted to each purchaser, without price or rent, to enable him to contribute, without loss, to such public roads as should be found necessary, and six per cent. was fixed as the permanent quantity to be added to every man's land for that purpose, and all grants were afterwards, with this additional quantity, for the express purpose of contributing to the establishment of the roads; it was held, that the State might constitutionally authorize a turnpike company to lay out a road through the land thus granted, without making further compensation; compensation having been originally made to each purchaser's particular grant. This mode of accommodating the public, was devised by the legislature, at the expense of private individuals, who, from a prospect of deriving some small profits to themselves, might be induced to do it. It was immaterial to the public, whether it was done by a general tax, to be levied on the people at once, or by the gradual payment of certain specified sums by way of toll on those only who used the road, the latter being considered as the most equal mode of defraying the charge of making and keeping such road in repair; for although every man has a right to the free use of a public road, yet every member of the community may be taxed for making that road, in any manner that the legislature may think reasonable and just.[1]

120. Where, in Pennsylvania, an alley was laid out and opened in a borough by road and street commissioners thereof, under a special act of the legislature, which authorized and required them to perform the said duty, but which provided no

---

1 M'Clenachan *v.* Curwen, 6 Binn. (Penn.) R. 509; and see Commonwealth *v.* Fisher, 1 Penn. R. 466, and 6 Whart. (Penn.) R. 44.

mode of compensating the owners of the lands through which the alley passed, for the damages sustained; it was held, that the special act was not unconstitutional, as it only interfered with a general road law, to the extent of the agency used in laying out and opening the alley, but that it did not withdraw the case from the operation of the general road law, providing for the assessment of the damages sustained by reason of laying out and opening the alley; that the special act was to be construed and treated as part of the general road law.[1]

§ 121. The right granted to the Commonwealth of Massachusetts, in 1786, to purchase the lands of the Indians, in the State of New York, was, and always has been, subject to the right of the State to take and appropriate the lands to which the right of purchase attached; otherwise a portion of the territory of the State would be beyond its right of sovereignty. When any of the land of the Indians are taken for roads, canals, &c., compensation is made to the Indians, who have not parted with the right to the preëmptors, and may never do so; and no compensation is paid to the preëmptors.[2]

§ 122. In all cases, where private property is to be taken, without the owner's consent, at the demand of a local corporation, it is essential to inquire, whether all the requisitions of the statute have been complied with; as Courts cannot allow any essential departure from them, without jeopardizing private rights, which have no adequate protection, except in Courts. The rule of law, that no man shall be deprived of his property without an opportunity of defending himself, is inflexible; and, upon this principle, it was held, that a report of commissioners of estimate and assessment, should not be confirmed, if it contain an assessment upon property in a city belonging to *unknown owners*. It may be sometimes necessary in proceeding

---

1 Sharett's Road, (Matter of,) 8 Barr, (Penn.) R. 99.

2 Wadsworth *v.* Buffalo Hydraulic Association, 15 Barb. (N. Y.) Sup. Ct. R. 83, 95.

*in rem*, to proceed against persons who are unknown; but the judicial power is restrained from doing so, without the intervention of the legislative power, and by some sort of substituted service prescribed for the judicial jurisdiction *in personam.*[1] So strict have been the Courts, that a judgment in partition has been held to be utterly void, because the record did not contain the averment that an affidavit was filed, stating that the owner was unknown.[2]

§ 123. The Revised Statutes of Massachusetts [3] provide for the case where *several parties* have *different estates or interests*, at the same time, in any land or buildings, and direct that the jury shall first determine the damage done to the whole as an entire estate in fee-simple, and then apportion the amount amongst the several and distinct interests therein. This the Supreme Court of the State has declared a very wise and useful provision, and one which should be carried into effect, according to its true intent and spirit, as one intended for the relief and benefit of those who *are liable to pay damages.*[4]

§ 124. The commissioners of estimate and assessment in New York, should consider separately the distinct existing interests in each portion of such private lands as are required for opening or widening a highway, as those of *landlord* and *tenant*, and make a separate award of the damages to each. The proper mode is, first, to estimate the damage to the fee, as if it were owned entire and unincumbered by one person, and then, apportion that amount among all the interests which such persons have in the property.[5] The rule applies to the case of *mortgagors* and *mortgagees*, and to undivided owners, as well

---

1 Flatbush Avenue, (Matter of,) 1 Barb. (N. Y.) Sup. Ct. R. 286.

2 Deming *v.* Corning, 11 Wend. (N. Y.) R. 647.

3 Chap. 24, §§ 48, 49, 50.

4 Walker *v.* Maine Railroad Co. 3 Cush. (Mass.) R. 20; and see Richardson *v.* Curtis, 2 Ibid. 341.

5 Coutant *v.* Catlin, 2 Sand. (N. Y.) Ch. R. 485.

as to that of *lessors* and *lessees*.[1] Where the report of the commissioners awards all the damages to one of several parties interested, and there is no award to either of the others, it is competent for the latter to prove their interest, and recover from the former their proportion of the award.[2] It is well settled, that the mortgagee may intervene and claim the award, although the whole amount of it is given to the mortgagor, where no notice of the right of the former is taken in the report.[3] The mortgagee need not be made a party to proceeding by the mortgagor, for the assessment of damages, provided he gives his assent thereto by a writing filed in the case.[4]

§ 125. In England, where the act of parliament speaks of owners and proprietors, in defining the parties entitled to compensation, these terms, it seems, are not to be understood simply of the owners of the inheritance, but may be taken to embrace generally the interests of all persons having a beneficial interest in the land, and of termors among the rest.[5] Where there is a change in the ownership of land, pending the settlement of a claim for damage done to such land by a railway company, it seems that the compensation for such damage, if *temporary*, belongs to the party who had the legal estate when the damage was done, but if *permanent*, goes with the land to the subsequent owner.[6] A party entitled to an *easement* over lands purchased by the company, cannot, under the general

---

[1] Wiggan *v.* Mayor, &c. of New York, 9 Paige, (N. Y.) Ch. R. 19; Railroad Company *v.* Hull, 1 Casey, (Penn.) R. 336.

[2] Matter of John Street, 19 Wend. (N. Y.) R. 659.

[3] Coutant, &c. *ub sup.*

[4] Meacham *v.* Fitchburg Railroad Co. 4 Cush. (Mass.) R. 291.

[5] Astor *v.* Miller, 2 Paige, (N. Y.) Ch. R. 68; and S. C. 5 Wend. (N. Y.) R. 603. A tenant for years, is an owner within the act of Pennsylvania constituting a plank-road company. Erie and Waterford Plank-Road Company, *v.* Brown, 1 Casey, (Penn.) R. 156. And see South Devon Railway, (case of,) 7 Eng. Law and Eq. R. 139.

[6] Lister *v.* Lobley, 6 Nev. and Man. R. 340; Walford on Railways, 188; and see Thicknesse *v.* Lancaster Canal Company, 4 M. & Welsb. R. 472.

provisions of a railway act, maintain an action for acts done upon those lands by the company, to the prejudice of his easement, (so far, at least, as such acts are done in the execution of the purposes of the act,) but ought, as soon as any damage is actually sustained, to claim compensation under the act.[1]

§ 126. Where, in England, there are different persons having several interests in the property required for the purpose of a highway, the compensation must be apportioned among the several parties, according to their respective interests, at least, if the jury are impanelled to do so; and an assessment of the compensation in one gross sum, would accordingly be bad.[2] And the like rule would seem to apply where the same party prefers a twofold claim, both for purchase-money and for damages, if the jury are required at the trial to make a separate assessment.[3] But if no demand is made at the time on the part either of the company or the claimant for a separate assessment, then it seems a verdict is not to be regarded as a nullity, for not adjudicating separately on each claim, even though the act expressly declares that the one claim shall be inquired into and assessed separately from the other; the act not being compulsory or in the nature of condition precedent.[4]

§ 127. Where land of a person deceased, is taken for a highway, the *heir*, and not the *administrator*, is entitled to damages for such taking, and he may prosecute for the recovery thereof; although the administrator has previously represented the estate to be insolvent, and afterwards obtained a

---

1 See judgment of Baron Alderson, in Cator *v.* Croydon Canal Company, 4 Y. & Coll. R. 405.

2 Rex *v.* Trustees of Norwich and Watton Road, 5 Adol. & Ell. R. 578; and S. C. 1 Nev. & Per. R. 32.

3 Walford on Railways, 204.

4 Ibid.; In the Matter of the London and Greenwich Railway Co. 2 Adol. & Ell. R. 683; and S. C. 4 Nev. & Man. R. 458; Corrigall *v.* London and Blackwall Railway Co. 21 Law Journ. R. 216; and S. C. 5 M. & Grang. R. 219.

license to sell the intestate's real estate for the payment of debts. But this supposes, that no act of legislation has provided for cases of this description.[1]

128. An *occupant* of premises required for the purposes of a highway, may have an interest in those premises, which, without strictly falling under the meaning of a legal interest, is yet highly valuable, and which, but for the passing of the act, he might have hoped to enjoy for a prolonged term, such as an interest in regard of the good will of a business, the hope of a beneficial renewal, tenant's fixtures, improvements, and the like.[2] An interest, however, of this kind is too slight and precarious to be made a ground for compensation, except there are conclusive words in the act of the legislature embracing it.[3] It will not, therefore, be included in the terms of an act which speaks simply of the value of the tenant's unexpired term and interest.[4]

§ 129. The grantor of a tide-mill and mill-pond, who had reserved the right of boating and rafting through the pond, and of using the same as a depot for lumber, it seems, has no such proprietary interest in the premises, by virtue of such reservation, as to entitle him to become, or to render it necessary that he should be made a party, under the Revised Statutes of Massachusetts, for the recovery of damages occasioned by the laying out and construction of a railroad through the granted premises. "We are not prepared to say," said Shaw, C. J., "that the legal distinction between an *estate* and an

[1] Boynton *v.* Peterborough and Shirley Railroad Co. 4 Cush. (Mass.) R. 467. Money, if paid into court by a railroad company, for land taken under the Land Clauses Acts, from a person who was under mental *imbecility*, and who continued in that state until his death, but was not the subject of a commission of lunacy, will be ordered, after his death, not to be reinvested, or considered as land, but to be paid to his executor. Flamark, *ex parte*, 3 Eng. Law and Eq. R. 243.

[2] Walford on Railways, 188.

[3] Ibid., referring to cases decided on Hungerford Market Company's Act, 2 B. & Adol. R. 341, 348; 4 Ib. 596, 600, n.; 9 Adol. & Ell. R. 463.

[4] Rex *v.* Liverpool and Manchester Railway Co. 4 Adol. & Ell. 650.

*easement* in the premises taken, will always determine whether one has or has not a proprietary interest, rendering it proper to make him a party or not, with the owners in a claim of damages. Possibly an easement for a mill privilege, for example, may be so large and valuable as to render an interest therein much more important than that of a *lessee* for years, or a *reversioner*."[1] In England, a party entitled to an *easement* over lands purchased by a railroad company, cannot, under the general provisions of a railway act, maintain an action for acts done upon those lands by the company to his easement, (so far, at least, as such acts are done in the execution of the purposes of the act,) but ought, as soon as any damage is actually sustained, to claim compensation under the act.[2]

§ 130. An *alien* resident, in one of the States of the United States, who owns land, under a special law of the State, may sustain a suit in the Circuit Court in relation to such land, and has a right to claim compensation, when it is taken for public use.[3]

---

1 Davidson *v.* Boston and Maine Railroad Co. 3 Cush. (Mass.) R. 91.

2 Walford on Railways, 188.

3 Bonaparte *v.* Camden and Amboy Railroad Co. 1 Bald. (Cir. Ct.) R. 205.

# CHAPTER III.

## HIGHWAYS BY PRESCRIPTION AND DEDICATION.



### I. Prescription.

§ 131. Prescription, in its more general acceptation, is defined to be "a title, acquired by possession, had during the time and in the manner fixed by law." It is also said that "a prescription by immemorial usage, can, in general, only be for things which may be created by grant; *for the law allows prescriptions only to supply the loss of a grant.*"[1] Now, inasmuch as the public cannot take by grant, prescription, in its strict sense, has no application to highways. "As the law now exists in this State," says Senator Furman, in Post *v.* Pearsall,[2] "and as it has in substance existed ever since the formation of our constitution, the only way that an *individual* can acquire a right in real estate is, by grant, or by an adverse possession of twenty years under a claim of title, in which case

[1] Cruise Dig. Tit. XXXI. Ch. 1, § 11.
[2] Post *v.* Pearsall, 22 Wend. (N. Y.) R. 444.

the law presumes a grant; and, as to the *public*, the only way in which they can at the common-law acquire an easement in the lands of another is by *dedication*." But, nevertheless, there are cases in which the doctrine of prescription has been applied to highways. Thus in the case of Odiorne *v.* Wade,[1] which was an action of trespass *quare clausum fregit*, the defendant having put in a plea of common highway from time immemorial, and proved the existence of the way for more than sixty years, there being no evidence showing its commencement, the Court held, that the duration of the way was sufficient to support the plea of prescription. And again, in the case of Reed *v.* Northfield,[2] Shaw, C. J., in delivering the opinion of the Court, said: "We think it clear upon principle, that public easements, as well as others, may be shown by long and uninterrupted use and enjoyment, upon the conclusive legal presumption from such enjoyment, that they were, at some anterior period, laid out and established by competent authority."[3] And, not unfrequently, an uninterrupted use of a way, on the part of the public, for a period of twenty years or more, is spoken of as constituting a title by prescription. But, more properly speaking, such use, unless by virtue of some statute,[4] is but a fact from which a dedication to the public may be presumed. These cases, therefore, have seemed to me to be more properly treated under the head of dedication.

---

1 Odiorne *v.* Wade, 5 Pick. 421.

2 Reed *v.* Northfield, 13 Pick. 94.

3 See also, Commonwealth *v.* Low, 3 Pick. 408; Stedman *v.* Southbridge, 17 Pick. 162; Folger *v.* Worth, 19 Pick. 108; Valentine *v.* Boston, 22 Pick. 75; Hicks *v.* Fish, 4 Mason, 310; Williams *v.* Cunningham, 18 Pick. 312; Brownell *v.* Palmer, 22 Conn. 107; State *v.* Gregg, 2 Hill, (So. Car.) R. 387.

4 In New York, and probably in many of the other States, there is a statutory provision to the effect, that all roads not recorded, which have been, or shall have been used as public highways, for twenty years or more, shall be deemed public highways. 1 R. S. 521, § 100; (3d ed. 636, § 120.)

## II. DEDICATION.—1. *Definition and History.*

§ 132. Dedication is an appropriation of land to some public use, made by the owner of the fee, and accepted for such use by or on behalf of the public. A common public road, originating in such an appropriation and acceptance, is a *highway by dedication.* The interest, which the public thus acquires, is merely an easement or right of passage over the soil; the original owner still retaining the fee, together with all rights of property not inconsistent with the public use, and becoming, whenever that use is relinquished or lost, revested with as absolute and exclusive a dominion as he possessed previous to the dedication.

§ 133. The doctrine of dedication is of purely common-law origin. In the civil law,[1] public parks, squares, bridges and highways were recognized, indeed, and protected by suitable legal regulations; but, in that law, there was no principle strictly analogous to that of dedication. In that law, the public right flowed from a higher source. The state or nation was the paramount lord of the soil; the individual held subject to its ultimate ownership. This relation led to the distinction between what is called the *dominium eminens* and the *dominium vulgare*, the former denoting the title which the public reserved to itself, the latter the right which *individuals enjoyed by its permission.* By an exercise of this reserved right of dominion in the State, the individual occupant might be devested of his estate, whenever the public safety or convenience demanded; and, instead of acquiring an easement, the public entered at once into an actual ownership of the land itself. In the common law, the principle of *dominium eminens* was not carried to the same extent, and hence the difference between the two systems as regards dedication. The earliest reported case, at common law, in which this doctrine is as-

---

[1] Poth. Pand. de Just. Lib. 43, tit. 8, art. 1.

serted, is that of Lade *v.* Shepard,[1] which was decided at Hilary Term, eighth year of the reign of George II., in the year 1835, although the readiness with which it is there assented to, would seem to imply that it was already a familiar and undoubted principle of the law. Since that time, however, the decisions have rapidly multiplied both in England and in the United States, and the doctrine, which then was announced as little more than a mere dictum of the Court, adapting itself to the increasing demands of the public travel, has now become one of the most important branches of the law relating to highways.[2]

## 2. *The Parties to Dedication.*

§ 134. A primary condition of every valid dedication, is that it shall be made by the owner of the fee. Thus, where land, as far back as living memory could go, had been used in all respects as a public street, yet, having been under lease for ninety-nine years, which had but just expired, it was held, that the permission of the tenants could not bind the landlord, and that there was no dedication, unless it was proved to have been made previously to the giving of the lease.[3] But subject to this condition, dedication may be made by any private individual,[4] by a corporation, provided such an act be not inconsistent with the limitations of its charter and the purpose for which it is incorporated,[5] or by a trustee, when compatible with the

---

1 Lade *v.* Shepard, 2 Strange, 1004.

2 Post *v.* Pearsall, 22 Wend. (N. Y.) R. 442.

3 Wood *v.* Veal, 5 Barn. & Ald. 454. *Vide* also, Ward *v.* Davis, 3 Sandf. Sup. Ct. R. 502; Baxter *v.* Taylor, 1 Nev. & M. 13.

4 Whether dedication can be made by, or presumed against a person laboring under any of the common-law disabilities,—idiocy, infancy, coverture, &c. does not appear to have been decided; but courts would probably be guided by the analogies of the Statutes of Limitations, in so far as they furnish analogies for such a case.

5 Great Surrey Canal Co. *v.* Hall, 1 Man. & Gr. 392.

scope and nature of his trust.[1] The object of the rule is to protect the owner of the fee against public easements, originating in the unauthorized acts of his tenants, or in the acts of intermediate proprietors, without his consent; and it will not be strictly applied when this object would not be subserved by so doing. Where, therefore, the land had been used for a public footway for upwards of fifty years, during the whole of which time it had been occupied by a succession of tenants, one of whom had frequently complained to the proprietor's steward, that the public used the footway, and thereby injured the land, and yet no action was brought either by the landlord or tenant against any one who used it, the Court left it to the jury to infer a dedication, instructing them, that after a long lapse of time, and a frequent change of tenants, from the notorious and uninterrupted use of the way by the public, it might be presumed that the landlord had notice of the way being used, and that it was so used with his concurrence, and that, in this case, there was express evidence of notice, notice to the steward being notice to the landlord.[2] For the same reason, the equitable owner of land, there being nothing but a naked fee outstanding in the trustees, may make a dedication which he cannot revoke when he afterwards comes into possession of the fee. In 1788, S. contracted with the Government of the United States for a patent for certain land, which, after some delay, occasioned by negotiations relative to payments, was, in 1794, issued to him and his associates; and, he being the only person named, vested the fee in him. In 1788, he sold his right to a portion of the land; and in 1789, the grantees of this right laid out a town, and set apart the *locus in quo* as a public common; in 1800, one of equitable owners took from S. a conveyance of the fee; yet it was held that he was bound by the dedication, the acqui-

---

[1] Rex *v.* Leake, 5 Barn. & Adolph. 469.

[2] Rex *v.* Barr, 4 Campb. 16; Wellbeloved on Highways, p. 61; Davis *v.* Stephens, 7 Carr. & Payne, 570.

sition of the mere naked fee giving him no right to revoke it.[1] And it has also been decided, that where the owners of the equitable estate makes a dedication, their trustee, holding but a legal title for their use, is bound to respect it.[2] And where land, over which a highway was claimed, had been sold and conveyed, but the vendor immediately took back the same estate to hold in fee and in mortgage, and afterward his executor entered for condition broken, and he, or those claiming under him, foreclosed the mortgage, so that he or they came in of the old estate of the mortgagee, the original vendor was held to be owner of the land, so far as related to a dedication thereof to the public, notwithstanding his conveyance.[3] In fact, the true rule seems to be, that acts of dedication, done with the knowledge and acquiescence of the owner of the fee, will be looked upon as his own acts, and that, for the purpose of dedication, the equitable owner will be regarded as the real owner of the fee rather than the mere naked trustee.

§ 135. The parties to a dedication are the individual proprietor and the public at large; and it has in some cases been objected that a grant, to be valid, must be to some specific grantee, and that, the public not being such, a dedication was void. To obviate this difficulty, the Courts have sometimes classed dedication with private grants for charitable and religious purposes, where, contrary to the general rule, the fee may remain in abeyance until there is a grantee capable of taking. But the better view seems to be, that dedication rests upon principles totally distinct from those which govern grants. No grant or conveyance can be necessary to pass the fee out of the owner of the land and let it remain in abeyance until a grantee shall come *in esse;* for there is no one contemplated by the party to take the fee either immediately or at

---

1 The City of Cincinnati *v.* White, 6 Peters, 431.
2 Williams *v.* First Presbyterian Society in Cincinnati, 1 Ohio State R. 478.
3 Wright *v.* Tukey, 3 Cush. (Mass.) R. 290.

any future day; the fee must remain either in the original proprietor or in some person to whom he shall convey it. By virtue of the appropriation which he has made and by that alone, he is precluded from reasserting any exclusive right over the land, so long as it remains in public use. His gift enures immediately to the public, and is limited only by the wants of the community at large.[1]

### 3. *In what Manner a Dedication may be qualified.*

§ 136. In Austin's case, Lord Hale remarked, "If a way lead to a market, and were a way for all travellers, and did communicate with a great road, it is an highway; but if it lead only to a church, to a private house or village, or to fields, there it is a private way."[2] This language would seem to imply, that no road can be a highway unless it be a thoroughfare; and, upon this point, the opinions of Judges have been somewhat divided. In the case of The Rugby Charity *v.* Merryweather,[3] which was an action of trespass, tried in 1790, it appeared that the *locus in quo* had been used as a common street for above fifty years, though no thoroughfare by reason of the houses at the end. Lord Kenyon, in answer to this objection, said: "And as to this not being a thoroughfare, that can make no difference. If it were otherwise, in such a great town as this, it would be a trap to make people trespassers." But in Woodyer *v.* Hadden,[4] decided in bank in 1813, the decision of Lord Kenyon was very much criticized, though it did not become necessary that it should be directly overruled. Lord Mansfield condemned the decision, and, in reply to Lord Kenyon's

---

1 City of Cincinnati *v.* White, 6 Peters, 431; Post *v.* Pearsall, 20 Wend. and 22 Wend. 425; State *v.* Wilkinson, 2 Vt. 480; New Orleans *v.* The United States, 10 Peters, 662; Williams *v.* First Presbyterian Society in Cincinnati, 1 Ohio State R. 478; Kennedy *v.* Jones, 11 Alabama R. 63.

2 1 Ventr. 189. *Vide* 1 Hawk. P. C. ch. 76, § 1.

3 The Rugby Charity *v.* Merryweather, 11 East, 375.

4 Woodyer *v.* Hadden, 5 Taunt. 126.

remark, that if it were not a highway it would be a trap to make people trespassers, suggested that its being open and inviting persons, there being no notice to warn them away, would support a plea of license. Two other of the Judges expressed their dissent still more strongly on this point, one of them asking, "How can a street like this, *which is no thoroughfare*, be deemed a public highway." Again, in the still later case of Wood *v.* Veal,[1] the Court leaned manifestly to the opinion that there could not be a public highway, which was not a thoroughfare, "because," as one of them, (Abbott, C. J.) remarked, "the public at large cannot be in the use of it." But afterwards, in the case of Jarvis *v.* Dean,[2] in an action of trespass in which the *locus in quo* is described as belonging to one of two unfinished houses standing in a new street leading from White Conduit Street to some fields, in which also there were houses; the jury, under the direction of the Court, found said street to be a highway. But it would seem probable, from the remarks of the Court, on a motion for a new trial, that this street communicated with public roads at both ends. And in Rex *v.* Lloyd,[3] Lord Ellenborough expressed the opinion that there might be a highway where there was no thoroughfare.

§ 137. In this unsettled state the law has remained in England until the recent case of Bateman *v.* Bluck.[4] In this case, a passage leading from the public street up to a court, called Hat and Mitre Court, in the parish of St. Sepulchre, which consisted of fourteen or fifteen houses, and through which there was no thoroughfare, was held by the full Court to be a public highway. And on this point Lord Campbell remarked: "There may or there may not be a highway under

---

1 Wood *v.* Veal, 5 B. & A. 454.

2 Jarvis *v.* Dean, 3 Bingh. 447.

3 Rex *v.* Lloyd, 1 Campb. 260. *Vide* Rex *v.* Downshire, 4 Ad. & El. 698.

4 Bateman *v.* Bluck, 14 Eng. Law & Eq. R. 69.

such circumstances, (where there is no thoroughfare.) It would be very wrong to hold that there can be no highway, even where there has been an express dedication to a public purpose, because the place is no thoroughfare. There may be a large square with only one entrance to it, and if the owner allows the public to use it without restriction for a great many years, he cannot afterwards turn round and say they are all trespassers." This case has undoubtedly settled the law in England in favor of the rule laid down in The Rugby Charity *v.* Merryweather.

§ 138. Upon American authority the law is not so unequivocally settled. A road, half a mile long, leading to a beach,[1] and a road leading to a dock and landing, or ferry,[2] have been held to be highways. And in the latter case it was said, that such a road does not cease to be a highway, though such ferry has been changed, and though some part of the way has been appropriated and built upon, if the passage continues open to the same dock and landing. But, in a more recent case, a street terminating upon private land and extending neither to another way, a mill, a market, nor other public place, was held to be incapable of dedication to the public as a highway.[3] But this decision was made previous to that of Bateman *v.* Bluck; and from the liberality which American courts have manifested in applying the doctrine of dedication not only to streets, but also to parks, squares, commons, and other places devoted to public use, it is reasonable to believe that they will not hesitate to adopt the latest English determination upon this subject.

§ 139. Dedication, to be valid, need not be absolute, but may be limited both as to the time and mode of enjoyment.

---

1 State *v.* Bartlet, cited by counsel in State *v.* Nudd, 3 Fost. (N. H.) R. 331.

2 Galatin *v.* Gardner, 7 Johns. 106.

3 Simmons *v.* Mumford, 2 R. I. Rep. 172. See Campbell *v.* Long, 28 Eng. Law & Eq. R. 30.

*Thus, as to limitation in point of time;* in the case of a bridge, used by the public at all times, on foot and with horses, but only occasionally with carriages, except in times of flood and frost, when it was unsafe to pass through the river; at which times carriages always passed over the bridge, which was, when carriages could pass the ford, sometimes barred by means of a post and chain which was locked; it was held, that the bridge was public; Lord Ellenborough saying, "Though it must be an absolute dedication to the public, still it may be definite as to time."[1] Yet there cannot be a dedication, subject to a power of resumption to the grantor, for that would be the reservation of a right inconsistent with the dedication to the public.[2]

§ 140. *And as to the mode of enjoyment;* it is undoubtedly the law, that there may be a dedication to the public for a limited purpose, as for a footway, horseway, or driftway.[3] And in a case where a land-owner suffered the public to use, for several years, a road through his estate, for all purposes except that of carrying coals, though it did not become necessary to decide whether such a limited dedication could be made, yet two of the Judges expressed an opinion favorable to its validity; one of them saying, "The public must take *secundum formam doni;* if they cannot take according to that they cannot take at all,"[4] and all agreeing that, if it were not a partial dedication, it was merely a license revocable.

§ 141. But still it may be questioned, whether the cases above referred to are absolutely conclusive upon these points,

---

1 Rex *v.* North Hampton, 2 M. & S. 262; Rex *v.* Hudson, 2 Stra. 909.

2 Fitzpatrick *v.* Robinson, 1 Hudson & Brook, 585; Blundell *v.* Cotterall, 5 B. & Ald. 315.

3 Poole *v.* Huskinson, 11 M. & W. 827; 1 Hawk. P. C. ch. 76, § 1; Gowen *v.* Philadelphia Exchange Co. 5 Watts & Serg. 141; Harper *v.* Charlesworth, 4 B. & C. 574; Hemphill *v.* Boston, 8 Cush. 195.

4 Marquis of Stafford *v.* Coyney, 2 B. & C. 257. See also Rex *v.* Lyon, 5 Dow. & Ry. 499; The State *v.* Trask, 6 Vt. 355.

except as regards a dedication for a footway or horseway, &c. It must be remembered that a dedication, to be complete, must be accepted by the public at large, and there is great difficulty in inferring such an acceptance, from mere user at least, where from the exclusion of one mode of use there is no evidence that the portion of the public, who have occasion to use it in that mode only or chiefly, have assented to the dedication.[1] But, whatever may be the better opinion upon these points, it is clear that there cannot be a dedication to a limited portion of the public, as to a parish or to the inhabitants of a particular neighborhood. This has been so held,[2] and would seem to flow naturally from the nature of the act. The parties to that act, as we have seen, are the donor and the public at large; and though it may be said, where the dedication is limited in the mode and time of enjoyment, that, inasmuch as the whole public can use it in that particular mode or time, their acceptance may be inferred from use; this cannot be said of a way from the use of which, in any mode and at any time, a large portion of the public are excluded. But though such a partial dedication will be simply void, having no operation against the intention of the owner, yet *primâ facie*, any dedication will be presumed to be in favor of the whole public, and it will be incumbent on the party denying it to prove the contrary.[3]

### 4. *What constitutes a Dedication on the part of the Donor.*

§ 142. We have now seen who may be the parties to a dedication and what may be its character; we come next to

---

1 Wellbeloved on Highways, pp. 50–56. Remarks of Abbott, C. J., in Barraclough *v.* Johnson, 3 Nev. & Perry, 233; Roberts *v.* Karr, 1 Campb. 262; Rex *v.* Leake, 2 Nev. & M. 595. In this case it was said, that land cannot be dedicated to the public as a highway, with a reservation of right of making cuts through the land when wanted for the purposes of draining.

2 Poole *v.* Huskinson, 11 M. & W. 827.

3 Penny Pot Landing *v.* City of Philadelphia, 4 Harris, (Penn.) R. 79.

consider how it may be made on the part of the donor, and upon what evidence established. No particular formality is required; it is not affected by the Statute of Frauds; it may be made either with or without writing, by any act of the owner, such as throwing open his land to the public travel, or platting it and selling lots bounded by streets designated in the plat, thereby indicating a clear intention to dedicate; or an acquiescence in the use of his land for a highway, or his declared assent to such use, will be sufficient; the dedication being proved in most, if not in all, cases by matter *in pais* and not by deed. The vital principle of dedication is the intention to dedicate,—the *animus dedicandi*, and, whenever this is unequivocally manifested, the dedication, so far as the owner of the soil is concerned, has been made. Time, therefore, though often a very material ingredient in the evidence, is not an indispensable ingredient in the act of dedication. "It is not like a grant presumed from length of time; if the act of dedication be unequivocal, it may take place immediately; for instance, if a man builds a double row of houses, opening into an ancient street at each end, making a street, and sells or lets the houses, that is *instantly* a highway."[1] If accepted and used by the public in the manner intended, the dedication is complete, precluding the owner and all claiming in his right, from asserting any ownership inconsistent with such use. Dedication, therefore, is a conclusion of fact to be drawn by the jury from the circumstances of each

---

1 The language of Chambre, J., in Woodyer *v.* Hadden, 5 Taunt. 125. *Vide* Poole *v.* Huskinson, 11 M. & W. 827; Jarvis *v.* Dean, 3 Bingh. 447; British Museum *v.* Finnis, 5 Carr & Payne, 460; Barraclough *v.* Johnson, 4 Ad. & El. 99; Cincinnati *v.* White, 6 Peters, 431; Regina *v.* East Mark, 11 Ad. & El. 876; Wright *v.* Tukey, 3 Cush. 290; Hobbs *v.* Lowell, 19 Pick. 405; State *v.* Wilkinson, 2 Vt. 480; Abbott *v.* Mills, 3 Vt. 521; Matter of Thirty-second Street, 19 Wend. 128; Matter of Thirty-ninth Street, 1 Hill, (N. Y.) R. 191; Pearsall *v.* Post, 20 Wend. 119, and 22 Wend. 425; Trustees of Dover *v.* Fox, 9 B. Mon. 201; Cole *v.* Sprowl, 35 Maine, 161; Macon *v.* Franklin, 12 Georgia, 239.

particular case; the sole question as against the owner of the soil being, whether there is sufficient evidence of an intention on his part to dedicate the land to the public as a highway.[1]

### 5. *What is sufficient Evidence to prove a Dedication.*

§ 143. What is sufficient evidence of this intention will best appear from an examination of the leading cases reported on this subject. There may be circumstances so unequivocal as to afford almost decisive proof of dedication. Thus, where the owner of land *built a street upon it*, which had been for several years used as a highway, the Court did not hesitate to pronounce this a dedication.[2] The fact of the acquiescence of the owner, in the free use and enjoyment of the way as a public road for the period of twenty years, would undoubtedly be deemed sufficient evidence in any case, though there were no further proof of an intention to dedicate.[3] In Rex *v.* Lloyd,[4] the passage was a narrow, oblong court, leading from one part of the street to another, without outlet elsewhere, the houses all the way around which had once belonged to the same person, and it had been open to the public as far back as could be remembered. Lord Ellenborough observed, that, "If the owner of the soil throws open a passage and neither marks, by any visible distinction, that he means to preserve all his rights over it, nor excludes persons from passing through it by positive prohibition, he shall be presumed to have dedicated it to the public. Although the passage in question was originally intended only for private convenience, the public are not now

---

1 Gould *v.* Glass, 19 Barb. (N. Y.) Sup. C. 195.

2 Lade *v.* Shepard, 2 Stra. 1004. See also Miles *v.* Rose, 5 Taunt. 705.

3 3 Kent's Commentaries, p. 451; Smith *v.* The State, 3 Zabriskie, (N. J.) 130; Denning *v.* Roome, 6 Wend. 65; Post *v.* Pearsall, 22 Wend. R. p. 450; The State *v.* Marble, 4 Ired. 318; State *v.* Sarstor, 2 Strob. 60; State *v.* Cardwell, Bus. (N. C.) R. 245.

4 Rex *v.* Lloyd, 1 Campb. 260.

to be excluded from it, after being allowed to use it so long without interruption." And where a circuitous road, which had been used by the public for more than forty years, was changed for a more direct route, the termini remaining the same, with the knowledge and assent of the owner of the soil, and the new road was used as the old had been for eight years, these facts were considered fully competent to prove a dedication of the new way by the owner as made for the very purpose of being used instead of the old way.[1] So, if a street has been used and built up along a particular line, and the adjoining owners have acquiesced in the line so built upon, and treated it as the true line of the street for forty or fifty years, they will not be permitted to deny the effect of their acts as a dedication, and to contract the lines of the street, on the ground that by so doing they make them conform to the original survey and lay-out of the street.[2] So, where a person laid off an alley fifteen feet wide from his lots, for his own convenience, and permitted the public to use it, and, the adjoining proprietors laying off an equal space and accommodating their improvements to it, it became a public thoroughfare of thirty feet wide, extending from one street to another, and was surveyed, and partly graded and paved by the city surveyor, without objection on the part of the owner, the said alley was held to be clearly dedicated to the public.[3] Also, in a case where a street in the city of New York was widened from forty to sixty feet, and accordingly used by the public for nineteen years, with the acquiescence of the owner, who paid an assessment for paving it to the full width, it was held, in a case made for the opinion of the Court upon a verdict taken by consent, that the circumstances were abundantly sufficient to warrant the presumption of dedication.[4] And in the case of

---

1 Larned *v.* Larned, 11 Met. 421.

2 Smith *v.* The State, 3 Zabriskie, (N. J.) R. 130.

3 Gamble *v.* St. Louis, 12 Missouri R. 617.

4 Denning *v.* Roome, 6 Wend. 651.

Regina *v.* Patrie,[1] the Court go so far as to say, that the enjoyment and user of a way by the public, with circumstances of publicity, for a period of six years, is evidence from which the assent of the owner, whoever he may be, is *primâ facie* to be inferred. But in a recent American case,[2] it was held, that without some clear and unequivocal manifestation of an intention to dedicate, dedication would not be presumed until after the lapse of twenty years, and this seems to be the view more generally taken by American courts.

§ 144. And where the evidence is not so conclusive, yet the jury may presume a dedication from circumstances indicative of an intent to dedicate, coupled with an uninterrupted user by the public for a period much less than twenty years. Thus in Jarvis *v.* Dean,[3] an unpaved and unlighted street, leading from White Conduit Street to some fields in which there were houses, and communicating with a road which passed over fields to Highgate, had been used as a public road for four or five years, and the inhabitants had paid highway and paving rates. The jury, being instructed that, if they thought the street had been used for years as a public thoroughfare with the assent of the owners of the soil, they might presume a dedication, did so, and their verdict was confirmed on a motion for a new trial. In Hobbs *v.* Lowell,[4] an ancient county road having been rendered impassable by a canal, a new road was opened by the corporation, in the same general direction, passing over the canal by a bridge, and falling into the old road at each extremity. The travel had been wholly diverted into this road, and

---

1 Regina *v.* Patrie, 30 Eng. Law & Eq. R. 207.

2 Hoole *v.* Attorney-General, 22 Ala. 190; Noyes *v.* Ward, 19 Conn. 250; State *v.* Thomas, 4 Har. (Del.) R. 568; State *v.* Gregg, 2 Hill, (S. C.) R. 587.

3 Jarvis *v.* Dean, 3 Bing. 447.

4 Hobbs *v.* Lowell, 19 Pick. 405. In this case, the Court overruled the opinion expressed in Hinckley *v.* Hastings, 2 Pick. 162, that in Massachusetts, highways by dedication were unknown. A similar view of the law has been taken in Maine, Estes *v.* Troy, 5 Greenl. 368, and subsequently overruled. Dwinel *v.* Barnard, 15 Shepl. 554.

had continued therein for six years, guide posts had been set in it by the local authorities, and all trace of the old road had disappeared. On a motion to the Superior Court, to set aside a nonsuit which had been ordered in this case, it was remarked, that the act of appropriation was as distinct and unequivocal as could possibly be without an instrument in writing, and a trial on the merits was directed. And where a road was laid out by the selectmen of a town, without compensation to the owner of the *land*, and used by the public for eighteen years, without dissent on his part, the jury were held to have properly presumed a dedication.[1] Also, twelve years' public use of a road, laid out by commissioners, but without a strict compliance with the prescribed formalities, has been considered sufficient evidence of its dedication.[2]

§ 145. In the case of The Rugby Charity *v.* Merryweather,[3] an uninterrupted *user* for eight years was considered to be in itself a sufficient proof of dedication, without reference to the intention of the owner, and although there was evidence of a contrary intention. This was an action of trespass, brought to try a right of way claimed by the Governor of the Foundling Hospital, in which the *locus in quo* was shown to have been a common street, though no thoroughfare, by reason of the houses at the end, for fifty years. The plaintiffs accounted for not having put up a bar or the like to denote that the way was not relinquished to the public at large, by showing that the *locus in quo* had been in lease for a long term, up to the year 1780. Lord Kenyon asked what the plaintiffs had to say to the time from 1780 till about two years ago, (the action was brought in

---

1 Pritchard *v.* Atkinson, 4 N. H. 1.

2 Colden *v.* Thurber, 2 Johns. 424. See further, Pritchard *v.* Atkinson, 3 N. H. 335; State *v.* Compton, 2 N. H. 513; Stacey *v.* Miller, 14 Mo. Rep. 478; Cole *v.* Sprowl, 35 Maine, 161; Dummer *v.* Selectmen of Jersey City, 1 Spencer, 86; Noyes *v.* Ward, 19 Conn. 250; Taylor *v.* Bailey, Wright, 646; Baker *v.* Clarke, 4 N. H. R. 380; Greeley *v.* Quimby, 2 Foster, (N. H.) R. 335.

3 The Rugby Charity *v.* Merryweather, 11 East, 375, note.

1790,) when they had put up a bar. In answer, it was said, that they had been in treaty with the Foundling Hospital respecting the allowing them the right of way, which was finally broken off. But Lord Kenyon said: "If this rested solely on the ground of a question of right between the plaintiffs and the Foundling Hospital, the former certainly would not have been barred by the time which elapsed from 1780 till the obstruction was put up, pending the treaty between them; but during all that time they permitted the public at large to have the free use of this way, without any impediment whatever, and therefore it is now too late to arrest the right; for this is quite sufficient time for presuming a dereliction of the way to the public. In a great case, which was much contested, six years was held sufficient." Here, the Court make no account of the owner's intention, and held, in fact, that dedication may be presumed after eight years' public use, even in the face of an adverse intention on his part, unless by some interruption of that use or other equally significant act, he notify the public of such adverse intention.

§ 146. But in Woodyer *v.* Hadden,[1] a street, which had been opened and partly paved for nineteen years, was held not to have been dedicated. In that case, the plaintiff had constructed a street leading out of a highway across his own close, intersected midway by another street, and terminating at the edge of the defendant's adjoining close, which for twenty-one years had been separated from the end of the street by the defendant's fence. The houses along the line of the street had been erected, and a foot pavement on each side of the way, and a horse pavement on one side, as far as the centre of the horse road, and extending the whole length of the street to the defendant's land, had been laid down for about eighteen or nineteen years before the trial; but the horse pavement, on the other side of the way, had at no time before the trial extended

[1] Woodyer *v.* Hadden, 5 Taunt. 126.

along more than a part of the street. The street was paved at private expense, but for some time before the trial it had been watched, lighted with parish lamps, and cleansed by the parish scavenger, the expense being defrayed by a parochial rate. Brewers' drays, and other carriages, bringing provisions and various articles for the use of the inhabitants, were accustomed to enter and leave the street without molestation, but there was no evidence that any carriages passed there, except in going to and from the houses on the street. Lord Mansfield being of the opinion, that the plaintiffs had not so far given up the street but that they might obstruct it, except when used for the purpose of the inhabitants of those houses which the plaintiffs had erected, the jury found, that the land had not been dedicated to the public, and returned a verdict for the plaintiffs. On a motion for a new trial, the verdict was confirmed, two of the Judges concurring with Lord Mansfield. "Although the same time," said Gibbs, J., "is not necessary to dedicate a highway as is required to establish a right of possession to land against an hostile claim, yet time is an ingredient. Now, in this case, I think there is not time enough to presume a dedication. The foot pavement was finished, the horseway was not completely finished; *there had been a negotiation for opening it and that had gone off.*" Heath, J., based his opinion still more distinctly upon the absence of a dedicative intent. "No act," he said, "is necessary on the part of the owner of the land, while his work is unfinished, to evince that under these circumstances he does not dedicate his property to the public. We know that in dedicating churches and churchyards, and anciently, temples, there is, after the work is completed, a formal act of dedication. I think here, by analogy, that not only until the work is completed, but until the owner has shown some intention of dedicating the soil to the public, his right continues of putting up a bar and excluding them; otherwise the building of every house and laying out a way to it, would establish a public way. *Affectus tuus nomen imposuit operi tuo.* No fact in this case shows that the owner meant to give the public any right over this land, beyond the right of passage to the respective houses." Chambre, J., dissenting from the rest of the Court, rested his opinion upon the case of The Rugby Charity *v.* Merryweather; and Mansfield, who followed him, in commenting on that case said: "I never could discover when the dedication began; Lord Kenyon says, during the lease there was no dedication, but that eight years' acquiescence afterward were sufficient; he says, that, in another case, six years were held to be enough, not naming the case; if six why not one? why not half a year? It would then become necessary for every reversioner coming into possession of his estate after a lease, instantly to put up fences all around his property, to prevent dedication." Indeed, so incompatible is Lord Kenyon's opinion with this and other subsequent cases, that it can hardly be considered authority upon this point at the present day.

§ 147. That dedication should not be presumed, without evidence of an unequivocal intention to dedicate, is still more strongly illustrated in the case of The Trustees of the British Museum *v.* Finnis,[1] where the jury refused to find it after thirty years' user by the public. The land in this case was a strip, five feet and four inches wide, extending by the south side of the Museum, outside the wall, and abutting on Great Russell Street. A witness recollected it to have been fenced in by a wooden railing, which, having decayed, was taken away and not replaced by any other fence, but he could not recollect accurately the date of its existence, (more than thirty years previous however.) The small stones, with which it was paved, were brought from the court-yard of the Museum; and, six or seven years previous to the trial, leave having been obtained from the committee of paving, to remove the pavement for the making of a sewer, part of the pavement was replaced by the committee, and part by the Trustees of the

[1] The Trustees of the British Museum *v.* Finnis, 5 Carr. & Payne, 460.

Museum. The servants of the Museum cleaned away the dirt up to the termination of the small stones, and to that line only. The Court instructed the jury, that if a man opened his land so that the public passed over it continually, they would, after a user of a very few years, acquire a right of way; and that, if he did not mean to dedicate it as a way, but only to give a license, he should do some act to show that he gave a license only; but that, there being an old way near his land, if, by the fences decaying, the public came on his land, that was no dedication; and directing the jury to take into consideration the fact, that the land *had been* fenced by the plaintiffs, that when repaired it was repaired by them, and still continued to be cleaned by their servants, left it to them to say whether there had been a total dereliction on the part of the plaintiffs, in favor of the public, or only a license. The jury found in favor of the plaintiffs. On the same principle, where the travelled path upon a public highway, which was established by immemorial use, separated into two tracks, thus leaving a triangular strip in the middle, over which the travel had never passed, partly on account of a declivity, and partly on account of some obstructions which had been placed there, it was held to be the right of the owner of the soil not to have it encumbered by the public without satisfactory evidence that it had been appropriated to public use.[1] But where a strip of land, from six to ten feet in width, lying between the beaten track of the road and the fence which enclosed land belonging to another person, had remained unenclosed ever since the laying out of the road; the Court said, the fair inference to be drawn from its situation, thus acquiesced in by the owner, was, that it had been abandoned to the public; and any other construction would convert it into a clap-trap to catch trespassers.[2]

---

[1] Sprague *v.* White, 17 Pick. 309; State *v.* Nudd, 3 Foster, (N. H.) R. 327.

[2] Gowen *v.* Philadelphia Exchange Co. 5 Watts & Serg. 141; Cleveland *v.* Cleveland, 12 Wend. 172; Valentine *v.* Boston, 22 Pick. 75.

§ 148. In Woodyer *v.* Hadden, that portion of the Court that thought there was no dedication, laid great stress upon the fact that the street was in an unfinished condition; and Lord Mansfield said, "to support any thing like a dedication, it must be finished as a perfect street." But that a street may be dedicated, while a portion of it is not prepared for use, has since been decided by the Supreme Court of the United States, in Barclay *v.* Howell's Lessee.[1] In that case, a suit was brought to recover a strip of land between Water Street and the River Monongahela. It appeared that the town of Pittsburg was originally platted into lots, streets, and alleys, from the junction of the Alleghany and Monongahela Rivers, extending up the latter to Grant Street. With the exception of Water Street, which lay along the bank of the Monongahela, all the streets and alleys of the town were distinctly marked by the surveyor, and their width laid down on the plat. On this plat the name of Water Street was given and its northern boundary, but to the south it was left open to this river, (there being no indication that it did not extend to the river's edge,) and it was testified to have been reserved for a public street, when the town was laid out, by the land-owner's agent. A portion of it had been used for a way, (the residue not being in a condition to be used without grading,) for thirty years, during which the public authorities had from time to time improved more and more of it, without any claim having been made on the part of the proprietor. The Court said: "If the dedication of these streets to the public was a matter of doubt, and a jury were about to inquire into the fact, it is admitted, that their not having been improved or used as streets, would be a circumstance which the jury might weigh against the proof of dedication. But it would most clearly be error for the Court to instruct the jury, that unless the ground claimed for these streets was in a situation to be used as streets, and had been so used, there could have been no dedication."

---

[1] Barclay *v.* Howell's Lessee, 6 Peters, (U. S.) R. 498.

§ 149. In this country, there is quite a large class of cases, in which dedication has been inferred from the sale of land, described by reference to a map or plat, in which the same is designated as laid off into lots, intersected by streets and alleys. It may be stated, as a general rule, that, where the owner of urban property, who has laid it off into lots, with streets, avenues, and alleys intersecting the same, sells his lots with reference to a plat in which the same is so laid off, or where, there being a city map in which this land is so laid off, he adopts such map, by sales with reference thereto, his acts will amount to a dedication of the designated streets, avenues and alleys to the public.[1] And in New York, where the highways are opened or accepted by a specific act, whereupon the fee of the soil becomes vested in the corporation, it has been held, that the proprietor, who has made such sales, is concluded from afterwards disposing of more than the naked fee of such street or alley, subject to the easement of a perpetual right of way in the public, or, at the least, in the purchaser, and, on acceptance of the street, is entitled to only nominal compensation.[2] In case of such a sale, the dedication will be presumed to extend, if not to all the vendor's land in the site of the street, yet to all his land in the same block, or, in other words, to the next cross-street or avenue on each side of the lots sold.[3] Moreover, if land be surveyed and laid off at the request of its several owners, according to a plan agreed upon by them, and

---

[1] Irwin *v.* Dixon, 9 Howard (U. S.) R. 10; Matter of Seventeenth Street, 1 Wend. 262; Matter of Lewis Street, 2 Wend. 472; Livingston *v.* The Mayor of New York, 8 Wend. 85; Wyman *v.* Mayor of New York, 11 Wend. 486; Matter of Furman Street, 17 Wend. 649; Matter of Thirty-second Street, 19 Wend. 128; Matter of Twenty-ninth Street, 1 Hill, 189; Ibid. 191; Hannibal *v.* Draper, 15 Mis. 639; People *v.* Lambier, 5 Denio, 9; Rowan *v.* Portland, 8 B. Mon. 232.

[2] Wyman *v.* Mayor of New York, 11 Wend. 486; Matter of Lewis Street, 2 Wend. 472; Trustees of Watertown *v.* Cowen, 4 Paige, Ch. R. 510; but see *post*, Chap. VII.

[3] Matter of Twenty-ninth Street, 1 Hill, 189.

sales effected and improvements made in reference to a street and landing designated in the survey, this will amount to a dedication of the street and landing to the public, and it is not essential that there should be a map of the survey. In such a case, all the proprietors with whom the plan was agreed upon, as well as those who have purchased with reference to it, have given a consideration for the dedication, and have an interest in its perpetuity, which cannot be defeated by the subsequent dissent of one of their number.[1] But a mere survey of the streets, without sale of lots or improvements thereon, and without allowing the streets to be occupied or used, is not sufficient to raise the presumption of dedication.[2] In some of the States of the Union, it has been provided by statute, that the proprietor of land, who lays it out in town or city lots, shall, by acknowledging and recording a plat or map of the same, vest the legal title of the land designated as streets in the corporation of the town or city for the use and benefit of the public. If the town or city has no corporate existence, the fee remains in abeyance, subject to vest in the corporation the moment it is created, and the purchaser of a lot, designated on such plat, takes no interest in the street, except in common with the public.[3] But, notwithstanding these statutes, dedication may still take place, as at common law.[4] And where such a plat is executed and recorded, but not acknowledged, and conveyances are made describing lots according to the plat, and referring to it as of record, this will not create a dedication of the streets, laid down thereon, by virtue of the statute. Such acts are only evidence of dedication as at common law, which

---

1 Godfrey *v.* The City of Alton, 12 Ill. 29.

2 United States *v.* Chicago, 7 How. (U. S.) R. 196; Bailey *v.* Copeland, Wright, 150.

3 Canal Trustees *v.* Havens, 11 Ill. 554; Hunter *v.* Middleton, 13 Ill. 50; Revised Statutes of Illinois, ch. 25, § 17–21; Revised Statutes of Michigan, (1833,) p. 531.

4 Manly *et. al. v.* Gibson, 13 Ill. 308; Sarjeant's Heirs *v.* State of Indiana, 4 McLean, 339.

may be rebutted by showing that the street has never been open to the public, that the city has had a restricted right of way therein by special grant, which it has released, and that portions of the street have been built upon by the owner since recording the plat.[1]

§ 150. There may be a dedication of the Crown lands of England or of the Government lands of the United States to the public as a highway, but in such a case it would seem that the circumstances, from which the consent to the user or the intention to dedicate are to be presumed, must be more than usually decisive. Thus, in Harper *v.* Charlesworth,[2] where a public footway over Crown land had been extinguished by an enclosure act, but for twenty years after the enclosure took place the public had continued to use the way, it was held that this user was not evidence of a dedication to the public, as it did not appear to have been with the knowledge of the Crown. In Regina *v.* East Mark,[3] however, the Court seemed rather inclined to discountenance the doctrine, that stricter evidence of dedication was required as against the Crown than as against an individual. In that case the road had once formed part of the waste of a manor and had been laid out as a private road under a private enclosure act, by virtue of which a portion of the waste had been allotted to the lord in lieu of his interest in the soil, the fee of the road being thereby vested in the Crown. It had been used by the public generally, ever since it had been set out, a period of about fifty years. It was contended that the jury should have been directed that much stronger evidence was necessary as against the Crown than as against the lord, who is likely to be present in the neighborhood and to be cognizant of his rights and of any

---

1 People *v.* Beaubien, 2 Dougl. (Mich.) R. 256.

2 Harper *v.* Charlesworth, 4 Barn. & Cress. 574.

3 Regina *v.* East Mark, 11 Adolph. & El. N. S. 876. See also Regina *v.* Patrie, 30 Eng. Law & Eq. R. 207; Rex *v.* Edmonton, 1 M. & Rob. 24.

invasion of them. The Court (Per Lord Denman, C. J.) said: "The Crown certainly may dedicate to the public and be bound by long acquiescence in public user. I think the public are not bound to inquire, whether this or that owner would be more likely to know his rights and to assert them; and that we have gone quite wrong in entering upon such inquiry. Enjoyment for a great length of time ought to be sufficient evidence of dedication, unless the state of the property has been such as to make dedication impossible." But, in the case of Phipps *v.* The State,[1] where a road, through uncultivated lands of the United States had been used as a highway for more than twenty years, the Court said: "We do not think this doctrine of dedication, inferred from user, is at all applicable to the extensive uncultivated domain of the United States. This domain is not in the actual, visible possession of anybody. There is no one to watch and guard against encroachment. It is impossible that the general government should know, whether its unseated lands are improperly used for highways or not. There cannot, therefore, exist that consent by the owner to the use of his land for a road, from which a dedication can be presumed." But, even in such a case, if there were circumstances sufficiently indicative of an intention to dedicate, the jury would undoubtedly be authorized to infer the fact of dedication from user for a less period than twenty years.

§ 151. Upon much the same principle, it has been decided that dedication of a road to the public, over the waste and unenclosed lands of an individual, ought not to be inferred from bare user alone. Thus, where a road, which had been in existence for more than fifty years, had originally passed entirely through woodland, the jury were instructed, that mere user by the public, however uninterrupted and long continued, would be insufficient to constitute it a public road, but must be

---

[1] Phipps *v.* The State, 7 Blackf. (Ind.) R. 512.

accompanied by acts which showed the use to have been claimed as a right and not by permission of the owner; such as working on it, keeping it in repair, and requiring the removal of obstructions.[1] The ground for the distinction is, that where the land is enclosed and cultivated, the mere use is an invasion and a trespass; but where it is woodland, those who travel it commit no trespass, until after notice to desist, and subject the owner to no loss or inconvenience; to prohibit such use would be considered churlish and would be ineffectual unless constant watch were kept; and, therefore, to subject him to the presumption of dedication from such use would be to exclude his property from the protection of the law. And, even though the land be enclosed and cultivated, dedication is not to be presumed so readily of agricultural as of urban property. Thus, it has been held, that the bare fact, that a farmer leaves a lane through his farm for his own convenience, and permits the public to use it as a highway for fifteen years, does not warrant the inference of dedication. "An intention to dedicate," it was said, "must be obvious, and the same acts which would warrant the inference in cities and towns, would be quite insufficient in sparsely settled agricultural districts."[2]

### 6. *What is sufficient Evidence to rebut the Presumption of Dedication.*

§ 152. Dedication being the joint effect of an intentional appropriation by the owner of the land and an acceptance by the public, it follows that no presumption of dedication can be made, where circumstances exist, which negative the presumption of an intent to dedicate. The most common method,

---

1 Hutto *v.* Tindal, 6 Rich. (S. C.) 396; Hoggs *v.* Gill, 1 McM. (S. C.) 329; State *v.* Thomas, 4 Har. (Del.) R. 568.

2 Stacey *v.* Miller, 14 Mo. R. 478; Badeau *v.* Mead, 13 Barb. Sup. Ct. R. 328; Hewins *v.* Smith, 11 Met. (Mass.) R. 241.

adopted to rebut such a presumption, is the placing of a gate or bar[1] across the road, to open and shut at pleasure; though the fact that there is such a gate, is not entirely conclusive, for the road may have originally been granted, reserving the right of keeping a gate across to prevent cattle straying.[2] In a case where a street had been made across an enclosed field, and soon after the houses were finished, a bar had been placed across the street to prevent carriages from passing, but had soon been knocked down, since which time the street had been used as a thoroughfare; the Court held, that the putting up the bar rebutted the presumption of dedication, which, to bind the land-owner, must have been made openly and with a deliberate purpose; and that, in this case, the street was to be considered only as a way for the use of the tenants inhabiting on each side of it.[3] So, where originally a gate had been erected across the way, but for twelve years had not been there, the jury, under the direction of the Judge, found that there was no dedication; and the Court of King's Bench, the following term, refused a rule *nisi* to set aside the verdict.[4] So, also, the parish being bound to repair all public roads, the fact of no repairs having been made by it, is a circumstance from which it may be inferred that a way is not public and therefore not dedicated.[5] And where a road had been made such pursuant to the provisions of an act of parliament, which was to continue in force for a limited period only, and the inhabitants of a parish, through which it passed, were thereby bound to do statute duty; it was held, that the performance of such statute duty, being compulsory, was not an adoption of the road by the parishioners, and that, at the expiration of the

---

1 Commonwealth *v.* Newbury, 2 Pick. 51; State *v.* Strong, 25 Maine, 297.

2 Davies *v.* Stephens, 7 Carr. & Payne, 570.

3 Roberts *v.* Karr, 1 Campb. 262, n.

4 Lethbridge *v.* Winter, 1 Camb. 262, n.

5 Davies *v.* Stephens, 7 Carr. & Payne, 570.

act, they were not bound at common law to repair such road.[1] So a road, set out by commissioners under a local act for the benefit of a particular class of persons, but which had been used by the public for seventeen years, was held not to have become a highway by dedication, it having been compulsory on the owner to permit a qualified passage; since, it was remarked, if this were a public road, it would follow, whenever such a road were set out, which happened to be convenient for passage, it would become almost immediately a public road, and the burden of repairing it would be thrown on the parish.[2]

§ 153. In Barraclough *v.* Johnson,[3] a lane was thrown open to the public, in pursuance of a private agreement with an iron company and the inhabitants of the hamlet, to the effect that the company should pay an acknowledgment of five shillings a year and supply cinders for the repair of the road, and that the hamlet should lead and spread them. The road remained open from 1814 to 1832, when, in consequence of disputes, it was closed by the proprietors. The jury, under the direction of the Judge, found by their verdict that there was no dedication, and, in refusing a motion to set it aside, the Court, per Lord Denman, C. J., said: "A dedication must be made with an intention to dedicate; the mere acting so as to lead persons into the supposition that the way is dedicated, does not amount to a dedication, if there be an agreement which explains the transaction; and referring to the agreement here, it is plain that there was only a license to use." And per Patterson, J.: "There must be a clear intention to dedicate in order to constitute a dedication. I do not mean to say that if the owner of land allows the public a right of way for a series of years, his saying once or twice during

1 Rex *v.* Mellor, 1 B. & Ad. 32.

2 Rex *v.* St. Benedict, 4 B. & Ad. 447.

3 Barraclough *v.* Johnson, 8 Ad. & Ellis, 99; 3 Nev. & Perry, 233.

that time, 'this is not a public highway,' without taking any further steps about it, would be such an indication as to prevent the user by the public being referred to dedication; but, even then, the question would be on the intention of the party." So the presumption arising from thirty years' use by the public of a private way was held to be rebutted by the fact, that the owner used it in like manner at the same time, repaired it at his own expense, paid taxes assessed thereon, stowed lumber on it, and exercised other acts of ownership over it.[1] Also, the fact that a street, which had been in general use for fifteen years, was originally laid out for the use and accommodation of the abuttors thereon, with the right reserved to them to alter or discontinue it, has been held sufficient to rebut the presumption of dedication.[2] And, indeed, in all cases this presumption, being merely an inference from circumstances indicative of an intent to dedicate, is open to rebuttal by evidence of circumstances indicative of a contrary intent.

§ 154. But the owner of the soil having once authorized this presumption, by his own acts or omissions, coupled with user by the public, will not be allowed by any subsequent act to make evidence to rebut it. This was so held in the case of The Grand Surrey Canal Company *v.* Hall,[3]—a very important case as regards what is sufficient evidence of an intention to dedicate. In that case, it appeared, that by the 41 Geo. III. c. 31, § 66, the incorporated company of the proprietors of The Grand Surrey Canal were required to make and maintain bridges over the canal, for the use of the owners and occupiers of adjoining land; and, also, where the canal was carried across any common highway, public bridleway, or footpath. After the passing of the act in 1801, the canal was commenced, and

---

1 Irwin *v.* Dixon, 9 How. (U. S.) R. 10.

2 Bowers *v.* Suffolk Manufacturing Co. 4 Cush. 332; State *v.* Trask, 6 Vt. 355; Stone *v.* Jackson, 32 Eng. Law & Eq. R. 349.

3 The Grand Surrey Canal Company *v.* Hall, 1 Man. & Gr. 392.

being carried in its progress through land belonging to one Rolls, over which there was a foot and bridle way, it became requisite, in pursuance of the act, to erect a bridge over the canal at the spot where it crossed such way. A swivel or swing bridge was accordingly built by the company in 1804. From 1810 to 1822, the public occasionally used the bridge as a carriage-way. In the latter year, a church was built near to the canal, and streets were formed leading to the bridge, which were repaired by the parish, and the neighborhood became very populous. From 1822 down to 1832, the public used the bridge as a carriage-way, without any other interruption than was caused by the bridge being swung back to allow vessels to pass. In 1832, the company began to exact a toll from all persons using the bridge with carriages, who were not tenants of the Rolls' Estate. In 1834, the company removed the swivel bridge, and erected a stone bridge in its stead. In an action of trespass against the defendant, for passing the bridge with a horse and chaise, without the license of the plaintiffs, it was contended that, inasmuch as the company was bound by the act to erect a bridge over the canal for the use of the tenants of the Rolls' Estate, as a carriage-way, the public must be presumed to have known, the statute being a public act, that there was no original intention on the part of the company to dedicate it to them. Lord Denman instructed the jury, that, if, in consequence of the acts of the company, an idea grew up in the mind of the public, that they intended to dedicate the bridge to the public use, such acts would amount to a dedication. The jury found a verdict for the defendant. On a motion for a new trial, on the ground of misdirection, the plaintiffs' counsel contending, that the proper question for the jury was, not what idea had grown up in the mind of the public, but whether the company had intended to dedicate the bridge to the public; the Court held, that the charge of the Judge, properly construed, purported that the jury were to consider whether what the public supposed to be a dedication, was a dedication in point of fact, and that, taken in connection with the discussion which took place between the counsel of the parties as to the intention of the company, it was impossible not to see that he must have left it to the jury to say whether the plaintiffs intended to dedicate the way to the public. It was further remarked, per Tindal, C. J., "If the matter were to rest on what had taken place since 1834, it could not be said that there had been a dedication to the public. But we must look back at what had occurred previous to that period, and if the public had acquired a right of way along the swivel bridge, subject only to the temporary interruption caused by the passing of barges up and down the canal, the circumstance of the company erecting a stone bridge in this place, cannot have the effect of destroying the right so acquired. It seems to me that there was evidence of a dedication to go to the jury, and I see no reason for saying that they have come to an improper conclusion; consequently, this rule must be discharged."

## 7. *Limits of Dedication.*

§ 155. Where there is no other evidence of dedication than mere user by the public, the presumption of dedication is not necessarily limited to the travelled path, but may be inferred to extend to the ordinary width of highways, or, if the road be enclosed with fences, to include the entire space so enclosed. Thus, where a private road was established by the award of commissioners of the width of eight yards, but, in fact, a space of sixty feet was left between the adjoining fences for nearly sixty years, the centre of which space had commonly been used by the public as a carriage-way, and had been repaired by the township for eighteen years, the Court held that it was properly left to the jury to say, whether or not the entire space had not been dedicated to the public.[1] But where the land is held in

---

[1] Rex *v.* Wright, 3 Barn. & Adolph. 681. See also, Cleveland *v.* Cleveland, 12 Wend. 172; Hannum *v.* Belchertown, 19 Pick. 311; Simmons *v.* Cornell,

common by the proprietors on opposite sides, no act showing an intent to dedicate by one of the proprietors, will be sufficient to establish a dedication without some corresponding act by the other.[1]

§ 156. In the case of the City of Cincinnati *v.* White,[2] it was said, that, where dedication is implied from use, "such use ought to be for such a length of time that the public accommodation and private rights might be materially affected by an interruption of the enjoyment;" but that, this being the case, and private and individual rights having been acquired with reference to it, "the law considers it in the nature of an *estoppel in pais*, which precludes the original owner from revoking such dedication. It is a violation of good faith to the public, and to those who have acquired private property with a view to the enjoyment of the use thus publicly granted." This language, used originally rather by way of illustration than as announcing a strictly legal principle, has been adopted and extended by some American Courts, so far as to convey the impression, that the right of the public to the use of a road may rest upon an *estoppel in pais* as against the owner.[3] Now, if by *estoppel in pais* any thing other than dedication be meant, this doctrine is not sanctioned by a single English decision; if dedication be meant, the use of the term estoppel, in this connection, is only productive of a confusion of ideas. The doctrine of *estoppel in pais*, in so far as it is applicable to real estate, rests upon the equitable principle, that the owner of land, who induces or suffers another to acquire an interest in or expend money upon such land under an erroneously supposed right so to do, shall thereby be precluded from denying the existence of such supposed right.

---

1 R. I. Rep. 519; Sprague *v.* Waite, 17 Pick. 309; Mount Vernon *v.* Lawrence, 35 Maine, 100.

1 Simmons *v.* Mumford, 2 R. I. Rep. 172.

2 City of Cincinnati *v.* White, 6 Peters, 431.

3 Noyes *v.* Ward, 19 Conn. 250; The Mayor of Macon *v.* Franklin, 12 Geo. 239; Cole *v.* Sprowl, 35 Maine, 161; 2 Greenl. Ev. § 662.

Such a principle may be applicable as between the owner of a private street, and individuals who have built upon the line of it, supposing it to be a public street, or intended for a public street, in so far as to estop him from interfering with the free use of the same; but the public acquires its right by the acceptance of a voluntary donation, and holds it against the owner, not because he is precluded by any equitable principle from asserting his title, but because he has no title which is not consistent with the public use. It is a right which the individual may confer without deed, without express declaration, by nothing more than an intention to that effect implied in his conduct. It is not, therefore, the indispensable condition of dedication, that the public have incurred expense in relation to the roads, and that it is essential to the public accommodation; these facts are strong, perhaps almost conclusive, evidence of dedication; but, in the absence of both facts, dedication may exist, which it could not do if it were dependent on an *estoppel in pais*. The public may not have expended a dime, it may be perfectly well accommodated by another road running between the same termini, and yet, if there be proof of an appropriation and an acceptance, there is a highway. Neither can the Court say to the jury, the public convenience requires that a given parcel of land shall be a highway, the public have used it as such and expended money upon it, and, therefore, the owner is precluded from asserting a private right to it. The most they can say, is, that these are facts from which the jury are authorized to infer an intention on his part to give the public the use of his land; and that, if they do infer such an intention, there exists a highway by dedication. This idea of an *estoppel in pais*, therefore, which occupies so prominent a place in a few American decisions, though it may furnish analogies for the guidance of the Court and jury in presuming an intention to dedicate, is foreign to the principle on which dedication rests, and does but form an excrescence to mar the simplicity of the doctrine as established by English authority.

## 8. *Acceptance.*

§ 157. It has been said, that dedication to be effectual, must be accepted, and this acceptance may be either of a part or of the whole of the land appropriated.[1] Such an acceptance may, undoubtedly, be made by a formal act of the body charged with repairing the highway, or by any act on its part sufficiently implying its acceptance; but whether such an acceptance may be made by the public generally, as evidenced by a mere use of the way, is a question upon which the decisions have not been entirely uniform.[2] The earliest reported case, in which this point appears to have been deliberately considered, was that of Rex *v.* The Parish of St. Benedict,[3] decided in 1821, in which the defendants were prosecuted for not repairing a highway. It appeared in this case that the road was originally made under the provisions of a local act, by a clause in which two private roads, therein particularly described, were directed to be set out for the use of such persons only as were entitled to use an old occupation road, running in the same direction as the latter of the two roads. The commissioners, acting in exe-

---

1 State *v.* Trask, 6 Vt. 355.

2 See The Glusburne Bridge case, 2 W. Bl. R. 685; 5 Burr. 2594; and Rex *v.* The West Riding of Yorkshire, 2 East, 342, and note, for the law as regards bridges on this point. In the latter case, it was held, that where a bridge, built under a turnpike act, in a highway, had been used by the public for about two years, the county were bound to repair it without any specific acceptance; "though," it was said, "if built in an imperfect and inconvenient manner, with a view to throw the onus of rebuilding or repairing immediately on the county, it might be treated as a nuisance and indicted as such."

3 Rex *v.* The Parish of St. Benedict, 4 Barn. & Ald. 447. Previous to this case, roads had been held to be highways, in cases where there appears to have been no other evidence of acceptance than public use. Lade *v.* Shepherd, Strange, 1004; Jarvis *v.* Dean, 3 Bingh. 446. Rex *v.* Lloyd, 1 Campb. 260, in which Lord Ellenborough remarks: "I think that if places are lighted by public bodies, this is strong evidence that the public have a right of way over them," which seems to have been the first intimation that an adoption by the parish would be more conclusive evidence of acceptance than mere general use, for he does not intimate that any adoption is necessary.

cution of this power, by their award, dated June 27, 1803, set out the road presented as one of these two roads. From the date of the award, however, until the finding of the presentment in 1820, the road had been used by the public without interruption as a carriage-way. The question was, whether, under these circumstances, this was a public road which the parish was bound to repair. In discussing this question, Bailey, J., said: "I do not accede to the doctrine that, because there is a dedication of the road by the owner of the soil, and the public use it, the parish is therefore bound to repair. I think there ought to be, in addition to that, evidence of an acquiescence by the parish in that dedication. In the case of bridges, there always is what is to be considered as an acquiescence by the county. The county is not liable except for bridges made in *highways;* the making of the bridge, and thereby obstructing the road, while the bridge is making, may be treated as a nuisance, and the county may, if it think fit, stop its progress by indictment, and the forbearing to prosecute in that way is an acquiescence by the county in the building of the bridge. But in the case of a parish, they have no power to prevent the opening of a road or to obstruct the public use of it. It would be most unjust if, by the public use of what was at first a private road, the burden of repairing it could be removed from the persons to whom the use of it was at first confined, and cast upon the parish. Admitting, therefore, that in this case there was a dedication to the public, and that the road was found to be a public benefit, I think that in consequence of the want of some act of acquiescence or adoption by the parish, they are not liable to the repair of the road."

§ 158. And in two subsequent cases,[1] in which this point came incidentally before the Court, the same view seems to

---

[1] Rex *v.* Mellor, 1 Barn. & Adolph. 32; and Rex *v.* Cumberworth, 2 Barn. & Adolph. 108.

have been taken. It was, however, admitted that where a way had been recognized as public in an act of parliament for making streets, squares, &c. it was not necessary that it should be adopted by the parish to make it a public way.[1] But in Rex *v.* Leake,[2] which was an indictment for not repairing a road, made by user on a dyke, built by trustees under an act of parliament, the absence of any acceptance by the parish was held to be immaterial. Per Parke, J.: "The absence of repairs by the parish is, indeed, a strong circumstance in point of evidence to prove, that the road is not a public one,—the fact of repair has a contrary effect. But the conduct of the parish, in acquiescing or refusing an acquiescence, is, in my opinion, immaterial in any other point of view. The judgment of Mr. Baron Bailey, in the case of Rex *v.* St. Benedict, was cited to the contrary; but I must say that I cannot accede to the doctrine, nor am I aware that there is any authority for it." Per Littledale, J.: "The adoption by a parish does not necessarily, as a matter of law, make the road public, nor does their refusal to adopt it, prevent its being so. If the parish have repaired it, it raises a strong presumption that it is a public highway. The adoption by the parish is no more than the use of it by the public. The parish are merely part of the public." And Denman, C. J., said: "I by no means think any act of adoption necessary to make a parish liable to repair a common road. I am of opinion, that if it is public, the parish is of common right bound to repair it." By this decision the law in England is probably settled, that no acceptance by the parish is necessary; at least in no subsequent case has the question been raised, though there have been later cases in which it does not appear that an acceptance by the parish was proved.[3]

---

1 Rex *v.* Lyon, 5 Dow. & Ry. 499.

2 Rex *v.* Leake, 5 Barn. & Adolph. 469; 2 Neville & Man. 583.

3 Regina *v.* Patrie, 30 Eng. Law & Eq. R. 207; Surrey Canal Co. *v.* Hall, 1 Man. & Gr. 392.

§ 159. In the United States, the cases in which this point has been directly raised, are comparatively few, and the decisions have hardly been sufficiently uniform or authoritative to establish any general rule; though some American Courts of high authority, influenced, however, by local statutes, incline against the view, that a highway may be established independently of the action of the body charged with its repair. In Massachusetts, in the case of Hobbs *v.* Lowell,[1] Shaw, C. J., remarked: "It is manifest that there is very little analogy between the character, powers, and duties of parishes in England and those of towns in this Commonwealth. Almost the only point of resemblance is, that they are respectively bound to repair all highways within their limits, where other provision is not made by law for the purpose. The great point of difference is, that in this Commonwealth, towns have the power in a certain course of proceedings, to lay out townways, which are in effect public highways, within their limits; they are also recognized as parties, in all proceedings for establishing new highways, for the support of which they are to be responsible." In that case, however, the Court were of opinion, that the town had by its acts recognized the road in question, and therefore gave no decisive opinion as to whether its acceptance was necessary. But in a case decided by the same Court, in 1849,[2] it was said: "If there were any doubts on this point previous to the statute of 1846, c. 203, it seems to me they must be removed by that statute. The statute provides, that no way heretofore opened and dedicated to the public use, and not already become a public way, shall become chargeable upon any city or town of this Commonwealth, unless such way shall be laid out and established by the city or town in the manner prescribed by the statutes of this Commonwealth." It was also decided that a way could not be-

---

1 Hobbs *v.* Lowell, 19 Pick. 405.

2 Bowers *v.* Suffolk Manufacturing Company, 4 Cush. 332.

come a highway until the town or city had incurred the obligation to maintain it by establishing it as such, but that, previous to that, the opening it to the public amounted only to a license and not to a grant or dedication.

§ 160. In Vermont, in a case where a way to a mill, built and maintained by the owner of the mill, had been in common use for more than twenty years, it was held, in an action against the town for insufficiency, that a public road was one laid out by proper authority, as the selectmen of the town or a committee appointed by the Supreme or County Court, the evidence of which is the survey, &c. or the record; and that an individual could not lay out a way and compel the town to adopt it.[1] In New York, it has been decided that "streets and roads dedicated by individuals to public use, but not accepted by the local public authorities or declared highways by statute, are not highways within the meaning of the highway acts, (acts which have been in force for more than half a century,) and there is no law by which any one can be compelled to keep them in repair."[2] And in Virginia, a road dedicated to the public must be accepted by the County Court on its records before it can be a public road.[3]

§ 161. In Indiana, in an action for damages suffered by reason of the insufficiency of a bridge, the Court said: "The bridge is upon the *Cumberland* or *National* road, and that road at the point where the bridge in question is situate, is not upon and along any street in Indianapolis, according to the original plat of the town, and there was no evidence upon the trial that the town had ever adopted the Cumberland road as a street. The town did not build this bridge, and certainly it is

---

1 Page *v.* Weathersfield, 13 Vt. 424; Blodget *v.* Royalton, 14 Vt. 288.

2 The City of Oswego *v.* The Oswego Canal Co. 2 Selden, 257; Badeau *v.* Mead, 14 Barb. 328; Clements *v.* West Troy, 16 Barb. 251. In the last case it was held, that acceptance could only be made by instituting the proceedings prescribed by statute for laying out and opening highways.

3 Kelly's case, 8 Grattan, 632.

not in the power of the general government, or of turnpike or plank-road companies, by running their improvements through the town and building bridges upon them to burden the town against her will, with the duty of keeping them in repair."[1] But in other States, the Courts, without having expressly decided, in any case in which the point has been controverted, that an acceptance by mere public user is sufficient, have nevertheless specified user as one of the modes in which an acceptance might be indicated.[2]

§ 162. But even where an acceptance on the part of the town is deemed necessary, this need not be by any formal proceeding, unless required by some statute, but may be implied from its acts recognizing the road as a public highway. Thus, in Hobbs *v.* Lowell,[3] the town, by forbearing to prosecute those who had stopped up an old highway and substituted a new one in its stead, and by setting up a guide-post in the new way, were held to have expressed their assent to its dedication. And, in a later case, it was held, that the passing of a vote by a city, appropriating money for a street, and the expenditure of any part thereof by the city officer, or by a committee intrusted with the expending of the money, was evidence of an acceptance by said city.[4] So, if a town should shut up an old road and leave no avenue for travel except a new road, which they make or cause to be made, or, if they put the same into the rate bills as a road on which a highway tax is to be worked, this is a sufficient adoption; but the

---

1 Indianapolis *v.* McClure, 2 Cart. (Ind.) R. 147.

2 Baker *v.* Clarke, 4 N. H. R. 380; State *v.* Nudd, 3 Fost. 327; Cole *v.* Sprowl, 35 Maine, 161; Curtiss *v.* Hoyt, 19 Conn. 154; The State *v.* The Town of Richmond, 1 R. I. Rep. 49; Remington *v.* Millard, Ibid. 93; Simmons *v.* Cornell, Ibid. 519; State *v.* Carver, 5 Strobh. (N. C.) R. 217; The People *v.* Beaubien, 2 Doug. (Mich.) R. 256; Manly *et al.* *v.* Gibson, 13 Ill. 308; Trustees of Dover *v.* Fox, 9 B. Mon. 201; Taylor *v.* Bailey, Wright, 646.

3 Hobbs *v.* Lowell, 19 Pick. 405.

4 Wright *v.* Tukey, 3 Cush. 290.

mere knowledge on the part of the selectmen of the town, that travellers suppose such road to be a highway, and their consent that they may travel it, do not amount to a recognition of it as such.[1] Neither would the mere assertion of a public right to a way by the prosecuting officer of the State by indictment for obstruction;[2] nor the declaration by a town council, that a given way is a highway, and the ordering the same to be repaired at the expense of the town, (such council not being the agent of the public for this purpose,) be sufficient to constitute such way a public highway.[3]

§ 163. An acceptance of a highway dedicated to the public may be made at any time, provided the gift continues and the tender is not withdrawn by the owner of the fee before an actual acceptance.[4] And where the offer of dedication is made to a city or town for acceptance on the part of the public, it will not be presumed to have been withdrawn until such city or town has had a reasonable time to elect whether they will accept or not. Thus, in the case of Crocket *v.* The City of Boston,[5] the plaintiff proposed to the city to give certain land, free of charge, for a street, provided said street should be established on a specified line, and that the proprietors of certain estates would give, and that the city would take from a certain other estate sufficient land for said purpose. And it was held, that, if such offer was accepted in a reasonable time, and the condition complied with, the proprietor would be estopped from claiming damages for his land; that it was not necessary that the offer should be accepted by a formal vote, but that it was sufficient, if seasonable measures were taken to secure the actual fulfilment of the conditions of the offer, by making the necessary orders for carrying the proposal into effect, and by

---

1 Blodgett *v.* Town of Royalton, 14 Vt. 288.

2 State *v.* Carver, 5 Strobh. 217; The People *v.* Beaubien, 2 Dougl. 256.

3 Remington *v.* Millerd, 1 R. I. Rep. 93.

4 Simmons *v.* Cornell, 1 R. I. Rep. 519.

5 Crockett *v.* The City of Boston, 5 Cush. 182.

actually accomplishing the same; and that a year and four months was not an unreasonable time for this purpose.

## 9. *Dedication of Bridges.*

§ 164. I have thus far treated of the dedication of roads and the dedication of bridges as identical; there is, however, one distinction between them which requires a passing notice. If the owner of land appropriate it to the public for a road, it is optional with the public to accept or decline its use. But if a private individual build a bridge in a road, the public has no choice but either to use it or abate it as a nuisance. Such a bridge, therefore, will not be presumed to have been accepted by the public until it be proved to be useful to the public. "This," say the Court in a leading case,[1] "is the grand criterion; if a man wantonly erects a useless or a mere ornamental bridge, neither he nor the public are bound to sustain it. And if it is principally for his own benefit and only collaterally of benefit to others, the public have nothing to do with it. But where it is of *public utility*, the public which reaps the benefit ought to sustain the burden of repairing it, else it would be a great discouragement to public-spirited persons to erect a beneficial bridge, provided they must either repair it themselves or it must run to ruin." And as an illustration of the case in which the benefit to the public is only collateral, it is said, if a man erects a mill for his own profit, and makes a new cut for the water to come to it, and makes a new bridge over it, and the subjects are to go over this as over a common bridge, this bridge ought to be repaired by him who has the mill, and not by the county, because he erected it for his own benefit.[2] So,

---

1 Rex *v.* The West Riding of Yorkshire, 2 W. Blackst. 685; 5 Burr. 2597.

2 1 Ro. Abr. 368, tit. Bridges, pl. 2; but see King *v.* Glamorgan, 2 East, 496, n.(a); Rex *v.* Kent, 2 Maule & S. 513. In the latter case, the authority relied upon for the dictum in Rolle was cited, but upon examination, it appeared that the liability

if such a bridge be built in a slight and incommodious manner, or under the color of public benefit, but in reality for the purpose of throwing the expense immediately on the county, it may be treated altogether as a nuisance and indicted as such. But, on the other hand, it is the rule that, "if a man builds a bridge, and it becomes useful to the county in general, the county shall repair it." And the fact, that such a bridge has been used for a considerable length of time, is *primâ facie* evidence that it is not a nuisance, and is at least sufficient to throw upon the inhabitants of the county the *onus* of showing who else is bound to repair, if they be not.[1] "Though," says Woodbury, J., in The State *v.* Compton,[2] "the use and repairs of it by the public may have been under a protest against their liability and for a shorter period than twenty years, the liability is still fixed, if the bridge be not indicted as a nuisance and be used by the public so long and so much as to evince its usefulness to them."[3] And even the fact that a bridge was built by trustees under a turnpike act, which authorized them to raise toll for the support of the roads, was held not to exempt the inhabitants of the county from this liability, there being no special provision exonerating them therefrom or transferring it to others.[4]

§ 165. Where, however, a bridge, although erected under

---

there was *ratione tenuræ*, and the Court laid down the rule broadly, that if a private person build a private bridge, which afterwards becomes of public convenience, the county is bound to repair it.

1 The King *v.* West Riding of Yorkshire, 2 East, 342; Reg. *v.* Wilts, 1 Salk. 359; Rex *v.* Buknol, 6 Mod. 151, n.; Rex *v.* St. Benedict, 4 B. & A. 450; Rex *v.* Devon, 1 R. & M. 144.

2 The State *v.* Compton, 2 N. Hamp. 513.

3 2 East, 342; Rex *v.* Lancashire, 2 B. & Adol. 813; Williams *v.* Cunningham, 18 Pick. 312. The property in the materials of the bridge when built and dedicated to the public, still continues in the builder, subject to the right of passage in the public, and if they are severed and taken away, he may maintain trespass. Harrison *v.* Parker, 6 East, 154.

4 Rex *v.* The Inhabitants of the West Riding of Yorkshire, 2 East, R. 342.

the provisions of a statute, is made for the furtherance of private schemes, and may be said to be in the nature of a *compensation* to the public for damage done to their highway; in such case, upon evidence to rebut the *primâ facie* presumption of public utility, arising out of the concurrence of the legislature, the party who built shall also be obliged to maintain the bridge. Thus, where a company, which was empowered by a local act to make a river navigable and to take tolls, and "to amend or alter such bridges or highways as might hinder the passage or navigation, leaving them or others as convenient in their room," deepened the river at a spot which had before that time been fordable by foot passengers, but which, in consequence of such deepening, became impassable for foot and almost for horses, and the company, thereupon being threatened with an indictment, built a bridge across the ford and repaired it till its destruction by a flood; it was held, that the company, and not the county, were bound to rebuild and keep in repair the bridge. And per Lord Ellenborough, C. J.: "The power given to the company to take or alter the old highway was upon condition of leaving another as convenient in its room, and if they do not perform the condition, they are not entitled to do the act; it is a continuing condition, and when the company thought proper, for their own benefit, to alter the highway in the bed of the river, so that the public could no longer have the same benefit of the ford, they were bound to give another passage over the bridge, and to keep it for the public."[1] And upon the same principle, where a canal company, under the authority of an act of Parliament, made for their own benefit a navigable cut and deepened a ford, which crossed the highway, and thereby rendered a bridge necessary for the passage of the public, which was accordingly built at the expense of the company in the first instance, it was

---

[1] Rex *v.* The Inhabitants of the County of Kent, 13 East, R. 220.

held, that the company were bound to maintain the same, and that the burden of repair could not be thrown upon the county. Per Lord Ellenborough, C. J.: "The act authorizes the company not only to alter, repair, and amend, but even to *discontinue* any of the works before authorized to be erected; amongst others, any bridge. And the inhabitants of a county can never have, by law, a permanent burden thrown upon them to repair a bridge, of which they have not the permanent use and enjoyment secured to them." And Le Blanc, J., said: "The authority given to the company to make the cut, which rendered the highway impassable without a bridge, must create an obligation in them to erect the bridge, though the word *authorize* in the act would not of itself create the obligation."[1]

§ 166. The observation of Le Blanc, J., in the last case, that even were nothing said in the act about building the bridge, yet its erection and reparation is required by law from the proprietors, as a compensation to the public, is fully confirmed in the case of Rex *v.* Kerrison.[2] Here the act empowered the commissioners for making navigable the River Waveney, to cut, dig, or use the ground or soil of any persons for the making, enlarging, straightening, or altering the channels of the river, or for making any new channel, &c., but was silent with respect to bridges or other such erections. By virtue of this act, the commissioners cut through a highway and rendered it impassable, and a bridge was built over the cut along which the public passed, and which had been repaired by the proprietors of the navigation. The Court of King's Bench held, that the proprietors, and not the county, were liable to repair. And per Lord Ellenborough, C. J.: "The undertakers of this navigation have a duty, as it seems to me,

---

1 Rex *v.* The Inhabitants of the Parts of Lindsey, in the county of Lincoln, 14 East, R. 319; and see Inhabitants of Cambridge and Somerville *v.* Charlestown Branch Railroad Co. 7 Met. (Mass.) R. 70.

2 Rex *v.* Kerrison, 3 M. & S. 526. As to a *partial* dedication of a bridge, see *ante*, § 139.

arising out of the execution of their own powers under the act. The act enables them to cut new channels, as occasion should require, and if occasion requires them to cut through a public highway, their duty is to furnish a substitute to the public by means of a bridge." And Le Blanc and Bayley, Justices, observed, That although the proprietors had a right to make a cut through the highway, and so far were not wrongdoers; yet if they had left it so, they would have been wrongdoers, and might have been indicted, and charged with cutting across the highway, and if they had pleaded the act of Parliament, the Court would have determined upon it, that they had power only to make the cut *sub modo*, that is, providing a substitute to the public.

### 10. *How a Dedication may be lost.*

§ 167. Dedication, having been rendered complete by acceptance, cannot be revoked by the donor or by any one claiming under him, so long as the land remains in the use to which it was dedicated.[1] A distinction has, however, been drawn in this respect between a dedication and a reservation; the latter being deemed revocable at the will of the land-owner. Thus, where water lots were granted by a city, and on a map, annexed to the grant, a square was designated, on one part of which the word "market" was written, and on another "reservation for a market," and a market having been erected there, remained for twenty years, when it was removed with the consent of the adjoining land-owners, and the space afterwards leased to a railroad company; these facts were said to indicate only a reservation for public use, and, it was said, there was this distinction between dedication and reservation; that,

---

1 Penny Pot Landing *v.* Philadelphia, 4 Harr. (Penn.) R. 79; Curtis *v.* Keesler, 14 Barb. 511; Adams *v.* Saratoga & Washington Railroad Co. 11 Barb. 414.

whereas the former was irrevocable and stripped the owner of all power inconsistent with the terms of the dedication, the latter imposed no obligations on the owner, who might exercise as complete dominion over the land as before the reservation.[1] But whether this distinction could be applied to public ways, as in the case just cited, is questionable; and it is not easy to perceive the precise shade of difference between what is here termed a reservation and what has commonly been denominated a license; though it is easy to see that, from analogous facts in the case of a road or street, the jury would be more likely to infer a dedication than a mere license.

§ 168. But, though a dedication cannot be revoked by the donor, the highway itself may be relinquished or discontinued by the public, or, according to some authorities, may be lost by long-continued non-user or by adverse possession for twenty years, though, according to other authorities, no lapse of time or cessation of user will deprive the public of the right of passage over a road, which has once been a highway, whenever they please to resume it. Upon the discontinuance or extinguishment of a highway, however it may happen, the land reverts to the owner of the fee discharged of the public easement or right of passage.[2]

---

1 Pitcher *v.* New York and Erie Railroad Co. 5 Sandf. 587.

2 *Post*, Chap. VII. *Abandonment and Reversion.*

# CHAPTER IV.

## ASSESSMENT OF ESTATES BENEFITED BY THE OPENING, WIDENING, OR IMPROVING STREETS.



### 1. *Difference between Taxation and Assessment.*

§ 169. It has been shown in a former chapter, that in recompensing an owner of private property, for appropriating a portion of it to public use, the benefit or advance in value given to the remaining portion by means of the use to which another portion of it is to be applied, may be taken into account by the appraisers, in awarding compensation. In this aspect, it may be, that where a corporation is authorized to take land by an act of the legislature, the appraisers under the act, are under no obligation to make any compensation whatever, *in money*, the benefit and the invasion of property being a fair offset each to the other.[1] But suppose that the benefit which the landowner reaps, *exceeds* the value of the land covered by the way,[2] and the way to be laid out, or when laid out, improved at the *public expense*, can the legislature constitutionally authorize, in

---

[1] Livermore *v.* Jamaica, 23 Vt. R. 341; Rexford *v.* Knight, 15 Barb. (N. Y.) Sup. Ct. R. 627; S. C. on Appeal, 1 Kernan, (N. Y.) R. 308; Pennsylvania Railroad Company *v.* Fisher, 8 Burr, (Penn.) R. 445.

[2] Commonwealth *v.* Sessions of Middlesex, 9 Mass. R. 388; Hill *v.* Mohawk and Hudson River Railroad Company, 3 Seld. (N. Y.) R. 152; Hill *et al.* *v.* Mohawk and Hudson River Railroad Company, 3 Seld. (N. Y.) R. 133,—Court of Appeals.

this case, an impost upon the owner, for the benefit he has thus received? The question, at first view, would seem to be one that respects the extent of the power of *taxation*, the distinction between which power and the power of *eminent domain*, has already been briefly stated.[1] Or it may be said to embrace another question, viz., whether an obligation imposed to pay for opening a *street*, for example, or of improving one, in a ratio to the benefit derived therefrom, is strictly a tax, it being no burden, though for practical purposes it may go by that designation, as it usually does.

§ 170. Such a distinction has been attempted upon the assumption that *taxes* are levied without discrimination, equally upon *all* the subjects of property, whilst assessments are only levied upon some specific property, the subject of supposed benefit conferred, to repay which the assessment is levied.[2] Thus Spencer, J., in delivering the opinion of the Superior Court of Cincinnati, was not prepared to concede, that "taxation" and "assessment" are in all respects identical, and must, therefore, be levied in the same mode. For he says: "An assessment is doubtless a tax, but the term implies something more; it implies a tax of a particular kind, predicated upon the principle of *equivalents*, or benefits which are peculiar to the persons or property charged therewith, and which are said to be assessed or appraised according to the measure or proportion of such equivalents. Whereas a simple tax is imposed for the purpose of supporting the government generally, without reference to any *special* advantage which may be supposed to accrue to the persons taxed."[3] And, in a case in New

---

1 See *ante*, Chap. II. § 77. See Rights of Taxation and Eminent Domain, treated of in the American Law Register for March, 1857, p. 289.

2 Wharton, in his Law Lexicon, says: "That a tax is money which a nation pays to its servants, for the management of its business, and is granted and controlled by the House of Commons."

3 Ridenow *v.* Saffin, 1 Handy, (Superior Court of Cincinnati,) R. 473. But the legislature, of course, has no right to impose a tax and apportion it, upon the

York, the same distinction was relied upon for the purpose of upholding *assessments* made upon certain churches which, by a statute of that State, are exempt from *taxation*.[1] But in a subsequent case this distinction was exploded, except as designating different modes of exercising the same power. "The difference," said Ruggles, J., in the case alluded to, "between general taxation and special assessments for local objects, requires that they should be distinguished by different names, although both derive their authority from the taxing power. They have always been so distinguished, and it is therefore evident that the word 'tax' may be used in a contract, or in a statute, in a sense which would not include a street assessment, or any other local or special taxation within its meaning. Several cases are found in which it has been adjudged to have been so used. But in no case has it been adjudged that street assessments are not made by virtue of the legislative taxing power. If there are expressions to the contrary, in some of the cases, it will be found that they are *dicta* inapplicable to the point decided, or if applicable, that they were unnecessary to the decision and not well considered."[2]

---

property of an individual, and appropriate it to the use of another. Such a case bears no analogy to a tax apportioned upon a particular territory, and which operates upon the public, although the territory and the public are comparatively small. Guildford, (Town of) *v.* Cornell, 18 Barb. (N. Y.) Sup. Ct. R. 615. The sections of the Constitution of New York, declaring that no person shall be disfranchised or deprived of any of the rights or privileges secured to any citizen of the State, unless by the law of the land, or the judgment of his peers, and that private property shall not be taken for public use, without just compensation, have no application or reference to the taxing power of the legislature. The legislature possesses the power to levy and apportion upon all the taxable persons and property within the State, or within any particular political district, or portion of it *principally benefited*. Town of Guildford *v.* Cornell, 18 Barb. (N. Y.) Sup. Ct. R. 615; Taylor *v.* Porter, 4 Hill, (N. Y.) R. 146.

[1] In the Matter of the Mayor, &c. of New York, for improving Nassau Street, 11 Johns. (N. Y.) R. 77; and see Canal Trustees *et al. v.* City of Chicago, 12 Ill. R. 403; Northern Liberties *v.* St. John's Church, 13 Penn. R. 105.

[2] The People *v.* Mayor, &c. of Brooklyn, 4 Comst. (N. Y.) R. 432; and see Nichols *v.* Bridgeport, 23 Conn. R. 189.

## 2. *Authority to Assess.*

§ 171. The position assumed by Ruggles, J., in delivering the unanimous opinion of the Court of Errors of New York, in the case from which we have quoted, was, that there never was any just foundation for saying that a tax to be valid must be apportioned "upon principles of just equality," and upon all the property in the same political district. "It is wrong," he says, "that a few should be taxed for the benefit of the whole; and it is equally wrong that the whole should be taxed for the benefit of a few. No one town ought to be taxed exclusively for the payment of county expenses; and no county should be taxed for the expenses incurred for the benefit of a single town. The same principle of justice requires that where taxation for any local object benefits only a portion of a city or town, that portion only should bear the burden. There being no constitutional prohibition, the legislature may create a district for that special purpose, or they may tax a class of lands or persons benefited, to be designated by the public agents appointed for that purpose, without reference to town, county, or district lines. General taxation for such local objects is manifestly unjust. It burdens those who are not benefited, and benefits those who are not burdened. This injustice has led to the substitution of street assessments in place of general taxation; and it seems impossible to deny that in the theory of their apportionment they are far more equitable than general taxation for the purpose they are designed for."[1] These prin-

---

[1] People *ex rel.;* Griffin *v.* Mayor, &c. of Brooklyn, 4 Comst. (N. Y.) R. 419, overruling the judgment given by the Supreme Court, in 6 Barb. (N. Y.) Sup. Ct. R. 209, and case between parties of the same name, in 9 Ibid. 535. The Revised Statutes of New York, it may be added, have an explicit adoption of the assessment principle in the provision, that "no non-resident tracts shall be assessed, unless the same will, in the judgment of the commissioners, be *enhanced in value by the highway-labor so assessed.*" See 9 Barb. (N. Y.) Sup. Ct. R. on p. 578. In Massachusetts, meadows, swamps, and low lands may be assessed among the proprietors for the expense of draining the same, without

ciples have been generally recognized, and followed out, as applicable to estates benefited by opening and improving streets, by the Courts of the State of New York, though not uninterruptedly. We proceed to give Judge Ruggles's review of the decisions in that State.

§ 172. "In the Matter of the Mayor, &c. of New York, for improving Nassau Street,[1] several churches were included within a street assessment, and they claimed to be exempted from its operation by the 28th section of the act of 1813, for the assessment of taxes.[2] By this section it is enacted, that 'no real estate belonging to any church shall be taxed by any law of this State.' The Court held, that all the provisions in the act, including the exemption, referred to general and public taxes to be assessed and collected for the benefit of the town, county, or State at large. This was the whole point decided. The Court proceeded, however, to observe, that to pay for the opening of a street in a ratio to the benefit or advantage derived from it, is no burden, and therefore no tax. 'That there is no inconvenience or hardship in it, and the maxim of law that he who feels the benefit, ought to feel the burden also, is perfectly consistent with the interests and dictates of science and religion.' Surely these are not *dicta* to be relied on to show that a street assessment is '*robbery*.' If they are to be regarded as authority, they prove that such an assessment, when considered in reference to the benefit in connection with the money exacted, is no grievance; but they do not show that the act of exacting the money, considered by itself, is not an exercise of the taxing power. The point decided was, that a street assessment was not such a tax as the exemption contemplated."

reference to any particular district, and in proportion to the benefit which each party derives from the work. Revised Statutes of Massachusetts, 673. The same power is given in Connecticut, by statute, to commissioners. Statutes of Connecticut, ed. of 1839, p. 544.

[1] In the Matter of the Mayor, &c. of New York, for improving Nassau Street, 11 Johns. (N. Y.) R. 77.

[2] 1 Revised Statutes of New York, 519.

§ 173. Another case[1] contains a dictum of C. J. Savage, founded on the case last cited, "that a street assessment is not a tax. But the case called for no such remark. The point decided was, that a covenant in a lease, by which a tenant bound himself to pay 'all such duties, taxes, *assessments*, impositions and payments as should, during the term, grow due and payable out of the demised premises,' made him liable to pay a village street assessment. This was a plain case, in which the lessee covenanted to pay all assessments, *eo nomine*, and whether they were taxes or not, was therefore not the question to be decided, nor material to the question. In Sharp *v.* Spier,[2] land had been sold under an assessment for constructing a well and pump, in the village of Brooklyn. The assessment was not charged on the lands sold, but upon the 'owners and occupants' of the lands intended to be benefited. By a section in the village charter, it was enacted, that 'whenever any tax of any description *on lands or tenements* in said village shall remain unpaid,' &c. such lands might be sold. The point decided was, that the sale was void. The assessment was upon the owners personally, and, of course, if the assessment was admitted to be a tax, there was no power to collect it by the sale, because the assessment was not on the land."

§ 174. "It is true that Bronson, J., who delivered the opinion, repeated the dicta found in the Matter of The Mayor of New York,[3] that an assessment is not regarded as a burden, but as an equivalent for benefit, and, therefore, cannot be regarded as a tax; but the decision rested clearly and safely on other grounds; although if it had stood on this alone it would have established nothing except that an assessment was not a tax within the meaning of the 7th section of the act incorporating the village. The question, whether street assessments

1 Bleeker *v.* Ballou, 3 Wend. (N. Y.) R. 263.
2 Sharp *v.* Spier, 4 Hill, (N. Y.) R. 76.
3 In the Matter of The Mayor of New York, 11 Johns. (N. Y.) R. 77.

are not made in virtue of the power of taxation, was not in that case decided. On the contrary, a question involving that point was expressly reserved as undecided, by Mr. Justice Bronson, who said: 'I have not overlooked the fact that street assessments are, by the third section of this act, made a lien or charge on the land. Whether that fact, taken in connection with the power conferred by the 7th section, will authorize a sale of land for street assessment, we are not now called upon to determine.'"

§ 175. But the point now more especially debated, was involved and decided in the Court for the Correction of Errors, in the case of the Mayor, &c. of New York *v.* Livingston.[1] "In that case, a street was opened in the city of New York, upon lands which had been previously dedicated by John R. Livingston to the public use for that purpose, but Mr. Livingston had never in any other way conveyed his title to the land within the limits of the street. He was the owner of the lands subject to the easement. He owned also lots of land adjoining the street, which, together with lots owned by other proprietors, were assessed for the opening and improving the street under a provision similar to that by which the assessment now in controversy was made in the city of Brooklyn. The amount of the assessment against him upon the adjoining lots was set off against the value of his interest in the lands within the street, and overbalanced it. He was charged in the assessment with the balance only. It did not appear that he was allowed, in adjusting the balance, less than the full value of his lands within the street subject to the easement. He complained of the whole proceeding. First, because he was not allowed the full value of the land taken for the street, without reference to the easement; and, secondly, he complained of the assessment, by which his lots adjoining the street were charged with his proportion of the expense of the improvement, in the same

---

1 The Mayor, &c. of New York *v.* Livingston, 8 Wend. (N. Y.) R. 85, 101.

manner as other adjoining lots were charged. The objection to the proceedings was, that they were unconstitutional. The late Chancellor, in his opinion, said: 'It was not denied that the legislature have the power to authorize the taking of private property for the purpose of public streets, upon making just compensation to the owners; but it is insisted by the plaintiff's counsel, that the increased value *of the adjacent property* cannot be set off against the loss or damage sustained by him in taking his property for a street, and be considered as a just compensation for the property so taken.' The Chancellor pronounced this objection untenable, and proceeded: 'The owner of property taken, is entitled to a full compensation for the damage he sustains thereby; but if the taking of his property for the public improvement is a benefit rather than an injury to him, he certainly has no equitable claim to damages. Besides, it is a well-settled principle, that where any particular county, district, or neighborhood is exclusively benefited by a public improvement, the inhabitants of that district may be taxed for the whole expense of the improvement, in proportion to the supposed benefits received by each. In this case, if the whole value of the property taken for a street in the city of New York is allowed to the individual owner, the proprietors of the adjacent lots must be assessed for the purpose of paying that amount; and if the individual whose property is taken, is the owner of a lot adjacent, that lot must be assessed ratably with the others. It therefore makes no difference whether he is allowed the whole value of the property taken in the first instance, and is assessed for his portion of the damage, or whether the one sum is offset against the other in the first place, and the balance is only allowed.' Senator Sherman delivered an opinion, concurring with the Chancellor in the result, and these opinions were sustained by the unanimous vote of the Court for the Correction of Errors."

§ 176. The above case affords an example of the exercise of the two powers before referred to, viz., of the power of eminent domain,[1] and the power of taxation; the first in taking the land for the use of the street, and the second in requiring contribution to defray the expenses of improving it, from that class of persons on whom the burden ought to fall. "The case affirms the validity of street assessments, in virtue of the latter power. In Owners of Ground Assessed *v.* Mayor, &c. of Albany,[2] the land of Mr. Betts, adjoining a square laid out in Albany, was assessed to pay the expenses, and Chief Justice Savage said: 'It cannot be conceded that any constitutional question properly arises in relation to Mr. Betts. *His property has not been taken for public use.*' And although he did not affirm or deny that the assessment was a tax, he affirmed the validity of the assessment against the objection of unconstitutionality expressly raised; and this could have been done on no other principle than that it was an exercise of the power of taxation."

§ 177. "In 1835, an act was passed, (ch. 309,) appointing commissioners, and authorizing them to 'assess the sum of $41,000 upon the owners of all the real estate situated in the city of Utica, in proportion to the benefits which each shall be deemed to have acquired by the location of the northern termination of the Chenango Canal, in the city of Utica, as nearly as the same can be estimated.' The statute authorized the assessments to be collected in the same manner as taxes in Oneida county were collected. The commissioners and collector were sued for attempting to collect the assessment. But the statute was held to be constitutional, and the assessment was adjudged to be within the lawful exercise of the power of taxation.[3] In Stryker *v.* Kelly,[4] there had been a street assessment in the city of New York, and its validity was strenuously

---

1 See *ante*, Chap. II. § 77.

2 Owners of Ground Assessed *v.* Mayor, &c. of Albany, 15 Wend. (N. Y.) R. 376.

3 Thomas *v.* Leland, 24 Wend. (N. Y.) R. 65.

4 Stryker *v.* Kelly, 7 Hill, (N. Y.) R. 9, 23.

contested. Mr. Justice Beardsley says: "This was local taxation for a local purpose, and falls within the legitimate exercise of the taxing power." In this opinion, Chief Justice Nelson concurred; and Bronson, J., agreed that the New York street law was free from constitutional objection, except on the ground of a provision therein which is not contained in the street laws of Brooklyn, under which the assessment now in question was made. We have, therefore, in that case the unanimous opinion of the Justices of the Supreme Court in favor of the validity of street assessments, so far as respects their constitutionality. The judgment in Stryker *v.* Kelly[1] was afterwards reversed, but upon a point not affecting the question now under consideration. The examination of the cases decided in this State terminates in the conclusion, (although several of the cases contain dicta to the contrary,) that street assessments, like that in controversy in this suit, have been adjudged, both in the Supreme Court and in the Court for the Correction of Errors, to be lawful and constitutional taxation."

§ 178. "Taxation similar to that now under consideration, has been sanctioned by long usage in the State of New York. In the Colony and State of New York, the system of taxation for local purposes, by assessing the burden according to the benefit, has been in force for more than one hundred and fifty years. It was applied to highways in the county of Ulster, in 1691.[2] The power was given to the corporation of New York in the same year.[3] This statute remained in force in 1773, when Van Schaack's edition of the statutes was published, and no evidence of its repeal is found until 1787, when it seems to have been revised and its provisions reënacted under the State Constitution.[4] The colonial statute was doubtless in force when

1 Stryker *v.* Kelly, 2 Denio, (N. Y.) R. 323.

2 Bradf. Laws, 45.

3 Ibid, 9.

4 Van Schaack's Law, 8, 9; 2 Jones & Var. 152; 1 Greenl. 443.

the State Constitution was adopted. It is not unworthy of remark, that in April, 1691, a bill of rights was passed for the security and protection of the people of the province. The statute authorizing the assessments first mentioned, was passed afterwards during the same year. In January, 1787, an act was passed, declaring the rights of the citizens of this State, and prohibiting, among other things, that any person should be deprived of his property except by due course of law. The statute of 1787, authorizing street assessments in the city of New York, was passed by the same legislature, and sanctioned by the same council of revision, which had assented to the bill of rights. Street assessments, upon the same principle, were authorized in the city of New York, in 1793,[1] and in 1795,[2] and in 1796,[3] and in 1801,[4] and in 1813.[5] The corporation of New York have had and exercised authority to make street assessments from the infancy of that city. Similar powers have been conferred on nearly every city, and on many of the villages in this State. It has also been applied to highways, to turnpike roads, and to the draining of marshes."

§ 179. "The system of taxation was in force in New York at the time of the making and adoption of its second and third constitutions, and has stood in our statute books along with the constitutions, from 1777 until now, without prohibition or restraint. Sales of real estate to large amounts have been made, and the lands so sold are now held on the faith of the validity of these assessment laws. Proceedings under them have been brought before the Supreme Court for review, continually during the last thirty years. They have been litigated often on the ground of irregularity, and sometimes upon constitutional objections. They have been confirmed in cases almost without number. If the uniform practice of the government, from its origin, can settle any question of this nature, the power of the

---

1 3 Greenl. 58.
2 Ibid. 244, 245.
3 Ibid. 333, 334.
4 2 K. & R. 130.
5 2 R. L. 407.

legislature to exercise this kind of taxation would seem to be established by it. Constitutional objections never prevailed against it until 1846, when the case of The People *v.* The Mayor, &c. of Brooklyn was decided."

§ 180. The case just referred to, was decided in 1846, and was overruled in 1851, by the Court for the correction of errors;[1] that Court deciding, that a statute which authorizes a municipal corporation to grade and improve streets, and to *assess the expense among the owners and occupants of land benefited by the improvements, in proportion to the amount of such benefit,* is a constitutional and valid law, and is not in conflict with the constitutional provision, that "no person shall be deprived of life, liberty, or property, without due process of law, nor shall private property be taken for public use, without just compensation."

§ 181. Taxation, as thus practised and sanctioned in the State of New York as constitutional, has been vindicated and enforced in Pennsylvania.[2] An act of the legislature of Pennsylvania not only authorized viewers to take into consideration the advantages of laying out a highway to land-owners, but it also authorized them to assess the lots benefited, for the advantage of those who may be injured by the improvement; and the Supreme Court of that State, in giving their opinion, by Rogers, J., upon this branch of the act, said: "The act goes still further. It not only authorizes the viewers to take into consideration the advantages, &c., but it also authorizes them to assess the lots benefited for the advantages of those who may be injured by the improvement, and it is of this the counsel chiefly complain. This is certainly a new feature which has been introduced into the statutes of this State, but I do not

---

1 People *v.* Mayor, &c. of Brooklyn, 4 Comst. (N. Y.) R. 419; and see the case appealed from, in 6 Barb. (N. Y.) Sup. Ct. R. 209; and see case between parties of the same name, in 9 Barb. R. 435.

2 Hancock Street, (Matter of extension of,) 6 Harris, (Penn.) R. 26.

conceive that the principle is new. It is copied from New York, where it has been in operation for some time, and where it has received the benefit of a judicial construction in the case of Livingston *v.* The Mayor, &c. of New York.[1] The owner of property taken, is entitled to a full compensation for the damages he sustains thereby, but if the taking of his property for the public improvement is a benefit rather than an injury to him, he certainly has no equitable claim for damages. Besides, it is a well-settled principle, that when any particular county, district, or neighborhood is exclusively benefited by a public improvement, the inhabitants of that district may be taxed for the whole expense of the improvement, and in proportion to the supposed benefit received by each. If the whole value of the property taken for a street is allowed to the individual owners, the proprietors of the adjoining lots must be assessed for the purpose of paying that amount; and if the individual whose property is taken is the owner of a lot adjacent, that lot must be assessed ratably with the others. If these principles are correct, and it cannot be doubted, it decides the question; for if a county, district, or town can be assessed for a public improvement, on the ground that they are particularly benefited, there can be no constitutional reason to exempt an individual from assessment on the same principle. It becomes a question of expediency, of which the legislature are the competent and exclusive judges, and not of right. This is a power which must be used with great caution; but these are considerations that must be addressed to the legislature, rather than to the Courts. The only restriction upon the power of the legislature, where the public at large, the inhabitants of any particular section of a state, or a town, or an individual, have an interest in the contemplated improvement, as citizens merely, is that the property shall not be taken without just compensation to the owner, and in the mode prescribed by law. . . That this

---

[1] Livingston *v.* Mayor, &c. of New York, 8 Wend. (N. Y.) R. 85.

great power may be abused, there can be no doubt, but that it has been in this case, we are not at liberty to suppose. The Court of Common Pleas affirmed the report of the viewers, on the ground, certainly, that the property of the defendant has been benefited to the amount of the assessment. There is, therefore, nothing contrary to natural right, and there is nothing in the constitutional objections which have been made."[1] The acts of the legislature of Pennsylvania, authorizing the paving and grading of streets in the city of Alleghany, and the assessment of the expenses of the same upon the owners of lots fronting on such streets, and prescribing the manner of collecting said assessments, were held to be a proper and constitutional exercise of the taxing power by the legislature.[2]

§ 182. In Connecticut, the Supreme Court of Errors has taken the same view of the law. Hinman, J., in delivering the opinion of the Court, thus expressed himself: "The only provision that can be found, at all bearing upon this subject, is the one already alluded to, that, 'the property of no person shall be taken for public use without just compensation therefor,' and this has respect to property taken by the right of eminent domain, as where the land itself is taken for a highway or other public work, or where property is directly taken for the use of the government, and has no reference to the collection of taxes, where money is taken as the contributive shares of individuals to the public burdens. The rule of taxation, which in this particular case was adopted, is certainly as equitable as any other. It attempts to aportion each man's tax to the benefit which he is to receive from the improvement, for which it is expended. Most of our highways are laid out by the selectmen of the towns, and the expense is borne by the town in which the highway is located, though in regard to

---

1 McMasters *v.* Commonwealth, 3 Watts, (Penn.) R. 292.

2 Schenley *v.* City of Alleghany, 1 Casey, (Penn.) R. 128; and the same held in Sharpless *v.* City of Philadelphia, 9 Harris, (Penn.) R. 147.

many of them, the inhabitants of the towns have a much less interest than the public beyond the local limits of the town; and, in regard to many others, they are principally for the accommodation of some, perhaps a small portion of the town's inhabitants. But the towns bear the burden, because the legislature has thrown it upon them. It might, with the same propriety, have thrown it upon the counties, or even upon the lesser territorial corporations, and although injustice may occasionally be done by compelling a small town to construct an expensive bridge for the benefit, principally, of persons outside of its limits, yet the general operation of the law is, perhaps, as equitable as any system which could be devised. At any rate, we have never heard it agitated, as a debateable point, that the system was so unjust as to be unconstitutional or illegal:"[1] And he was of the opinion that these principles were deducible from the acknowledged right of the public, in taking land for a highway, to consider the benefits thereby accruing to the owner as a partial or complete offset to his claim for compensation. "This," he adds, "is, in effect, but one way of taxing an individual, peculiarly benefited by the laying out of a highway, for a portion, and it may be only a portion of his just share of the whole tax, for the public improvement. If you can, in this way, tax one individual for the whole or a part of his share of the public burden, it seems to follow, that you can, for the same reason and on the same ground, viz., the special and peculiar benefit he has received or is to receive by the improvement, tax every other individual who is similarly situated. And if you can tax him to the extent of the full value of the land actually taken, there is no reason that will limit the tax to that precise amount, or to any amount short of the full value of the benefit he receives, provided all others, similarly situated, are taxed proportionably."

---

[1] Nichols *v.* Bridgeport, 23 Conn. R. 189.

In Maryland, also, a similar statute has been decided to be constitutional.[1]

§ 183. In Ohio, a city council, pursuant to the act incorporating the city, may assess a special tax upon the owners of property in the city, benefited by the opening of a street; but it cannot be done unless there be an ordinance, that the person thus assessed, shall have, if he desire it, a review, with the privilege of naming two of the persons composing the board of review.[2] Again, the act of Assembly, in Ohio, conferring upon cities a power to levy assessments for the improvement of streets upon the property abutting thereon, in proportion to the number of feet *front* so abutting, is held not to be in conflict with the constitutional provision in regard to taking private property for public use; also, that it does not conflict with that provision of the State Constitution, which declares, that "laws shall be passed taxing by uniform rule, all moneys &c.; and all real and personal property, according to its true value in money.[3]

§ 184. In New Jersey, a statute was enacted, giving power to the common council of Newark, to direct any public street opened by an individual on his own lands to be graded, put in repair and made fit for travel, and to assess the whole expense thereof upon the lands of the person opening the street. This act was passed in 1849, and, by virtue of its provisions, a street, opened in 1847 by the voluntary act or dedication of the owners of lands through which it passed, was graded and repaired by the city and the expense assessed upon the owners. It was contended that the act was retrospective and uncon-

---

1 Alexander *v.* The Mayor of Baltimore, 5 Gill, (Md.) R. 383.

2 Cuberston *v.* City of Cincinnati, 16 Ohio R. 574, and see Burnet *v.* Same, 3 Ohio R. 73.

3 Ridenour *v.* Saffin, 1 Handy, R. (Superior Court of Cincinnati,) 464, and see likewise Bonsall *v.* Town of Lebanon, 19 Ohio R. 421; Scovill *v.* The City of Cleveland and others, 1 McCook, (Ohio) R. 126.

stitutional. But the Court held the act to be valid, and per Nevins, J.: "If land owners see fit, for their own benefit and advantage, to throw out a portion of their lands, and mean that the same shall be recognized and used as a public street, they are bound by every fair principle to put it in a condition to be safely used as such, and have no right to assess upon the public the expense of having this done. The corporation, under the act of 1849, may enforce this duty by assessing upon the land owners this expense, whether the dedication was made before or after the passage of the act."[1] And, in the same State, where it was provided that the expense for improvements in opening, altering, widening, filling up, &c. streets, shall be assessed upon and paid by the lands and real estate benefited by the same, it was held, that the consent of the owners, or a majority of them, of certain lots to be assessed, was not necessary for such purposes.[2]

§ 185. In Tennessee, power was given by statute to the mayor and aldermen of Franklin to cause foot-pavements and sidewalks to be constructed by the owners of adjoining lots, and in case of their neglect so to do, when duly required, to contract themselves, and pay for the construction or repair of the same, the amount paid to constitute a charge against such owners. A case arose under a municipal ordinance, made by virtue of the power given by the statute, in which it was contended that the ordinance was in the nature of a tax levied upon the owners of lots, and as such, that it was unconstitutional because unequal. But Green, J., delivering the opinion of the Court, said, "We do not think that this law levies a tax. A tax is a sum which is required to be paid by the citizen annually for revenue for public purposes. But this ordinance leaves no sum of money to be paid by the citizens. It requires a duty

---

1 The State *v.* Dean, 3 Zabriskie, (N. J.) R. 335.

2 State, (Mann, prosecutor,) *v.* Mayor, &c. of Jersey City, 4 Zabriskie, (N. J.) R. 662.

to be performed for the well-being and comfort of the citizens of the town. It is in the nature of a nuisance, to be removed. And if an ordinance were to require that each owner of a lot in town should remove nuisances from his lot, and on failure to do so the town constable should remove the nuisance, and the party should pay the expense of the work, it would hardly be suggested that the expense so incurred would be a tax. And yet such a case is in principle analogous to the one before us. The ordinance in question is therefore not unconstitutional on the ground of being an unequal tax."[1] In Massachusetts and Illinois, statutes containing similar provisions have passed the ordeal of the Courts.[2]

§ 186. In Mississippi, a statute was enacted "to provide for the erection, repair, and preservation of levees on the Mississippi River, in the county of Inaquena, which authorized "a uniform tax, not exceeding ten cents per acre upon all lands lying on or within ten miles of the river in said county, subject to taxation; and a uniform tax of not exceeding five cents per acre on all lands in said county subject to taxation, lying ten miles from the Mississippi River." It was contended that the statute was repugnant to the provisions of the constitution of that State, which declared that "all freemen are equal in rights," and that "no men or set of men are entitled to exclusive, separate, public emoluments or privileges, from the community, but in consideration of public services," and also that "private property shall not be taken for public use with-

1 Mayor and Aldermen *v.* Maberry, 6 Humph. (Tenn.) R. 368. Affirmed in Washington *v.* The Mayor and Aldermen of Nashville, 1 Swan, (Tenn.) R. 177; Goddard's case, 16 Pick. (Mass.) R. 505, in which the Court upholds an ordinance of the City of Boston requiring the occupants or overseers of lots to remove the snow from the adjoining sidewalks, or in default thereof to pay not less than one nor more than four dollars, was referred to as an analogous case.

2 Lowell *v.* Hadley, 8 Met. (Mass.) R. 180; Lowell *v.* French, 6 Cush. (Mass.) R. 223; Morris *v.* The City of Chicago, 11 Ill. R. 650; and see McIntyre *v.* State, 5 Blackf. (Ind.) R. 384.

out just compensation," and therefore void. But these objections were overruled by the High Court of Errors and Appeals and the statute sustained.[1]

§ 187. The idea, in Kentucky, that an assessment of this kind must be made to embrace all the property within the *city* or *ward*, in which the improvement is made, seems to have originated from the opinion of a Judge of the Court of Appeals of that State in the case of Sutton's Heirs *v.* City of Louisville.[2] But that opinion was founded mainly on a clause in the constitution of that State, which is peculiar; and in respect to this point, the opinion was afterwards modified by the same Judge, and the principle in effect abandoned in the case of the City of Lexington *v.* McQuillan's Heirs.[3] The charter of the last mentioned city contained a provision which authorized the mayor and common council to cause the streets therein to be paved or turnpiked at the expense of the estates fronting such streets, and when the work was completed, to apportion the expense equally among the lot owners. McQuillan's heirs were charged with a sum which greatly exceeded the *proportionate* cost of the entire work done opposite the lots of ground respectively in the same square, in consequence of a deep cut and stone wall made opposite to their lot; and the Court held, that the *apportionment* of the expenses was irregular and erroneous, because the *ratio* of contribution was required by the charter to be equal among the lot owners. But the act was held to be valid and constitutional on the ground that each square, so far as its streets and sidewalks are concerned, might be considered a distinct municipality or local public. Such was the view taken by Ruggles, J., in giving the opinion of the Court of Appeals of New York, in Mayor, &c. of Brooklyn.[4]

---

1 Williams *v.* Commack, 27 Miss. (5 Cush.) R. 209.

2 Sutton's Heirs *v.* City of Louisville, 5 Dana, (Ken.) R. 28.

3 City of Lexington *v.* McQuillan's Heirs, 9 Dana, (Ken.) R. 513, 516.

4 The People *v.* Mayor, &c. of Brooklyn, 4 Comst. (N. Y.) R. 429; Court of

### 3. *Proceedings under authority to Assess.*

§ 188. We have already seen that in proceedings to take private property for public use, *in invitum*, and under the provisions of positive law, every requisite of the statute must be complied with and should appear on the face of the proceedings under which the property is attempted to be taken. The same principle applies to proceedings under authority to assess for benefits.[1] In construing such a statute, the leading rule is to examine all its parts, and, if possible, reconcile and give effect to all its provisions.[2] An *interested* Judge is, upon principle, incompetent to act and decide and of course unable to serve. The body, authorized to appoint the assessors, has, by implication, the power to remove them and appoint others in their places.[3]

§ 189. If no notice is required to be given by the statute of the time when the assessors meet to make an estimate of the benefits conferred, no notice need be given. Their duties are analogous to the duties of town assessors; and there is no more necessity of their giving notice than in the case of ordinary assessors of taxes.[4] But where notice is required to be given by statute, it must be given as prescribed or the proceedings of the assessors will be void. Thus, where by a city ordinance, the owners of lots bounding on streets were to be

---

Appeals; and see Slack *v.* Maysville and Lexington Railroad Co. 13 B. Mon. (Ken.) R. 1.

1 *Ante*, Ch. II.; Barney *v.* City of Buffalo, 15 Barb. N. Y. Sup. Ct. R. 457; Rex *v.* Haslingfield, 2 M. & Sel. R. 558; Matter of Hamilton Avenue, 14 Barb. (N. Y.) Sup. Ct. R. 405; Hill *et al.* *v.* Mohawk and Hudson Railroad Co. 3 Seld. (N. Y.) R. 152; Flatbush Avenue (Matter of) 1 Barb. (N. Y.) S. C. R. 286; 5 Denio, (N. Y.) R. 206; Dunlap *v.* Mount Sterling, 14 Ill. R. 251; Mitchell *v.* Kirtland, 7 Conn. R. 229; Hobart *v.* Frisbie, 5 Conn. R. 592.

2 Nichols *v.* Bridgeport, 23 Conn. R. 189.

3 Laimbeer *v.* The Mayor, &c. of New York, 4 Sandf. (N. Y.) Sup. Ct. R. 109.

4 Nichols *v.* Bridgeport, *supra;* Curry *v.* Mount Sterling, 15 Ill. R. 320; Stewart *v.* Board of Police of Hinds County, 25 Miss. 479.

charged with the expense of sidewalks constructed in front of their lots, in case they should neglect of themselves to construct the same, after thirty days' notice so to do, it was held, that a notice requiring the construction of such a sidewalk within seventeen days, would not entitle the city to charge the lot-owners with the expense thereof, notwithstanding more than thirty days elapsed after the giving of the notice before the construction by the city.[1]

§ 190. But in a case where it was required that the report of the commissioners should contain "the names of the persons interested in the premises and a statement of their respective interests," and the proportion of the expense of the improvement which each ought to bear," it was held, that a report in which certain lots were designated, not by the names of the owners but by less specific designations, was invalid, because in disregard of the statute, and also for the more general reason that the parties thus indefinitely indicated would be deprived of their property without an opportunity of defending themselves. It sometimes becomes necessary, it was remarked, especially in proceedings like this, *in rem*, to proceed against persons who are unknown; but Courts have no power to do so, unless the legislature has interposed, and by some sort of substituted service, given the Court jurisdiction over the person. Without some such statutory provision, if any of the owners are unknown, a lawful assessment cannot be made, nor can the Courts confirm such a report without violating one of their most sacred principles of action; that, namely, of giving the party interested an adequate opportunity of being heard in defence of his right.[2]

---

1 Washington *v.* The Mayor and Aldermen of Nashville, 1 Swan, (Tenn.) R. 177; The Owners of Ground, &c. *v.* The Mayor of Albany, 15 Wend. (N. Y.) R. 374.

2 Flatbush Avenue, (Matter of,) 1 Barb. (N. Y.) R. 286; but see John and Cherry Streets, (Matter of,) 19 Wend. (N. Y.) R. 659; William and Anthony Streets, (Matter of,) Ibid. 678.

§ 191. Where an act provided, that damages caused by the laying out of streets in a city should be appraised by three judicious freeholders of said city, it was held, that the fact that the appraisers were *freeholders*, was a jurisdictional fact, which could only be shown by the appointment itself, or the record of it, and, if it did not so appear, the appraisal was void, the want of jurisdiction being an objection which was not and could not be waived by an appeal from the appraisal by the party interested. But, it was further held, the invalidity of the appraisal did not affect a subsequent assessment for benefits, regularly made, under another section of the same act, by a different tribunal. For although it is true that an assessment consists in finding the excess of the benefit over the injury, and cannot therefore be made until it is first ascertained what is the amount of the injury, yet the assessors are not bound to resort to the appraisers to ascertain this fact, but may and must, of necessity, determine it for themselves.[1]

§ 192. The constitution of New York contains a provision as follows: "When private property shall be taken for any public use, the compensation to be made therefor, when such compensation is not made by the State, shall be ascertained by a jury, or by not less than *three commissioners* appointed by *a court of record*, as shall be prescribed by law." By the charter of the city of Utica, in proceedings to lay out, widen, &c. streets within the city, power was given to the common council to appoint *five disinterested freeholders* of said city, to ascertain and report a description of the real estate required to be appropriated, with the names of the owners and the *recompense* which should be made to them respectively therefor, and also to report what, if any benefit each parcel of land would receive. This provision of the charter was held to be repug-

---

[1] Nichols *v.* Bridgeport, 23 Conn. R. 189; and see Williams *v.* Cammack, 27 Miss. (5 Cush.) R. 209.

nant to the section of the constitution, above quoted. The word *jury*, as used in that section is to be taken in its usual meaning, and imports, necessarily, the idea of a body having the usual characteristics, and acting substantially through the accustomed forms by which the powers of a jury are exercised.[1]

§ 193. The appointment of commissioners of estimate and assessment, does not operate like a notice of *lis pendens*, so as to prevent an owner of land from going on to improve it, by erecting buildings thereon. Therefore, where such commissioners, appointed under a resolution for the widening a street in the city of New York, allowed the value of a certain parcel of land taken for that purpose, but refused to allow any thing for damages to a building thereon, on the ground that it had been erected after the passage of the resolution, it was held that their action, in refusing to allow for damages to the building, was erroneous. It was said, that it would be unjust to require every owner of land to refrain from building on his own land, or to conform his new building to a plan merely proposed by the city, when the city does not bind itself to adopt an improvement, either by passing a resolution to have it done, or by having commissioners appointed to carry it out, but may, even after delaying several years, and after the new building had been made to conform to the proposed plan, discontinue the proceeding at any time before the confirmation of the commissioners' report by the Supreme Court.[2]

§ 194. In New York, it has been held, that it is not the duty of the commissioners to pass upon conflicting claims of title, where they depend either upon strongly controverted

---

1 Clark *v.* The City of Utica, 18 Barb. (N. Y.) R. 451.

2 In the Matter of widening Wall Street, 17 Barb. (N. Y.) Sup. Ct. R. 617; Matter of 4th Avenue, 3 Wend. (N. Y.) R. 452; The Corporation of New York *v.* Mapes, 6 Johns. (N. Y.) Ch. R. 46; Matter of Canal Street, 11 Wend. (N. Y.) R. 154; 20 Ibid. 618; 18 Johns. R. 546. But see Matter of Furman Street, 17 Wend. (N. Y.) R. 649.

facts, or difficult questions of law. These are matters which should be settled by courts and juries, and the commissioners may, in such cases, report without specifying the names or the *estates* or *interests* of the owners, and generally say, that the land belongs to unknown owners; and the Court, after settling the principles upon which the assessment is to be made, will send back the report, if necessary, for revisal and correction. When land, required for the contemplated improvement, is held for a term of years under lease, it is the duty of the commissioners to consider in their estimate all the covenants and conditions in the lease. Consequently, if there be a covenant for a renewal, this is the subject of estimate and assessment, for though it is true that such a covenant does not create a *legal* estate in the land, yet a Court of Equity regards it as an estate, and the statute provision for all parties and persons *interested* in the land, requiring a just and *equitable* estimate of their loss and damage, is broad enough to embrace the equitable interest created by the covenant for a renewal. Where the owner has the unrestricted power of alienation, and the property may be converted to any new use at his pleasure, the only safe and practical course for the commissioners, is to disregard the present use of the property, and the purpose of the owner, in relation to its future enjoyment, and adopt, as their only standard, the *market value* of the land taken or benefited. In the case of *churches* and lands, which can only be used for a *cemetery*, a different rule applies, and inasmuch as the benefit to them must be small, in comparison with that to other property, they ought, therefore, not to contribute in like proportion.[1]

§ 195. An act of the legislature of Pennsylvania, required the viewers to *ascertain* and determine what lots in the vicinity of the extension of a street would probably be benefited by the

---

1 Coutant *v.* Catlin, 2 Sandf. (N. Y.) Ch. R. 485; William and Anthony Streets, 19 Wend. (N. Y.) R. 678; Furman Street, 17 Ibid. 668; Matter of the Mayor, &c. 11 Johns. (N. Y.) R. 77; Albany Street, 11 Wend. (N. Y.) R. 150.

opening of the street, and the damage occasioned by such opening, to be divided and apportioned upon such lots; and the viewers having reported, that they had agreed and adjudged, that each of certain lots, described in the report and schedule, and on a portion of a map of the city attached, are, in their judgment, benefited and increased in value to the amount assessed upon each of said lots, and that the amount be, and the same is, hereby assessed and adjudged to be paid by the said lots, the owners, or reputed owners, being shown in the report or schedule, and the amount assessed upon each lot being stated; it was held, that this was a sufficient compliance with the terms of the act.[1]

§ 196. Under a section of a city charter, providing for the improvement of streets, by an assessment to be laid upon ground bounding on such streets, the committee of estimate and assessment need not be appointed before adopting the ordinance for its construction. Such assessment, under the said section, need not be levied upon all the lands on such street, but only upon those bounding on the improvement. It is no objection to such assessment, that it exceeded the actual expense of the work, provided it was in accordance with the estimate, made in good faith.[2]

§ 197. A suggestion was thrown out by Ch. J. Nelson, in Elmendorf *v.* Mayor, &c. of New York,[3] that, by the construction of the statute of the State, (2 R. S. 407, §§ 175, 176,) the assessment might be made after the work had been done, though the point was not decided. But in the subsequent case of Doughty *v.* Hope,[4] Ch. J. Bronson was unable to perceive how a distinction could be made, as to time, between the estimate and the assessment, and, as he construed the

---

1 Extension of Hancock Street, (Matter of,) 6 Harris, (Penn.) R. 26.

2 Scovill *v.* City of Cleveland, 1 McCook, Ohio R. (N. S.) 126.

3 Elmendorf *v.* Mayor, &c. of New York, 25 Wend. (N. Y.) R. 693.

4 Doughty *v.* Hope, 3 Denio, (N. Y.) R. 249.

statute, both should precede the making of the improvement. But this was only directory; and if the improvement be made before the estimate and assessment, it would not prejudice the title of a purchaser under a sale for non-payment of the assessment. In Wetmore *v.* Campbell,[1] however, it was held not to be necessary to cause an estimate of the expense of constructing a public sewer to be made, and the amount thereof to be assessed upon the owners and occupants of premises liable to such assessment, previously to entering upon the construction of the work, but that the same might be done for the first time after the work is completed. Since the decision of the case of Stryker *v.* Kelly,[2] the former practice of requiring a party, before bringing error from an order confirming the report of the commissioners of estimate and assessment, to sue out a *certiorari* to the justices as commissioners, is not followed—the order of confirmation being now considered the act of the Court, and not of statute commissioners.

§ 198. The charter to a city conferred a general authority upon the common council to cause the streets, avenues, and squares, in certain wards in the city, to be graded, levelled, paved or macadamized, and to cause cross-walks to be made, &c. The corporation of the city contracted for the grading and regulating one of the avenues, at a specified price, to be paid out of the moneys which were to be collected for an assessment made for such improvement. The Court of Chancery held, that it was the duty of the officers of the corporation to see that a proper assessment was made for the improvement, and that the money was paid thereon, and paid over to the contractors, within a reasonable time after the completion of the improvement; and the Court also held, that the officers of the

1 Wetmore *v.* Campbell, 2 Sandf. (N. Y.) Sup. Ct. R. 341; and, to the same effect, see Laimbeer *v.* The Mayor, &c. of New York, 4 Ibid. 109; Manice *v.* New York, 4 Seld. (N. Y.) R. 120.

2 Stryker *v.* Kelly, 7 Hill, (N. Y.) R. 9.

corporation, having unreasonably neglected to compel a proper assessment to be made, the contractors were entitled to payment out of the general funds of the corporation; and that such general funds be reimbursed out of the proceeds of the assessment, when made.[1]

§ 199. Commissioners, appointed under the charter of the city of Buffalo, are not authorized to assess upon the real estate of those benefited by a canal about to be made, the cost or expense of constructing the same, in addition to their estimate and assessment of damages.[2]

§ 200. In New York, upon the coming in of the report of commissioners of estimate and assessment, it is the usual practice for the Court to confirm the report, unless the commissioners have violated some positive rule of law, or have not properly appreciated the legal interests of the owner, tenant, or other party interested in the premises. It is not the province of the Court, any more than of the commissioners, to inquire into the policy or expediency of the improvement ordered by the corporation; though, doubtless, a *certiorari* would lie for want of jurisdiction or error on the face of the proceedings.[3] It is, however, the duty of the Court to refuse confirmation, and send back the report, if it plainly appear that the substantial benefits to the persons assessed are not, at the least, equal to all the damage which others will sustain, or that property is not, and cannot be benefited to the extent of the amount assessed upon it, although the effect may be to postpone the improvement, or defeat it altogether.[4] To determine whether such be the case, affidavits of disinterested persons, in respect to the amounts of *benefit* and *damage*, estimated and assessed,

---

1 Cumming *v.* Mayor, &c. of Brooklyn, 11 Paige, (N. Y.) Ch. R. 596.

2 Barney *v.* City of Buffalo, 15 Barb. (N. Y.) Sup. Ct. R. 467.

3 Parks *v.* The City of Boston, 8 Pick. (Mass.) R. 218; Canal Street, 11 Wend. (N. Y.) R. 154.

4 Fourth Avenue, 3 Wend. (N. Y.) R. 453; Albany Street, 11 Ibid. 150; Furman Street, 17 Ibid. 663.

will be received and considered, provided the same have previously been submitted to the commissioners; but, unless there be a plain and decided preponderance of evidence against the judgment of the commissioners, the report will be confirmed. The report is not only viewed with the same favor as the verdict of a jury, that is, is sustained until it be affirmatively and clearly shown to be unwarranted by the evidence, but is regarded with still greater consideration, inasmuch as the commissioners are authorized to act upon personal view and individual knowledge, and even upon information derived from persons not under oath. Their report receives the consideration due to the result of the labors of men selected for their intelligence, integrity, and peculiar qualifications to discharge the duties of their appointment, who, after gathering information from every possible source, have formed and pronounced their judgment. "A review," said Bronson, J., in delivering the opinion of the Supreme Court of New York, "was given to this Court, for the purpose of seeing that the commissioners exercise their authority in the form prescribed by law, and for the correction of any error in the *principle* upon which they have proceeded in making their award. After what has been done in other cases, I will not say that we cannot go beyond this, and examine questions of value. But there must be something more than the *opinions* of witnesses against the judgment of the commissioners,—we must have facts. There must be something like demonstration that the commissioners have fallen into error."[1]

§ 201. Affidavits, which have not been submitted to the commissioners, are inadmissible on appeal, when offered for the purpose of *attacking* or setting aside the report, but will be

---

1 In the Matter of William and Anthony Streets, 19 Wend. (N. Y.) R. 678; In the Matter of John and Cherry Streets, Ibid. 659; In the Matter of Pearl Street, Ibid. 651.

received in its support.[1] The affidavits of owners of property, taken or assessed for benefit, giving their estimates of value or benefit, cannot be received either by the commissioners or the Court; being parties, they cannot be witnesses. Commissioners are authorized, both at common law and by statute, to put their witnesses under oath. Parties interested, who have omitted to lay their proofs before the commissioners, are concluded, unless they show a *want of knowledge* of the proceedings on the part of the corporation, in which case the report will be remitted, so that there may be an opportunity to be heard. So if the commissioners in the course of their proceedings make new parties, by assessing persons for benefit who were not before assessed, by the New York statute such parties are entitled to notice, and, if it be omitted, the report will be sent back, that they may have an opportunity of being heard.[2]

---

1 In the Matter of William and Anthony Streets, *supra*.

2 In the Matter of John and Cherry Streets, 19 Wend. (N. Y.) R. 659.

# CHAPTER V.

## DAMNUM ABSQUE INJURIA.



§ 202. When a highway has once been legally established, the public acquire complete control of the soil, over which it passes, for all the purposes of its proper enjoyment and maintenance. For these purposes they may do with it as the individual may do with his own land, and, so long as they keep within the sphere of its legitimate uses, are amenable to no stricter rule of damages. And, as it often happens that the lawful use of the land of one individual results in injury to the contiguous land of another, so these uses of the soil of a highway may result in injury to land along the line of the way, and, as in the former case, so in the latter, the party injured will be entitled to no redress. The injury thus resulting is, in the language of the law, *damnum absque injuria*. But while this is so, it is nevertheless true, that the law exacts from both individual and public a careful and just use of their own; the maxim of the law, *Sic utere tuo ut alienum non laedas*, being alike applicable to both. To state briefly, therefore, in what way an individual may use his own property, so as to incur or to escape a liability for the damages which may result therefrom to his neighbors, will aid us in determining the liability of the public or its agents for damages resulting to individuals from the use of the common highways.

### 1. *Where Injuries result from the Acts of Individuals.*

§ 203. No individual, in the enjoyment of his own property, can lawfully trespass or encroach, even unintentionally, upon the property of another. Thus, if one having a hedge on his own land adjoining another's close cut the thorns, and they, *ipso invito*, fall upon his neighbor's land, from which he removes them as soon as possible, he may be treated as a trespasser. And if he lop a tree and the boughs fall against his will on the land of another; or if in building his house a piece of timber fall on the house of his neighbor, or if he so build his house that it throws water off upon the house of his neighbor;[1] or if, in blasting rocks for a lawful purpose upon his own land, fragments of the rock fall on the house or land of a neighbor;[2] in all these cases an action lies, for the reason, it is said, that he who is damaged ought to be recompensed.

§ 204. The same principle applies to the use of a stream of flowing water. The rule of law is, that each proprietor, over whose land it passes, has a right to the advantage of its natural flow, undiminished in quantity and uninjured in quality. Though, therefore, a man may use the water of a stream while it is passing through his land, he cannot rightfully divert the water from the land of another lower down the stream; nor can any proprietor below throw back the water without the license or grant of the proprietor above.[3] And

---

[1] Lambert *v.* Bessey, T. Raymond's Rep. 421; Penruddocke's case, 5 Rep. 100; Fay *v.* Prentice, 1 C. B. 828; E. C. L. R. 50; Hayraft *v.* Creasy, 2 East, 104; Scott *v.* Shepherd, 3 Wils. 403.

[2] Hay *v.* The Cohoes Company, and Tremain *v.* The Same, 2 Comst. (N. Y.) R. 159, 163.

[3] Mason *v.* Hill, 5 B. & Ad. 1; Gardner *v.* Village of Newburgh, 2 Johns. (N. Y.) Ch. R. 162; 3 Kent, Com. p. 439, note *a*, 5th edit.

where A., having land through which a river runs to B.'s mill, lops the trees growing on the river's side, and the loppings accidentally impede the progress of the stream, which hinders the mill from working, A. will be liable.[1] But if, by digging in his own ground, he intercept or drain off the water collected from underground springs in his neighbor's well, he will not be liable.[2]

§ 205. So the owner of land, under color of enjoying his own, may not set up a nuisance which deprives another of the enjoyment of his property.[3] Nor can he, under the color of enjoying his own, protect himself from the consequences of his own negligence, unskilfulness, or malicious misconduct. It has, therefore, been held, that an action lies against a party for so negligently constructing a hayrick on the extremity of his land, that in consequence of its spontaneous ignition his neighbor's house was burnt down; and, in such a case, the proper criterion, it is said, for the guidance of the jury is, whether the defendant has been guilty of gross negligence, viewing his conduct with reference to the caution which a prudent man would, under the given circumstances, have observed.[4]

§ 206. But where, in using his own property, an individual does not invade or appropriate that of another, nor erect a nuisance, nor conduct with negligence, unskilfulness, nor malice, he cannot be made answerable for the consequences which ensue. Thus, as has been said,[5] "he may set fire to his fallow ground; and though the fire run into and burn the woodland

---

1 Lambert *v.* Bessey, T. Raymond, Rep. 422.

2 Acton *v.* Blundell, 2 M. & W. 324; South Shield Waterworks Company *v.* Cookson, 15 L. J., Ex. 315.

3 Deane *v.* Clayton, 7 Taunt. 497; Ded d. Bish *v.* Keeling, 1 M. & S. 95.

4 Vaughan *v.* Menlove, 3 Bing. N. C. 468; Turberville *v.* Stampe, Ld. Raymond, 264; S. C. 1 Salk. 13; Bradbee *v.* Mayor of London, 5 Scott, N. R. 119; Dodd *v.* Holme, 1 Ad. & Ellis, 493.

5 Per Bronson, Ch. J., in Radcliff's Executors *v.* Mayor, &c. of Brooklyn, 4 Comst. (N. Y.) Appeals Rep. 195.

of his neighbor, no action will lie;[1] he may open and work a coal mine in his own land, though it injure the house which another has built at the extremity of his land,[2] he may build on his own land though it stop the lights of his neighbor;[3] and even though he build for the very purpose of stopping the lights,[4] he may pull down his own house, though the adjoining house fall for the want of the support which it before had; and he may do it without shoring up the adjoining house, that being the business of the owner;[5] he may pull down his own walls, though the vaults of his neighbor be thereby destroyed;[6] he may build a house and make cellars upon his soil, whereby a house in the adjoining soil falls down;[7] and he may dig in his own land, though the house which his neighbor has previously erected at the extremity of his land, be thereby undermined and fall into the pit."[8] It has, however, been said, that each proprietor has a natural right to the use of his land, in the situation in which it was placed by nature, surrounded and protected by the soil of the adjacent lots, and if, therefore, another dig so near, that thereby his land shall go into the pit, an action brought for that will lie.[9]

---

1 Clark *v.* Foot, 8 Johns. (N. Y.) R. 421.

2 Partridge *v.* Scott, 3 M. & Welsb. 220; Acton *v.* Blundell, 12 Id. 352.

3 Parker *v.* Foot, 19 Wend. (N. Y.) R. 309.

4 Mahan *v.* Brown, 13 Wend. (N. Y.) R. 261.

5 Peyton *v.* Mayor and Commonalty of London, 9 B. & C. 725; Grocers' Company *v.* Donne, 3 Bing. N. C. 34; Davis *v.* London & Blackwall Railway Company, 2 Scott, N. R. 74.

6 Chadwick *v.* Tower, 6 Bing. N. C. 1.

7 Com. Dig. Action on the Case for Nuisance, C.

8 2 Rolle's Ab. Trespass, I. pl. 1; Wyatt *v.* Harrison, 3 B. & Ad. 871; Panton *v.* Holland, 17 Johns. (N. Y.) R. 92; Lasala *v.* Holbrook, 4 Paige, (N. Y.) Ch. R. 169; Thurston *v.* Hancock, 12 Mass. R. 220.

9 Lasala *v.* Holbrook, 4 Paige, (N. Y.) R. 169; but see Partridge *v.* Scott, 3 M. & W. 220.

### 2. *Where Injuries result from the Acts of the Public or its Agents at Common Law.*

§ 207. Such are the principles that determine the liability of individuals in the enjoyment of their property, and they reflect much light upon the liability of the public in reference to highways. It is evident that, in their strictest application, they allow a wide margin for injuries which are without a remedy. In the case of highways, this margin is susceptible of a still greater extension. The public acts, and is amenable, only through its officers, whose powers are commonly defined by statutes, and who, so long as they do not exceed those powers, cannot be held to answer for the consequences of their acts, unless the statutes themselves are void. In England, where the legislature is not restrained by a written constitution, the sanction of a statute is always a justification; in the United States, it is so unless the statute be repugnant to the constitution of the State or of the Union. But neither in the United States nor in England will a statute shelter from liability the officer, who, while acting under its authority, by his own negligence, unskilfulness, or wilful malice, occasions a mischief which, by the exercise of proper care and diligence, might have been avoided. In illustration of these views there are numerous decisions both in England and in this country.

§ 208. In England, the leading case is that of The Governor and Company of the British Cast Plate Manufacturers *v.* Meredith and others.[1] The plaintiffs, in this case, were the owners of a certain messuage and a yard with three warehouses built therein, on the north side of High Ground Street, communicating with the street by a gateway, leading through and under the messuage. The defendants, who acted as paviors under the authority of an act of parliament, by raising the

---

1 The Governor and Company of the British Cast Plate Manufacturers *v.* Meredith and others, 4 Term Rep. 794.

grade of the street lessened the height from the pavement to the centre of the arch of the gateway, so much as to make it necessary to take down and heighten the arch for the admission of wagons and other carriages to the warehouses, for the purpose of loading and unloading as they had previously done. It was contended, on the authority of Leader *v.* Moxton and others,[1] that the defendants were liable to make good to the plaintiffs, any actual damage sustained by their acts; for, it was said, it could never be supposed to be the intention of the legislature, that the avenue to one man's house should be blocked up for the convenience of his neighbors, without some compensation. But Kenyon, C. J., remarked: "If this action could be maintained, every turnpike act, paving act, and navigation act, would give rise to an infinity of actions. If the legislature think it necessary, as they do in many cases, they enable the commissioners to award satisfaction to the individuals who happen to suffer. But if there be no such power, the parties are without remedy, provided the commissioners do not exceed their jurisdiction. But it does not seem to me that the commissioners acting under this act have been guilty of any excess of jurisdiction." And per Buller, J.: "There are many cases in which individuals sustain an injury, for which the law gives no action; for instance, pulling down houses or raising bulwarks for the preservation and defence of the kingdom against the king's enemies. The civil law writers indeed say, that the individuals who suffer have a right to resort to the public for a satisfaction; but no one ever thought that the common law gave an action against the individual who pulled down the house, &c. This is one of those cases to which the maxim applies, *salus populi suprema est lex.* If the thing

1 Leader *v.* Moxton and others, 3 Wilson, 461; 2 Bl. Rep. 924, S. C.; Kenyon, Ch. J., in the above case, doubts the accuracy of this report; but the decision is explicable on another principle; the defendants having, in the opinion of the Court that rendered it, abused their authority and acted arbitrarily and oppressively.

complained of were lawful at the time, no action can be sustained against the party doing the act. In this case express power was given to the commissioners to raise the pavement; and, not having exceeded their power, they are not liable to an action for having done it."

§ 209. In Boulton *v.* Crowther,[1] the same doctrine was asserted. The defendant, by changing the grade of a turnpike road, had rendered the entrance gates to the plaintiff's premises unavailable for the use of persons with carts and carriages, and had allowed a part of the materials of the road to fall into the plaintiff's premises, and to damage his hedge and plantations. The grading had been done by the order of the trustees of the road, acting in pursuance of a statute, which authorized them to carry or improve the road through or over any private land, tendering or making satisfaction to the owner thereof, and the persons interested therein, for the damages sustained thereby. It was contended, that although the trustees had not taken any of the plaintiff's land, yet, as they had rendered it of less value to him, in consequence of raising the road in some parts, and lowering it in others, they were liable, although the act had not provided a compensation for a consequential damage, accruing to a party in a case where no part of his land was taken. The jury having found for the defendant, upon instructions, that the action was not maintainable, if the trustees used proper care and caution, and did nothing oppressive and arbitrary, a motion for a new trial to the Court in bank was refused. And per Holroyd, J.: "The act done being itself lawful, can only become unlawful in consequence of the mode in which it is carried into execution; and

---

1 Boulton *v.* Crowther, 2 Barn. & Cress. 703. For other English cases, see Sutton *v.* Clark, 6 Taunt. R. 34; Dore *v.* Gray, 2 Term R. 358; The King *v.* Bristol Dock Company, 6 Barn. & Cress. 181; Harman *v.* Tappenden, 1 East, R. 555; The Wardens, &c. *v.* Donne, 3 Scott, R. 356; Roberts *v.* Read, 16 East, R. 215; Hall *v.* Smith, 2 Bing. 156; Warburton *v.* The London and Blackwell Railway Company, 1 Railway Cases, 558.

here the jury have, by their verdict, negatived the fact of the act having been done carelessly, wantonly, or oppressively."

§ 210. It has been urged in favor of this immunity of public officers, that they ought not to be subject to damages for their acts, because, unlike individuals, they derive from them no private emolument. In giving an opinion, in the case just referred to, Littledale, J., mentions this as one of the grounds of his decision. "I agree," he says, "that a private individual must so use his own land as not to injure that of another, but the private individual acts for his own benefit, and he ought not to obtain a benefit at the expense of his neighbor. But where an act of parliament vests a power in trustees or commissioners to be exercised by them, not for their own benefit, but for that of the public, and gives no compensation for a damage resulting from an act done by them in the execution of that power, the legislature must be taken to have intended, that an individual should not receive any compensation for the loss resulting to him from an act so done for the public benefit." And in the earlier case of Sutton *v.* Clark,[1] the same reason had been advanced. The defendants, who were the trustees of a turnpike road, and were empowered to make watercourses, to prevent the road from being overflowed, on the recommendation of their surveyor, made a wide channel from the road, gradually narrowing and conducting the water into the ordinary fence-ditches of the plaintiff's land, which were insufficient to discharge it, and his land was consequently overflowed. Gibbs, Ch. J., in delivering the opinion of the Court, said: "This case is perfectly unlike that of an individual, who, for his own benefit, makes an improvement on his own land, according to his best skill and diligence, and not foreseeing it will produce an injury to his neighbor, if he thereby unwittingly injure his neighbor, he is answerable. The resemblance fails in the most

---

1 Sutton *v.* Clark, 6 Taunton, R. 29.

important point of comparison, that his act is not done for a public purpose, but for private emolument. Here the defendant is not a volunteer; he executes a duty imposed on him by the legislature, which he is bound to execute. He exercises his best skill, diligence, and caution in the execution of it, and we are of the opinion, that he is not liable for an injury which he did not only not foresee, but could not foresee. He has done all that was incumbent on him, having used his best skill and diligence." But though this may be an argument to support the policy of such an exemption, the all-sufficient reason for the exemption is, that the act is done under lawful authority, and being so done, if done in a proper manner, no legal wrong has been committed to be redressed. And this has been expressly so decided in an American case, in an action against a municipal corporation, for causing the plaintiff's lot to be overflowed by stopping up a watercourse, where the Court declared, that if the city was authorized to stop up the watercourse, an action would not lie, although it was done by the city in an attempt to improve their own private property.[1]

### 3. *Where Injuries result from the Acts of the Public, or its Agents, in the United States.*

§ 211. The law of England is likewise the law of the United States, except in so far as it has been modified by the constitutional provision that private property shall not be taken for public uses, without just compensation. The States, which have not engrafted this provision upon their constitutions, have as unlimited a power in this particular as the English parliament.[2] With reference to this provision, injuries, resulting from the use and improvement of highways, may be divided into two

---

1 Mayor, &c. *v.* Randolph, 4 Watts & Serg. (Penn.) R. 514; but see Mayor, &c. *v.* Bailey, 2 Denio, (N. Y.) R. 450.

2 The State *v.* Dawson, 3 Hill, (S. C.) R. 100; but see Martin, *ex parte*, 13 Ark. (8 Eng.) R. 198.

classes, viz.; first, injuries which result from changes in the surface of highways, and confined within their established limits; second, injuries which result from changes extending beyond their established limits into land adjoining. Injuries of the first class plainly do not fall strictly within the constitutional restriction. That applies to the *taking* of property, not to the *use* of property after it has been taken. And, provided the changes are carefully and properly made, with a view to the better adaptation of the soil to the purposes of a highway, it is not easy to see why, even independently of direct statutory sanction, upon the general principles which control the enjoyment of property, they should not be held to be *damnum absque injuria;* if, as has been assumed, the public may do with the soil of a highway, in furtherance of its legitimate use, what the individual may do with his own land.[1] But injuries of the second class, being such as result from changes made outside the established limits of the highway, as where a watercourse is diverted or flowed back upon adjoining lands, fall within the analogies of that class of injuries which, at common law, expose the individual to an action for damages, and, consequently, require a statute for their justification.[2] They are not, moreover, by any means so plainly beyond the operation of the constitution; for it is somewhat difficult to perceive, why the diversion of a stream of water, or the flooding of adjoining land, for the sake of improving a highway, in so far as the stream or the land becomes thereby less valuable, is not, *pro tanto*, a *taking* of them for public use. The constitutional taking does not import an absolute privation of all right on the part of the original owner in the land taken; for, if so, then the laying out of a highway is not a taking; and, if any degree short of absolute privation be a taking, why is not every degree, to the extent to which it goes, equally so, and equally deserving of compensation. It has, however, been decided,

---

1 See *ante*, § 202.

2 See *ante*, § 204.

that neither of these clases of injuries are subject to compensation by force of the constitution. To some of these decisions I now ask the attention of the reader.

§ 212. In Callendar *v.* Marsh,[1] the defendant, a surveyor of highways, in the lawful discharge of his functions as prescribed by statute, dug down the streets by the plaintiff's dwelling-house in Boston, and took away the earth, so as to lay bare the foundation walls of the house and endanger its falling, in consequence of which, the plaintiff was obliged, at great expense, to build up new walls, and otherwise secure the house, and render it safe and convenient of access, as before. In an action for the damages thereby sustained, it was contended, that the statute under which the defendant justified, was void, as being repugnant to that clause of the constitution which secures to individuals, whose property is taken for public use, a reasonable compensation therefor, and was, consequently, no defence for the defendant's acts. But the Court held, that this provision of the constitution was confined to the direct loss of property sustained by the individual, and to such expenses as are necessarily incident to the very act of taking it. That the highway having been legally established, although the right or title in the soil remained in him from whom the use was taken, yet the public acquired the right, not only to pass over the surface in the state it was in when first made a highway, but the right also to repair and amend it, and, for this purpose, to dig down and remove the soil sufficiently to make the passage safe and convenient. That in no case could a person be liable to an action as for tort for an act which he is authorized by law to do; and, therefore, the act, authorizing the defendant, as surveyor, to make the alterations in the highway complained of, being constitutional, he was not responsible for the consequences.

§ 213. In Radcliff's Executors *v.* Mayor, &c. of Brooklyn,[2]

---

1 Callender *v.* Marsh, 1 Pick. (Mass.) R. 417.

2 Radcliff's Executors *v.* Mayor, &c. of Brooklyn, 4 Comst. (N. Y.) R. 195.

the defendants, the corporation of the city of Brooklyn, regularly laid out and opened a street, and thereby acquired title to the land over which it passed. Afterward, they proceeded to grade the street, in order to bring it into public use, and, in so doing, removed a high bank which constituted a natural support to the premises of an adjoining owner, so that a portion of his land fell. There was no allegation of malice, or want of care or skill, and it was held, that the adjacent owner could not maintain an action on the case for the damages sustained by him. In delivering the opinion of the Court, Bronson, Ch. J., after an admirable review of the authorities, remarked: "The opening of a street in a city, is not, necessarily, an injury to the adjoining land-owners. On the contrary, it is in almost every instance a benefit to them. The damage which they sometimes sustain, because the level of the street does not correspond with the level of their land, is usually more than compensated by the increased value which the property acquires from having a new front on a street. In some instances, the land-owner will suffer a heavy loss; and this case may, perhaps, be one of the number; but it is *damnum absque injuria*, and the owner must bear it. He often gets the benefit for nothing, when the value of his land is increased by opening or improving a street or highway; and he must bear the burden in the less common case of a depreciation in value in consequence of the work. It may be added, that when men buy and build in cities and villages, they usually take into consideration all these things which are likely to affect the value of their property, and particularly what will probably be done by way of opening and grading streets and avenues. Whether in cases of this kind, the legislature ought, as a matter of equity, to provide for the payment of such damages as are merely consequential, we are not called upon to decide. It is enough for us to say, that a law which makes no such provision, is not, for that reason, unconstitutional and void."

§ 214. The principles laid down in the two preceding

cases, have been often recognized as sound,[1] and extended to still other changes in the use of highways. Thus it has been frequently held, that the occupation of a street in a city for a railway track, authorized by statute, and laid under the direction of the city authorities, does not entitle the owner of adjacent land to the damages which result to that land, or to any business or trade conducted thereon, in consequence of such occupation.[2] So, likewise, it has been decided in New York, that a public highway taken by a plank-road corporation, by virtue of a statute and its act of incorporation, does not cease to be a public highway; and when the corporation has paid the commissioners of highways for the interest of the public in the road, it succeeds to all the rights of the town commissioners to make such repairs in the road as the public interest requires, whether such repairs consist in excavations or embankments, to bring the road to a proper grade, and thus to improve its condition as a public thoroughfare; and any inconvenience or damage which any person may suffer in the proper and reasonable repairs of such public highway by the corporation, in the legitimate exercise of the powers conferred by the statute, is *damnum absque injuria*, and no action lies therefor.[3] The

---

1 O'Conner *v.* Pittsburgh, 18 Penn. (Harris,) R. 187; Green *v.* The Borough of Reading, 9 Watts, (Penn.) R. 382; Graves *v.* Otis, 2 Hill, (N. Y.) R. 466; Taylor *v.* City of St. Louis, 14 Missouri R. 20; Round *v.* Mumford, 2 R. I. Rep. 154; Henry *v.* Pittsburgh and Alleghany Bridge Company, 8 Watts & Serg. (Penn.) R. 85; Matter of Furman Street, 17 Wend. 667; Gossler *v.* Corporation of Georgetown, 6 Wheat. (U. S.) R. 593; Humes *v.* Mayor, &c. of Knoxville, 1 Humph. 403; Lebanon *v.* Olcott, 1 N. H. 339.

2 Hamilton *v.* The New York and Harlem Railroad Company, 9 Paige, (N. Y.) Ch. R. 171; Drake *v.* The Hudson River Railroad Company, 7 Barb. (N. Y.) Sup. Ct. R. 508; Plant *v.* Long Island Railroad Company, 10 Ibid. 26; Chapman *v.* Albany and Schenectady Railroad Company, 10 Ibid. 360; The Lexington and Ohio Railroad *v.* Applegate, 8 Dana, 289; Wetmore *v.* Story, 22 Barb. (N. Y.) Sup. Ct. R. 414.

3 Benedict *v.* Goit, 3 Barb. (N. Y.) Sup. Ct. R. 449; Chagrin Falls and Cleveland Plank-road Company *v.* Cane *et al.*, 2 Ohio, (Warden,) N. S. Rep. 419.

rationale of these decisions is, that the owner of the land when he parted with the easement, did so in view of the powers which the public thereby acquired, and of the changes to which it might be subjected, and must be presumed to have received compensation accordingly; and that subsequent purchasers must have purchased in view of all the advantages and disadvantages, which might ensue from the same cause, and cannot, therefore, when injured, be entitled to damages, any more than they can be subject to them when benefited.

§ 215. For similar reasons, where erections are made under the authority of the law in a navigable river, which is one species of common highways, a party who is *consequentially* injured thereby is not entitled to damages. Thus, as we have seen, the proprietors of one toll-bridge cannot prevent the building of another over the same river on the ground that their tolls will be thereby diminished;[1] and the erection of a railroad in a river below high-water mark is not the subject of damages to the riparian proprietor.[2] In Lansing *v.* Smith,[3] the plaintiff brought an action to recover damages for the construction of a basin in Hudson River, in the city of Albany, authorized by statute, and for the erection of temporary bridges and a sloop-lock, as auxiliary thereto, alleging that the beneficial enjoyment of his dock, and of his right of way to and from the same, had been essentially impaired by that operation. The remedy was refused, and the Court, in giving judgment, said: "The right of way of the plaintiff to and from his dock is not denied. All that is contended for on the part of the defendants is, that the mode in which that right is to be exercised, is subject to be controlled and regulated by the legislature, as, in their judgment, the interest and convenience of the

---

1 *Ante*, § 94.

2 *Ante*, § 98. But see Sinnickson *v.* Johnson, 2 Harr. (N. Y.) R. 129, and Wetmore *v.* Story, 22 Barb. (N. Y.) S. C. R. 414.

3 Lansing *v.* Smith, 8 Cowen, (N. Y.) R. 148; 4 Wend. (N. Y.) R. 3.

public may require. In all such regulations, a due regard is undoubtedly to be paid to the interest of individuals. But every great public improvement must, almost of necessity, more or less affect individual convenience and property; and where the injury sustained is remote and consequential, it is *damnum absque injuria*, and is to be borne as a part of the price to be paid for the advantages of the social condition."

§ 216. But the power of the public, or of municipal corporations acting in the public behalf, over highways, is not restricted to their use for the mere purpose of transit. It extends to the promotion of the public convenience by the laying of water-pipes and gas-pipes in the streets of cities; and to the promotion of the public health by the construction of drains and sewers, or making any other changes therein. And any injury which results to individuals from such a use of the public streets, unless there be a lack of proper care, is *damnum absque injuria*. Thus, it has been decided that a city has the right to fill up a watercourse, if that be the best means of remedying a nuisance which it occasions, and that the fact, that a riparian proprietor is thereby deprived of his right to pass and repass upon the watercourse from his land to the sea, or is damnified by the noisome smells generated by the stagnation of the water, does not entitle him to damage. Such a proceeding stands on the same footing as quarantine or fire regulations, from which if the individual receives damage, the law presumes him to be indemnified by sharing their advantages, and holds it to be *damnum absque injuria*.[1] And it makes no difference though the regulation thus made be of such a character as to suspend the enjoyment of the property in the sole mode in which the party plaintiff is entitled to use it.[2] Nor can the city, by covenants with individuals, divest itself of the power of making such a regulation. The city

---

1 Baker *v.* Boston, 12 Pick. (Mass.) R. 184.

2 Stuyvesant *v.* The Mayor, &c. of New York, 7 Cowen, (N. Y.) R. 588.

sustains a twofold capacity,—as a corporation with power to contract and be bound by its contracts, and as a special legislature charged with the care of the public health and morals; and its acts done in the former capacity are subject to its legislative action, in the same manner as the acts of an individual.[1]

§ 217. Also, as we have before said, an action does not lie where damages are sustained by the overflowing of the land of an individual in consequence of the repair or improvement of a highway. No public work, however important, it was remarked in a case of this description, could be constructed without being the source of endless litigation if such remote and consequential damages would lay the foundation of an action at law.[2] In Wilson *v.* Mayor, &c. of New York,[3] the defendants, in grading one of the streets of the city, raised it about eighteen inches without making any drain or sewer, thereby obstructing the former flow of water from the plaintiff's lots, so that the water ran from the street and avenue and from the adjacent lots upon her premises. Yet the Court held, that, the defendants being authorized to do what had been done, if the plaintiff was thereby incommoded, it was *damnum absque injuria*, and gave her no right of action against those who had only exercised a legal power vested in them for the public convenience and welfare. And it was said that, though the power was given to the city to make common sewers, drains, and vaults, in any part thereof, yet the exercise of that power being discretionary, the city was not liable for damages resulting from a neglect to exercise it.

§ 218. But, while such has been the usual course of de-

---

1 Presbyterian Church *v.* City of New York, 5 Cowen, (N. Y.) R. 538.

2 City of St. Louis *v.* Gurno, 12 Missouri R. 415.

3 Wilson *v.* Mayor, &c. of New York, 1 Denio, (N. Y.) R. 555; and see State *v.* The Inland Lock Navigation Company, 2 Johns. (N. Y.) Rep. 283; Boughton *v.* Carter, 18 Ibid. 405. In Delaware it has been held, that a Canal Company is not liable for damages occasioned by a mere accidental breach of their canal. Higgins *v.* Ches. & Del. Canal Co. 3 Harring. (Del.) R. 441.

cision, it has prevailed not without dissent,[1] and in two States, at least, has been overruled. In Connecticut, in Hooker *v.* The New Haven and Northampton Company,[2] the injuries complained of were caused by the flowing of water from the waste wier of a canal over the adjoining land of others upon and through the land of the plaintiff. In the construction of the canal and waste wier, the defendants had strictly pursued their charter, and were found to have acted with proper prudence and care in thus discharging the water. It was contended that the defendants, having acted under the authority of law, and not having *taken* the plaintiff's property, were not liable for the consequential damages resulting from their acts. But the majority of the Court were of the opinion, that it was not to be intended, from any thing in the charter, that the legislature had given the defendants power to take away or essentially impair the rights of other persons, for which they had made no provision; that the injury, though consequential, flowed from their act in throwing their surplus water upon the

1 Dissenting opinions in Charles River Bridge *v.* Warren Bridge, 7 Pick. (Mass.) R. 344; 11 Peters, (U. S.) R. 420; and in City of St. Louis *v.* Gurno, 12 Missouri R. 415; *Ante*, § 93. "Even if the damage be merely *consequential* or *indirect*," says Chancellor Kent, "as by the creation of a new and rival franchise in a case required by public necessities, the same compensation is due, and the cases of Thurston *v.* Hancock, 12 Mass. Rep. 220, and Callender *v.* Marsh, 1 Pick. Rep. 418, are erroneous, so far as they contravene such a palpably clear and just doctrine. If A. be the owner of a mill, and the legislature authorize a diversion of the watercourse which supplies it, whereby the mill is injured or ruined, is not that a consequential damage to be paid for? The solid principle is too deeply rooted in law and justice to be shaken." Kent, Com. 340, note *c.* (5th ed.); Gardner *v.* The Village of Newburg, 2 Johns. (N. Y.) Ch. R. 166; Stevens *v.* The Proprietors of the Middlesex Canal, 12 Mass. R. 466; Rowe *v.* The Granite Bridge Corporation, 21 Pick. (Mass.) R. 344; Fletcher *v.* The Auburn and Syracuse Railroad Co. 25 Wend. (N. Y.) R. 462; Boughton *v.* Carter, 18 Johns. (N. Y.) R. 405.

2 Hooker *v.* The New Haven and Northampton Company, 14 Conn. R. 146; but see dissenting opinion in that case, and Hollister *v.* The Union Company, 9 Conn. R. 436; Nicholson *v.* The New York and New Haven Railroad Co. 22 Conn. R. 174.

plaintiff's land, and thus depriving him of the use of it; and they were, therefore, bound to allow a just compensation for the damages. In Ohio, the liability for damages of this kind is still more unequivocally maintained. "That the rights of one," is the language of the Supreme Court of that State, "should be so used as not to impair the rights of another, is a principle of morals, which, from very remote ages, has been recognized as a maxim of the law. If an individual exercising his lawful powers commit an injury, the action on the case is the familiar remedy; if a corporation, acting within the scope of its authority, should work wrong to another, the same principle of ethics demands of them to repair it, and no reason occurs to the Court why the same remedy should not be applied to compel justice from them."[1] And, in a subsequent case against a municipal corporation for an injury occasioned by the grading of a street, where the defendants were acting within the scope of their corporate authority, the Court, in referring to the language just cited, indorsed it in its fullest extent, and expressed the hope "that, by the light of such example and assurance, the whole subject-matter of corporations will, in the end, be reduced to the control of incontestable principle."[2]

### 4. *Liability for the want of due care and diligence in acts performed under lawful authority.*

§ 219. But, as has been remarked, though a party act under lawful authority, he is not protected from the damages which result from his own malice, unskilfulness or negligence. In a very early case, where commissioners, who were empowered by act of parliament to grade and repair a street in such manner

---

1 Rhodes *v.* City of Cleveland, 10 Ohio R. 159.

2 McCoombs *v.* The Town Council of Akron, 15 Ohio R. 474. And see Goodloe *v.* City of Cincinnati, 4 Ohio R. 500; Smith *v.* City of Cincinnati, Ibid. 514; Savill *v.* Giddings, 7 Ibid. 212; Hickox *v.* Cleveland, 8 Ibid. 543.

as they should think fit, caused it to be raised six feet in front of the plaintiff's houses, it was said by the Court: "Every man of common sense must understand, that this act of parliament ought to be carried into execution without doing such enormous injury to individuals, as hath been manifestly done to the plaintiff in this case. Whenever a trust is put in commissioners by act of parliament, if they misdemean themselves in that trust, they are answerable criminally in the King's Bench; if they aggrieve and damnify the subject, as they have done in the present case, they are answerable in this Court *civiliter* in damages to the party injured."[1] It is the implied condition of a grant of authority, that the authority shall suffer no abuse in the execution.[2]

§ 220. Neither is a party, who deviates in the slightest degree from the legal authority under which he claims to act, entitled on account of that authority, to any exemption from liability, even though such a deviation be less injurious than an exact observance of the authority would have been. Thus, where a railroad corporation was authorized by its charter to raise or lower any highway, which in its course the railroad might pass, so that, if necessary, the road might pass under or over or across the same, and it was provided that the town council of the town, where the highway was located, should have power to require of the corporation to do it in such a manner as should be satisfactory to them, by requesting any alteration or amendment which should be necessary for that purpose, and should have power to enforce such request by complaint to the Court of Common Pleas, in case of non-compliance on the part of the corporation; it was held, that the corporation was not justified in widening a highway, or diverting its course, or supplying its place with a new way, so that the railroad would

---

1 Leader *v.* Moxon, 3 Wilson, 461; 2 W. Blackst. Rep. 924, S. C.

2 Mearls *v.* Commissioners of Wilmington, 9 Ired. (N. C.) R. 73; Jones *v.* Bird, 5 Barn. & Ald. 837; *Ante*, § 209, 214, and the cases there cited.

be passed at a point different from its intersection with the original way, even though the change was approved or acquiesced in by the town council, and was for the convenience of the public, and that in such case they were liable in damages to private individuals who had suffered a special injury by their act.[1]

§ 221. When damages of this kind accrue in the prosecution of a work by the order of a municipal corporation, the corporation is liable for the acts of its servants and agents, in the same manner as an individual.[2] Municipal corporations are

---

1 Hughes *v.* The Providence and Worcester Railroad Company, 2 R. I. Rep. 493; Spencer *v.* London and Birmingham Railway Company, 1 Railway Cases, 150; Regina *v.* Eastern Counties Railway, 2 Adol. & Ellis, N. S. 569; and see *post*, Chapter VI.

2 Delmonico *v.* The Mayor, &c. of New York, 1 Sandf. (N. Y.) Sup. Ct. R. 22; The Mayor of Memphis *v.* Lasser, 9 Humph. (Tenn.) R. 759; Ross *v.* City of Madison, 1 Smith, (Ind.) R. 98; Radcliff's Executors *v.* Mayor of Brooklyn, 4 Comst. (N. Y.) R. 195. In England, it has been held, that the trustees, appointed under a public road act, are not responsible for an injury occasioned by the negligence of the men employed in making or repairing the road. Waterhouse *v.* Keen, 6 Clark & Fin. 894; 1 Rob. 911. And in the case of Harris and Ux. *v.* Baker, 4 M. & S. 27, the trustees of a public road were empowered and required, by an act of parliament, to place lamps along the road, if they should think necessary, and to make contracts for the cleansing of the road, and to take a night-toll for the purpose of enabling them to light and watch the same. The highway had been cleansed, and the scrapings had been left in round heaps, on both sides of the road. One evening, after it was dark, there being no lamps by the road side, the plaintiff's wife, having occasion to cross the way, in her passage fell over one of these heaps and broke her arm. And it was held by the Court of King's Bench, that the clerk to the trustees was not liable to an action under the above circumstances. Per Lord Ellenborough, C. J.: "If, by omitting to put up lamps where it is necessary, the trustees are guilty of a breach of public duty, they may be indicted. But to hold that every trustee of a road is liable in damages for such an accident as this, would, I conceive, be going further than any case warrants." But although the trustees themselves may not be liable to make compensation for damage occasioned by acts ordered by them to be done, which are within the scope of their authority, if they proceed with sufficient caution, yet it should seem from the case of Hall *v.* Smith and others, 2 Bing. R. 156, that the agent who is appointed to execute such acts, is answerable for any negligence in their performance. This was an action brought against the clerks to certain commissioners, for lighting, paving, and watching the town of Birmingham, and also against the surveyor and contractor employed

charged with a twofold duty in regard to highways; first, they are to decide when, where, and what repairs and improvements

---

by them, and a laborer who was employed by the contractor. It appeared that the defendants dug a deep ditch in a certain street, placed a quantity of rubbish near the same, and left it at night, without any guard, fence, light, or signal; and that the plaintiff, not knowing thereof, fell into the ditch with great force whilst riding across the street, whereby he broke his thigh, and his horse was much injured. On the trial, the jury found a verdict for the laborer, and against all the other defendants. Upon motion, the Court of Common Pleas set aside the verdict, as against the clerks to the commissioners, but confirmed it as against the surveyor and contractor. In the course of a most able judgment, Best, C. J., observed, that, "As to the surveyor and contractor, it was admitted, that the verdict found against them must stand. The question to be decided was, whether the clerks to the commissioners were to have a verdict entered for them. The action is not maintainable against these defendants, unless it could have been supported against the commissioners. Now, if commissioners, under an act of parliament order something to be done, which is not within the scope of their authority, or are themselves guilty of negligence in doing that which they are empowered to do, they render themselves liable to an action; but they are not answerable for the misconduct of such as they are obliged to employ. If the doctrine of *respondeat superior* were applied to such commissioners, who would be hardy enough to undertake any of those various offices, by which much valuable, yet unpaid, service is rendered to the country? The maxim of *respondeat superior* is bottomed on this principle, that he who expects to derive advantage from an act which is done by another for him, must answer for any injury which a third person may sustain from it. The commissioners here had authority to make the trench which occasioned the damage to the plaintiff; and they are not answerable for the negligent execution of an order properly given." So in the case of Jones *v.* Bird and others, 5 B. & Ald. R. 837, the plaintiff brought his action against the defendants, who were employed under the commissioners of sewers. It appeared that the sewer, which it was necessary to repair, passed close to five houses adjoining to that belonging to the plaintiff, and that a stack of chimneys belonging to one of those houses was built upon the arch of the sewer. In the execution of the work, it became necessary to rebuild this arch, and in order to support the chimneys in the meantime, a transum and two upright posts were placed under them, in order to support them, but without success; the chimneys fell, and, in consequence of their fall, the adjoining houses, including the plaintiff's house, fell also. There was no specific notice given to the owner of the house to which the chimneys belonged of their dangerous state, or that it would be necessary for him to take them down. But there was a general notice to the inhabitants to secure their houses while the sewer was repairing. The jury, at the trial, were of opinion, that the defendants had conducted themselves negligently in their execution of the work intrusted to them, and accordingly found a verdict for the plaintiff; which verdict the Court of King's Bench refused to

are to be made in them; secondly, they are to procure them to be made. The former is a judicial or legislative duty, in the discharge of which they are exempt from civil responsibility, so long as they do not exceed their jurisdiction. The latter is a purely ministerial duty, in the performance of which they derive no immunity from their character as a municipality, for any want of due care and diligence on the part of their agents.[1] On the other hand, even though the act from which the damage ensues was planned and advised by their surveyor, they are primarily liable.[2] They are also liable for a neglect to perform, as well as for negligently performing, a duty which is incumbent upon them.[3] And where the injury was occasioned by an erection unskilfully constructed *upon the land of a city, and for its benefit*, the city was held to be liable for the damages, although the persons who constructed the same were not its agents nor under its control.[4]

---

disturb. Per Bayley, J.: "The defendants were bound to conduct themselves in a skilful manner." And per Best, J.: "Here, too, the action was brought against the parties who negligently executed, and not against the party giving the order, as in Sutton *v.* Clarke." From this observation, it may be inferred, that, in the case alluded to, the surveyor would have been considered liable, although the trustees were held not to be responsible.

1 Rochester White Lead Company *v.* The City of Rochester, 3 Comst. (N. Y.) R. 463; Lloyd *v.* The Mayor, &c. of New York, 1 Selden, (N. Y.) R. 369; Wilson *v.* The Mayor, &c. of New York, 1 Denio, (N. Y.) R. 555; Martin *v.* Mayor of Brooklyn, 1 Hill, (N. Y.) R. 545.

2 Rochester White Lead Company *v.* The City of Rochester, *supra.*

3 Mayor of New York *v.* Furge, 3 Hill, (N. Y.) R. 612.

4 Bailey *v.* Mayor of New York, 3 Hill, (N. Y.) R. 531; 2 Denio, (N. Y.) R. 433. This decision was made upon the authority of Bush *v.* Steinman, 1 Bos. & Pul. 404, in which it was held, that the defendant, *as proprietor of the land,* was liable for an injury occasioned by the depositing of lime in the highway, in front of his house, and for his benefit, although by one who was not in his service.

# CHAPTER VI.

## NUISANCES AND THEIR REMEDIES.



### I. NUISANCES.

§ 222. A PUBLIC nuisance may be defined to be an offence against the public, either by doing a thing to the annoyance of the public, or by neglecting to do a thing which the common good requires. Of this description are nuisances in highways, which may be committed, either positively, by actual obstructions, or negatively, by want of reparations. The latter, or negative kind, can of course be committed only by those upon whom an obligation lies to keep highways in repair; the former, or positive kind, can be committed by any person indiscriminately; but either kind, to be embraced by the definition, must be such as annoys the whole community or travelling public in general, and not merely some particular individual. Being offences against the public, they are indictable only, and not actionable, except where an individual has suffered a special damage beyond what is common to himself with the rest of the public, in which case he may seek redress by a private action.

#### 1. *Illegal Obstructions.*

§ 223. At common law, any act or obstruction, which unnecessarily incommodes or impedes the lawful use of a highway by the public, is a nuisance. Thus, it is a nuisance at common law to dig a ditch or make a hedge across a highway, to suffer adjoining ditches to be foul, by reason whereof it is impaired, or to suffer the boughs of trees, growing near, to overhang it in such a manner as to incommode the passage,[1] to erect a gate[2] or fence[3] across it or a building[4] on it, to deposit lime[5] or gravel[6] in it, though but for temporary convenience, to pile logs or lumber[7] therein, or in any manner unreasonably to obstruct the public passage. Even the substitution of a gate for a stone stile of less height across a public footway is a nuisance, though other gates have been previously placed across other parts of the way;[8] as also would be the continuance of a gate, authorized by statute,

---

[1] 1 Hawk. P. C. Ch. 76, §§ 48 and 50.

[2] James *v.* Hayward, Cro. Car. 184; Greasly *v.* Codling, 2 Bingh. R. 263. In James *v.* Hayward, Croke, J., dissenting from a majority of the Court, was of opinion, that "the law accounts not such petty troubles nuisances; for it appears that there are many gates in divers highways which have been always allowed, and if it were a nuisance in itself there should not be any gate, for there cannot be any prescription for a nuisance." But to this it has been answered, that the erecting of a gate is a nuisance because it interrupts the free and open passage which the public before enjoyed and are entitled to; but where such a gate has continued time out of mind, it shall be intended, that it was set up at first by consent on a composition with the owner of the land on the laying out of the road, in which case the people had never any right to a freer passage than what they still enjoy. See 1 Hawk. Ch. 75, § 9, and the authorities there cited. Where the fee of a public street is in private persons, they may lawfully make a race-way across it to convey water to a factory; but in so doing they must not disturb the servitude or easement of way. 3 Barb. (N. Y.) Sup. Ct. Rep. 42.

[3] Gregory *v.* Commonwealth, 2 Dana, (Ky.) R. 417; Kelly *v.* Commonwealth, 11 S. & R. (Penn.) R. 345.

[4] Stetson *v.* Faxon, 19 Pick. (Mass.) R. 147; Barker *v.* Commonwealth, 19 Penn. (Harris.) R. 412.

[5] Bush *v.* Steinman, 1 Bos. & Pul. R. 404.

[6] Burgess *v.* Gray, 1 Man., Gr. & Scott, R. 578.

[7] Mould *v.* Williams, 5 Ad. & El. R. 469; 1 Hawk. P. C. Ch. 76, §§ 48 and 50.

[8] Bateman *v.* Burge, 6 Car. & P. R. 391. See Clark *v.* Lake, 1 Ham. (Ill.) R. 229.

after the expiration of such statute.[1] It has also been held a nuisance at common law to carry an unreasonable weight on a highway, with an unusual number of horses. And an information for that offence, stating that the carrier went "with an unusual number of horses," without setting forth what number, has been held good, because the nuisance was caused by the excessive weight which was carried.[2]

§ 224. To destroy, stop up, or divert the course of an ancient highway, is a nuisance at common law; nor is it any the less a nuisance, though a new and better way be substituted in its place. Such a change can be made only under the king's license obtained upon a writ of *ad quod damnum*, or in the mode provided by statute. Where, therefore, the change has been made without due authority, the public may, at any time, return to the old path, and remove any obstruction there, or indict the person who caused or continued such obstruction, and it is immaterial how long it has been shut up or disused. And, on the other hand, the proprietor may, at any time, close up the substituted way, or, after notice, (for without such notice a plea of license would be permitted,) treat persons who travel it as trespassers; unless the public use has been continued under such circumstances as will support the inference of a dedication by the owner.[3] So it would seem, that to obliterate a highway by ploughing,[4] or even to use a common pack and horse-way with a cart, in such a manner as to furrow and cut it up, is a nuisance.[5] And to open trenches in the streets of a city, for the purpose of laying gas-pipes, is an indictable nui-

1 Adams *v.* Beach, 6 Hill, (N. Y.) R. 271. See also Runyon *v.* Bordine, 2 Green, (N. J.) R. 36; Wales *v.* Stetson, 2 Mass. R. 143; Justice *v.* Commonwealth, 2 Virg. Cas. 171.

2 Com. Dig. Chimin. A. 3; Rex *v.* Egerly, 3 Salk. R. 183.

3 Rex *v.* Ward, Cro. Car. 266; Rex *v.* Inhabitants of Flecknow, 1 Bur. R. 465; Thomas *v.* Sorrell, Vaugh. 346; Allen *v.* Lyon, 2 Root, (Conn.) R. 213; State *v.* Duncan, 1 McCord, (So. Car.) R. 404; Hone *v.* Widlake, Yelv. R. 141; but see *post* Chap. VII.

4 Griesley's case, 1 Ventr. 4.

5 Regina *v.* Leech, 6 Mod. R. 145.

sance, though the pipes be laid and the road restored with reasonable dispatch.[1]

§ 225. But to constitute a nuisance, it is not necessary that there should be an actual physical obstruction to the public use of the highway; it is enough if there be something that occasions imminent peril to those that travel it. Thus, if a house on the highway be ruinous and likely to fall down, it is a nuisance, and the occupier, although he be but a tenant at will, is bound to repair it; for, as has been remarked, "as the danger is the matter that concerns the public, the public are to look to the occupier and not to the estate, which is not material in such case as to the public."[2] And so to assemble a large number of persons near a highway for the purpose of shooting, with the noise and disturbance consequent upon such assemblage, is a nuisance.[3]

§ 226. The public are entitled not only to a free passage along the highway, but to a free passage along any portion of it, not in the actual use of some other traveller. Therefore it is no excuse for one who layeth logs of timber along a highway, that he laid them only here and there, so that the people might have a passage by windings and turnings through the logs.[4] Yet it is said to be no nuisance for the inhabitants of a town to unlade billets, &c. in the street before their houses, unless they suffer them to continue there an unreasonable time after they are unloaded.[5]

§ 227. But the right to lade and unlade carriages in the highway is entirely subordinate to the right of passage and must not be exercised in such a manner as unreasonably to

---

1 Regina *v.* Sheffield Gas Company, 22 Eng. Law and Eq. R. 518.

2 Regina *v.* Watts, 6 Salk. 357. See also, United States *v.* Hart, Peters, (Cir. Ct.) Rep. 390, in which it was held, that driving a carriage through a crowded and populous street in such a manner as to endanger the safety of the inhabitants, is an indictable offence at common law, and amounts to a breach of the peace.

3 King *v.* Moore, 3 B. & Ald. 184.

4 1 Hawk. P. C. Chap. 76, § 49.

5 Ibid.

abridge or incommode this latter right. Thus in Rex *v.* Russell,[1] it appeared that one or two, and sometimes three large wagons of the defendant were, for several hours both day and night, standing in a street thirty-seven feet wide, before his warehouse, and usually occupied one half of the street, so that no carriages could pass on that side next the warehouse, though two carriages might pass on the opposite side, the gutter being in the middle of the street; that the wagons were loaded and unloaded in the street, and the packages thrown down on the same side of the street, so as frequently, with the wagons, to obstruct even foot passengers, and oblige them to cross the gutter to the other side. It was argued, that partial obstructions of this kind, which arose out of the necessary means of carrying on trade and business, did not constitute a nuisance, the public passage not being impeded, though narrowed thereby. But the language of the Court was: "That the primary object of the street was for the free passage of the public, and any thing which impeded that free passage, *without necessity*, was a nuisance. That if the nature of the defendant's business were such as to require the loading and unloading of so many more of his wagons than could be conveniently contained within his own private premises, he must either enlarge his premises, or remove his business to some more convenient spot."

§ 228. The same principle was recognized in Rex *v.* Cross,[2] where the defendant was indicted and found guilty for keeping coaches at a stand in the street, waiting for passengers; and, again, in Rex *v.* Jones,[3] where the defendant, a timber merchant, occupied a small yard close to the street, and, from the smallness of his premises, was obliged to deposit the long pieces of timber in the street, and to have them sawed up there before they could be carried into the yard. In the latter case, it having been contended, that this was necessary for his trade,

---

1 Rex *v.* Russell, 6 East, R. 427.
2 Rex *v.* Cross, 3 Campb. R. 226.
3 Rex *v.* Jones, Ibid. 230.

and that it occasioned no more inconvenience than draymen letting down hogsheads of beer into the cellar of a publican, Lord Ellenborough said: "If an unreasonable time is occupied in the operation of delivering beer from a brewer's dray into the cellar of a publican, this is certainly a nuisance. A cart or wagon may be unloaded at a gateway, but this must be done with promptness. So as to the repairing of a house; the public must submit to the inconvenience occasioned necessarily in repairing the house; but, if this inconvenience be prolonged for an unreasonable time, the public have a right to complain, and the party may be indicted for a nuisance. The defendant is not to eke out the inconvenience of his own premises by taking the public highway into his timber yard; and, if the street be narrow, he must remove to a more commodious situation for carrying on his business." But it has been held, that the necessity, to justify what would otherwise be a nuisance, need not be absolute, but that it is enough if it be reasonable; and that, in accordance with this principle, a merchant may place his goods in the street for the purpose of removing them to his store in a reasonable time, though he has no right to keep them in the street for the purpose of selling them there, because there is no necessity for it.[1]

---

[1] Commonwealth *v.* Passmore, 1 S. & Raw. (Penn.) R. 219. In Rex *v.* Ward, 4 Ad. & El. R. 405, Lord Denman, in speaking of a hoard erected for repairing a house, said, "That the hoard is placed for the safety of those possessing the right of way; it protects them from inevitable danger if it leaves them a free passage, and leads them another way if the whole street is necessarily obstructed. Every way to which houses adjoin, must be considered as set out, subject to these occasional interruptions, which resemble the temporary acts of loading coals in keels, alluded to in Rex *v.* Russell, 6 B. & C. R. 566. And see Bradbee *v.* London, 5 Scott, N. R. 79. In repairing or rebuilding a house, care must be taken that the encroachment on the highway be not unreasonable; for if the owner of a house employ his own servants, or even contract with a builder to rebuild or repair his house, and the latter erect a shed so far out into the street as to encroach unreasonably on the highway, the owner would be guilty of a nuisance. Bush *v.* Steinman, 1 B. & P. R. 407. But building a house higher than it was before, whereby the street becomes darker, is not a public nuisance on account of the darkening only. Rex *v.* Webb, 1 Ld. Raym. R.

§ 229. The navigation of public rivers is regulated by the same principle. The right of each citizen to use such river as a highway, must, everywhere, within reasonable limits, accommodate itself to the same right in the public at large. The refusal of such reasonable accommodation is a nuisance. Thus, where a man obstinately refused to move his ship from opposite a wharf, although it would have been just the same if he had moved a little one way or the other, it was held, that he had abused his right, and that the party injured was entitled to recover. So, although the right to a fishery in a river is subordinate to the right of navigation, yet if one, using the river for the latter purpose, act wantonly and maliciously for the purpose of injuring the fishery, he is liable for the damage resulting from his acts.[1] Vessels have a right to use a warp in getting in or out of a harbor, but this must be done in a way not to interfere with the free navigation of other vessels. They may extend their warp across the entire channel, but, on the approach of another vessel, it is their duty to take notice of such approach, and lower their warp, so as to give ample space in the ordinary travelled part of the channel for her to pass, and to give timely notice of the space so left. If they neglect to lower their warp, and to give such notice, the approaching vessel is not liable for interference with the warp, although in fact ample space be left her to pass in some portion of the ordinary travelled part of the channel. But if, on the receipt of

---

737. An indictment will not lie for obstructing a highway, by holding a fair or market, if there has been an uninterrupted custom for twenty years. Rex *v.* Smith, 4 Esp. R. 109 ; Rex *v.* Canfield, 6 Esp. R. 136. And so a custom to erect a booth or stall, during the period of a fair or market, on any part of a public street or highway, (sufficient space being left for the public to pass,) is a good custom. Elwood *v.* Bullock, 13 Law J. N. S. 330. But a sale by a constable under an execution, in a public street, is a nuisance, notwithstanding a custom so to do for fifteen years. Commonwealth *v.* Milliman, 13 S. & R. (Penn.) R. 403. And see Wilkes *v.* Humgerford Market, 2 Bingh. R. N. C. 281.

[1] Anonymous, Durham Assizes, in note to 1 Campb. R. 516.

such notice, she chooses to take her course in a part of the channel other than that indicated by the notice, and so becomes entangled in the warp and cuts it, she will be liable for the damage, unless it can be shown that this is done in the belief, on the part of those in command, that there is depth of water over the warp sufficient to pass in the course taken, and that an honest, though mistaken, judgment is exercised in the matter, without any design or intention of interfering with the warp; it being the *primâ facie* presumption that the disregard of notice is reckless and wilful.[1]

§ 230. A nuisance, in the legal sense, is a culpable act or omission that occasions an obstruction, not the obstruction itself. Consequently, a person, who accidentally breaks or overturns a loaded wagon in the highway, is not guilty of nuisance, though there be an obstruction;[2] while, on the other hand, a person who does some act, which is the natural occasion of an obstruction on the part of others, is guilty of nuisance, though the act in itself be no obstruction. In Rex *v.* Carlisle,[3] the defendant, who was a bookseller in Fleet Street, having been distrained on for the non-payment of a church-rate, put into one of his windows the effigy of a bishop of the established church, under which was written "Spiritual Broker," and in the other window, a man in ordinary dress, under which was written "Temporal Broker," and afterwards

---

1 Potter and others *v.* Pettis, 2 R. I. Rep. 483, per Greene, C. J.

2 If a vessel be sunk in a river, by misfortune or inevitable accident, and without fault on the part of the owner, it is not indictable as a public nuisance, should the wreck not be removed. Rex *v.* Watts, 2 Esp. Rep. 675. But in such case, the owner is bound to place a buoy over the wreck; and to station a watchman near the obstruction, to point out the danger, is not sufficient. "It is a peremptory law of navigation," said Lord Ellenborough, "that when any substance is sunk in a navigable river so as to create danger, a buoy shall be placed over it for the safety of the public; and this was the proper and specific notice, which all understand and are bound to obey. A verbal communication," he added, "might be easily misunderstood, and was likely to lead to confusion and mischief." Hammond *v.* Pearson, 1 Campb. Rep. 515.

3 Rex *v.* Carlisle, 6 Carr. & Payne, R. 636.

added a figure of the devil, through the arm of which was tucked that of the bishop. The exhibition attracted a crowd to look at it, so that passengers, particularly old persons and females, were obliged to go off the footpath into the carriage-way, as there was not room for them to walk on the foot pavement. Park, J., admitting that the defendant had a right to do as he chose on his own premises, provided he did nothing to injure or annoy his neighbors or the public, instructed the jury that, if the exhibition caused the footway to be obstructed, so that the public could not pass as they ought to do, this was an indictable nuisance, and that it was not essential that the figures should be libellous, or that the crowd attracted should consist of idle, disorderly and dissolute persons. And, in reply to certain arguments addressed to the jury, he further said: "The defendant has compared this exhibition to the procession of the Judges going to Saint Paul's; however, in that case, the crowd who look at the procession, move on with it, and do not stand obstructing the street, as they have done in this case. The defendant has also observed upon the Lord Mayor's Day; however, that is but one day in the year; and if, instead of that, the Lord Mayor's Day lasted from October to December, I should say it ought to be put a stop to."

§ 231. In the case above referred to, Park, J., remarked: "One question is, whether this act of the defendant was at all necessary for the *bonâ fide* carrying on of his trade; for if it was, and he did not take up more time in the doing of it than was necessary, the law would do what it could to protect him." Undoubtedly, as man in the pursuit of his lawful business would be excused for acts, which, if wantonly done, would render him punishable for a nuisance;[1] but even in such a

---

[1] It is not impossible, that this consideration may have had weight with the Court, in quashing the indictment, in Rex *v.* Sannon, 1 Bur. R. 516, in which the defendant was charged with keeping a person upon an ancient common footway in London, to deliver out certain printed bills of her occupation, to persons passing that way, which she did for the space of four hours and more

case, the claims of private business must yield to the superior right of the public, whenever they would lead to an unreasonable interruption. Thus, in a recent case in New York, in which the nuisance complained of was occasioned by the congregation of carts in the public street, for the reception of slops from a distillery; it was insisted for the defendants, first, that, their business being lawful, they had a right to use, in carrying it on, so much of the public highway as was necessary for that purpose, provided they used reasonable diligence and dispatch; and, second, that they, not being the owners of the carts and teams there assembled, and having no control over them, were not responsible. But the Court held, as to the first point, that private interest must be made subservient to the general interest of the community, and that, if this business could not be carried on in any other manner at that place, so advantageously either to individuals or the public, the defendants must either enlarge their premises, or remove their business to some more convenient spot; and, as to the second, that, having furnished the occasion of the assembling, they were liable for the natural consequences.[1]

§ 232. It has been held, where the highway has been laid out and established of a certain width by statute, to be no justification, on an indictment for this offence, that the obstruction is placed in a part of the highway which has not been prepared, and cannot be used for travel, by reason of ledges of rocks and stones, and that said obstruction does not obstruct or hinder the travel thereon. The Court distinguished between the right of the public, or town, as against the individual, for an obstruction, and the right of the individual, by private action, under

---

together on every of several days specified, whereby said footway was greatly impeded and obstructed. The Court, without difficulty, we are told, quashed the indictment, though attempted by two or three counsel to be supported.

1 The People *v.* Cunningham, 1 Denio, (N. Y.) R. 524. And see Rex *v.* Moore, 3 B. & Ald. R. 184.

the statutes, as against the town for a defect or want of repair. The latter, it is said, "only requires a road of proper width, and kept in good repair. But the town, on the other hand, to enable itself to discharge its obligation to the public, requires the full and entire width of the whole located highway. The space between the made road and the exterior limits of the located highway, may be required for various purposes; as for making and keeping in repair the travelled path; for making sluices and watercourses; for furnishing earth to raise the road, and, not unfrequently, from the location of the road, and from its exposure to be obstructed by snow, the entire width of the located road is required to be kept open, to guard against accumulations of snow that might otherwise wholly obstruct the public travel at such seasons. For these and other uses, in aid of what is the leading object, the keeping in good repair the made or travelled road, the general easement in the public, acquired by the location of a highway, is coextensive with the exterior limits of the located highway; and the question of nuisance or no nuisance does not depend upon the fact, whether that part of the highway, which is alleged to have been unlawfully entered upon and obstructed by the defendant, was a portion of the highway capable of being used by the traveller."[1]

§ 233. In an indictment for a nuisance, the gravamen of the charge is the injury which the public have incurred in the enjoyment of their free right of passage in consequence of the act complained of; and, therefore, it has been argued, that if a benefit accrues to the public by reason of such act, which fully or more than compensates for the injury, there is no ground for indictment. This was the view urged upon the Court in Rex *v.* Morris,[2] in which case it appeared that the defendant, the proprietor of a colliery, had constructed a railroad from it to a

1 Commonwealth *v.* King, 13 Met. (Mass.) R. 115. An indictment and conviction are proper for obstructing a road established by re-location, even if it has not been used as a highway. Harrow *v.* The State, 1 Iowa (Green,) R. 439.

2 Rex *v.* Morris, 1 B. & Ad. R. 441.

seaport town, four hundred yards long, and laid upon a turnpike road, which it narrowed so far that in some places there was not a clear space for two carriages to pass. The public being allowed the use of the railroad upon paying toll, it was contended that, inasmuch as it was upon the whole a convenience to the public, by facilitating the conveyance and lessening the price of coals, and by saving the turnpike road from wear, it was not indictable. But Lord Tenterden, C. J., said: "Supposing that doctrine to be sound, which I am not prepared to say, how does it apply in this case? Here is a road for carts bringing down coals to Swansea, and it is for the convenience of an individual, who sends coals there for sale, to make a railway along the public road for their conveyance in wagons. It is said, indeed, that all persons may use this railway who will pay for so doing, but no man has a right to tell the public, that they shall discontinue the use of such carriages as they have been accustomed to employ, and adopt another kind, in order to pass along a new description of road, paying him for the liberty of doing so." It will be observed here, that Lord Tenterden, without either admitting or denying the doctrine contended for, contented himself with simply pointing out its inapplicability; the other Justices, Parke, J., and Patterson, J., did not even give it a passing consideration.

§ 234. In support of this doctrine, the counsel for the defendant in the above case relied very much upon the authority of Rex *v.* Russell.[1] This was an indictment for obstructing the navigation of the River Tyne, by the erection of staiths on the river, for the delivery of coal into vessels. In his charge to the jury, Bayley, J., said: "The use of a public water is not for passage only, but for many other purposes, and many of those purposes are entitled to supersede the right of passage, and to narrow the right of passage to those parts which may not be requisite for greater and more beneficial purposes. Where there is a space of water of very considerable extent,

---

[1] Rex *v.* Russell, 6 B. & C. R. 566.

some part may be most usefully applied for the purposes of commerce, and that which is so applied may be over and above that which is sufficient for navigation; and where a great public benefit results from the abridgment of the exercise of the rights of passage, the great public benefit makes that abridgment no nuisance, but a useful, beneficial, and proper purpose." And he suffered the jury to take into their consideration, as part of the public benefit, the possible reduction of prices at the staith, the possible reduction of prices in the London market, and the improved quality in which the coals would arrive there. Upon a motion for a new trial, Holroyd, J., and Bayley, J., sustained this charge. Lord Tenterden, C. J., was of the opinion, that the public benefit resulting from the better price and condition of the coals, could not properly be taken into consideration in the question raised by this indictment, which question was, he said, "whether the navigation and passage of vessels on this public navigable river, was injured by these erections." Lord Tenterden, therefore, when he refused to assent to this doctrine in Rex *v.* Morris, must be considered to have still retained the opinion here expressed, and to have intimated something more than a mere reluctance to acknowledge the authority of this case. And, indeed, it is not easy to understand by what legal principle this neutralization of a public wrong by a public benefit is effected. The principle, if sound, is certainly anomalous, for of no other offence could it be pleaded in justification that the public are benefited by its commission. And if any material abridgment of the public right can be authorized by reason of a compensatory benefit resulting therefrom, why may there not be a resultant benefit so preponderating as to authorize its entire destruction? But this, it will be admitted, could be justified by nothing short of a license from the sovereign power in the State.[1]

---

1 See, on this subject, Rex *v.* Grosvenor and others, 2 Starkie, 511, and Pilcher *v.* Hart, 1 Humph. (Tenn.) R. 524. In the later case, it was held, in ac-

§ 235. But, whatever doubts may have previously existed upon this subject, they are, at least in England, put at rest by the decision of the Court of King's Bench in The King *v.* Ward. There the defendant, having been indicted for a nuisance in a navigable river and common highway by erecting an embankment across the stream and waterway of the river, the jury found that the embankment was a nuisance, but that the inconvenience was counterbalanced by the public benefit arising from the alteration. The Court held, that this finding amounted to a verdict of guilty. Denman, C. J., subjected the case of Rex *v.* Russell to a very searching criticism. "In the infinite variety of active operations," he said, "always going forward in this industrious *community*, no greater evil can be conceived than the encouragement of capitalists and adventurers to interfere with known public rights from motives of personal interest, on the speculation that the changes made may be rendered lawful by ultimately being thought to supply the public with something better than what they actually enjoy. There is no practical inconvenience in abiding by the opposite principle, for daily experience proves that great and acknowledged public improvement soon leads to a corresponding change in the law, accompanied, however, with the just condition of being compelled to compensate any portion of the public which may suffer for their advantage." [1]

---

cordance with Rex *v.* Russell, that a permanent erection in a navigable stream, would not be a nuisance, if the general and public advantages arising from its erection greatly exceeded any slight inconvenience therefrom. But in Arundell *v.* McCulloch, 10 Mass. 70, a bridge over a navigable river, which had existed fifty years, was held to be a nuisance, not having been authorized by the legislature. To the same effect, see Charlestown *v.* Middlesex, 3 Met. (Mass.) R. 202; Commonwealth *v.* Charlestown, 1 Pick. (Mass.) R. 180; Simmons *v.* Mumford, 2 R. I. Rep. 174. It would seem, if the principle laid down in Pilcher *v.* Hart, be correct, it would have at least been alluded to in these cases.

[1] The King *v.* Ward, 4 Adolph. & Ellis, R. 384.

§ 236. Besides the acts, which are nuisances at common law and which are held not to be abolished by statutory enactment, the statute remedy being merely cumulative;[1] there are others which are made such by statute. These it is not proposed to enumerate. In many instances they are the same with those already treated of as nuisances at common law; and sometimes depend upon the nice interpretation of special statutes.

## 2. *Legalized Obstructions.*

§ 237. But not only may nuisances be made such by statute, but also obstructions, which at common law are nuisances, may by statute cease to be such. This most frequently happens in cases where power is granted to railroad, canal, or turnpike companies to pass over or along highways. Such statutes are strictly construed, and parties acting under them can do only that which they authorize, and in the precise way and manner therein prescribed. Therefore, a railroad company, which was authorized to raise or lower a highway in order that it might be crossed without obstructing or impeding the safe and convenient use thereof, was held not to be justified in widening or diverting its course or supplying its place with a new way, so that the railroad would be passed at a point different from its intersection with the original way, even though the change was for the convenience of the public.[2] Where, however, a railroad company were directed, in case they cut through a highway, to make a new road as convenient as the road to be cut through or as near thereto as might be, they were held not to be bound to make it absolutely as convenient if

---

1 Commonwealth *v.* King, 13 Met. (Mass.) R. 115; State *v.* Wilkinson, 2 Vt. R. 480.

2 Hughes *v.* The Providence and Worcester Railroad Co. 2 R. I. Rep. 493; and see Rex *v.* Morris, 1 B. & Ad. R. 441; Reg. *v.* Eastern Counties Railway, 2 Ad. & El. R. N. S. 569.

that could be done only by a very disproportionate and unwarrantable expenditure.[1]

§ 238. By a railway act, a company was empowered "to divert or alter any roads or ways in order the more conveniently to carry the same over or under the railway." The company, in carrying the road under the railway, had entered a skew bridge, which diverted the road to an angle of 45°, instead of 34°, which was the angle made at that particular point by the old line of the road. At the trial of an indictment against the company's engineer for so doing, the learned Judge directed the jury that, if the public sustained inconvenience by the alteration, they should find for the Crown; but that, if the work was done in a mode in which an experienced engineer would do it, having reasonable regard to the interests both of the company and the public, the company had a right to make such diversion. The jury having found for the defendant on the ruling, the Court refused to grant a new trial.[2] In that case it was observed, that "conveniently" means both for the company and the public.

§ 239. Where a company were authorized to use locomotive engines upon a railway made parallel and adjacent to an ancient highway, whereby the horses of persons using the highway were frightened, it was held that such interference with the rights of the public must be taken to have been contemplated and sanctioned by the legislature, since the words of the statute authorizing the use of the engines were unqualified, and the public benefit derived from the railway, (whether it would have excused the alleged nuisance at common law or not,) showed at least an express provision of the legislature

---

1 Reg. *v.* Scott, 3 Ad. & El. R. N. S. 543.

2 Reg. *v.* Sharpe, 3 Railw. Cas. 33; and see Reg. *v.* Eastern Counties Railway Co. 3 Railw. Cas. 22; Clarence Railway Co. *v.* Great North of England, Clarence and Hartlepool Junction Railway Co. 13 M. & W. R. 706; 3 Railw. Cas. 426.

giving such an unqualified authority was not unreasonable.[1] That which is authorized by an act of the legislature cannot be a nuisance.[2]

§ 240. But an authority, thus given, must be exercised with proper skill and care, and with the observance of such precautions as the character of the obstruction, or the statute which authorizes it demands.[3] Where the charter of a railroad company required them to purchase a turnpike road running parallel to the proposed railroad, and to assume the liabilities of that corporation, before they should be permitted to run cars upon their own road; and gave them the right to lay their railroad track across and along the bed of the turnpike, but required them "to restore the road to its former state, or in a sufficient manner not to impair its usefulness;" and the company, by virtue of these provisions, laid the track of the road by the side of the turnpike road for some distance; it was held, that, if the proximity of the railroad to the turnpike rendered it dangerous to persons travelling with teams on the latter, it was the duty of the defendants to protect them against that danger, and, if such protection could not be afforded by a fence or screen, to move the tracks of their respective roads at a greater distance from each other.[4]

§ 241. And this power of legitimating obstructions, which

---

1 Rex *v.* Pease, 4 B. & Adol. R. 30; Bordentown and S. Amboy Turnpike Co. *v.* Camden and Amboy Railroad Co. 2 Harr. (N. J.) R. 314.

2 The First Baptist Church, &c. *v.* The Utica and Schenectady Railroad Co. 6 Barb. (N. Y.) Sup. Ct. R. 313; Williams *v.* The New York Central Railroad Co. 18 Barb. (N. Y.) R. Sup. Ct. R. 222.

3 Bordentown and S. Amboy Turnpike Co. *v.* Camden and Amboy Railroad Co. *supra*.

4 Moshier *v.* The Utica and Schenectady Railroad Co. 8 Barb. (N. Y.) Sup. Ct. R. 427; and see The Attorney-General *v.* The Great Northern Railway Company, 3 Eng. L. & Eq. R. 263. The English statute requires the railroad company to maintain gates, whenever their track crosses a public road, and to employ proper persons to open and shut them; and to keep them constantly closed except when horses, &c. passing along such road have to cross the railway.

would otherwise be regarded as nuisances, is not of such sovereign character that it may not be delegated either by a specific act or by a general grant of authority. Thus, it is a usual provision of our railway charters that the companies may lay their tracks across or upon public roads or streets with the consent and under the direction of the town and city authorities. Municipal corporations have also large powers of this description, by virtue of the authority with which they are invested for the regulation and repair of highways. They have an undoubted right, for instance, to obstruct and even entirely discontinue a highway for the temporary purpose of repairing or regrading it. And in cities and villages there are many uses, aside from their mere use for foot-passengers and vehicles moved by animal power, to which the municipal governments may devote the streets under their control for the promotion of health, trade, commerce and the public convenience. Sewers and drains may be constructed, and water-pipes and gas-pipes laid in them by their authority.[1] "By the Dongan Charter," it is said, "the city of New York was invested with 'full power, license and authority to establish, appoint, order and direct the establishing, making, laying out, ordering, amending and repairing of all streets, lanes, alleys, highways, &c. in and throughout the city, necessary, needful and convenient for the inhabitants of said city and for all travellers and passengers there.' This power has never been withdrawn or essentially changed. The corporation yet has the exclusive right to control and regulate the use of the streets in the city. In this respect it is endowed with legislative sovereignty. The exercise of that sovereignty has no limit, so long as it is within the objects and trusts for which the power is conferred."[2]

---

1 Chapman *v.* Albany and Schenectady Railroad Co. 10 Barb. (N. Y.) Sup. Ct. R. 360; Plant *v.* Long Island Railroad Co. 10 Barb. (N. Y.) Sup. Ct. R. 26.

2 Per Harris, J., in Milhau *v.* Sharp, 17 Barb. (N. Y.) Sup. Ct. R. 435.

§ 242. In the State of New York it has been much mooted, whether the use of streets by railroads is a use to which such streets can be legitimately applied without express authority. And it has been said, if not definitively decided, that the laying a railroad in a street or highway is only a new and improved method of making use of the public easement over land dedicated or appropriated pursuant to law for a street or highway. "The use of a street for a railroad," it has been said, "consists merely in adapting its surface to a particular mode of conveyance; and when so adapted, the running of a railroad car is no more an exclusive appropriation of the street, than the running of any other species of conveyance would be. If the additional facilities for passage and repassage, which a railroad furnishes, will have the effect of increasing the use of the street, and thus cause some inconvenience to persons doing business, or residing in its neighborhood, yet, if it is not diverted from the purposes for which it was opened and laid out, no right of any person will be violated." [1]

§ 243. But while such are the views advanced by the New York courts, it does not seem to have been decided, in any case where that precise point has been raised, that municipal corporations, exclusive of express legislative authority, have the power to establish a railroad in a public street. In the Trustees of the Presbyterian Society of Waterloo *v.* The Auburn and Rochester Railroad Company,[2] the defendants, under

---

1 Williams *v.* New York Central Railroad Co. 18 Barb. (N. Y.) Sup. Ct. R. 222; but see Rex *v.* Morris, 1 B. & Ad. R. 441; Ante, § 233.

2 Trustees of the Presbyterian Society of Waterloo *v.* The Auburn and Rochester Railroad Co. 3 Hill, 567, recognized in Seneca Road Co. *v.* The Auburn and Rochester Railroad Co. 5 Ibid. 170. In Hamilton *v.* The New York and Harlem Railroad Co. 9 Paige, 171, an injunction to restrain the defendants from using their road laid in the streets of New York was refused, upon the ground that the defendants in constructing their road had complied with their charter, and that it did not interfere materially with the use of the streets and was not therefore a nuisance which the plaintiffs, owners of adjacent property, were entitled to have restrained.

the sanction of their charter, constructed their railroad upon the highway in front of the plaintiff's premises and without making him compensation, and it was held, that the plaintiff was owner of the soil of the highway, subject only to the public easement, and that the defendants could not use the highway for a railroad track without making compensation. In New Jersey and in Mississippi this decision has been directly affirmed; and, in Mississippi, the railroad was laid in the streets of a city, which is an important fact, as the cases which support the right of subjecting a highway to the use of a railroad have relied much upon an alleged distinction between highways in the country and in cities.[1]

§ 244. In Drake *v.* The Hudson River Railroad Company,[2] railway tracks were being laid in Canal and Hudson streets, in the city of New York, in compliance with the charter and with the assent of the city government. The plaintiffs, who were owners of land fronting on said streets, applied for an injunction to restrain the laying of the tracks. It appeared that the fee of the soil in the highway was vested in the city corporation; so that the only ground upon which the plaintiffs could claim the injunction, was the consequential damage to them as adjoining proprietors. But the Court, being of the opinion that the railway was an authorized and legal use of the highway and not a nuisance, held that the plaintiffs were not entitled to compensation for such damage and dismissed the application. Plant *v.* Long Island Railroad Company[3] was a similar case. The plaintiff, who was the owner of a retail dry

---

1 Starr *v.* Camden and Atlantic Railroad Co. 4 Zabrisk. (N. J.) R. 592; Donnaher *v.* The State of Mississippi, 8 S. & M. (Miss.) R. 649; and see The Clarence Railway Co. *v.* The Great North of England, Clarence, and Hartford Junction Railway Co. 4 Ad. & El. N. S. 46; Fletcher *v.* The Auburn and Syracuse Railroad Co. 25 Wend. (N. Y.) R. 462; but *ad contra*, Case of Trenton and Philadelphia Railroad Co. 6 Whart. (Penn.) R. 25.

2 Drake *v.* Hudson River Railroad Co. 7 Barb. (N. Y.) S. C. R. 508.

3 Plant *v.* Long Island Railroad Co. 10 Barb. (N. Y.) S. C. R. 26.

good store upon Atlantic Street, in the city of Brooklyn, brought an action on the case for the injury to his property and trade caused by the construction of a tunnel through the street. It appearing that the defendants had proceeded properly under their charter and with the consent of the city, and their right to the soil in the street without compensation not being in question, the Court held, that the damage to the plaintiff, if any there were, was merely *damnum absque injuria*, and would not support an action. In both these cases it was explicitly declared, although not necessary to the decision, that the use of the street with railroad cars, in a manner not unreasonably to obstruct the public travel, was a legitimate use of the public easement in the street, and that the city, when the streets were established, acquired the right to appropriate the land to all such legitimate uses as custom and the public good required.

§ 245. Several of the other New York cases, in which the same views were advanced, will be found to be open to the same criticism.[1] But in Williams *v.* New York Central Rail-

---

[1] Chapman *v.* Albany and Schenectady Railroad Co. 10 Barb. (N. Y.) S. C. R. 360. In this case the Court, while going the full length of preceding decisions on this point, say: "In whatever aspect this case may be considered, it seems to me that it must be held to belong to that numerous class of cases in which it has been held that persons acting under legal authority to grade or improve streets are not answerable for *consequential damages* which may be sustained by those who own land adjacent to the street, provided such authority is exercised with proper care and skill." In Adams *v.* Saratoga and Washington Railroad Co. 11 Barb. (N. Y.) S. C. R. 414, in which these views were reaffirmed, judgment was given against the plaintiff, who brought ejectment for land in the highway taken by the defendants, under their charter, for a railway, but without compensation to the owner of the fee, upon the ground that ejectment would not lie, the plaintiff not having the right of possession, but that trespass for the damages was the proper action. And in Milhau *v.* Sharp, 15 Barb. (N. Y.) S. C. R. 193, and 17 Ibid. 437, it was held to be beyond the authority of the Board of Aldermen of New York to grant to the defendants, an unincorporated company, power to establish a railroad in Broadway with certain exclusive privileges designed to be perpetual in their duration, upon the ground that such a grant was a surrender of a portion of their municipal authority and could only

road Company,[1] the question came before the Court in a more direct form. The action was brought to recover damages occasioned by the construction and use of the defendant's railroad on Washington Street, in Syracuse, by an owner of lands bounding on said street, and who claimed the fee of the soil to the centre. . The Court, having adjudged that the laying of the railroad was authorized by the defendant's charter and by the municipal authorities of Syracuse, say: "But it is insisted that the railroad acquired no right to occupy or use the street in question, notwithstanding the assumed permission of the municipal authorities of Syracuse, because no provision was made for compensation to the original proprietor of the land dedicated, pursuant to the provision of the constitution requiring compensation to be made to the owner of private property taken for public purposes. The answer to this is, that the property of the plaintiff has not been taken within the intent and meaning of the constitution. The original owner of the land in this case dedicated it to the public use, and although the legal presumption is, that the fee of the land is in the owner, yet the easement is wholly granted to the public. In the city of New York it has been repeatedly held, that the corporation has power to grant to a railroad company the privilege of laying their track through the streets of the city, and that the prohibition of the constitution which is against taking private property without compensation, does not apply to a case, where the complaint is, that the injuries are consequential and incidental upon the use which the party complained of is about to make or has made of the granted right; and that to allow a street in a city to be used for a railroad

---

be made with the sanction of the legislature. See also Stuyvesant *v.* Plousal, 15 Barb. (N. Y.) S. C. R. 244.

[1] Williams *v.* New York Central Railroad Co. 18 Barb. (N. Y.) S. C. R. 222, said to be under review in the Court of Appeals in The Attorney-General *v.* Sharpe, New York Daily Times, Jan. 10, 1857; and see also Wetmore *v.* Story, 22 Barb. (N. Y.) S. C. R. 444.

track, either upon its natural surface or by tunnelling, is not a misapplication of it, provided such use does not interfere with the free use of it as a highway for passage and repassage. The legislative authority is competent to declare the uses to which highways may be appropriated, and to impart to municipal corporations, both permissive and restraining powers over the subject-matter. They have exercised the power in both forms, and the appropriate authority has declared, in this case, that the use of Washington Street by the railroad of the defendants is a legitimate and proper mode of enjoying the easement dedicated to the public. It is insisted with pertinency and force on the part of the defendants that there is an inherent power in every government to take property for public use, except where the power is retained by an express and precise constitutional provision. If, therefore, neither the constitution or the laws have been transcended, in a given case, no individual can sustain a suit against a party exercising a right granted to him by competent authority."

§ 246. Against this strong current of dicta and decision may be quoted the language of Denio, C. J., used in a recent case, in which it was held, that a grant of right to establish a railroad in Broadway, in New York city, was not in the terms in which they assumed to make the grant, within the power of the municipal corporation, because it amounted to a franchise or monopoly. "The feature," he says, "which most widely distinguishes a railroad from an ordinary highway or street is, that the former is a strict monopoly, entirely excluding all idea of competition. A traveller who would go upon a railroad must take his seat in the carriage of the proprietors of the road and pay them the price of his transportation. The nature of the subject requires a unity of control and management, which precludes the existence of competing carriages. There may be rival roads, but there can be no rivalry on the same road; and no more than one road can exist in Broadway without excluding altogether every other kind of travellers with

19 *

carriages. We may be allowed, without the testimony of witnesses, to know enough of the method of operating railroads, to say, that their carriages are quite unlike the vehicles used on other roads. They are necessarily large machines occupying the space which would be required for several carriages of any other kind, and containing passengers enough to fill a great many of the carriages used on other streets or roads. I have mentioned these particulars which distinguish a railroad from every other species of way for the purpose of explaining the reason why, in my judgment, *the establishment of such a road is not within the jurisdiction conferred upon the public authorities by the general laws relative to highways, or upon the corporation of New York, over the roads and streets in that city.* The power of the corporation over this subject is necessarily very large. It may lay out, open, alter, repair, and amend and regulate streets, lanes, alleys, and highways, and may direct the draining, ditching and paving of them; and, moreover, the common council are commissioners of highways; and they may discontinue and close up streets in the manner specified in the statutes.[1] But this power relates to and is confined to streets, &c. as such. Every thing which is fairly within the idea of regulating, altering, repairing or amending the streets with a view to their uses and purposes as streets may be exercised by the corporation, but the converting of a street or a part of a street into a piece of machinery for transporting persons with which the existence of a street has no natural or necessary connection is not, in my judgment, at all within the purview of the charters and acts of the legislature to which I have referred. If an existing street can be converted into a railway, I see no reason why the corporation may not authorize the laying out of a railroad where at present no street exists. They have as ample power to lay out and establish streets as

---

[1] The Montgomerie Charter, Kent Charters, pp. 15, 99, and note 31 at p. 235; R. L. 1813, §§ 193 to 197; Laws, 1818, ch. 213; Laws, 1824, ch. 39.

to alter and amend them; and if they can consider a railway as falling within the legal notion of a street, the power extends as well to the laying out of new railroads as to changing the present streets into railroads. They can exercise the right of eminent domain in the opening of new streets; and if a railroad is only an improved species of street, the power could be rightfully applied in constructing a railroad wherever it might be considered that the public good would be promoted by it."[1]

§ 247. In Kentucky, in the case of The Lexington and Ohio Railroad *v.* Applegate,[2] the question came before the Court in regard to the city government of Louisville, and, in that case, the right of the city to authorize the location, construction, and use of a railroad through the streets, was affirmed. The owners of property on the streets, it was maintained, held or acquired the same subject to all the consequences which might result, whether advantageously or disadvantageously, from any public and authorized use of the streets, in any mode promotive of, and consistent with, the purposes of establishing them as common highways in towns, and compatible with the reasonable enjoyment of them by all others entitled thereto. "The onward spirit of the age," said Robertson, C. J., in delivering the opinion, "must to a reasonable extent have its way. The law is made for the times and will be made and modified by them. The expanded and still expanding genius of the common law should adapt it here, as elsewhere, to the improved and improving condition of our country and our countrymen. And therefore railroads and locomotive steam cars—the offspring, as they will also be the parent of progressive improvement—should not, in themselves, be considered as nuisances, although, in ages that are gone, they might have been so held, because they would have

1 The Attorney-General *v.* Sharp, reported in the New York Daily Times, January 10, 1857, from a copy furnished by F. Keenan, Reporter; and see Regina *v.* Charlesworth, 22 Eng. Law & Eq. R. 235.

2 The Lexington and Ohio Railroad *v.* Applegate, 8 Dana (Ky.) R. 289.

been comparatively useless and therefore more mischievous." Indeed the weight of the authorities, at present, seems to be, that a railroad in a street is not *per se* a nuisance, and that it may be so conducted and regulated as to be considered not only a lawful but even an improved mode of using the public easement, though there still remains no little uncertainty in the law on this point.[1]

§ 248. A very common kind of nuisances, which cease to be such when authorized by the legislature, is that of bridges over navigable rivers. In the United States, as has been already stated, an act of the legislature authorizing the erection of such bridges, within the limits of the State, is clearly constitutional.[2] This power, however, is subordinate to the power vested in congress, "to regulate commerce with foreign nations, and among the several States, and with the Indian tribes," and any exercise of the power by a State, which in any manner conflicts with laws passed in pursuance of this provision, is to that extent unconstitutional. In a New York case, it was contended, that an act authorizing the erection of a bridge across a navigable river, at a point below where the coasting trade was carried on by licensed vessels, was repugnant to the act of congress regulating that trade, and, therefore, void; and the bridge, built in compliance with its provisions, a nuisance. But in that case, it was held, that both the State and the General Government have rights which they may exercise over and upon navigable waters, and that it is the duty of both so to exercise their several portions of the sovereign power, that the greatest good may result to the citizens at large; and that a bridge with a draw, which shall be opened free of expense for every vessel sailing under a license as a coasting vessel, while it affords the necessary accommodations for citizens in the vicinity, or for travellers, does not impede the navigation in any

---

1 See *Ante*, § 33, and note.

2 *Ante*, § 41, and the authorities there cited.

essential degree, nor come in collision with any law passed by congress for the regulation of commerce.[1]

§ 249. In The United States *v.* The New Bedford Bridge,[2] it was decided, that an indictment would not lie in the Courts of the United States for the obstruction of a navigable river by a bridge. Woodbury, J., in delivering the opinion, expressed his conviction, that the power conferred on congress to regulate commerce abroad, and between the States, authorizes it to keep open and free all navigable rivers, from the ocean to the highest ports of delivery or entry, and protect the intercourse between two or more States, on all our tide waters, and to this end to pass acts for the removal and punishment of unauthorized obstructions. But, he held, congress has not yet exercised this power by declaring such obstructions to be offences, and until it does declare them to be such, and prescribes the extent of punishment and place of trial, though the subject-matter is within the powers granted to the general government, no particular Court has any right to try a person for causing the obstruction, or to affix any punishment to them. But he intimated the objection against treating as a crime what has *not* been made so by any clause in the constitution, or any act of congress, does not apply to a civil suit; and, consequently, when an individual suffers special damage by such an obstruction, he may have civil redress by a suit, though the obstruction be authorized by a State, if it is contrary to the constitution, or conflicts with some clause in the acts of congress, such as a coastwise license.

§ 250. The doctrine, that an individual, who suffers special damage, may proceed civilly against the party who causes such

---

1 The People *v.* Saratoga and Rensselaer Railroad Co. 15 Wend. (N. Y.) R. 113; Gibbons *v.* Ogden, 9 Wheat. (U. S.) R. 203; Wilson *v.* The Blackbird Creek Marsh Co. 2 Peters, (U. S.) R. 245; State of Pennsylvania *v.* Wheeling Bridge Co. *et al.* 13 Howard, (U. S.) R. 518.

2 The United States *v.* The New Bedford Bridge, 1 Woodb. & Min. (Cir. Ct.) Rep. 401.

an obstruction, was established in the case of The State of Pennsylvania *v.* The Wheeling Bridge Company *et al.*[1] This was a bridge over the Ohio River, erected under the authority of a statute of Virginia. The State of Pennsylvania, having constructed lines of canal and railroad, and other means of travel and transportation, in the diminution of the revenues from which they would be specially injured by this obstruction of the Ohio River, proceeded on the Equity side of the United States Court for an injunction to have the bridge abated as a nuisance. It appeared that the bridge, which was a suspension-bridge, was so constructed as not to be an obstruction to the free navigation of the river by any vessels propelled by sails, which then were, or were likely to become engaged in the commerce or navigation of the river; and that, of the two hundred and fifty steam vessels which plied upon the river, only seven of the larger sized packets were interrupted; and this interruption was occasioned by the height of the chimneys, and might be remedied by shortening the chimneys, or by contriving them so that they could be lowered in passing under the bridge, though not without considerable injury and expense to the vessels. The Court decided that, the Ohio being a navigable stream, subject to the commercial power of congress, and over which that power has been exerted, if the act of Virginia authorized the structure of the bridge, so as to obstruct navigation, it could afford no justification to the Bridge company. "Congress," said McLean, J., "have not declared in terms that a State, by the construction of bridges, or otherwise, shall not obstruct the navigation of the Ohio; but they have regulated navigation upon it, as before remarked, by licensing vessels, establishing ports of entry, imposing duties upon masters and other officers of boats, and inflicting severe penalties for the neglect of those duties, by which damage to life or property has resulted."

[1] The State of Pennsylvania *v.* The Wheeling Bridge Co. *et al.* 13 Howard, (U. S.) R. 518.

And the Court determined, that the complainant was entitled to have the navigation of the said river made free, either by the abatement or elevation of the bridge, so that it would cease to be an obstruction, in ordinary stages of high-water, to the largest class of steam vessels navigating the Ohio River; and decreed accordingly.[1]

§ 251. If a bridge, erected under the sanction of a State statute, is a nuisance whenever it obstructs the free navigation of a public river, it follows that, even though not open to objection when first erected, such a bridge may subsequently become a nuisance. Congress, under its constitutional power to regulate commerce, may make it so by subsequent legislation; or, in the lapse of time, it may become such by causing accumulations of sand and a shoalness in the channel, so as to obstruct passing and repassing with vessels; or, by an increase in the size of vessels and steamboats, or in the height of their masts or chimneys, or by a large addition in their number, or a change in the modes of navigation, so as to render that which at first afforded ample accommodations for their passage wholly insufficient for this purpose.[2]

### 3. *Want of Reparation at Common Law.*

§ 252. This species of nuisance, as has been remarked, can only be committed by those upon whom an obligation lies to

---

1 As an additional ground for this decision, the Court referred to the compact made by Virginia with Kentucky, at the time of its admission into the Union, "that the use and navigation of the River Ohio, so far as the territory of the proposed State, or the territory that shall remain within the limits of this Commonwealth lies thereon, shall be *free* and common to the citizens of the United States," which compact, by the sanction of congress, had become a law of the Union. But though the existence of this compact afforded a second ground, there is no intimation that the ground, which has been stated in the text, would not have been a sufficient basis for the decision.

2 The United States *v.* The New Bedford Bridge, 1 Woodb. & Min. (Cir. Ct.) R. 401.

keep highways in repair. In England, the inhabitants of the several parishes at large are *primâ facie* and of common right bound to repair all highways lying within them, unless by prescription or otherwise they can throw the burden upon particular persons; and if it be sought to charge a particular division of a parish, it must be shown how they are bound.[1] So stringent is this obligation, that if others, before liable, become unable through insolvency to make the repair,[2] or if an inferior district of a parish, bound by prescription to repair the roads within it, be expressly exempted by statute,[3] the common-law liability re-attaches upon the parish. No agreement by the parish with any person for the making of the repairs, and no statute imposing an obligation to repair upon other parties, will exonerate the parish from its liability, or do more than give it a remedy over against the parties so charged.[4] Indeed, so conclusive is this obligation at common law, that an indictment, stating that particular persons ought to repair, without averring a special cause for charging them, is bad. It must show *how* they are bound; and it is not enough to show that they immemorially ought to repair; it should be shown that they have repaired.[5] The parish, if it would discharge itself, must point out the party who is liable, by special plea; for under the plea of not

---

1 1 Hawk. P. C. c. 76, §§ 5, 6, 7, 8; 1 Ventr. 90; Austin's case, 1 Ventr. 189; Rex *v.* The Mayor, &c. of Warwick, 2 Show. R. 201; Rex *v.* Ragley, 12 Mod. R. 409; Anonymous, 1 Ld. Raymond, R. 725; Rex *v.* Great Broughton, 5 Burr. R. 2700; Rex *v.* Stoughton, 2 Wms. Saunders, R. 159 *c;* Rex *v.* Ecclesfield, 1 B. & Ald. R. 348; Rex *v.* St. Andrew, 1 Mod. R. 112; Rex *v.* Eastington, 5 Ad. & El. R. 765.

2 Anonymous, 1 Ld. Raym. R. 725.

3 Rex *v.* Sheffield, 2 T. R. 108; Rex *v.* Oxfordshire, 4 B. & C. R. 194.

4 Rex *v.* St. George, Hanover Square, 3 Campb. R. 222; Rex *v.* Liverpool, 3 East, R. 86; Rex *v.* Scarisbrook, 6 Ad. & El. R. 509; Rex *v.* Neatherthong, 2 B. & Ald. R. 179.

5 Rex *v.* Great Broughton, 5 Burr, R. 2700; Rex *v.* Penderryn, 2 T. R. 513; Rex *v.* Mile End, Str. 163; Regina *v.* Scott, 2 Ld. Raym. R. 222; Regina *v.* Frydden, 10 Eng. Law and Eq. R. 402.

guilty, it can only prove that the way is in good repair.[1] Former conviction against a parish is conclusive evidence of its liability to repair.[2]

§ 253. But although, in England, a parish is *primâ facie* and of common right liable to repair all highways within its limits, yet particular persons or districts of the parish may be burdened with this charge, in exemption of the parish at large; first, in respect of enclosure, and secondly, by prescription.

§ 254. *As to Liability in respect of Enclosure.* If a common highway is so founderous and out of repair as to become impassable, or even dangerous or incommodious to travellers, the public have a right to go upon the adjacent land, whether it be sown with grain or not.[3] An enclosure of the highway takes away that liberty and convenience; and, therefore, if the owner of land not enclosed, next adjoining to a highway, encloses his land on both sides, he is bound to make a *perfect good way* as long as the enclosure lasts; and he is not excused by showing that he has made the way as good as it was at the time of the enclosure; because if it was then defective the public might have gone on the adjoining land.[4] So if one encloses land on one side which has been anciently enclosed on the other side, he ought to repair all the way; but if there is no such ancient enclosure on the other side, he ought to repair but half the way.[5] Also, it seems that, if, after one has enclosed a highway, he suffers it to be so much out of repair as to be impas-

---

1 Rex *v.* Stoughton, 2 Wms. Saund. R. 159; Rex *v.* St. Andrews, 1 Mod. 112; Little Bolton *v.* Regina, 12 Law J., N. S., M. C., 104. As to the liability of extra-parochial places, see Reg. *v.* Kingsmoor, 2 B. & C. R. 190; Reg. *v.* Midville, 4 Ad. & Ell. R., N. S. 240.

2 Regina *v.* Nether Hallam, 29 Eng. Law & Eq. R. 200.

3 1 Roll. Abr. 390, (A.) pl. 1, and (B.) pl. 1; Absor *v.* French, 2 Show. 28; Taylor *v.* Whitehead, Doug. R. 749.

4 1 Roll. Abr. 390, (B.) pl. 1; Duncombe's case, Cro. Car. 366; Styles, 364; 2 Ld. Raym. R. 1170.

5 Rex *v.* Stoughton, 1 Hawk. P. C. 76, § 7.

sable, it is lawful for passengers to make gaps in his hedges, and to avoid the ill way, so that they do not ride further into his enclosed grounds than is needful for avoiding the bad way.[1] Where, however, the way is altered or changed, and enclosed by a legal proceeding, or is enclosed under the authority of an act of parliament for dividing and enclosing open common fields, the person who encloses is not bound to repair it, unless in the case of a writ *ad quod damnum* the jury impose such a condition upon him, or unless the new way lies in another parish.[2] And if the owner destroy his enclosures and again open the way, it seems that he will be freed from the repair thereof; and the burden shall thereupon revert to the parish.[3] In the case of footpaths, all stiles between different enclosures must be kept in good repair by the occupiers of the field; and it is sufficient to indict him as occupier, and not as owner, for the public are not obliged to search out who is owner.[4]

§ 255. *Of Liability by Prescription.* A particular person cannot be bound to such a duty by a general prescription, from what his ancestors have done, if it be not in respect of the tenure of his land, taking of toll or other profit; for the act of the ancestor cannot charge the heir without profit. Where, therefore, this liability is pleaded as chargeable on particular persons, the plea must state the *consideration* on account of which such persons are bound to repair; for the parish being liable as of common right, cannot exonerate themselves unless they show that the burden is cast upon some other persons, under an obligation equally durable with that which would have bound the parish, which obligation must arise in respect of some consideration of a nature as durable as the burden cast

---

1 Berni's case, Sir W. Jones, 296; 3 Salk. R. 180.

2 *Ex parte* Vernon, 3 Atk. R. 771; Rex *v.* Flecknow, 1 Burr, R. 465; 2 Wms. Saund. R. 160, n. 12; Rex *v.* Commissioners of Llandillo, 2 T. R. 232.

3 2 Wms. Saund. R. 160.

4 1 Salk. 357, pl. 3; 7 Mod. Rep. 55.

upon them.[1] But, though in the case of individuals there must be such a consideration, it is said that a corporation aggregate may be compelled to do it by force of a general prescription, "that it ought and hath used to do it," without showing that it used to do so in respect of the tenure of certain lands, or for any other consideration; because such a corporation, in judgment of law, never dies; and, therefore, if it were ever bound to such a duty, it needs must continue to be always so; neither is it any plea, that such a corporation have always done it out of charity, for what it hath always done, it shall be presumed to have been always bound to do.[2] Likewise, a particular district or division of a parish may be bound by prescription to repair the highways within its limits, and a plea alleging this fact need not state any consideration for the liability, though in order to charge it with the repair of a highway, the highway must be stated in the indictment to be situated therein. But such a charge is said more properly to be considered as originating in a custom than a prescription; the distinction between which is, that a prescription is always alleged in the person; a custom ought always to be alleged in the land or place; a prescription ought to have, by common intendment, a lawful beginning; a custom may be good although the particular reason of it cannot be assigned, for it suffices if no good reason can be assigned against it. Custom, therefore, being the ground of the liability, must be specially alleged in an indictment against a district or township, for not repairing.[3] So, it seems, that several

---

1 Bac. Abr. Highways, (F.,) 13 Rep. 33; Rex *v.* St. Giles, Cambridge, 5 Maule & S. R. 260; Regina *v.* Blakemore, 9 Eng. Law & Eq. R. 541.

2 1 Hawk. P. C. c. 76, § 8; c. 77, § 2; Rex *v.* Liverpool, 3 East, R. 86; Rex *v.* Stratford-upon-Avon, 14 East, R. 348; Rex *v.* Gloucester and Birmingham Railway Company, 9 Carr. & P. R. 469; Rex *v.* Machynlleth, 2 B. & C. R. 166.

3 Rex *v.* Ecclesfield, 1 B. & Ald. R. 348; Rex *v.* West Riding of Yorkshire, 4 B. & Ald. R. 623; Rex *v.* Machynlleth, 2 B. & C. R. 166; Rex *v.* Heage, 1 Gale & D. R. 548; 2 Ad. & E. R., N. S. 128; Regina *v.* Barnoldswick, 4 Ad. & E. R., N. S. 499; Rex *v.* Hatfield, 4 B. & A. R. 75; Rex *v.* Great Broughton, 5 Barr. R. 2700.

townships may be chargeable conjointly with the repair of a highway; and that one parish may by prescription be bound to repair a highway in another parish.[1] But if a way be enlarged, it seems that those who were before liable by prescription to repair it, shall not have their burden increased on account of such enlargement, but that the repair of the new part of the way shall be made at the expense of the parish.[2]

§ 256. Where lands, bound to the repair of a bridge or highway *ratione tenuræ*, are conveyed to several persons, every one of the grantees, being a tenant of any parcel, is liable to the whole charge, and must have contribution from the others. And the grantees are chargeable with the repair, though the grantor should convey the land or manor discharged of the burden, in which case the grantees must have their remedy over against the grantor. And the reason seems to be, because the whole manor or land, being once chargeable with the repair, the law will not suffer the owner to apportion the charge, so as to make the remedy for the public more difficult, since the necessity of the case requires the greatest expedition in cases of this nature; or, by alienations to insolvent persons, to render the remedy against such persons quite frustrate. And though such land or manor come into the hands of the crown, yet the obligation or duty continues; and any person afterwards claiming the whole, or any part of it, under the crown, will be liable to an indictment for not repairing.[3]

§ 257. *Repair of Bridges.* In England, at common law, all public bridges are *primâ facie* repairable by the inhabitants of the county without distinction of foot, horse or car-

---

1 Rex *v.* Bishop of Auckland, 1 Adol. & Ell. R. 749; 12 Mod. R. 409; Vin. Abr. Chirain, B. pl. 2.

2 Rex *v.* St. Pancras, Peake, R. 286; Rex *v.* Townsend, 1 Doug. R. 421; 2 Camp. R. 494; 12 East, R. 368.

3 Regina *v.* Buccleugh, 1 Salk. R. 358; Rex *v.* Buckeridge, 4 Mod. Rep. 48; 3 Vin. Abr. Apportionment, S., pl. 9; 1 Hawk. P. C. c. 77, § 3; Rex *v.* Oxfordshire, 16 East, R. 223.

riage bridges, unless they can show that others are bound to repair particular bridges; the liability of a county in this respect being the same as that of a parish with respect to highways.[1] Bridges, to be repairable by the county, must, however, be public; that is, built in a highway and common to all the king's subjects; and must, further, be erected over such water as answers the description of *flumen vel cursus aquæ;* that is, water flowing in a channel between banks more or less defined, although such channel may be occasionally dry.[2] Whenever such a bridge is built, though it be the work of a private individual, undertaken for his own convenience, or even of the trustees under a turnpike act, who are empowered to raise tolls for the support of the roads, if it becomes useful to the county in general, the county shall repair it.[3] But this duty of reparation does not oblige a county to widen bridges which have become too narrow for the convenient use thereof by the public.[4] And though it *primâ facie* attaches upon the county, yet may it be transferred to bodies politic, smaller districts, or individuals, by reason of prescription, custom, or the tenure of land, upon precisely the same principles as apply in this respect to highways in general.[5] And if part of a bridge lie within a franchise, those of the franchise may be charged with the repairs for so much; also, by a special

---

1 1 Hawk. P. C. c. 77, § 1; 2 Inst. 701; Rex *v.* W. R. of Yorkshire, 5 Burr. 2594; 2 W. Bl. 685; Lofft. 238; 2 East, 342; Rex *v.* Salop, 13 East, 95; Regina *v.* Southampton, 14 Eng. Law & Eq. R. 116.

2 Rex *v.* Kent, 2 East, R. 342; Rex *v.* Northampton, 2 Maule & S. R. 262; Rex *v.* Devon, R. & M. R. 144; Rex *v.* Buckinghamshire, 4 Campb. R. 189; Rex *v.* Oxfordshire, 1 B. & Adol. R. 289; Rex *v.* Derbyshire, 2 Ad. & El. R., N. S. 745; Rex *v.* Trafford, 1 B. & Ad. R. 874; 8 Bing. R. 204; Rex *v.* Whitney, 4 Nev. & M. R. 594; 7 Carr. & P. R. 208.

3 2 Inst. 701; 1 Salk. R. 359; Glasburne Bridge case, 5 Burr. R. 2594; 2 W. Bl. R. 685; 2 East, R. 353, n.; 2 East, R. 356, n.; 2 East, R. 342; Rex *v.* Lancashire, 2 B. & Adol. R. 813; Rex *v.* Kent, 2 Maule & S. R. 513.

4 Rex *v.* Cumberland, 6 T. R. 194; 3 Bos. & P. R. 354; Rex *v.* Devon, 4 B. & C. R. 670.

5 See *Ante*, § 253, *et seq.*

tenure, a person may be charged with the repairs of one part of a bridge, and the inhabitants of the county be liable to repair the rest.[1] And if a foot bridge or horse bridge, with the repair of which an individual or township is charged, be enlarged to a carriage bridge, the reparation thereof shall be made as to the new by the county, and as to the old part by the individual or township *pro rata*.[2] By Stat. 22 Hen. VIII. c. 5, § 9, the inhabitants of a county are bound to repair to the extent of three hundred feet of the highway at each end of the bridge; and *primâ facie* a party, who is liable by prescription to repair a bridge, is also liable to repair the highway to the same extent.[3]

### 4. *Want of Reparation in the United States.*

§ 258. Such, in England, is the obligation of maintaining and repairing highways and bridges at common law. In the United States, at common law, this obligation does not exist; but in most of the States is imposed by statute on the several towns in which the highways are situate. In England, it was incident to a peculiar form of territorial organization, originating like itself in immemorial usage; and when the American colonists left that organization behind them, they necessarily left the incidental obligation with it. "There is," says Selden, J., in delivering the judgment of the Supreme Court of New York, "no very close correspondence between the nature and object of the organization of towns in this State and that of parishes in England. While the former are exclusively

---

1 1 Hawk. P. C. c. 77, § 1.

2 Rex *v.* W. R. of Yorkshire, 2 East, R. 353; Regina *v.* Brecknockshire, 3 Eng. Law & Eq. R. 402.

3 Ibid.; Rex *v.* W. R. of Yorkshire, 7 East, R. 588; 5 Taunt. R. 284; 3 Smith, R. 437; Reg. *v.* Lincoln, 8 Ad. & E. R. 65. See the very excellent treatise of Leonard Shelford, Esq. on Highways, pp. 34 to 42, and 44 to 52, of which this and the preceding sections relating to the common-law liability to repair highways is little more than an abridgment.

political in their character, the latter were primarily ecclesiastical, and only incidentally political through the connection in England between the church and the government. But again, towns were known in England and recognized as political bodies as well as, and distinct from, parishes; and a single parish might and frequently did embrace a number of towns. The obligation, however, to repair the roads never rested upon the towns as such, unless by force of some statute or special usage and prescription. It is clear, therefore, that towns, in this country, do not succeed to the duty of repairing highways in consequence of any special correspondence between their nature, organization, and functions, and those of parishes in England; but if at all, it must be because, by our statutes, certain powers are given to and certain duties imposed upon towns, or rather upon their officers, in regard to roads, and because the making and repairing of roads are, to a considerable extent, accomplished through our town organizations. But it is difficult to see how this common-law obligation, the sole foundation of which is prescription or immemorial usage, can be made to attach to bodies of modern statutory creation, unknown to the common law as they exist here. The corporate powers of towns, in this State, are clearly and fully defined by our statutes, and their obligations can only be coextensive with their powers."[1]

§ 259. But though the towns in this country are amenable to no other rule, and only to the precise measure of obligation prescribed by statute; yet, in kind and degree, that obligation is very much the same as at common law, or differs only by its severer stringency.[2] Convenience and safety are the essential

---

1 Morey *v.* Newfane, 8 Barb. (N. Y.) S. Ct. R. 645; Loker *v.* Brookline, 13 Pick. (Mass.) R. 343; Commonwealth *v.* Springfield, 7 Mass. R. 13. But see Commonwealth *v.* Hopkinsville, 7 B. Mon. (Ky.) 38; City of Talahassee *v.* Fortune, 3 Flor. R. 19; People *v.* Albany, 11 Wend. (N. Y.) R. 539; State *v.* Murfreesboro, 11 Humph. (Tenn.) R. 217.

2 In Massachusetts, Maine, and Rhode Island, the obligation imposed by

conditions of a well-maintained highway, both at common law and by statute. Whether or not any given highway fulfils those conditions is a mixed question of law and fact, to be determined by the jury upon the circumstances of each particular case, under proper legal instructions from the Court.[1] In determining this question it is the duty of the jury to consider the location of the road, the geographical features of the country, the difficulty of keeping it in a better condition without an unreasonable expense, the season of the year and the kind and amount of travel having occasion to pass over it. A road which would be safe and convenient in the country might be totally unsafe and inconvenient in the city. And this distinction applies not only to the width, but also to the hardness, smoothness, and evenness of the street. A street thickly built with shops and houses, crowded at once with heavy and bulky loads, lighter teams and wagons, horse wagons, market carts, and all the variety of light conveyances for the transportation of persons going necessarily at very different rates of speed, with the ordinary exigencies of frequently crossing, recrossing, and stopping for purposes of business at the various shops and houses, might in a few hours be crushed and broken up, if made of materials which yet would maintain a smooth and unbroken surface in a thinly settled place, and would become completely choked, if of no greater

---

statute is, that the towns shall keep their highways in repair, "so that the same may be safe and convenient for travellers, with their teams, carts and carriages at all seasons of the year." Rev. Sts. of Massachusetts, ch. 25, sect. 1; Rev. Sts. of Maine, tit. 111, sect. 57; Public Laws of Rhode Island, p. 323, sect. 1. In Vermont and Connecticut, the obligation is to keep the highways "in good and sufficient repair." Comp. Sts. of Vermont, ch. 23, sect. 1; Rev. Sts. of Conn. tit. 24, ch. 1, sect. 1.

[1] Green *v.* Danby, 12 Vt. R. 338; Kelsey *v.* Glover, 15 Vt. R. 708; Rice *v.* Montpelier, 19 Vt. R. 470; Fitz *v.* Boston, 4 Cush. (Mass.) R. 365; Merrill *v.* Hampden, 26 Maine R. 234; City of Providence *v.* Clapp, 17 How. (U. S.) R. 161; Sessions *v.* Newport, 23 Vt. R. 9.

width than would furnish ample room for the travel of such place.[1]

§ 260. This obligation on the part of the town extends not only to the ordinarily travelled path of the highway, but also to the gutters and margins, and in cities to the sidewalks. But the measure of this obligation, as in the case of the travelled path, varies with the circumstances of each particular road; the nature of the country, whether rough, smooth, or hilly; the amount of travel and the places near on which carriages could be turned out. It has, however, been said that the extent of the responsibility of towns for defects and obstructions exterior to the wrought or travelled way, and for injuries suffered from such defects or obstructions, in the use of that portion of the way, is mainly a question of law, calling for special instructions from the Court.[2] It is not required that towns—at least in the country—should incur the expense of having the whole width of a highway, of two or four rods, passable safely with wheels on the sides, or even a double track for wheels over all public roads including causeways and bridges.[3] In many cases, as has been remarked, all the property of the town would be insufficient for that purpose. There may be ledges of rocks, ravines and watercourses in the road, and towns are not expected in all cases to bridge the whole width of the road, to fill up ravines or cut down ledges of rock. The most that could be required in a road so difficult by nature, is, that the sides should be in such a state as would admit of the passing of carriages when they meet without unusual delay

---

1 Hull *v.* Richmond, 2 Woodb. & M. (Cir. Ct.) R. 337; Fitz *v.* Boston, 4 Cush. (Mass.) R. 365; Church *v.* Cherryfield, 33 Maine R. 460.

2 Rice *v.* Montpelier, 19 Vt. R. 470.

3 Kelsey *v.* Glover, 15 Vt. R. 708; Green *v.* Danby, 12 Vt. R. 338; Cobb *v.* Standish, 14 Maine R. 198; Johnson *v.* Whitefield, 18 Maine R. 286; Bigelow *v.* Weston, 3 Pick. (Mass.) R. 267; Hull *v.* Richmond, 2 Woodb. & M. (Cir. Ct.) R. 337; Coggswell *v.* Lexington, 4 Cush. (Mass.) R. 307; Snow *v.* Adams, 1 Cush. (Mass.) R. 443.

or trouble. "If a road," says Woodbury, J., in the case of Hull *v.* Richmond, "was on a steep mountain's side, or was carried up from the bed of a stream against a steep cliff of rocks or through a narrow notch or gorge among the hills, a double track would seldom be expected, though places should be made at no great distances for persons to turn out entirely, and others, where, by each turning out in part, each could safely pass. Some of these distances, like the Jew's Leap, in Africa, or the Notch of the White Hills, or some modern tunnels, might be so far apart as to require a horn to be blown or a loud halloo made to apprise others at the other end to wait. Some of them, where the road was straight, might be seen, by common vigilance, for some distance, as travellers approach, and a stop be made by either at the first convenient spot for two teams to pass each other. There must be an accommodating spirit and cautious watchfulness on these matters, in order to avoid difficulties, and more especially must these be attended to in large falls of snow in winter."[1]

§ 261. It has, however, been said that while the town has done its duty, when it has prepared a pathway of suitable width in such a manner that it can be conveniently travelled with teams and carriages; the citizens are not thereby deprived of the right to travel over the whole width of the way as laid out, without being subjected to other or greater dangers than may be presented by natural obstacles or those occasioned by making and repairing the travelled path. Thus, a town is liable for an injury caused by a cedar log lying in its highway on the side of the travelled part.[2] And an obstruction, without the travelled path, which would be likely to frighten horses, would undoubtedly be indictable, when, but for that fact, it would not be regarded as a nuisance. But

---

[1] Hull *v.* Richmond, 2 Woodb. & Min. (Cir. Ct.) R. 343.

[2] Johnson *v.* Whitfield, 6 Shep. (Maine) R. 286. And see Commonwealth *v.* Belding, 13 Met. (Mass.) R. 10.

where an injury was caused by large loose stones lying outside the gutter, and seven feet and eight inches from the cart rut, in a highway thirty-four feet in width, the plaintiff, who sued for special damages incurred thereby, was nonsuited.[1]

§ 262. It is, moreover, no justification for a defect or obstruction that it is without the travelled path, if from its nature or position it is dangerous to such as use the road. Thus, in Cobb *v.* Standish,[2] in an action for the loss of a horse, in a deep mud hole, filled with water, partly within and partly without the limits of the located highway, and which, to the common observer, had the appearance of being a convenient watering place for horses, Weston, C. J., remarked: "Towns are not obliged to furnish watering places for the public convenience, but when they are provided by nature in the highway, they ought not to be suffered to become pitfalls, first to allure and then to destroy horses or other animals turned aside to partake the refreshment to which they are thus invited." And if a road pass over a bank or bridge or along the verge of a precipice, it is the duty of the town properly to guard the edge of the road by walls or railings.[3] Though, if the town has no power or right to erect such a barrier against danger, it is not answerable for the consequences which follow from the want of it.[4]

§ 263. In cities the sidewalks are considered a part of the public streets, and as such are to be kept, like the streets themselves, in a safe and convenient state of repair through their entire width. And this obligation is not varied or discharged by the exercise of the right of an adjoining owner of land, to use the street or sidewalk for some private purpose, not inconsistent with the right of the public. Thus, the owner

---

1 Howard *v.* North Bridgewater, 16 Pick. (Mass.) R. 189.

2 Cobb *v.* Standish, 2 Shep. (Maine) R. 198.

3 Bliss *v.* Deerfield, 13 Pick. (Mass.) R. 102; Hunt *v.* Pownal, 9 Vt. R. 411; Palmer *v.* Andover, 2 Cush. (Mass.) R. 600; Kelsey *v.* Greene, 15 Vt. R. 708.

4 Jones *v.* Waltham, 4 Cush. (Mass.) R. 299.

of adjoining land may build thereon and construct his cellar in such a way that the doors, windows, and passage-ways communicate with the street through apertures opening in the sidewalks; but it is nevertheless the duty of the city to guard against the danger which might result therefrom. And the fact that similar apertures have existed, for a long time and to a great extent in the same city, would not authorize the jury to find them not such defects as would charge the city, if they in reality cause the sidewalks to be *dangerous*, though it might be admissible as evidence tending to prove that they were not unsafe nor inconvenient. In the case of Bacon *v.* The City of Boston, where there was an aperture thirty-seven inches long and fourteen inches in width for a cellar window, made in a sidewalk six and a half feet wide, which the plaintiff stepped into and injured his ankle; the Court said: "It is true, that when a road of suitable width is made and kept in a proper state of repair, and guarded with proper barriers to protect travellers using the same, if a traveller voluntarily leaves the made road or usually travelled path, and thereby encounters pitfalls or obstructions, endangering his person or his property, he can have no remedy against the town for an injury thus received without the limits of the travelled way. But the case supposed is not one of city travel. The law as to the extent of repair and what will constitute obstructions rendering a public way unsafe or inconvenient for the traveller must depend in a good degree upon the locality of the road. In the present case, the entire sidewalk was only six and a half feet in width. A sidewalk of this width, in the city of Boston, should be for its whole extent so constructed and fitted for use as to be safe for all persons passing over it."[1] So, an awning projecting over a sidewalk, though built by the owner of the building, to which it is attached, is a defect for

---

[1] Bacon *v.* The City of Boston, 3 Cush. (Mass.) R. 174; Raymond *v.* Lowell, 6 Cush. (Mass.) R. 524.

which the town or city is liable, if through decay, insecurity or other cause, it is dangerous to travellers.[1]

§ 264. The general duty of towns to keep their highways safe and convenient extends as well to defects and obstructions occasioned by falls and drifts of snow as by any other cause.[2] The liability of towns for this species of obstruction was very thoroughly discussed and expounded in the case of The City of Providence *v.* Clapp, decided in the Supreme Court of the United States. In that case, the obstruction consisted of a ridge of hard-trodden snow and ice, on the centre of the sidewalk, along which the plaintiff was passing in the night time, and by means of which he fell across the ridge, breaking his thigh bone in an oblique direction. In addition to the usual obligation imposed, the statute under which the action was brought specially directed, that when the highways were blocked up or incumbered with snow, so much thereof should be removed or trodden down as would render the road passable. In view of this provision, it was contended that the towns and cities were bound only to keep their highways and streets open, in case of falls of snow, so as to be passable for travellers, and not to keep them from being slippery from ice or trodden down snow. But the Court were of the opinion that the liability of the city was not modified by this special provision; that when a fall of snow took place, it was the duty of the city to use ordinary care and diligence to restore it to a reasonably safe and convenient state; that the law did not prescribe how this should be done, whether by treading down or removing the snow; and that it was for the jury to find, as matter of fact, whether the sidewalk, at the time in question,

---

1 Drake *v.* The City of Lowell, 13 Met. (Mass.) R. 292; Brady *v.* The City of Lowell, 3 Cush. (Mass.) R. 121; The City of Providence *v.* Clapp, 17 How. (U. S.) R. 161.

2 Loker *v.* Brookline, 13 Pick. (Mass.) R. 346; Holman *v.* Townsend, 13 Met. (Mass.) R. 297; Green *v.* Danby, 12 Vt. R. 338; Brailey *v.* Southborough, 6 Cush. (Mass.) R. 141; State *v.* Fryeburg, 3 Shep. (Maine) R. 405.

was in a reasonably safe and convenient state, having reference to its uses. And it was also held, that in determining this question the jury might take into consideration the ordinances of the city, not as prescribing a binding rule, but as evidence that a removal, and not a treading down of the snow, was reasonably necessary.[1]

§ 265. "The powers of the towns and of the city," said Mr. Justice Nelson, in delivering the opinion of the Court, "are as ample for the purpose of removing obstructions from the highways, streets and sidewalks, arising from falls of snow and accumulations of ice, as those arising from any other cause; and the reason for the removal, so that they may be safe and convenient for travellers, is the same in the one case as in the others. The 13th section of the act which gives the personal remedy, makes no distinction in the two cases; and, in the absence of some plain distinction pointed out by the statute, it would be exceedingly difficult, if not impossible, to state one. It is conceded, that an obstruction from falls of snow or accumulations of ice must be removed by the towns and cities, so as to make the highways and streets passable, and that this is a duty expressly enjoined upon them. The question is, what sort of removal will satisfy the requirement of the statute? It is admitted, that, as it respects every other species of obstruction, the repairs must be such that the highways and streets may be safe and convenient for travellers; and that this is a question of fact to be determined by the jury. Is an obstruction by snow or ice to be determined by any other rule, or by any other tribunal? The counsel for the defendant suggests, that as it respects such safety and convenience for travellers in case of falls of snow, the statute should be construed as meaning merely, that the snow should be trodden down or removed, so that the highways and streets should not be so blocked up or incumbered as not to be safely and conveniently open and

---

1 The City of Providence *v.* Clapp, 17 How. (U. S.) R. 161.

passable. But it is quite clear, that this would be a very indefinite and uncertain rule to guide either the officers, whose duty it is to remove these obstructions, or the jury in passing upon them, when the subject of legal proceedings. The suggestion may be very well as an argument to the jury, for the purpose of satisfying them that the repairs, in the manner mentioned, were such as to fulfil the requirement of the statute, but to lay it down as a rule of law, in the terms stated, might, in many cases, and under the circumstances, fall far short of it."

§ 266. "The treading down of snow when it falls in great depth, or in case of drifts, so that the highway or street shall not be blocked up or incumbered, may, in some sense, and for the time being, have the effect to remove the obstruction; but as it respects the sidewalks and their uses, this remedy would be, at best, temporary; and, in case of rains or extreme changes of weather, would have the effect to increase rather than remove it. It is but common observation and knowledge of those familiar with the climate of our northern latitudes, that not unfrequently the most serious obstructions arise from the great depth of snow and changes in the temperature of the weather; and that simply treading down the snow, and leaving it in that condition without further attention, would have the effect to render the highways and sidewalks utterly impassable. In the case also of obstructions from snow, the sidewalks may frequently require its removal, so as to make a safe and convenient passage for the pedestrian, when, at the same time, the treading of it down in the street would answer the purpose for the traveller with his team. The nature and extent of the repairs must necessarily depend upon their location and uses; those thronged with travellers may require much greater attention than others less frequented. The just rule of responsibility, and the one, we think, prescribed by the statute, whether the obstruction be by snow or by any other material, is the removal or abatement, so as to render the highway, street or sidewalk, at all times, safe and convenient, regard being had to its locality and uses."[1]

§ 267. So inflexible is the obligation upon the towns to keep their roads safe and convenient, that they are not released, though another party be bound to the same duty by statute. In Currier *v.* Lowell,[2] the defect was an excavation in the highway, made by its intersection with a railroad. The statute, authorizing the construction of the railroad, required that it should be so constructed as not to impede or obstruct the safe and convenient use of any highway across which it might pass; and provided, that the selectmen of the town, in case it was not constructed at the point of intersection with the highway in such a way as to be satisfactory to them, might require any alteration or amendment which they might think necessary, and, if the company did not comply with the requirement, might make the alteration or amendment themselves, and be entitled to a remedy over against the corporation for the expense thereof. The Court held, that this requirement of the act of incorporation did not discharge the liability of the town; that the work being required to be done to the satisfaction of the selectmen, who, if dissatisfied, might make the necessary alterations themselves; the case stood, in regard to travellers, as if the town itself were making extensive repairs on its highway, which it would be their duty to make within a reasonable

---

1 City of Providence *v.* Clapp, 17 Howard, (U. S.) R. 168–170; and see Church *v.* Cherryfield, 33 Maine R. 460. Since the decision in the City of Providence *v.* Clapp, the law relating to highways in Rhode Island has been amended, by limiting the liability of towns respecting the removal of snow from the highways. No town or city will hereafter be liable for "any injury to persons or property, caused by snow or ice obstructing any or any part of the highways therein, unless notice of the existence of the particular obstruction shall have been given to the surveyor of highways, in writing, for at least twenty-four hours before the injury was caused; and such town or surveyor shall not thereupon have commenced the removal of such obstruction, or caused any sidewalk which may have been obstructed by ice to be rendered passable, by spreading ashes or other like substances thereon."

2 Currier *v.* Lowell, 16 Pick. (Mass.) R. 170.

time, and, in the meanwhile, to guard the place of danger against exposure, and that, therefore, they were the party immediately liable to the traveller, who was injured by the want of proper precautions. And, in this case, the town was held to be liable, notwithstanding it had given notice to the superintendent of the work on the railroad, that a barrier must be put up for the protection of travellers on the highway, and such superintendent had promised that this should be done. In a more recent case in Vermont, where the obstruction was caused by the construction of a railroad across a highway under a similar statutory provision, it was said, that the town, though not required to keep the highway passable, since this might be impracticable, was bound to see that a suitable by-way was provided for the public, and to take all proper and reasonable precautions to guard them against passing upon the highway, while it remained unsafe by reason of the operations of the railroad company in the construction of their road.[1] And in case such a by-way be made by the railroad company, and used by the public with the acquiescence of the town, the town will be liable for injuries caused by the defects of such by-way; there being in law no necessary privity between the traveller and any one but the towns, as to the sufficiency of the highways.[2]

§ 268. This duty, however, is not so absolute as to admit of no qualifications. In those States which require an acceptance by the town, the town is not liable for any defect or want of repair until it has made such acceptance.[3] If a road has been

1 Willard *v.* Newbury, 22 Vt. R. 458; Lowell *v.* Boston and Lowell Railroad Company, 23 Pick. (Mass.) R. 24; Kimball *v.* Bath, 38 Maine R. 219; and see Rex *v.* St. George, Hanover Square, 3 Campb. R. 222; Rex *v.* Oxfordshire, 4 B. & C. R. 194; Rex *v.* Netherhong, 2 B. & Ald. R. 179. But see Sawyer *v.* Northfield, 7 Cush. (Mass.) R. 490.

2 Ibid.

3 Blodget *v.* Royalton, 14 Vt. R. 28; Bowman *v.* Boston, 5 Cush. 1; Page *v.* Weathersfield, 13 Vt. R. 424; Indianapolis *v.* McClure, 2 Cart. (Ind.) R. 147; Southerland *v.* Jackson, 30 Maine R. 462.

discontinued, the liability of the town ceases, and is not revived though the road be afterwards repaired by the town surveyor.[1] And where a town was allowed a year to open a new road, it was held not to be liable for defect before the expiration of the year, though such road had been partially made and thrown open to the public.[2] If a way be dedicated for a foot-way, and accepted as such, the town is not liable for defects which make it unsafe for horses.[3] And in any case, the town is liable only for the want of ordinary care and diligence; and, whether or not it has exercised that, is a question of fact for the jury, unless there be some definite statute provision upon the subject.[4] If, for instance, a road has sustained an injury, by the operation of causes over which the town has no control, reasonable time must be afforded to put it in a convenient and safe condition; or, if it be rendered impassable by the making of necessary repairs, the town will be excused, provided they use suitable precautions to put the public on their guard.[5] But it will be no justification for them, if they unreasonably protract the time of putting such road in a safe and convenient state,

---

1 Tinker *v.* Russell, 14 Pick. 279.

2 Lowell *v.* Moscow, 3 Fairf. (Maine) R. 300; see Calder *v.* Chapman, 8 Barr, (Penn.) R. 522; Farrow *v.* The State, 1 Iowa, 439. In the latter case, it was held, that in Iowa an indictment will lie for obstructing a road established by location, survey, and recording a plat thereof, though it has never been open and used as a highway. But it is hardly probable that any liability can attach to the town or other party chargeable with repair, before the road has been opened.

3 Hemphill *v.* The City of Boston, 8 Cush. (Mass.) R. 195.

4 City of Providence *v.* Clapp, 17 How. (U. S.) R. 161; Hull *v.* Richmond, 2 W. & M. Cir. Ct. R. 344; Reed *v.* Northfield, 13 Pick. (Mass.) R. 94. Where a defect in a highway, for an injury occasioned by which to person or property the town would be liable, is found to exist on the Lord's day, it is the duty of such town to cause the defect to be repaired immediately, or to adopt measures to guard against the danger, until such repair can be made; and work, labor, or business for this purpose, is a work of necessity within the statute respecting the observance of the Lord's day. Flagg *v.* Millbury, 4 Cush. (Mass.) R. 243.

5 Kimball *v.* Bath, 38 Maine R. 219.

that there is another parallel road open and in good repair, which might be used in its place.[1]

§ 269. Neither does this duty extend so far as to make it incumbent upon towns to restore a road, when the soil itself has been entirely removed or destroyed by the action of natural causes. In a recent English case,[2] it appeared that a public highway originally ran down to the sea, at right angles to the shore, the land gently sloping to the water's edge. By the encroachments of the waves, a portion of the land and road was swept away, so that there was left a cliff twenty feet high above the beach, the road running to the edge, and there terminating abruptly. The highway was kept in proper repair by the parish to the very edge of the cliff. The Court held, that an indictment would not lie for not repairing that portion of the road which had been entirely washed away; and per Maule, J.: "We are clearly of opinion, that there is no highway to repair. There appears to have been a road running down to the sea; natural causes, without default of any one, have washed away and destroyed the road in great part, so that where that has taken place, the subject of repair no longer exists. An indictment for non-repair of a highway, charges that there is a common and public highway, and complains, not that it has been destroyed, but that it is out of repair. The several authorities which have been cited,[3] (and they are confirmed by common sense,) show that if there be no longer any highway, if there be nothing which can be effectually restored, by what may fairly be termed repairs, the case does not exist in which a liability is cast upon the parish. In the present case, it is found, that all that part of the highway which exists is in good repair,

---

1 State *v.* Fryeburg, 3 Shep. (Maine) R. 105; Frost *v.* Portland, 11 Maine R. 271; Jacobs *v.* Bangor, 4 Shep. (Maine) R. 187.

2 Regina *v.* Inhabitants of Hornsea, 25 Eng. Law and Eq. R. 582.

3 The Queen *v.* Bamber, 5 Q. B. Rep. 279; The Queen *v.* Paul, 2 Moo. & R. 307; The King *v.* Montague, 4 B. & C. R. 598.

and that which is not passable could not be made good without considerable engineering works, which, I think, the parish were not bound to execute."

§ 270. The duty of repairing bridges, as of roads, is in the United States regulated by statute. In the New England States, this duty, for the most part, devolves upon the towns, unless some particular person is specially charged therewith.[1] If a bridge be built by an individual, and dedicated to the public, and by them used for so long a period as to evince its usefulness, though for less than twenty years, and though during that period the public have used and repaired it under protest against their liability, yet it becomes a public bridge which the town will be bound to repair.[2] And, in repairing, towns and individual proprietors must preserve their bridges in such strength as will support the variety of business and travel for which they may be ordinarily required, having regard to the wants and usages of the community where they may be located.[3] A bridge, carried away by a flood, must be rebuilt within a reasonable time, regard being had to the importance of the road, the magnitude of the work, the opportunity of procuring materials, and other circumstances connected with its reconstruction.[4] In case of gross neglect, the party injured by the defectiveness of a bridge, may recover exemplary damages.[5]

§ 271. But though, as a general rule, the repair of high-

---

1 Lobdell *v.* New Bedford, 1 Mass. 153; Norwich *v.* Commissioners, 13 Pick. (Mass.) R. 60; Lewis *v.* Litchfield, 2 Root, (Conn.) R. 436; State *v.* Franklin, 9 Conn. 32; State *v.* Compton, 2 N. Hamp. R. 513; Bardwell *v.* Jamaica, 15 Vt. R. 438; Schoolbred *v.* Charleston, 2 Bay, (So. Car.) R. 63; Sampson *v.* Gooikland Justices, 5 Gratt. R. 241.

2 State *v.* Compton, 2 N. Hamp. R. 513.

3 Richardson *v.* Royalton, &c. Turnpike, 6 Vt. 496; Townsend *v.* Susquehannah Railroad Company, 6 Johns. (N. Y.) R. 189.

4 The People *v.* Tisdale Turnpike Company, 23 Wend. (N. Y.) R. 254; Briggs *v.* Guilford, 8 Vt. R. 267.

5 Whipple *v.* Walpole, 10 N. Hamp. R. 130.

ways and bridges devolves upon the towns where they are situated, yet that obligation may, in particular instances, rest upon individuals or corporations. An individual who builds a bridge over a public highway for his own exclusive benefit,[1] or a corporation who, in pursuance of their charter, build a turnpike road or bridge, and take toll from passengers, thereby become bound to keep the road or bridge in repair.[2] The taking toll is in itself *primâ facie* proof of the obligation.[3] And where a company have established their gates, and taken toll for many years, they cannot defend themselves when indicted for not repairing their road, on the plea that the part of the road out of repair has not been so made as to be accepted, since a part of the toll so taken is considered by law as a compensation for making this part of the road.[4] And such company, so long as they continue to take toll, cannot discharge themselves from liability to individuals by simply giving notice of danger; to give the notice such an effect, they must likewise refuse to take the toll.[5]

---

1 Heacock *v.* Sherman, 14 Wend. (N. Y.) R. 58; Dygert *v.* Schenck, 23 Ibid. 446; Waterbury *v.* Clark, 4 Day, (Conn.) R. 198; Sawyer *v.* Northfield, 7 Cush. (Mass.) R. 490; but where an individual builds a bridge over a private way for his own benefit, he is not indictable for neglecting to repair it, though it be generally used by the public. State *v.* Seawell, 3 Hawks. (N. C.) R. 193.

2 Goshen and Sharon Turnpike Co. *v.* Sears, 7 Conn. 86; Townsend *v.* The Susquehannah Turnpike Co. 6 Johns. (N. Y.) R. 90; Bartlett *v.* Crozier, 15 Ib. 250; The Wayne County Turnpike Co. *v.* Berry, 5 Ind. (Porter,) R. 286; Noyes *v.* Turnpike Co. 11 Verm. 531; Kane *v.* People, 3 Wend. (N. Y.) R. 363; State *v.* Patton, 4 Iredell, (N. C.) R. 16. In the last two cases, the president and directors were held to be personally liable as for a misdemeanor, and punishable with fine and imprisonment.

3 State *v.* Wayne, 1 Hawks. (N. C.) R. 451.

4 Commonwealth *v.* The Worcester Turnpike Co. 3 Pick. (Mass.) R. 326. But a turnpike company are not bound to repair a bridge on the line of their road, not included in the parts completed and licensed. New Jersey *v.* Morris Turnpike Co. 1 South. (N. J.) R. 165; Sherwood *v.* Weston, 18 Conn. R. 32.

5 Randall *v.* The Proprietors of the Cheshire Turnpike, 6 N. Hamp. R. 147.

§ 272. A private liability to repair a highway, where it exists, is coextensive with that of towns, its measure in both cases being an exercise of ordinary care and diligence in the construction and preservation of the way.[1] It does not extend to accidents, unless these accidents result from a want of this ordinary care and diligence, nor to injuries which are occasioned by the negligence of the party injured. Thus it has been held, that a turnpike company is not liable for damages sustained by one who overloads a bridge, if it be of sufficient ordinary strength.[2] Where, by statute, it was provided, that a turnpike company should not be liable for damages occasioned by the breaking of their bridge, to any person, who, without the consent of the toll-gatherer or agent of the company, should drive over the bridge a loaded wagon of more than forty-five hundred pounds weight, it was held, that such consent could not be implied from the frequent unchallenged passage of the wagon with more than that weight, but that the consent must be obtained upon notice expressly given.[3] But this liability may, of course, be enhanced by statute. Thus where it was provided, that a turnpike company should be liable "to pay all damages that might happen to any person from whom toll is demandable, for any damages which should arise from defect of bridges, or want of repair of said turnpike road," the Court held, that the company was liable for any injury or accident to travellers, unless they themselves were chargeable with negli-

---

1 Townsend *v.* Susquehannah Turnpike Co. 6 Johns. (N. Y.) R. 90; Baxter *v.* Winooski Turnpike Co. 22 Vt. (7 Washb.) R. 114; Mathews *v.* Winooski Turnpike Co. 24 Vt. (1 Deane,) R. 480; Ward *v.* Newark and Pompton Turnpike Co. 1 Spencer, (N. J.) 323; Talmadge *v.* Zanesville and Marysville Road Co. 11 Ohio R. 197. In this case, it was held, where a coach was upset by reason of a defect in the road, and the passengers injured, that the company was liable for damage to the coach, but not for damages recovered against the coach proprietors for injury to the passengers.

2 Richardson *v.* Royalton Turnpike Co. 5 Verm. 580.

3 Pomeroy *v.* Fifth Massachusetts Turnpike Corporation, 10 Pick. (Mass.) R. 35.

gence, even though from some unforeseen and unavoidable cause the road happened to be out of repair. "It is founded," the Court say, "on the consideration, that the toll is an adequate compensation for the risk assumed, and that by throwing the risk upon those who have the best means of taking precautions against it, the public will have the greatest security against actual damage and loss."[1] In proceeding criminally against an individual, the indictment must set forth *how* the liability accrued.[2]

§ 273. At common law, it is obligatory upon a canal company to take reasonable care to keep their canal free from obstructions, so that all persons who navigate the same may do so without danger. Thus, where a boat was sunk in a canal, and the company, after reasonable notice thereof, neither raised the same, nor placed any signal, or gave notice of the obstruction, the company was held liable for the damage done to the plaintiff's ply-boat, by reason of a collision therewith. And it was remarked by Lord Denman, C. J., "We do not feel the smallest doubt that this action may be maintained. The only one of the numerous cases cited, that appeared to point the other way, is Harris *v.* Baker,[3] where trustees of a road were held not liable to an action for a personal injury arising from the plaintiff's wife falling, in the night time, over a heap of scrapings placed on the road side by a defendant, who placed no light to give notice of the obstruction. But that case may be distinguished, as the action was against public officers who derived no benefit from the road. The present defendants, on the contrary, invite the whole public to navigate their canal, in consideration of the tolls paid. They have lawful power to make the canal in all respects fit for navigation, and particularly

1 Yale *v.* Hampden and Berkshire Turnpike Corporation, 18 Pick. (Mass.) R. 355.

2 State *v.* New Jersey Turnpike Co. 1 Harr. (N. J.) R. 222; State *v.* King, 3 Ired. (N. C.) R. 411; State *v.* Wayne, 1 Hawks. (N. C.) R. 451.

3 Harris *v.* Baker, 4 M. & Sel. R. 27.

to remove the kind of obstructions by which the plaintiffs suffered. It is the same in principle as if they announced the carrying on of a business at premises accessible only by a certain road over their land, which was open to the public for that purpose, but which they only, and not the public, had a right to repair, and then left that road in so bad a state that a person's leg was broken when he came to transact business with them there. A more familiar example, and not of very rare occurrence, is that of a shopkeepker who leaves a trap-door open in his shop, and causes a customer to fall down and suffer injury."[1]

## II. Remedies.—1. *Abatement.*

§ 274. A nuisance in the common highway may be *abated*, that is removed or destroyed, by any individual who wants to use it in a lawful way; and he may even enter upon the land of the party erecting or continuing the nuisance, for the purpose of removing it, doing as little damage as possible to the soil or buildings.[2] The reason why the law allows this private and summary method of doing one's self justice is, because injuries of this kind, which obstruct or annoy such things as are of daily convenience and use, require an immediate remedy; and cannot wait for the slow progress of the ordinary forms of justice.[3] But although any one may abate a common nuisance obstructing a highway, and remove the

---

[1] The Company of Proprietors of the Lancaster Canal Navigation *v.* Parnaby and others, 1 Railway and Canal Cases, 695; 11 Ad. & E. 223; 3 Nev. & Per. 523.

[2] 1 Hawk. P. C. 75, § 12; 2 Roll. Abr. 144, 145; 5 Rep. 101; 9 Rep. 55; James *v.* Hayward, Cro. Car. R. 184; Arundel *v.* M'Culloch, 10 Mass. R. 70; Mann *v.* Marston, 3 Fairf. (Maine) R. 32; State *v.* Knapp, 6 Conn. R. 418; Cool *v.* Crommett, 13 Maine R. 250; Loder *v.* Arnold, 2 Salk. R. 458; Hart *v.* Mayor of Albany, 9 Wend. 571; Moffett *v.* Brewer, 1 Iowa (Green) R. 348.

[3] 111 Black. Com. p. 5 and 6.

materials, yet he cannot convert them to his own use.[1] And the right also seems to be qualified by the exception, that it cannot lawfully be exerted if its exercise involve a breach of the peace.[2] When such is the case, the party erecting the nuisance must be proceeded against according to the ordinary form of criminal procedure. Neither does this right of abatement, as has been held, go to the extent of justifying the removal of every encroachment upon the highway unless such encroachment at the same time annoys and obstructs its lawful use. Thus, in New Hampshire, in the case of Hopkins *v.* Crombie,[3] where the frame and cellar of a building extended about ten feet into the highway, but did not cover or obstruct any of the travelled part thereof, the Court held the encroachment not to be such a nuisance as could, at common law, be abated by an individual unless it actually obstructed his passage. And although, in that State, such an encroachment was declared by statute to be a common nuisance and exposed the offender to indictment, and fine upon conviction, yet the Court were of the opinion that it was not any the more abateable for this reason. So, it has been held, that if property, (as oysters,) be placed in the channel of a public navigable river so as to create a public nuisance, a person navigating is not justified in damaging such property by running his vessel against it, if he has room to pass without so doing; for an individual cannot abate a nuisance if he is no otherwise injured by it than as one of the public. And, therefore, the fact that such property is a nuisance is no excuse for running upon it negligently.[4] And in Burnham *v.* Hotchkiss,[5] which was similar in its circumstances to Hopkins *v.* Crombie, the

---

1 1 Hawk. P. C. c. 76, § 187.

2 Day *v.* Day, 4 Maryland R. 262.

3 Hopkins *v.* Crombie, 4 N. Hamp. R. 520.

4 Colchester (Mayor, &c. of) *v.* Brook, 7 Ad. & El. R. N. S. 339.

5 Burnham *v.* Hotchkiss, 14 Conn. R. 311.

Court held, that whether or not a given obstruction is a nuisance is a question of fact for the jury, and that the abatement was not justifiable unless the public travel was, by reason thereof, actually obstructed, hindered, or endangered. In this case two out of the five Judges dissented from this opinion, and Waite, J., in delivering the dissenting opinion, contended: "All erections on a highway, whether in the place used for travel or not, are nuisances, and may be abated, unless they are actually *beneficial.*" And this view is not unsupported by authority.[1] But, whatever may be the better opinion thereon, inasmuch as every proprietor adjoining a highway has a right of reasonable access thereto, the exemption does not extend so far as to prevent him from abating, as a nuisance, any obstruction which essentially interferes with such reasonable access, whether it be in or out of the travelled part of the highway.[2] Where an obstruction in a highway is authorized by an act of the legislature for a limited period, it becomes abateable as soon as that period expires;[3] and it has been said, that a nuisance, however long-continued, never ceases to be abateable by reason of its antiquity.[4]

## 2. *Indictment.*

§ 275. Indictment is the appropriate remedy both against individuals for positive obstructions and against towns for want of repair. An obstruction, on the part of an individual,

---

1 Lancaster Turnpike Co. *v.* Rogers, 2 Barr. (Penn.) R. 114; Rung *v.* Shoneberger, 2 Watts (Penn.) R. 23; Dimmett *v.* Eskridge, 6 Munf. (Ohio) R. 308; Gunter *v.* Gearey, 1 Cal. R. 462; Wetmore *v.* Tracy, 14 Wend. (N. Y.) R. 250.

2 Hubbard *v.* Deming, 21 Conn. R. 357.

3 Adams *v.* Beach, 6 Hill, (N. Y.) R. 271.

4 Arundel *v.* M'Culloch, 10 Mass. R. 70; but see *post*, Chap. VII. It has been held that a turnpike corporation have a right to remove fences or other encroachments upon their road and are not compelled to resort to a remedy by action. Estes *v.* Kelsey, 8 Wend. (N. Y.) R. 555.

is, as we have seen, a common-law offence, and is punishable as such, even though a statute exists imposing a penalty for the offence, unless an intent is evinced to exclude the common-law punishment; for, as a general rule, the simple addition of a penalty by statute for an offence at common law is merely cumulative, and, in the absence of a plain meaning to the contrary, such statute detracts nothing from the ordinary remedies at law.[1] And, whatever may be the law in regard to abatement, it would seem that the author of a nuisance within the limits of a highway is liable to indictment, whether such nuisance actually obstruct the public travel or not. "By the location of a public highway with certain defined exterior limits," it has been said, "the public acquire an easement co-extensive with the limits of such highway. Whoever obstructs the full enjoyment of that easement, by making deposits within such limits of the located highway, of timber, stones, or other things, to remain there and occupy a portion of such public highway, is guilty of a nuisance at common law."[2] Where such a nuisance exists, both the party who created it and the party who continues its use or maintenance are liable to indictment;[3] and it is no defence for a master or employer that a nuisance is caused by the acts of his servants, if such acts are done in the course of their employment; nor, on the other hand, is it any defence for the party causing a nuisance that

---

1 Renwick *v.* Morris, 7 Hill, (N. Y.) R. 575; State *v.* Wilkinson, 2 Vt. R. 480; Commonwealth *v.* King, 13 Met. (Mass.) R. 115; State *v.* Hogg, 5 Ind. R. 515; Rex *v.* Balm, Cowp. R. 648. But see Commonwealth *v.* Turnpike Co. 2 Virg. Cases, 361, where it was held, that where a penalty, and the method of recovering it, is prescribed, by the act incorporating a turnpike company, against the person intrusted with repairing the road, the prescribed remedy must be pursued and the company is not criminally liable.

2 Commonwealth *v.* King, 13 Met. (Mass.) R. 115.

3 State *v.* Yarnell, 12 Ired. (N. C.) R. 130; 1 Hawk. P. C. c. 76, § 157; Rex *v.* Stoughton, 2 Saunders, R. 158-9, note; King *v.* Kerrison, 3 M. & Sel. R. 526.

he was only acting as an agent or overseer for another.[1] It is also no defence that a nuisance has existed for more than twenty years,[2] or that a new road has been opened and used a number of years in the place of the road obstructed.[3] Where the indictment is against the town for neglect to repair, it must be brought under the statutes imposing that duty upon them; for, though there is a close resemblance of the duties and liabilities of towns to those of parishes in England as to roads, and of counties as to bridges, yet those duties and liabilities do not in this country exist at common law.[4]

§ 276. In an indictment for the non-repair of a highway, it is sufficient to allege compendiously that it is a common highway, without showing how it became so, or that it has been so from time immemorial.[5] Although it is not necessary to state the *termini* of the highway,[6] yet, if they are stated, they must be proved, and care must be taken that the description is so framed as neither to exclude the parish, or town, liable, nor to seem repugnant to itself; for if the highway be described as between two places, both of them are necessarily excluded.[7] The words "*from*" and "*unto*" seem to have an exclusive as well as inclusive meaning.[8] In an indictment for a nuisance in obstructing a highway "leading *from* the township of D. *into* the town of C." by placing a gate across it, the ter-

---

1 State *v.* Bell, 5 Porter, (Ala.) R. 365.

2 Elkins *v.* State, 2 Humphrey, (Tenn.) R. 543; Com. *v.* Tucker, 2 Pick. (Mass.) R. 44; People *v.* Cunningham, 1 Denio, (N. Y.) R. 524; Russell on Crimes, (Amer. ed.) 274; Mills *v.* Hall, 9 Wend. (N. Y.) R. 315.

3 Commonwealth *v.* Belding, 13 Met. (Mass.) R. 10.

4 State *v.* Canterbury, 8 Fost. (N. H.) R. 195.

5 3 T. R. 265; 2 Saund. R. 158, *n.* (4). The State *v.* Harsh, 6 Black. (Ind.) R. 346.

6 Rouse *v.* Bardin, 1 H. Bl. R. 351; Rex *v.* St. Weonard's, 6 C. & P. 582; The State *v.* Hageman, 1 Green, (N. J.) R. 314.

7 2 Saund. R. 158, *n.* (6); Regina *v.* Fisher, 8 C. & P. R. 612; The State *v.* Newfane, 12 Vt. R. 422.

8 Rex *v.* Knight, 7 B. & C. R. 412.

mini D. and C. are excluded, and therefore if it appear that the gate was put in the township of D. the defendant must be acquitted.[1] An indictment for an obstruction of a public way, describing it as from A. towards and unto B. is satisfied by proof of a public way leading from A. to B. though turning backwards between A. and B. at an acute angle; and though the part from A. to the angle be an immemorial way and the part from the angle to B. be recently dedicated. B. was a church, and the path from A., after passing the point at which the obstruction took place, reached the churchyard, but not the church, before reaching the angle; it was held, by Denman, Ch. J., and *semble per* Coleridge, J., that this proof would not have supported an indictment describing the whole as an immemorial way.[2]

§ 277. An indictment for non-repair of a highway, stated that there was a queen's highway for carriages, &c., "leading from Abingdon, in the county of Berks, towards and unto the village of East Hendred in the same county," a part of which was out of repair. The part of the road charged to be out of repair was a portion of a lane called F. lane, and it was proved, that, to go from the town of Abingdon to the village of East Hendred with a carriage, a person must go four miles along the C. turnpike road, then all along F. lane, and then across W. turnpike road, and for a short distance go along a road which goes from the W. turnpike road to the village of East Hendred. It was held, that the description of the road was sufficient. It was not incorrect, as by this way a person would go from Abingdon to East Hendred, and by the plan it appeared to be the nearest way for a carriage to go from the one place to the other, and a road is not less a highway

---

1 Regina *v.* Botfield, 1 Carr. & M. R. 151; Regina *v.* Fisher, 8 Carr. & P. R. 612.

2 Rex *v.* Devonshire, (Marchioness of,) 4 Ad. & El. R. 232.

because part of it is a turnpike road.[1] In an indictment for non-repair, where it was alleged, "that, from the time whereof the memory of man runneth not to the contrary, there was, and yet is, a common and ancient highway, &c., and the only other allegation as to time was, that a part of said highway, situate, &c., "on the 1st day of January in the twelfth year aforesaid and continually afterwards, until the taking of this inquisition, was, and yet is," out of repair, so that the liege subjects of the queen could not, during the time aforesaid, nor yet can go, return, pass, &c., it was held, that the allegation of immemoriality might be rejected as surplusage, and that, without it, sufficient appeared on the face of the indictment, as to time, to support the liability charged.[2]

§ 278. In an indictment for non-repair, it is not necessary to name the owners of the land over which the highway is laid, and if part are named, and others omitted, it will not vitiate the proceedings.[3] Though the commissioners of public roads are liable to criminal prosecution for neglect of duty, yet in New York they cannot be indicted for not repairing a bridge, unless they wilfully and unlawfully refuse to employ funds that they have on hand; and the *having such funds* should be averred in the indictment.[4] An indictment against an overseer of highways ought to state when he was elected, when his office commenced and when it terminated, that he was in office during the period complained of, and that the road was within his district.[5] A mere error of judgment is not sufficient to subject commissioners to an indictment for a

---

[1] Regina *v.* Steventon, 1 Carr. & K. R. 55; Shelford on Highways, p. 235.

[2] Regina *v.* Turweston, 1 Eng. Law & Eq. R. 317.

[3] State *v.* Dover, 10 N. Hamp. R. 394.

[4] The People *v.* Adsit, 2 Hill, (N. Y.) R. 619; The State *v.* The Commissioners, Walker, (Miss.) R. 368; but see The State *v.* Harsh, 6 Blackf. (Ind.) R. 346.

[5] The State *v.* Hageman, 1 Green, (N. J.) R. 314.

palpable omission of duty.[1] An indictment against a supervisor charging that he neglected to keep the roads in his district in repair, without describing the particular roads or parts thereof suffered to be out of repair, is bad for uncertainty. So in an indictment for not putting up guide-boards at crossings, it should be alleged at what crossings the neglect occured. And where a supervisor is bound to keep a road in repair, as far as the labor of persons bound to work thereon will enable him so to do, the indictment must show affirmatively that he could command the labor for that purpose.[2] An indictment against a turnpike company, for not keeping their road in repair, should show how they are bound to do so.[3] A misdescription, which occasions no ambiguity as to the road intended, is immaterial.[4] Where, after the finding of the bill, and before the trial, the selectmen of the town indicted for non-repair, made a new road and discontinued the one described in the indictment, it was held, that this did not defeat the prosecution against the town.[5]

§ 279. All common nuisances are regularly punishable by fine and imprisonment; but as the removal of the nuisance is usually the chief end of the indictment, the Court will adapt the judgment to the nature of the case. Where the nuisance, therefore, is stated in the indictment to be continuing and does in fact exist at the time of the judgment, the defendant may be commanded by the judgment to remove it at his own cost.[6]

---

1 Eyman *v.* The People, 1 Gilman, (Ill.) R. 4.

2 The State *v.* McMurrin, 1 Carter, (Ind.) R. 44; Lequat *v.* The People, 11 Ill. R. 330.

3 The State *v.* New Jersey Turnpike, 1 Harr. (N. J.) R. 222; The State *v.* Patton, 4 Ired. (N. C.) R. 16.

4 Harrow *v.* The State, 1 Iowa (Green) R. 439; Alexander *v.* The State, 16 Alabama R. 661; The State *v.* Lemay, 8 Eng. (13 Ark.) R. 405; The State *v.* Town of Fletcher, 13 Vt. 124.

5 The State *v.* The Town of Fletcher, 13 Vt. 124.

6 2 Roll. Abr. 84; 1 Hawk. P. C. c. 75, § 14; Rex *v.* Pappineau, 1 Str. R.

But in case it does not appear by the indictment that the nuisance is a continuing nuisance, such judgment will not be awarded. If, however, the nuisance still continue, the defendant may be again indicted for continuing it.[1]

### 3. *Injunction.*

§ 280. *In favor of the Public.* In addition to these more ordinary remedies, it is now well settled, that a Court of Equity may take jurisdiction of public nuisances by an information filed by the Attorney-General.[2] This jurisdiction is grounded upon the greater efficacy and promptitude of the remedies administered in Courts of Equity, enabling them to restrain such nuisances as are only threatened or are in progress, as well as to abate such as already exist, to effect their final suppression by perpetual injunction, to arrest irreparable mischief, and prevent multiplicity of suits.[3] The instances of the exercise of this remedy are, however, rare, and it will be withheld whenever there is any doubt of the fact of the nuisance, until the fact has been established by a jury.[4] And, even where the nuisance is proved to exist, the jurisdiction is confessedly one of delicacy, and demands great caution in its exercise. "If," says Chancellor Kent, "a charge be of a criminal nature or an offence against the public, and does not

---

686; Rex *v.* Stead, 8 T. R. 142. Upon the law of Practice and Pleadings in indictments for nuisances, *vide* Woolwych on Ways, pp. 220–252; 111 Archbold's Criminal Practice and Pleading, 609–51.

1 111 Archbold's Criminal Practice and Pleading, 609–51.

2 Attorney-General *v.* Richards, 2 Anstr. R. 603; Attorney-General *v.* Johnson, 2 Wilson, Ch. R. 101 to 103; Attorney-General *v.* Forbes, 2 Mylne & Craig, R. 123; Attorney-General *v.* Burridge, 10 Price, R. 350; Id. 378; Attorney-General *v.* Manchester Railway, 1 Railway Cases, 436; Story's Commentaries on Eq. Jur. Vol. II. § 921.

3 Ibid. § 924.

4 Attorney-General *v.* Cleaver, 18 Ves. R. 217; Earl of Ripon *v.* Hobart, 1 Cooper, Sel. Cas. 333; S. C. 3 Mylne & Keen, R. 169.

touch the enjoyment of property, it ought not to be brought within the direct jurisdiction of this Court, which was intended to deal only in matters of civil right, resting in equity or where the remedy at law was not sufficiently adequate. Nor ought the process of injunction to be applied, but with the utmost caution. It is the strong arm of the Court; and to render its operation benign and useful, it must be exercised with great discretion, and when necessity requires it."[1]

§ 281. "The very fact," says Chancellor Vroom, of New Jersey, "that there may be a doubt on the subject, by intelligent jurists, should be sufficient to induce caution on the part of the Court. In cases of public nuisance, there is an undis-

---

[1] Attorney-General *v.* Utica Insurance Co. 2 Johns. (N. Y.) Ch. R. 370. In this case, Chancellor Kent remarks, that the jurisdiction of Courts of Equity, in cases of public nuisance, had lain dormant for a century and a half, or from the time of Charles I. down to the year 1795, when it was invoked in the case of Attorney-General *v.* Richards, 2 Anst. 603, in which case, the injury charged was a public nuisance of a particular kind, termed purpresture, which means an encroachment upon, and an enclosure of, the property of the *crown*, in a highway, river or harbor, and, from the fact that the precedents cited in that case were of the same description, he seems to have been of the opinion that the jurisdiction was limited to the case in which the nuisance was not only serious and dangerous but upon the *soil* of the crown, and, therefore, an injury to property like the case of a private nuisance. But, in the Attorney-General *v.* Forbes, 2 Mylne & Craig, 129, 130, Lord Cottenham said: "With respect to the question of jurisdiction, it was broadly asserted, that an application to this Court to prevent a nuisance to a public road was never heard of. A little research, however, would have found many such instances. Many cases might have been produced, in which the Court has interfered to prevent nuisances to public rivers and to public harbors. And the Court of Exchequer, as well as this Court, acting as a Court of Equity, has a well-established jurisdiction, upon a proceeding by way of information, to prevent nuisances to public harbors and public roads; and, in short, generally, to prevent public nuisances." So, also, in the city of Georgetown *v.* The Alexandria Canal Company, 13 Peters, (U. S.) R. 98. Barbour, J., in delivering the opinion of the Supreme Court of the United States, remarks, that this "jurisdiction has been finally sustained, upon the principle that Equity can give more adequate and complete relief than can be obtained at law." And see Rowe *v.* Granite Bridge Co. 21 Pick. (Mass.) R. 344; Commonwealth *v.* Rush, 14 Penn. 372; Hale *v.* Attorney-General, 22 Alabama R. 190; Spooner *v.* McConnell, 1 McLean, (Cir. Ct.) R. 337; Putnam *v.* Valentine, 5 Ohio R. 188; Eden on Injunctions, 157–262.

puted jurisdiction in the Common-Law Courts by indictment; and a Court of Equity ought not to interfere in a case of misdemeanor, when the object sought can be as well attained in the ordinary tribunals." Accordingly, the Chancellor refused an injunction sought by the Attorney-General of New Jersey, upon a bill or information, charging the defendants with being in the act of erecting a bridge over the Passaic River, which is a navigable stream, in such a way as to interfere materially with the navigation, and calling upon the Court, on the ground that such bridge would be a serious detriment to the community, and a public nuisance, to interfere and prevent the further erection of the same, and also to order the same to be obviated and abated. In this case, it appeared that the bridge had been already in great part completed; and the Court, being of the opinion that an injunction is only a *preventive remedy*, and cannot be applied correctively to an injury, already done, so as to remove it, held, that the appropriate remedy was by indictment at common law.[1]

§ 282. Where, however, the public owns, not only an easement in the soil, but also the soil itself, an application for equitable relief, will meet with greater favor. Thus, in The Attorney-General *v.* The Cohoes Company, in which the defendants were charged with having commenced cutting through the embankment of the Erie and Champlain Canals, for the purpose of drawing water for the supply of mills erecting by

---

[1] The Attorney-General *v.* The New Jersey Railroad and Transportation Co. 2 Green, (N. J.) Ch. R. 136. "The rule," says the learned reporter, "admits of exceptions, and as applied to the abatement or removal of nuisances, either public or private, it seems not to be universally true that the remedy by injunction cannot be applied." And he cites, among other cases, Attorney-General *v.* Richards, 2 Anst. 603; The East India Co. *v.* Vincent, 2 Atk. R. 83; Robinson *v.* Lord Byron, 1 Bro. C. C. 588; Attorney-General *v.* Parmenter, 10 Price, R. 378; Van Bergen *v.* Van Bergen, 2 Johns. (N. Y.) Ch. R. 272; 3 Johns. (N. Y.) Ch. R. 282; Hammond *v.* Fuller, 1 Paige, (N. Y.) Ch. R. 197.

the Cohoes Company below such embankment, and in which the defendants denied, on oath, that any injury would result; Chancellor Walworth said: "The Court has jurisdiction to restrain any purpresture or unauthorized appropriation of the public property to private uses, which may amount to a public nuisance, or may injuriously affect or endanger the public interest. And where the officers intrusted with the protection of such public interests, acting under the sanction of their official oaths, believe the intended encroachment will prove injurious to the navigation of the canals, private persons should not be permitted to interfere with the waters or embankments of the canals contrary to law, upon a mere opinion, although under the sanction of an oath, that the intended trespass upon the public rights would not be an injury to the public."[1]

§ 283. *In favor of the private Individual.* Courts of Equity, also, pursuing the analogy of the law, will take jurisdiction in case of a public nuisance, at the instance of a private person, where he is averred and proven to be in imminent danger of suffering a *special injury*, for which, under the circumstances of the case, the law would not afford an adequate remedy.[2] In the leading case of Crowder *v.* Tinkler, Lord Eldon stated as the reason for granting an injunction to restrain the establishment of a powder magazine in a populous neighborhood and contiguous to the plaintiff's paper mills, that

---

1 The Attorney-General *v.* The Cohoes Company, 6 Paige, Ch. R. 133; Story's Eq. Jur. § 921, 922.

2 Georgetown *v.* Alexandria Canal Co. 12 Peters, (U. S.) R. 91; Rowe *v.* Granite Bridge Co. 21 Pick. (Mass.) R. 344; Bigelow *v.* The Hartford Bridge Co. 14 Conn. R. 565; O'Brien *v.* Norwich and Worcester Railroad Co. 17 Conn. R. 372; Frink *v.* Lawrence, 20 Conn. R. 117; Spooner *v.* McConnell, 1 McLean, (Cir. Ct.) R. 337; Putnam *v.* Valentine, 5 Ohio R. 190; Corning *v.* Lowerre, 6 Johns. (N. Y.) Ch. R. 439; Spencer *v.* London and Birmingham Railway Co. 8 Sim. R. 392; Sampson *v.* Smith, Id. 272; Coats *v.* Clarence Railway Co. 1 Russ & Mylne, R. 181; Coulson *v.* White, 3 Atk. R. 21; Anon. 3 Atk. R. 750; Barnes *v.* Baker, Amb. 158; Story, Eq. Jur. § 924 a; 1 Railway Cases, 480.

the complaint was to be considered as of, not a public nuisance simply, but what, being so in its nature, was attended with extreme probability of irreparable injury to the property of the plaintiffs, including also danger to their existence.[1] But in the later cases the practice of the Courts seems to have become somewhat more liberal, and in Corning *v.* Lowerre, Chancellor Kent granted an injunction, to restrain the obstruction of a street in the city of New York by building a house thereon, in favor of the owners of lots on and adjoining the street, upon the simple ground that it worked a *special* injury to them.[2]

§ 284. In applications for injunction, on the ground of *special* injury, it is not necessary that the Attorney-General should be a party, although the nuisance is one which subjects the author of it to indictment.[3] Thus, in Sampson *v.* Smith, the Vice-Chancellor said: "Here the plaintiff represents that something has been done which is highly injurious to himself, and also to certain other individuals; which averment it was not necessary for him to make. In a case so constituted, I do not see, if the Attorney-General were a party, that I could make a decree which would bind the question between the defendant and the public; and, unless having the Attorney a party, would enable me to make a decree which would bind the public, through the Attorney-General, it appears to me that it is not necessary to make him a party."[4] But where the application is made to prevent a public nuisance, merely from apprehended danger to the community, it must be in the name or on behalf of the people. And an injunction, it has been said, will not be issued on the application of an individual to prevent the perpetration of an act prohibited by a public statute, merely

1 Crowder *v.* Tinkler, 19 Vesey, R. 616.

2 Corning *v.* Lowerre, 6 Johns. (N. Y.) Ch. R. 439; and see cases above cited.

3 Spencer *v.* Birmingham and London Railway Co. 8 Simons, R. 193; 11 Con. Ch. R. 392; Georgetown *v.* Alexandria Canal Co. 12 Pet. (U. S.) R. 91.

4 Sampson *v.* Smith, 8 Simons, 272; 11 Con. Ch. R. 433.

because it might diminish the profits of a trade or business pursued by the applicant in common with a considerable class of his fellow-citizens, although the statute may have been designed principally for the protection of the interests of such class.[1]

### 4. *Case for Special Damage.*

§ 285. It is a general rule, that a private action cannot be maintained for a public injury. The reason of this restriction is to prevent a multiplicity of suits, which would ensue, if every one in his own person might redress the public grievance. But if any individual, from a common nuisance, suffers a more special damage than any other, in such case, and because of his special damage, he shall have his separate action on the case.[2] Thus, an individual who receives a bodily hurt, or suffers a damage to his horse or carriage in consequence of a direct collision with an obstruction in the highway, is specially damnified, and may maintain an action against the author of the obstruction. But there are cases in which it is not so easy to distinguish the damage which is peculiar to the individual, from that which is common to him with the rest of the public. Thus, it has been held, that the being put to the necessity of going a circuitous route, or the being delayed on a journey by which some important affair is neglected, are not sufficient of themselves to warrant this action.[3] But if, in addition thereto, the plaintiff, having in part made his journey, is turned back and obliged to proceed by a very circuitous route, or, meeting the obstruction, is withheld from removing it so that he may

---

1 Smith *v.* Lockwood, 13 Barb. (N. Y.) S. C. R. 209.

2 Vin. Abr. tit. Chimin. Common, D. 2; 1 Coke, Inst. 56 a; Chichester *v.* Letheridge, Willes, R. 71; Fineaux *v.* Hovenden, Cro. Eliz. 664; Pain *v.* Patrick, Carth. 191; 3 Mod. 289; 2 Carter (Ind.) R. 162; 5 Black. (Ind.) R. 35; Payne *v.* Rogers, 2 Hen. Bl. Rep. 349.

3 Hubert *v.* Groves, 1 Esp. R. 148; Pain *v.* Patrick, Carth. R. 194; Barr *v.* Stevens, 1 Bibb, (Kentucky) R. 273.

pass, this will be sufficient.[1] And, in an early case, it was determined that an individual, who was prevented by an obstruction from carrying his corn over the most convenient road from the field where it was sowed to the place of his residence, in consequence whereof the corn was spoiled by a fall of rain, was entitled to a private action for the damage.[2] So, where a wharfinger, under a special contract to deliver coal at a particular place, was impeded, in going to and fro with his carts, by the keeping open a swing bridge on his way for unreasonable spaces of time and was in consequence obliged to provide additional carts and obtain another wharf in a different situation, he was held to have suffered special damage.[3] Diversion of custom from a shop or colliery, by an obstruction of the road leading to the same, is such a special grievance as will warrant a private action. Thus, where the plaintiff was a bookseller, whose customers consisted mainly of persons frequenting an adjoining thoroughfare, which was blocked up by the continuance of an authorized obstruction after the expiration of the act authorizing the same, the Court remarked, that the plaintiff, in addition to a right of way which he enjoyed in common with others, had a shop on the roadside, the business of which was supported by those who passed; that all who passed had the right of way, but all had not the shop; and held, that for this loss of custom he was entitled to his remedy.[4] In Rose *v.* Miles, the plaintiff, while navigating his barges laden with goods along a public navigable creek, was obstructed by the defendants' mooring their barge across, and obliged to unload and carry his goods over land, by reason

---

1 Griesley *v.* Codling, 2 Bingh. R. 263; Chichester *v.* Letheridge, Willes, R. 71. See, also, Hart *v.* Basset, T. Jones, R. 156; Hughes *v.* Heiser, 1 Binney, (Penn.) R. 463.

2 Maynell *v.* Saltmarsh, Keb. R. 847.

3 Wiggins *v.* Boddington, 3 Carr. & Paine, R. 543.

4 Wilkes *v.* Hungerford Market Co. 2 Bingh. R. N. C. 281; Iveson *v.* Moore, 1 Ld. Raymond, R. 486.

of which he incurred considerable expense. Lord Ellenborough, distinguishing this case from Hubert *v.* Groves, in which Lord Kenyon held it not to be enough that the plaintiff had been put to the necessity of going a circuitous route, by the circumstance that the plaintiff in this case had commenced his course upon the creek and was in the act of using it when obstructed, said: "If a man's time or his money are of any value, it seems to me that this plaintiff has shown a particular damage."[1] In Pierce *v.* Dart,[2] the nuisance was the building of a fence across a public highway near the residence of the plaintiff. The Court said: "In considering the special damage we must lay out of view the fact that the road was more contiguous and therefore more beneficial to the plaintiff than to others. He might have been more injured by the obstruction on this account than others; but it is not such an injury as the law will notice. The right of action for obstructing a highway can never be determined by the distance at which the party resides from it."[3] And in this case it was said to be the principle to be extracted from all the cases, that any the least injury to an individual, as an expense of time or labor, &c. entitles him to an action. "It is a special damage as contradistinguished from the injury of the public in general, which is theoretical or resting in presumption of law only. In the case at bar the plaintiff was certainly put to some expense. There was delay and labor in abating the nuisance so that he might proceed on the road."[4]

§ 286. At common law, however, this liability was confined to individuals who either actually obstructed the highway, or being bound to keep it in a safe and unobstructed state, omitted

1 Rose *v.* Miles, 4 M. & Sel. R. 101.

2 Pierce *v.* Dart, 7 Cowen, (N. Y.) R. 609.

3 *Vide* Bradbee *v.* Christ's Hospital, 4 Man. & Gr. R. 714.

4 Stetson *v.* Faxon, 19 Pick. (Mass.) R. 147; Thayer *v.* Boston, Ibid. 511; Lansing *v.* Wiswall, 5 Denio, (N. Y.) 213; Lansing *v.* Smith, 8 Cowen, (N. Y.) R. 146.

that duty, and did not extend to parishes, townships, or counties, for want of reparation. The reason given in an ancient case for this restriction is, that such a defect is a public matter, which ought to be reformed by presentment.[1] In Russell *v.* The Men of Devon,[2] this reason is adopted and the additional one given, that parishes and counties being merely *quasi* corporations, there is no corporation fund, and no legal means of obtaining one, out of which satisfaction could be made, so that if damages were recoverable they must be levied on one or two individuals, who would have no means whatever of reimbursing themselves; for if they were to bring separate actions against each individual of the parish or county for his proportion, it would be better that the injured party should be without remedy, in accordance with the general principle of law, that it is better that an individual should sustain an injury than that the public should suffer an inconvenience. In the United States, the same doctrine has been affirmed.[3] But in several of the States, provision is made by statute for the recovery of damages by private suit against towns, in favor of individuals who have sustained any injury in person or property, in consequence of the insufficiency of any highway or bridge repairable by such towns. In those States it is held, that the liability being created solely by statute, cannot be extended beyond the statute measure thereof.[4]

§ 287. Thus, in Massachusetts, a statute which provides

---

1 Broke's Abr. title Sur le Case, pl. 93.

2 Russell *v.* The Men of Devon, 2 Term Rep. 667; Makinnon *v.* Penson, 25 Eng. Law & Eq. R. 457.

3 Mower *v.* Leicester, 9 Mass. R. 247; Riddle *v.* Proprietors of Locks and Canals on Merrimack River, 7 Mass. R. 169; Loker *v.* Brookline, 13 Pick. R. 343; Morey *v.* Newfane, 8 Barb. (N. Y.) Sup. Ct. R. 646; Lynn *v.* Adams, 2 Cart. (Ind.) R. 143; Bartlett *v.* Crozier, 17 Johns. (N. Y.) R. 439; Hedger *v.* Madison, 1 Gilm. (Ill.) R. 567; Reed *v.* Belfast, 20 Maine R. 246.

4 Chidsey *v.* Canton, 17 Conn. R. 475; Sawyer *v.* Northfield, 7 Cush. (Mass.) R. 490; Tisdalè *v.* Norton, 8 Met. (Mass.) R. 388; Brady *v.* Lowell, 3 Cush. (Mass.) R. 121; Kelsey *v.* Glover, 15 Vt. R. 708; Farnum *v.* Concord, 2 N. Hamph. R. 392.

indemnity for any person "who shall receive any injury in his person or property by reason of any defect or want of repair," &c., has been held to embrace only injuries sustained while using the highway, and not the damage which a party sustains in consequence of not being able to use it, because of the neglect of the town to keep it in a proper state for such use. Therefore, the damage sustained by the owner of land, from being deprived of convenient access thereto by a defect in the highway, is not remediable under such a statute.[1] And where a highway was obstructed by snow, the plaintiff was not allowed to recover for the expense, trouble, and loss of time in extricating his team. In that case, Shaw, C. J., in commenting on the language of the statute, said, it meant "physical injury in his person, or in his horse, or other material object, which can be denominated property, and does not extend to expenses incurred, or loss, unless they are incident to such physical injury and constitute one item of the damage caused by it."[2] In Maine, under a similar statute, it has been determined that a father cannot recover for the loss of the services of his minor son; nor a husband for the loss of the services or society of his wife, or for expenses incurred on account of such an injury to her; for it would not be an injury to his person nor a damage to his property, within the meaning of the statute.[3] But for his own loss of time and medical expenses, where he has suffered in his person, he is entitled to compensation, and, by joining his wife in a suit, may recover for her loss of time and expenses; the common-law rule, that the husband alone can recover, not being in force under the statute.[4]

---

1 Smith *v.* Dedham, 8 Cush. (Mass.) R. 522; Holman *v.* Townsend, 13 Met. (Mass.) R. 297.

2 Brailey *v.* Southborough, 6 Cush. (Mass.) R. 141.

3 Reed *v.* Belfast, 20 Maine R. 246; Sanford *v.* Augusta, 32 Maine R. 536; but see Weeks *v.* Shirley, 33 Maine R. 271; Harwood *v.* Lowell, 4 Cush. (Mass.) R. 310; Chidsey *v.* Canton, 17 Conn. R. 475.

4 Sanford *v.* Augusta, 32 Maine R. 536.

§ 288. In Maine, also, it has been determined that a person travelling with a hired horse, which is injured by reason of a defect in the road, may recover in his damages the value of the horse, which he has paid its owner. "The hirer," said Shepley, C. J., in announcing the judgment of the Court, "acquires a special property in the article hired, and is regarded as the owner of it for the purpose of recovering damages of one who has injured it while in his possession. This rule, it is said, cannot be applicable to the present case; for if the horse was injured without any fault of the hirer, the loss could not fall upon him but upon the owner. And if the loss were occasioned by any fault or neglect of the hirer, he would not be entitled to recover of the defendants. These positions, although founded upon acknowledged principles of law, do not show that the plaintiff is not entitled to recover. They assume that the hirer of a horse would not be guilty of any fault, as respects the owner, by driving him upon a highway defective and unsafe. This cannot be admitted. And yet, so far as it respects those liable to keep the highway in repair, he could not be chargeable with any neglect or fault. The relations existing between the hirer and owner, and between the hirer and those liable to keep a highway in repair, are not the same. The argument, therefore, although very plausible is not sound."[1]

§ 289. The statutes of Massachusetts and Maine provide that the towns shall have had reasonable notice of the defect in order to be liable for an injury occasioned thereby. In reference to what amounts to reasonable notice, in Reed *v.* Northfield,[2] it was remarked: "It has often been held, in giving a

---

1 Littlefield *v.* Biddeford, 29 Maine R. 310. The statute gives a remedy to any person, "who shall receive any bodily injury or suffer any damage in his property through any defect or want of repair," &c. Under that statute bodily pain is a part of the injury for which damage may be recovered. Verrill *v.* Minot, 31 Maine R. 299; Mason *v.* Ellsworth, 32 Ibid. 271.

2 Reed *v.* Northfield, 13 Pick. (Mass.) R. 94.

construction to this act, that notice to the town of the defect of a highway may be inferred from its notoriety and from its continuance for such a length of time as to lead to the presumption, that the proper officers of the town did in fact know, or with proper diligence and care might have known, the fact. This latter is sufficient, because this degree of care and vigilance they are bound to exercise, and, therefore, if in point of fact they do not know of such defect, when by ordinary and due vigilance and care they might have known it, they must be responsible as if they had actual notice." In some cases it has been thought to be sufficient notice to the town that some principal or tax-paying inhabitant thereof had actual knowledge of the defect; and in a recent case in Maine, knowledge of the defect by two of its inhabitants *capable of communicating information of it*, was held to be evidence of notice to the town, and it was considered not to be necessary that they should be among the principal men or that they should be assessed for public taxes.[1]

§ 290. But whether the action be brought at common law against an individual who has committed some positive nuisance whereby the plaintiff has suffered a special damage, or under the statute, against the town for injuries sustained by reason of some defect or want of repair; in either case the plaintiff, to recover, must be shown not to have *contributed* to the injury by his own fault or by the want of ordinary care.[2] The town that suffers its highways to be out of repair, or the party who obstructs the same, is answerable to the public by

---

1 Mason *v.* Ellsworth, 32 Maine R. 271; Springer *v.* Bowdoinham, 7 Greenl. (Maine) R. 422; Hull *v.* Paris, 10 Shepl. (Maine) R. 556; French *v.* Brunswick, 8 Shepl. (Maine) R. 29; Lobdell *v.* New Bedford, 1 Mass. R. 152.

2 Butterfield *v.* Forrester, 11 East, R. 60; Flower *v.* Adams, 2 Taunt. R. 314; Smith *v.* Smith, 2 Pick. (Mass.) R. 621; Wood *v.* Waterville, 4 Mass. R. 422; Moore *v.* Abbot, 32 Maine R. 46; Tisdale *v.* Norton, 8 Met. (Mass.) R. 388; Noyes *v.* Norristown, 1 Vt. R. 353; Rice *v.* Montpelier, 19 Vt. R. 470; Brown *v.* Maxwell, 6 Hill, (N. Y.) R. 592, and cases cited in note; and see *post*, Chap. VIII.

indictment, whether any person be injured or not; but not to an individual, unless he has received some particular damage by reason thereof; and, where he has been careless, it cannot be known whether the injury be imputable to the fault of the party defendant, or to the negligence of the party complaining.[1] "Two things," says Lord Ellenborough, "must concur to support this action; an obstruction in the road by the fault of the defendant and no want of ordinary care to avoid it on the part of the plaintiff."[2] If, however, the injury be such as could not have been avoided by the exercise of ordinary care, or was wantonly caused by the defendant, it would seem that the plaintiff, though negligent, is entitled to recover.[3] The degree of care required of the plaintiff is such care as persons of common prudence generally exercise; and whether in any given case he has exercised this degree of care is a question of fact, or a mixed question of law and fact, to be determined by the jury under the direction of the Court.[4] The burden of proving the exercise of such care rests upon the plaintiff, though it need not be directly shown, but may be inferred by the jury from the circumstances of the case.[5]

§ 291. Where the injury is the result of a deviation from the travelled or wrought track of the road, this in itself is con-

---

1 Smith *v.* Smith, 2 Pick. (Mass.) R. 621; Farnum *v.* Concord, 2 N. Hamp. R. 292.

2 Butterfield *v.* Forrester, 11 East, R. 60.

3 Bridge *v.* The Grand Junction Railway Co. 3 M. & W. R. 244; Davies *v.* Mann, 10 M. & W. R. 645; Kennard *v.* Burton, 25 Maine R. 39; Farrar *v.* Green, 32 Maine R. 574; Brownell *v.* Flager, 5 Hill, (N. Y.) R. 282.

4 Kelsey *v.* Glover, 15 Vt. R. 708; Allen *v.* Hancock, 16 Vt. R. 230; Reed *v.* Northfield, 13 Pick. (Mass.) R. 94; Bigelow *v.* Rutland, 4 Cush. (Mass.) R. 247; Farnum *v.* Concord, 2 N. Hamp. R. 292.

5 French *v.* Brunswick, 8 Shep. (Maine) R. 29; Foster *v.* Dixfield, 6 Shep. (Maine) R. 380; Cobb *v.* Standish, 2 Shep. (Maine) R. 198; Merrill *v.* Hampden, 26 Maine R. 234; but see Beaty *v.* Gilmore, 4 Harris, (Penn.) R. 463; Beach *v.* Parmenter, 11 Ibid. 196. In the declaration it is enough to aver that the injury was caused by a defect, without averring the exercise of ordinary care. May *v.* Princeton, 11 Met. (Mass.) R. 442.

sidered such negligence as ordinarily will exempt the town from liability, unless the plaintiff be forced aside by an accident or is obliged to turn out for some other sufficient reason. Thus, in a case where the plaintiff, while travelling in a sleigh in the night time, deviated from the centre of the road, which was bare, to the margin, which was covered with snow and had been travelled, and was injured by a hole dug without the travelled path; the Court held, that if the plaintiff diverged without necessity, merely for the benefit of the snow, or if the horse took the same direction from a natural instinct or from an inability to see the road on account of the darkness, the town should not be held responsible for the consequences which ensued.[1] So, if a person knows there is an obstruction in a street and voluntarily encounters it, though in consequence of the darkness of the night or of the rise of water over the street, he cannot see the obstruction, he will not be considered to be in the exercise of such care as will entitle him to recover against the town.[2] But a traveller is not bound to look a great distance ahead in order to guard against obstructions which ought not to be suffered to exist. Thus, a traveller, who lost his horse upon a causeway, which, from a distant eminence he might have discovered to have been covered with water, but which, when he had descended, was out of sight until he had proceeded too far to retreat or go on with safety, was held to be entitled to recover for the loss of his horse if he then used ordinary care in endeavoring to extricate him.[3]

§ 292. In the case of Erie City *v.* Schwingle,[4] the carriage of the plaintiff was upset, whilst passing along a way deviating from the street on which he had passed, and leading to the

---

1 Rice *v.* Montpelier, 19 Vt. R. 470; Tisdale *v.* Norton, 8 Met. (Mass.) R. 388.

2 Mount Vernon *v.* Dusouchett, 2 Cart. (Ind.) R. 586; Shepardson *v.* Coleman, 13 Met. (Mass.) R. 55; Jacobs *v.* Bangor, 4 Shep. (Maine) R. 187.

3 Thompson *v.* Bridgewater, 7 Pick. R. 188.

4 Erie City *v.* Schwingle, 10 Harris, (Penn.) R. 384.

crossing of a stream in a borough, the bridge over which had been carried away by flood, by which accident his leg was broken. It was held, that although there were other streets in the borough, by which the plaintiff could have safely reached the point towards which he was going when the accident occurred, yet if the officers of the borough permitted the street to be used without warning the public of its imperfect condition, they cannot charge the plaintiff with inexcusable negligence or want of ordinary care in using it. "They invited him," said the Court, "into that street, by not closing it up, by allowing it to be used without objection, and by putting certain repairs upon it, which made it not safe, but passable with skilful driving and good luck. Culpable negligence or want of ordinary care on the part of the plaintiff would have been a defence. No proof of that kind was offered, except what may be inferred from the plaintiff's not going around some other way. We are very clear in the opinion, that that amounts to nothing in the circumstances of this case."

§ 293. But a traveller who goes entirely out of the highway, because it has become dangerous or impassable by reason of want of repair, into the adjoining land, and there receives an injury, cannot recover against the town for the injury received. "Due care and diligence," say the Court, "are to be used to avoid danger, and if the traveller, with full knowledge that the road is out of repair, shall, with rashness, or, as it is sometimes called, fool-hardiness, rush into danger, he is remediless. Wherever, therefore, the road is notoriously a dangerous one, and unsafe for travelling, it becomes the duty of the traveller, upon being apprised of the actual state of things, whether this be indicated by a bar being thrown across the road, or other equally effective mode of giving notice, to abandon the route, and make use of some other public way; otherwise he proceeds at his own peril."[1]

---

[1] Tisdale and Wife *v.* Norton, 8 Met. (Mass.) R. 388.

§ 294. In Wood *v.* Waterville, this principle was applied to a case in which the plaintiff was a surveyor of the highway, through a defect in which the damage resulted. In that case, the plaintiff's mare, in passing and travelling in said highway, through a defect or want of necessary repair of a pole-bridge or causeway in the same, fell down and broke one of her legs. On the trial of an action against the town, evidence was offered that the plaintiff was the surveyor of the defective way, and rejected. After verdict for the plaintiff, a new trial was moved for on that ground; and Parsons, C. J., in delivering the opinion of the Court, after stating the power and duties of the surveyor under the statute, continued: "From this view of the act, it is clear that the surveyors are bound to repair the highways, but at the expense of the town. And if the town had raised sufficient money, or if it was in the power of the surveyor to assess sufficient, and the ways have not been repaired through his neglect of duty, and by that neglect a defect has existed from which he has sustained damage, it would be a very unreasonable construction of the act, to enable him to recover double damages of the town; as it would reward him for his own faulty misconduct. We are, therefore, satisfied that the evidence offered ought to have been admitted. If the plaintiff had neglected to spend the money raised by the town, or if the town had refused to raise any money, and the plaintiff had neglected to assess and expend a sufficient sum, he ought to be barred of his action."[1]

§ 295. In Vermont and in Massachusetts, it has been determined, that the town may be liable for an injury which is primarily imputable to a pure accident. Thus, in Kelsey *v.* Glover, a frightened horse, running driverless, was crowded against the plaintiff's horse, by an obstruction on the road. The Court directed the jury, that towns are bound to build and repair their roads in such a manner, that they will be reason-

---

1 Wood *v.* Waterville, 4 Mass. R. 422.

ably safe from the consequences of such accidents, as may be justly expected, occasionally, to occur on such roads, and that, in this case, if an insufficiency of the road, as thus explained, coöperated to produce the injury to the plaintiff's horse, the town was liable. And these directions, upon a motion for a new trial after verdict for the plaintiff, were affirmed.[1] In a still earlier case, where the plaintiff and his wife were precipitated over the edge of an insufficiently-guarded precipice, the Court, after acknowledging the principle, that the plaintiff would not be entitled to damages if guilty of any negligence, either in driving or in the construction or repair of his carriage or harness, whereby the injury was, in any manner, hastened or produced,—remarked as follows: "In every case of damage, occurring on the highway, we could suppose a state of circumstances, in which the injury would not have occurred. If the team had not been too young, or restive, or old, or too headstrong, or the harness had not been defective or the carriage insufficient, no loss would have intervened. It is against *these* constantly occurring *accidents*, that towns are required to guard in building highways. The traveller is not bound to see to it that his carriage is always *perfect*, and his team of the *most manageable* character, and in the *most perfect training* before he *ventures* upon the highway. If he could be always sure of all this, he would not require any further guaranty of his safety, unless the roads were absolutely impassable. If the plaintiff is in the exercise of ordinary care and prudence, and the injury is attributable to the insufficiency of the road, conspiring with some accidental cause, the defendants are liable."[2]

---

[1] Kelsey *v.* Glover, 15 Vt. R. 708; see also, Halley *v.* Winooski Turnpike Co. 1 Aik. (Vt.) R. 74. There can be no recovery on the part of a person who is so intoxicated as to be incapable of carefully conducting himself and his team. Cassedy *v.* Stockbridge, 21 Vt. R. 391. But where a woman is the driver, it will be for the jury to determine from the character of the horse and the capacity of the driver whether there is not an exercise of ordinary care. Cobb *v.* Standish, 2 Shep. (Maine) R. 178.

[2] Hunt and Wife *v.* Pownal, 9 Vt. R. 411.

And in Massachusetts, in a case almost identical with this in its essential features, the Court said: "It seems to us that where the loss is the combined result of an accident and of the defect in the road, and the damage would not have been sustained but for the defect, although the primary cause be a pure accident, yet if there be no fault or negligence of the plaintiff, if the accident be one which common prudence and sagacity could not have foreseen and provided against, the town is liable."[1]

§ 296. But in Maine, a contrary doctrine seems to have obtained. In the case of Moore *v.* Abbot,[2] the Judge instructed the jury, that if they should be satisfied the accident happened by the joint effect of a defect in the way, and a defect in the harness, rendering it unsuitable or unsafe, although such defect in the harness was not known, and the plaintiff was not in fault, for want of knowledge, the plaintiff would not be entitled to recover. The Court, in refusing to set aside a verdict obtained for the defendants, said: "An injury cannot be determined to have been occasioned by a defect in the way, so long as it remains certain that some other cause contributed to produce the injury." A different rule "would make the town when its ways are not in repair, an insurer against injuries, not occasioned by its own negligence, but partly by inevitable accident."[3] But, in that State, where the injury was the result of two defects, one of which frightened the horse and rendered him unmanageable, and the other, coöperating with the unmanageableness of the horse, produced the injury, the town was held to be liable.[4]

---

1 Palmer *v.* Andover, 2 Cush. (Mass.) R. 600.

2 Moore *v.* Abbot, 32 Maine, R. 46.

3 Moore *v.* Abbot, 32 Maine R. 46; Farrar *v.* Greene, 32 Maine R. 574; Libbey *v.* Greenbush, 20 Maine R. 47. The statutes of Massachusetts and Maine provide a remedy for injuries occasioned "through any defect or want of repair;" that of Vermont for injuries occasioned "by means of any insufficiency or want of repair."

4 Verrill *v.* Minot, 31 Maine R. 299.

§ 297. In any case, however, the liability of towns for injuries, is limited to injuries from such defects as are indictable,[1] though it extends as well to obstructions placed on the way, as to inherent defects.[2]

§ 298. We have seen, that the town is primarily liable for injuries occasioned by obstructions placed upon a highway by an individual. In such case, the town is entitled to be indemnified for the damages, which it has paid, by the author of the obstruction; and, where several injuries result from the same obstruction, each successive recovery against the town constitutes a distinct claim for indemnity against the author of the obstruction, the town being entitled in no case to recover probable damages beyond the specific damages assessed in the judgments against it.[3] But, in Massachusetts, under a statute which provides double damages for injuries happening after reasonable notice to the town of the defect, the town is held entitled to recover to the amount of single damages only against the individual who caused the nuisance. This is the extent to which he would be liable to the party injured; and the damages are held to be doubled by reason of the neglect of the town; and although there be, in fact, no actual negligence, yet by reason of their constructive negligence, they alone are responsible for the increased amount of damages.[4] Where the defect was occasioned by a cellar-way opening upon a sidewalk, it was held that the occupant of the building, and not the owner, was liable over to the town for the damages, unless there had been an express agreement between the landlord and tenant, that the former should keep the premises in repair, in

---

1 Merrill *v.* Hampden, 26 Maine R. 234; Howard *v.* North Bridgewater, 16 Pick. (Mass.) R. 189.

2 Frost *v.* Portland, 11 Maine R. 271; Bigelow *v.* Weston, 3 Pick. (Mass.) R. 291; Snow *v.* Adams, 1 Cush. (Mass.) R. 443.

3 Newbury *v.* Conn. and Pass. Rivers Railroad Co. 25 Vt. R. 377.

4 Lowell *v.* Boston and Lowell Railroad Corporation, 23 Pick. (Mass.) R. 24; Lowell *v.* Short, 4 Cush. (Mass.) R. 275.

which case, to avoid circuity of action, the landlord would be liable in the first instance.[1]

§ 299. Where the duty of repair devolves upon individuals or private corporations, they are liable for injuries which result from any defect, which might have been prevented by the exercise of ordinary care and diligence. And when their liability is regulated by statute, they, like towns, will be liable for any injuries occasioned by a non-compliance with the requirements of the statute.[2] Thus it has been held, that where there is a failure on the part of a turnpike company to comply with an express requirement of the statute, either as to the width of the road, or the mode of its construction, and a person travelling over it sustains an injury in consequence of such omission, the turnpike company is liable, unless it appears that the plaintiff could have avoided the injury by the exercise of ordinary care and prudence. In such a case there is no question involved of want of skill or care on the part of the company, but the omission to comply with the statutory requirement, is a nuisance for which a party injured, without negligence on his part, may claim damages.[3]

§ 300. From what has been already said, it is obvious, that the party injured by a nuisance in the highway, has his option to proceed in this action, either against the town under the statute, or against the author of the nuisance; and, if the author commit the same in the course of his employment, as the servant of another, either against him or his employer. And, from the case of Bush *v.* Steinman, it would seem, that a person may be liable in this action for a nuisance committed by another, if committed for his benefit, even though he is not

1 Lowell *v.* Spaulding, 4 Cush. (Mass. R.) 277.

2 Townsend *v.* Susquehannah Bridge Co. 6 Johns. (N. Y.) R. 90.

3 Wilson *v.* Susquehannah Turnpike Road Co. 21 Barb. (N. Y.) Sup. Ct. R. 68; citing Harlow *v.* Humiston, 6 Cowen, (N. Y.) R. 189; Dygert *v.* Schenk, 23 Wend. (N. Y.) R. 446.

his immediate employer, and exercises no authority over his actions. In that case, the plaintiff was injured by a quantity of lime deposited in the highroad. The defendant, having purchased a house by the road side, (but which he had never occupied,) contracted with a surveyor to put it in repair for a stipulated sum; a carpenter having a contract under the surveyor to do the whole business, employed a bricklayer under him, and he again contracted for a quantity of lime with a lime-burner, by whose servant the lime in question was laid in the road. The defendant was held to be liable. "Where a civil injury of the kind now complained of has been sustained," it was remarked, "the remedy ought to be obvious, and the person injured should have only to discover the owner of the house which was the occasion of the mischief; not be compelled to enter into the concerns between the owner and other persons, the inconvenience of which would be more heavily felt than any which can arise from a circuity of action." And Rooke, J., said: "He who has work going on for his own benefit, and on his own premises, must be civilly answerable for the acts of those whom he employs. It shall be intended by the Court, that he has a control over all those persons who work on his premises, and he shall not be allowed to discharge himself from that intendment by any act or contract of his own. He ought to reserve such control, and if he deprive himself of it, the law will not permit him to take advantage of that circumstance, in order to screen himself from an action."[1]

---

[1] Bush *v.* Steinman, 1 Bos. & Pul. R. 404, citing Michael *v.* Alestree, 2 Lev. R. 172; Stone *v.* Cartwright, 6 Term R. 411; Littledale *v.* Lord Lonsdale, 2 H. Bl. R. 267; and see Bailey *v.* Mayor of New York, 3 Hill, (N. Y.) R. 531; 2 Denio, (N. Y.) R. 433.

# CHAPTER VII.

## THE FEE IN HIGHWAYS.



### 1. *The Rights of the Owner of the Fee.*

§ 301. AT common law, as we have already had frequent occasion to remark, a highway is simply an easement or servitude, carrying with it, as its incidents, the right to use the soil for the purposes of repair and improvement, and, in cities, for the more general purposes of sewerage, the distribution of light and water, and the furtherance of public morality, health, trade, and convenience. The owner of the land, over which the highway passes, retains the fee and all rights of property not incompatible with the public enjoyment, and, whenever the highway is abandoned or lost, recovers his original unencumbered dominion.[1] He may sell the land subject to the ease-

---

[1] Roll. Abr. 392; Comyn's Dig. tit. Chimin. (A. 2.); Lade *v.* Shephard, 2 Str. 1004; Goodtitle *v.* Alker, 1 Burr. 133; Gore *v.* West, 7 Taunt. 39; Cooke *v.* Green, 11 Price, 736; Doe d. Pring *v.* Pearsy, 7 B. & Cr. 304; Cro. Jac. 190; 4 Bacon's Abr. 668; Maynell *v.* Surtees, 31 Eng. Law & Eq. R. 485; United States *v.* Harris, 1 Sumner, (Cir. Ct.) R. 21; Chatham *v.* Brainard, 11 Conn. R. 60; Harris *v.* Elliott, 10 Peters, (U. S.) R. 25; Howard *v.* Hutchinson, 1 Fairf. (Maine) R. 335; Bingham *v.* Doane, 9 Ham. (Ohio) R. 165; Kennedy *v.* Jones, 11 Alabama R. 63; Harrington *v.* County Commissioners of Berkshire, 22 Pick. (Mass.) R. 263; Barclay *v.* Howell's Lessee, 6 Peters, (U. S.) R. 498. In Buel *v.* Clark, 1 Root, (Conn.) R. 49, the question was, whether lands left for a highway by the proprietors in the original laying out of

ment; and a deed of a farm of land, "reserving only the highway through the said farm," conveys the land subject only to the easement.[1]

§ 302. "The owner of the soil," said Foster, J., in Goodtitle *v.* Alker,[2] "has right to *all above* and *under* ground, except only the right of passage for the king and his people." And Mansfield, J., in the same case, quoting from Rolle's Abridgment, remarked, "That the king has *nothing but the passage* for himself and his people; but the *freehold and all profits* belong to the owner of the soil, so do all the trees upon it and mines under it, which may be extremely valuable. The owner may carry water in pipes under it. The owner may get his soil discharged of the servitude or easement of a way over it, by a writ of *ad quod damnum*. It is like the property in a market or fair. There is no reason why he should not have a right to all remedies for the freehold; subject still, indeed, to the servitude or easement. An assize would lie, if he should be disseized of it; an action of trespass would lie for an injury done to it." So it was held, that the trustees of a turnpike road could not consent to the turning of a public footpath into their highway, because, said Kenyon, C. J., "The soil was not vested in them, but remained in the persons who were entitled to it before the act passed by which they were appointed. The trustees have only the control of the highway."[3] In another case the plaintiff had declared generally for a trespass on his close called "Shepherd's Lane." The trespass proved was, that the defendant had depastured

---

their lots, that are not wanted for the use of a highway, belong to the proprietors of the town, and may be taken up by the proprietors and laid out into lots; or whether they belong to the town—by Court and jury they belong to the proprietors,—and verdict and judgment was for the plaintiff to recover accordingly. Brown *v.* Freeman, Ib. 118.

[1] Fairfield *v.* Williams, 4 Mass. R. 427; Whitbeck *v.* Cook, 15 Johns. (N. Y.) R. 483; Peck *v.* Smith, 1 Conn. R. 103; Hart *v.* Chalker, 5 Ib. 311.

[2] Goodtitle *v.* Alker, 1 Burr, 133.

[3] Davison *v.* Gill, 1 East, R. 64.

his cattle all along the lane, as well in the parts opposite to the plaintiff's close, as in other parts; and a motion was made to set aside the verdict, because, at most, he was only entitled to the soil and freehold of half the lane opposite to his own enclosures; but, *per Curiam:* "The plaintiff had an exclusive right to part of 'Shepherd's Lane;' and if the defendant meant to drive him to confine the trespass complained of upon the face of his declaration to that part of the lane which was his, he should have pleaded soil and freehold in another, which would have obliged the plaintiff to new assign."[1]

§ 303. The principles of the common law, in this respect, have been recognized and adopted by the American courts. The language of Parsons, Ch. J., in Perley *v.* Chandler,[2] is an exact statement of these principles. "By the location of a way over the land of any person," said that learned jurist, "the public have acquired an easement, which the owner of the land cannot lawfully extinguish or unreasonably interrupt. But the soil and freehold remain in the owner, although encumbered with a way. And every use to which the land may be applied, and all the profits which may be derived from it, consistently with the continuance of the easement, the owner can lawfully claim. He may maintain ejectment for the land thus encumbered; and if the way be discontinued, he shall hold the land free from the encumbrance. Upon these principles there can be no doubt but that the owner of the land can sink a drain, or any watercourse below the surface of his land covered with a way, so as not to deprive the public of their easement. And it is a common practice for the owners of water-mills, or of sites for water-mills, to sink watercourses for the use of their mills in their own land under highways, care being taken to cover the watercourses sufficiently,

---

1 Steevens *v.* Whistler, 11 East, R. 51; Doe d. Jackson *v.* Wilkinson, 3 B. & Cr. 413.

2 Perley *v.* Chandler, 6 Mass. R. 454.

so that the highways remain safe and convenient for passengers." "If a highway be located over watercourses, either natural or artificial, the public cannot shut up these courses, but may make the road over them by the aid of bridges. But when a way has been located over private land, if the owner should afterwards open a watercourse across the way, it will be his duty, at his own expense, to make and keep in repair a way over the watercourse, for the convenience of the public; and if he should neglect to do it, he may be indicted for the nuisance; and upon the conviction, the nuisance may be prostrated by filling up the watercourse, if he shall not make a convenient way over it." So it has been held by the same Court, that the herbage belongs exclusively to the owner of the soil and he may maintain trespass against one who puts his cattle in the highway to graze. And it was said by Putnam, J., in delivering the opinion of the Court: "It is not lawful, therefore, for the public to put their cattle into the highway to graze. For wherever one would justify taking the property of another, in virtue of a license or of a way, he must plead and prove that he pursued the authority, or used the way as a way and not for any other purpose.[1] So in 22 Edw. IV. 8, pl. 24, it was said by one of the Court, that if one drive a herd of cattle along the highway, where trees, or wheat, or any other kind of corn is growing, if one of the beasts take a parcel of the corn, if it be against the will of the driver, he may justify; for the law will intend that a man cannot govern them at all times as he would; but if he permitted them or continued them, &c., then it is otherwise."[2]

---

1 Dovaston *v.* Payne, 2 H. Bl. R. 527.

2 Stackpole *v.* Healy, 16 Mass. R. 33; Cool *v.* Crommet, 1 Shep. (Maine) R. 250. In Avery *v.* Maxwell, 4 N. Hamp. R. 36, the same doctrine was announced. But in that case it was contended that the common law was in this respect altered by the statute of January 14, 1795, entitled, "An act to prevent damage being done by horses, mules, and jacks," which prohibits horses and mules from going at large without being fettered with good and sufficient

§ 304. The law has, also, been well expressed by Platt, J., in delivering the opinion of the Supreme Court of New York, in Jackson *v.* Hathaway.[1] "Highways," he remarked, "are regarded in our law as *easements.* The public acquire no more than the right of way, with the powers and privileges incident to that right; such as digging the soil and using the timber and other materials found within the space of the road, in a reasonable manner, for the purpose of making and repairing the road and its bridges. When the sovereign imposes a public right of way upon the land of an individual, the title of the former owner is not extinguished; but is so qualified that it can only be enjoyed subject to that easement. The former proprietor still retains his exclusive right in all mines, quarries, springs of water, timber and earth, for every purpose not incompatible with the public right of way. The person in whom the fee of the road is, may maintain trespass, or ejectment, or waste. But when the sovereign chooses to discontinue or abandon the right of way, the entire and exclusive enjoyment reverts to the proprietor of the soil." Accordingly, it has been held, that the owner of the fee may maintain trespass against one who builds on the highway;[2] or who digs up and removes the soil;[3] or cuts down trees or timber growing

---

fetters, under a penalty. It was urged that as horses were by this law prohibited from going at large without fetters, it was by implication a license to permit them to go at large with fetters. But the Court were of the opinion that, admitting the legislature had the power to authorize one man to turn his horse to graze upon the land of another, which was very questionable, still it would be a forced and unnatural interpretation of this statute to construe it to give a license of that nature. Every man had a right to turn his horses into the highway to graze, where he owned the soil over which the highway was laid, and this statute was intended to regulate the exercise of that right and not to give any new right.

1 Jackson *v.* Hathaway, 15 Johns. (N. Y.) R. 447.

2 Peck *v.* Smith, 1 Conn. R. 103; Costelyou *v.* Van Brundt, 2 Johns. (N. Y.) R. 357.

3 Gidney *v.* Earl, 12 Wend. (N. Y.) R. 98; Willoughby *v.* Jenks, 20 Ib. 96.

thereon; and though a surveyor may, as the agent of the town, cut such trees to be used in the repair of the way or in order to improve it; yet if he cuts them for his own use, he is a trespasser.[1] So it has been held to be trespass for a ferry-man to land his passengers or boats, or for any other person to unlade or receive freight at the terminus of a highway, without the consent of the owner of the soil.[2] And a railroad company cannot lay their railroad on a highway, at least in the country, though authorized by their charter, without making compensation to the owner.[3] A highway upon land is in its nature an encumbrance and a breach of a covenant, which stipulates that the land is free of encumbrances.[4]

§ 305. In Adams *v.* Rivers,[5] trespass was maintained by the adjoining owner against a person who came upon the side-walk and there remained using abusive language towards him, and refusing to depart. The language of the Court, per Willard, J., was as follows: "The defendant committed a trespass while standing on the sidewalk by the plaintiff's lot where he lived, and using towards him abusive language. While so engaged he was not using the highway for the purpose for which it was designed, but was a trespasser. He stood there but about five minutes. It was not shown that he stopped on the sidewalk for a justifiable cause; on the contrary, it was rendered probable that it was for a base and wicked purpose. It was, therefore, a trespass. Suppose a strolling musician stops in front of a gentleman's house, and plays a tune or sings an obscene song under his window, can

---

1 Babcock *v.* Lamb, 1 Cowen, (N. Y.) R. 238; Makepeace *v.* Worden, 1 N. Hamp. R. 16.

2 Chambers *v.* Fury, 1 Yeates, (Penn.) R. 167; Cooper *v.* Smith, 9 Serg. & Rawle, (Penn.) R. 31; Chess *v.* Manown, 3 Watts, (Penn.) R. 219.

3 See *ante*, § 243, *et seq.*

4 Pritchard *v.* Atkinson, 3 N. Hamp. R. 335; Kellogg *v.* Ingersoll, 2 Mass. R. 97; Wilson *v.* Wilson, 2 Vt. R. 68.

5 Adams *v.* Rivers, 11 Barb. (N. Y.) Sup. Ct. R. 390. But see O'Linda *v.* Lathrop, 21 Pick. (Mass.) R. 292.

there be a doubt that he is liable in trespass? The tendency of the act is to disturb the peace, to draw together a crowd, and to obstruct the street. It would be no justification that the act was done in a public street: The public have no need of the highway but to pass and repass. If it is used for any other purpose not justified by law, the owners of the adjoining land are remitted to the same rights they possessed before the highway was made. They can protect themselves against such annoyances by treating the intruders as trespassers." So an individual, who, without lawful authority from the town, reconstructs a highway, making it safe and convenient in parts not before actually travelled, is a trespasser.[1]

§ 306. At common law, we have remarked that the owner of the fee is entitled to the herbage growing in a highway; and the question has been raised whether this right can be constitutionally taken away or qualified without compensation therefor. In New York, an act was passed empowering the electors of each town, at their annual town meeting, "to make rules and regulations for ascertaining the sufficiency of all fences in such town; and for determining the times and manner in which cattle, horses, or sheep shall be permitted to go at large on highways." In pursuance of this act a resolution was passed at the town meeting of the town of Pierpont, in these words: "*Voted*, that all orderly neat cattle have a right to run at large from the 1st of May to the 1st of November in each year." And also another in these words: "*Voted*, that all fences shall be equal in strength to a good rail fence four and a half feet high." In an action of trespass, for the entry of cattle from the highway into the plaintiff's close, through fences which were proved to be insufficient, the defendant justified under the act and resolutions above cited. For the plaintiff it was objected that the act and resolutions

---

1 Hunt *v.* Rich, 38 Maine R. 195; Ruggles *v.* Lesure, 24 Pick. (Mass.) R. 187.

were in derogation of the clause in the constitution, which provides that private property shall not be taken for public use, without just compensation, and therefore void. But the objection was overruled and the act and resolutions were pronounced constitutional by the Supreme Court of that State.[1]

§ 307. "The question," said Willard, J., in delivering the opinion of the Court, "whether the act under consideration is in conformity to the constitution or not has never been distinctly passed upon by this Court, and I am not aware of any case in which it has been necessarily involved. We have *dicta* from highly respectable sources, adverse to the power but accompanied with no examination of our recent legislation on the subject. Thus, in Holladay *v.* Marsh,[2] which arose before the revised statutes, Chief Justice Savage intimates a doubt whether it was competent for the legislature to authorize a town to permit domestic animals to depasture the highway. And he observes that the public have simply a right of passage over the highway and have no right to depasture it. The owner of the land through which the road runs is still the owner of the soil and of the timber, except what is necessary to make and repair bridges; and, he asks, if the owner of the soil owns the timber, why not the grass? In Gidney *v.* Earl,[3] it was held, that where a road runs through a man's close, *primâ facie*, the fee of the land over which the road passes, belongs to him. "The law," says Nelson, J., "will not presume a grant of a greater interest or estate than is essential to the enjoyment of the public easement; the rest is parcel of the close." In the Tonawanda Railroad Co. *v.* Munger,[4] Beardsley, Ch. J., expresses similar views, concluding with the opinion that the legislature "do not possess the power

---

1 Griffin *v.* Martin, 7 Barb. (N. Y.) Sup. Ct. R. 297.
2 Holladay *v.* Marsh, 3 Wend. (N. Y.) R. 142.
3 Gidney *v.* Earl, 12 Wend. (N. Y.) R. 98.
4 The Tonawanda Railroad Co. *v.* Munger, 5 Denio, (N. Y.) R. 255, 264.

in question, whether compensation be made or not, but certainly in no case unless compensation is made." This opinion is not essential to the decision of the cause before him, as the action was for killing cattle, not on a public highway, but on a railroad where they were confessedly trespassers. In White *v.* Scott,[1] McCoun, J., took occasion, incidentally, to remark, when speaking of a town ordinance similar to the one in this case, "that the power of a town meeting cannot be lawfully exercised beyond allowing the owners of the soil to turn their own animals out to feed on such parts of the highway as they respectively own, under such safeguards, rules, and regulations as shall prevent any obstruction of the public use or travel, and as shall at the same time avoid collisions and trespasses by the beasts of one owner upon the property of another." And he further intimates, that a town ordinance, like the one in question, is void, as extending beyond the authority which the electors of the town in their collective capacity possess under the statute. The learned Judge does not consider the act of the legislature unconstitutional, but he gives a construction to it entirely novel, and which defeats the main object and policy of the law. Under his construction, the act does not empower the towns to pass ordinances allowing cattle, sheep, and horses to run at large on the highway, but merely to adopt regulations with respect to the *time* and *manner* in which the owner of the freehold may depasture the road which passes through his own close. He views the act as restrictive of the right which might otherwise be enjoyed. He assumes, however, that the act would be unconstitutional, if it allowed the towns to treat the public highways, in any respect, as a common of pasture. Under this narrow construction of the act, none but the great landholders could derive any benefit from it. The poor tenants and other inhabitants, not owners of the soil, would be entirely excluded."

---

[1] White *v.* Scott, 4 Barb. (N. Y.) Sup. Ct. R. 56.

§ 308. "In none of these cases was the point we are considering necessarily involved or in fact decided by the Court. In all the cases in which the constitutionality of the act in question has been doubted, the reasons assigned have been, that the soil and grass growing on a highway belong to the owner of the land, through which the road passes, and that the public have merely a right of passage; and that the effect of the town by-law is to take the private property of the owner of the land, without compensation, for the use of those who permit their cattle to run at large on the highway. This was the ground taken in the cases just cited, and by Judge Cowen in his treatise and in the note before cited,[1] and in all the adjudged cases to which we have been referred. Whatever may have been the force of this argument prior to the revised statutes, it is obvious that since the 1st of January, 1830, it is based upon a false assumption. It takes for granted that the owner of the land receives compensation merely for the easement or right of passage. This is not so. The statute which regulates the compensation to be made to the owner through whose lands public highways are laid, does not confine the damages to what arises from parting with a mere right of way. By the 65th section of the act relative to highways, bridges, and ferries, (2 R. S. 515,) when the owner of the soil and the commissioners of highways cannot agree upon the damages, a jury composed of twelve disinterested freeholders, residing in some other town, are directed to be summoned "*to assess the damages sustained by the laying out of such road.*" These damages will depend on the quantity of interest which is vested in the public. It might be competent for the legislature to take the entire fee of the land; in which case the compensation would be increased accordingly. It is presumed that the public become vested with such interest as

[1] 1 Cowen, on the Civil Jurisdiction of Justices of the Peace, p. 383, *et seq.*; Bush *v.* Brainard, 1 Cowen, (N. Y.) R. 78 and note 1.

the legislature authorize them to use. The existing law, if we consider, as we should, the act relative to towns and the highway acts as part of an entire system, empowers the commissioners not only to take the right of passage, but the right of permitting cattle, horses, and sheep, to go at large on the highway, in such times and manner, as the electors of the town in their annual town meeting shall determine. The damages of the owner of the soil are regulated by what he relinquishes to the public. He thus is compensated not only for parting with the right of way, but for parting with the right of pasturage. Hence the main argument on which the objection to the law rests is untenable."

§ 309. "It cannot with truth be said, that a by-law, like the one in question, takes the property of one man and gives it to another, or even to the public, without compensation. The owner of the soil is not deprived of the pasturage, any more than he is of the way. He can enjoy both in common with his neighbors. In agricultural districts, and especially in new countries, the public benefit resulting from permitting cattle, horses and sheep to run at large in highways, probably overbalances the increased expense of acquiring a title to the road. The intrusting the power of regulating the exercise of this right to the electors of the town, in their annual town meeting, is in conformity to the analogy of our system of government, and will rarely ever lead to abuse. To no other persons could it more safely be confided. No danger is to be apprehended that towns will multiply highways for the purpose of acquiring common of pasture. The right of pasturage is a mere incident to the road, and the latter cannot, in general, be laid out without the consent of the owner of the soil, over which it passes, except on the certificate upon oath of twelve reputable freeholders of the town, not interested in the land nor of kin to the owner, that such road is necessary and proper. It is not to be presumed that these gentlemen will give a false certificate for the sake of an incidental advantage, for which their town must pay an equivalent. (1 R. S. 514, §§ 60, 61.) Moreover, the public have a guaranty against reckless and improvident applications of this kind, in the equitable and impartial remedy provided for making the assessment of the damages." (Id. § 65.)[1]

§ 310. Turnpike roads, railroads and canals, like ordinary highways, are, as a general rule, simple easements, the fee remaining in the owner of the soil, and, upon their abandonment, reverting without further encumbrance. During the existence of such road or canal, the rights of the owner of the fee are subject to the same rule as in the case of ordinary highways.[2] Thus it has been held, that trespass lies against the servant of a turnpike company, for cutting and removing thatch growing within the limits of the road, or against one for ploughing on the road, though if done for the repair of the road, that is a good defence.[3] A turnpike company have, however, the right to erect and maintain a toll-house within the limits of their road, provided it does not incommode the public travel. They have not only a right to use the surface of the land for the purpose of travel, but may make such use of the land below the surface as may be necessary to secure and maintain the proper enjoyment of their franchise; posts may be sunk in the earth for the gate to swing upon; the soil may be excavated to drain the road. "And," adds Parker, Ch. J., "we are of the opinion, also, that a toll-house may be placed there, and that, if convenient, this may be made so as to accommodate the toll-

---

1 *Ante*, § 303, and note; Wells *v.* Howell, 19 Johns. (N. Y.) R. 385.

2 Davison *v.* Gill, 1 East, 69; Rex *v.* Mersey Navigation, 9 B. & C. 95; Rex *v.* Thomas, Ib. 114; Tippets *v.* Walker, 4 Mass. R. 595; Fisher *v.* Coyle, 3 Watts, (Penn.) R. 407; Bridge Turnpike Co. *v.* Stoever, 2 W. & Serg. (Penn.) R. 548; Parker *v.* The Inhabitants of Framingham, 8 Met. (Mass.) R. 260; Worcester *v.* Western Railroad Co. 4 Met. (Mass.) R. 564; Haswell *v.* Vermont Central Railroad Co. 23 Vt. 228; Hooker *v.* Utica and Minden Turnpike Road Co. 12 Wend. (N. Y.) R. 371, and the cases annexed; The State *v.* Hampton, 2 N. Hamp. 25; State *v.* New Boston, 9 Ib. 410.

3 Adams *v.* Emerson, 6 Pick. (Mass.) R. 57; Robbins *v.* Borman, 1 Ib. 122. But see Prather *v.* Ellison, 10 Ohio R. 396.

gatherer with a dwelling-house; and that all things necessary for this may be also lawfully done; such as the cutting down the trees, digging a cellar, well, &c., under the restriction before-mentioned, that the public highway be not too much straitened."[1] But the company cannot, by implication, have a right to build toll-houses beyond the limits of their road.[2]

§ 311. But though the interest of the public in highways, and of incorporated companies in turnpike roads, railroads and canals, is generally limited to a mere easement, there is nothing to prevent the appropriation, if necessary, of the fee of the soil. This, though not without much doubt and contrary decision, seems now to be the established law in the United States. In The People *v.* White,[3] the right is denied. The land in that case had been taken for the construction of a canal, in pursuance of a statute, providing that the fee-simple thereof should be vested in the people of the State. The land was afterwards abandoned, and the canal located in a different place. "If," reasoned the Court, "the State might retain the land thus compulsorily taken, after it had been abandoned for the purpose of a canal, it might sell it to some other private citizen." This, in effect, would be taking the property of one citizen and transferring it to another, which, if not a violation of the letter, would be of the spirit of the constitution, for the constitution, by authorizing the appropriation of private property to public use, impliedly prohibited its appropriation to any private use. But in Hayward *v.* The Mayor of New York,[4] the preceding case, though neither cited nor alluded to, was in substance overruled. This was the case of land taken under a statute for an almshouse, and *the fee simple absolute* vested in

1 Tucker *v.* Tower, 9 Pick. (Mass.) R. 109; Bridge Turnpike Co. *v.* Stoever, *supra.*

2 Thompson *v.* Proprietors of Androscoggin Bridge, 5 Greenl. (Maine) R. 62.

3 The People *v.* White, 11 Barb. (N. Y.) Sup. Ct. R. 26.

4 Hayward *v.* The Mayor of New York, 3 Selden, (N. Y.) R. 214, Court of Appeals; 8 Barb. (N. Y.) Sup. Ct. R. 486.

the corporation of the city of New York. Twenty-six years after the appropriation, it was abandoned for the purpose of an almshouse, and sold. The representatives of the original owner claimed a resulting use of the land, and denied the right of the city to the proceeds of the sale. *More land*, it was argued, cannot be taken for the public use, than is declared necessary, and is actually applied to it.[1] It results, that a fee cannot be taken when an easement or an estate for years or for a limited time will suffice. There is no difference between taking more land and taking a larger estate than necessary.[2] The principle is exemplified in the case of highways, which are easements;[3] of turnpikes, a fee limited to a use;[4] of railroads;[5] of public dams and canals;[6] of sites for forts, temporary possessions during war.[7] But the Court were of the opinion that, as incident to the right of eminent domain, the State has the power to determine, not only that lands shall be taken, but also the quantity of interest which shall be taken; whether an estate for years, for life, or in fee; whether a right of reversion shall be left in the owner, or whether a mere easement shall be taken without divesting the fee and general ownership of the land. Such a power is necessary to secure the useful exercise and

---

1 In the Matter of Albany Street, 11 Wend. (N. Y.) R. 150, 151; In the Matter of Cherry Street, 19 Ib. 667.

2 Benlow *v.* Townsend, 1 Mylne & Keene, 506. When before the Supreme Court, the case was said to be distinguishable from that of a turnpike, inasmuch as a turnpike company is bound, as a condition of its existence, to continue the road for the public use, and when it ceases to be a company, the title must, *ex necessitate*, vest in some one else, and it would seem reasonable that it should revert to the original owner. The Court of Appeals, however, do not indorse this distinction, but sustain the claim of the city, as will be seen, upon principles applicable alike to every species of appropriation.

3 Jackson *v.* Hathaway, 15 Johns. (N. Y.) R. 447; United States *v.* Harris, 1 Sumner, (Cir. Ct.) R. 1; per Edmunds, J., in Peck *v.* Smith, 1 Conn. R. 125.

4 Estes *v.* Kelsey, 8 Wend. (N. Y.) R. 555; Hooker *v.* Utica Turnpike Co. 12 Ib. 371.

5 Beekman *v.* Saratoga Railroad Co. 3 Paige, (N. Y.) R. 46, 64, 76.

6 Varick *v.* Smith, 5 Paige, (N. Y.) R. 146; 4 Law Reporter, (N. S.) 177.

7 Van Horne's Lessee *v.* Dorrance, 2 Dallas, 311.

enjoyment of the right of eminent domain. One case might require but a temporary use; another case might require the permanent and apparently perpetual occupation and enjoyment of the property by the public. The right to take must be co-extensive with the necessity of the case, and the measure of compensation should, of course, be graduated by the nature and duration of the estate or interest of which the owner is deprived. To hold otherwise, would be to pay the owner in full for his lands, and also to allow him to reclaim them, greatly enhanced in value, perhaps, by improvements placed upon them by the public.[1]

§ 312. The rights, which this ownership of the fee, where it exists, gives, are subject in practice to endless modifications, depending upon the exigencies of the public, and the location of the highway. The more ancient decisions limited the rights of the public to that of passage and repassage, and treated any interference of the soil, other than was necessary to the enjoyment of this right, as a trespass. But the modern decisions have very much extended the public right, and, particularly in the streets of populous cities, have reduced the interest of the owner of the soil to a mere naked fee of only a nominal value.[2] "These streets," says Edwards, P. J., speaking of the streets of New York city, and announcing what seems to be the modern doctrine in regard to the streets of a city, "for many years, have been used for the construction of sewers, and for

---

1 Affirmed in Rexford *v.* Knight, 1 Kernan, (N. Y.) R. 308; 15 Barb. (N. Y.) Sup. Ct. R. 627, which was the case of a canal; and see The Commonwealth *v.* Christian Fisher, 1 Penrose & Watts, (Penn.) R. 462; case of Philadelphia and Trenton Railroad, 6 Whart. (Penn.) R. 25, 44; Railroad *v.* Davis, 2 Dev. & Batt. (N. Car.) R. 451; Bonaparte *v.* Camden and Amboy Railroad Co. 1 Baldwin, (Cir. Ct.) R. 206. In the latter case, it was said, if the soil be taken by the sovereign power of the State, without the owner's conveyance, it would revert upon the discontinuance of the road; because the power of the State is only to take land for public purposes. Munger *v.* Tonawanda Railroad Co. 4 Comst. 349.

2 *Ante*, § 241, *et seq.*

the laying of water and gas-pipes, and no one has ever seriously questioned the right of the city to authorize their use for such purposes, and no adjoining owner, as far as I am aware, ever pretended to claim compensation for such use. These urban servitudes, as they have been called, are the necessary incidents of a street in a large city; and whether the streets be laid out and opened upon property belonging to the corporation, or whether they became public streets by dedication, or by grant, or upon compensation being made to the owner of the fee, they have all the incidents attached to them which are necessary to their full enjoyment as streets. It is an elementary principle of the law, that where a power, right, or thing is granted, either to a natural or an artificial person, all the incidents are granted which are necessary to the enjoyment of the power, right, or thing. And whether the corporation be the owner of the fee of the streets in trust for the public, or whether it be merely the trustee of the streets and highways as such, irrespective of any title to the soil, it has the power to authorize their appropriation to all such uses as are conducive to the public good, and do not interfere with their complete and unrestricted use as highways; and, in doing so, it is not obliged to confine itself to such uses as have already been permitted. As civilization advances, new uses may be found expedient. It was upon this principle that the existing railways in this city and in Albany, and the tunnels in the city of Brooklyn and in the village of Whitehall, have been sanctioned."[1]

### 2. *Presumptions from Adjacent Ownership.*

§ 313. Where the land, bounding on the opposite sides of a highway, belongs to the same person, the presumption is, that he owns the fee of the entire highway; where it belongs to different persons, the presumption is, that each owns to the centre

---

[1] Milhau *v.* Sharp, 15 Barb. (N. Y.) Sup. Ct. R. 210.

of the way,—*ad medium filum viæ*.[1] And so of the waste land on each side of the way, unless, indeed, it communicate with other larger wastes belonging to the lord of the manor.[2] The presumption, however, is not artificial and of positive institution, but is founded on the supposition that the way was originally granted by the adjoining proprietors in equal proportions, and may be rebutted by proof of the contrary. Where, therefore, an adjoining owner enclosed a portion of the highway, which he continued to cultivate, so enclosed, for twenty-eight years, it was held, that even on the supposition that the public easement was thereby discharged, the line of separation between the opposite proprietors remained, as it was, previous to the enclosure, the centre of the original highway.[3] In Headlam *v.* Headley,[4] the plaintiff, as adjoining proprietor, claimed a slip of greensward, across which extended a highway, whose width, including the greensward, was about sixty or seventy yards. It appeared that this greensward had been generally treated as waste land, and as a portion of a neighboring common, to which on one extremity it adjoined, and that it had been used as a common for cattle for a long space of time, by persons in the next village. There was no evidence that the plaintiff had exercised any acts of ownership over it; but he rested his claim upon the general presumption of law. It was said by Bayley, J.: "It is difficult in many cases to discover the origin of roads. They are sometimes made over

1 Stevens *v.* Whistler, 1 East, 51; Cooke *v.* Green, 11 Price, 736; Witter *v.* Harvey, 1 McCord, (So. Car.) R. 67; Willoughby *v.* Jenks, 20 Wend. (N. Y.) R. 96; Bingham *v.* Doane, 9 Ham. 165; 3 Kent, Comm. (5th ed.) p. 432; Copp *v.* Neal, 7.

2 Steele *v.* Prickett, 2 Stark. R. 463; Doe *v.* Pearsey, 7 B. & C. 304; Grose *v.* West, 7 Taunt. 39; Barrett *v.* Kemp, 7 Bing. 332; Scoones *v.* Monell, 1 Beav. 251.

3 Watrous *v.* Southworth, 5 Conn. R. 305; Peck *v.* Smith, 1 Conn. R. 127; Rex *v.* Edmonton, 1 M. & Rob. 124; Rex *v.* Hatfield, 4 Ad. & El. 164; Poole *v.* Huskisson, 11 Mees. & W. 827.

4 Headlam *v.* Headley, Holt, R. 463.

waste or common lands, in which case, the rights of the soil, subject to the public easement, are in the lord of the manor. In other cases, they are allotted by the owners of adjoining lands, and then the property in the soil continues in such owners, subject to the rights of passage. I think the presumption of the private rights of the plaintiff are negatived by the circumstances of this case, so far at least as to make it incumbent on him to adduce some evidence of property, or act of ownership, from which property may be inferred. In the absence of such evidence, I shall direct the jury to presume the *locus in quo* to be common land or waste." In Illinois, where by statute the recording by the proprietors of a plat of land, laid out into town or city lots, intersected by streets, passes the fee in the streets to the corporation, it has been held, that the purchasers of a lot designated upon such a plat, only acquires a title to the land included within the actual limits of the lot as designated. He takes no interest in the street, except in common with the public, and cannot claim title to the centre of it.[1]

### 3. *Boundaries by Highways.*

§ 314. "The established inference of law," says Chancellor Kent,[2] "is, that a conveyance of land bounded on a public highway, carries with it the fee to the centre of the road, as part and parcel of the grant. The idea of an intention in a grantor to withhold his interest in a road to the middle of it, after parting with all his right and title to the adjoining land, is never to be presumed. It would be contrary to universal practice; and it was said in Peck *v.* Smith, that there was no instance where the fee of a highway, as distinct from the adjoining land, was ever retained by the vendor. It would require an express declaration, or something equivalent thereto,

---

1 Canal Trustees *v.* Havens, 11 Ill. R. 554.

2 3 Kent, Com. (5th ed.) p. 433.

to sustain such an inference; and it may be considered as the general rule, that a grant of land bounded upon a highway or river, carries the fee in the highway or river to the centre of it, provided the grantor at the time owned to the centre, and there be no words or specific description to show a contrary intent." The soil under the highway, if it passes at all, passes as parcel of the land, and not as an appurtenant.[1] Therefore, whether the soil passes or not, is purely a question of intention, to be ascertained in each particular case from the descriptions contained in the deed, explained and illustrated by all the other parts of the conveyance, and by the localities and subject-matter to which it applies.[2]

§ 315. It may be stated, as the fair conclusion from the authorities, that a grant of land, described as bounded generally "by," or "on," or "along" a highway, carries the fee to the centre of the highway, if the grantor owned so far;[3] and, on the other hand, where the descriptive words are "by the side of," "by the margin of," or, "by the line of," or expressions equivalent thereto, the soil of the way is excluded.[4] This rule, however, has not uniformly prevailed. In Massachusetts, for instance, the Courts have more generally favored a construction which excludes the way. Thus, in Sibley *v.* Holden,[5] where

---

1 Parker *v.* The Inhabitants of Framingham, 8 Met. (Mass.) R. 266; United States *v.* Harris, 1 Sumner, (Cir. Ct.) R. 21; Webber *v.* Eastern Railroad Co. 2 Met. (Mass.) R. 147; Witter *v.* Harvey, 1 McCord, (So. Car.) R. 67.

2 Webber *v.* The Eastern Railroad Co. 2 Met. (Mass.) R. 151.

3 Bucknam *v.* Bucknam, 3 Fairf. (Maine) R. 463; Johnson *v.* Anderson, 6 Shep. (Maine) R. 76; Peck *v.* Smith, 1 Conn. R. 103; Chatham *v.* Brainard, 11 Conn. R. 103; Styles *v.* Curtis, 4 Day, (Conn.) R. 228; Reed *v.* Leeds, 19 Conn. R. 182; Reed's Petition, 13 New Hamp. R. 381; Hunt *v.* Rich, 38 Maine R. 195; Id. 309.

4 Hughes *v.* The Providence and Worcester Railroad Co. 2 R. I. Rep. 508; Jackson *v.* Hathaway, 15 Johns. (N. Y.) R. 447; Jones *v.* Cowman, 2 Sandf. (N. Y.) R. 234; Child *v.* Starr, 4 Hill, (N. Y.) R. 369; Union Burial Ground *v.* Robinson, 5 Whart. (Penn.) R. 18; Noble *v.* Cunningham, 1 McMullin, (So. Car.) R. 289.

5 Sibley *v.* Holden, 10 Pick. (Mass.) R. 249.

the description was, "beginning at a stake and stones *on the southerly side of a town-road*," and, after giving other boundaries, returning "to said road; *thence by said road easterly to the place of beginning;*" the Court were of the opinion, that the boundary first given, must be taken to be the side of the road, and so of the returning boundary, otherwise the line would be diagonal, neither by the side nor by the centre, and repugnant to the last clause, "by said road to the place of beginning." In Tyler *v.* Hammond,[1] a small lot of land was described as bounded "northwesterly on Ann Street," &c., the courses and distances being given in feet and inches. "This," said the Court, "is a very particular description of the land intended to be conveyed, in respect to which there can be no doubt or uncertainty. The lines are short, and were measured, no doubt, with great exactness, and, therefore, a mistake in the side-lines of twenty or thirty feet cannot be supposed; and, besides, I do not understand that any error appears by reference to the boundaries, at least not so as to affect the present question." The highway was held to be excluded. In O'Linda *v.* Lothrop,[2] where two parcels of land, lying on opposite sides of a narrow strip, designed for a street, were described in the grant as bounded, the one south on a "street," and the other north "on an intended street," it was held, that the fee of the narrow strip did not pass. And in Parker *v.* The Inhabitants of Framingham,[3] a grant of land, "bounded by the Worcester turnpike road," was held not to pass the fee to the centre of the road, for the reason that the grantor was strongly interested in not putting it in the power of the grantee to shut up the road in case the turnpike was discontinued.

§ 316. In New York, the rule, as laid down by Oakley, J.,

1 Tyler *v.* Hammond, 11 Pick. (Mass.) R. 193.

2 O'Linda *v.* Lothrop, 21 Pick. (Mass.) R. 292.

3 Parker *v.* The Inhabitants of Framingham, 8 Met. (Mass.) R. 260; and see Webber *v.* Eastern Railroad Railroad Co. 2 Met. (Mass.) R. 151; Clap *v.* M'Neil, 4 Mass. R. 589; Alden *v.* Murdock, 13 Mass. R. 256.

in Herring *v.* Fisher,[1] is, that where a deed or grant of land is bounded *on* a highway, or *runs along* a highway, or when the boundary lines run *to* a highway, it conveys the land to the centre of the road, if there be no words or specific description to show the contrary; and such words or specific description, must be of a very decided and controlling character. And in that case, the boundary, described as *running along a road*, was held to run through the centre thereof, notwithstanding a map or plat referred to represented the boundary as the external line of the road. Where, however, the boundary is expressly by the side of the road, the highway will be held to be excluded.[2] In Warner *v.* Southworth,[3] where land was granted, bounded by an artificial ditch and embankment, the Court of Errors of Connecticut, in analogy to the rule under discussion, held, that the grant extended to the middle of the ditch. And Judge Daggett, in delivering the opinion of the Court in that case, said: "Doubtless, had the bounding line been a stone wall, six feet in width at the bottom, the grant would have extended to the centre of it." So it has been held, that though there be no mention of the highway, yet if the land be in fact bounded thereon, the construction is the same, carrying the grant to the centre.[4]

§ 317. In the State of New York, there is a class of cases, originating in appeals from assessments of damages for land appropriated as streets in the city of New York, in which a construction somewhat novel, if not peculiar to that city, has been adopted. The owner of city land, it has been held in these cases, which is platted into lots and intersected by streets, when he sells the lots bounding them on the streets, does not

---

1 Herring *v.* Fisher, 1 Sandf. (N. Y.) R. 344, 348; Hammond *v.* McLachlan; The Same *v.* Peugnet, Ib. 323; Adams *v.* Saratoga and Washington Railroad Co. 11 Barb. (N. Y.) Sup. Ct. R. 416; Adams *v.* Rivers, Ib. 390.

2 *Ante*, § 314, note.

3 Warner *v.* Southworth, 6 Conn. R. 471.

4 Champlin *v.* Pendleton, 13 Conn. R. 23.

thereby part with the fee in the streets, but still retains the same, subject, however, to an implied right of passage in the purchasers of the adjacent lots, by virtue of which he is estopped from ever closing up the streets.[1] But in Hammond *v.* McLachlan,[2] the Court entirely repudiates this doctrine, and refuses to recognize any distinction between grants of land bounded on highways in the city and in the country. "We have looked into the cases," says Oakley, Ch. J., delivering the opinion of the Superior Court of the city of New York, "all of which arose on applications to the Supreme Court, to set aside or to confirm assessments, or awards for damages on opening streets; and the question mooted has always been, whether the grantor of lots bounded on the streets, was entitled to remuneration for his interest in the ground taken for the street. The first case was that of Mercer Street, and there it was held, that the grantor was entitled to have awarded to him the full value of the ground so taken for the street. The Supreme Court soon began to recede from that position, and afterwards overturned it entirely, and finally held, that such owner was only entitled to a mere nominal allowance, and awarded nothing to him, or a nominal sum. In these cases, the Court incidentally speaks of the fee of the ground in the street remaining in the grantor when he conveys lots bounded on the street; but in no one is it distinctly decided as between grantor and grantee, that the former retains any title to the land within the lines of the street. And, we conclude, there is nothing in these street cases which amounts to an

---

1 Mercer Street, 4 Cowen, (N. Y.) R. 442; Seventeenth Street, 1 Wend. (N. Y.) R. 262; Lewis Street, 2 Ib. 472; Livingston *v.* Mayor, &c. of New York, 8 Ib. 85; Wyman *v.* The Same, 11 Ib. 487; Furman Street, 17 Ib. 650; Thirty-second Street, 19 Ib. 128; Twenty-ninth Street, 1 Hill, (N. Y.) R. 189; and see New Orleans *v.* United States, 10 Peters, (U. S.) R. 663; O'Linda *v.* Lothrop, 21 Pick. (Mass.) R. 292; White *v.* Hanigan, 1 Magruder, (Md.) R. 540.

2 Hammond *v.* McLachlan, 1 Sandf. (N. Y.) R. 323, 342.

authority for establishing such a distinction as that claimed by the plaintiffs. We see no reason for holding a different construction in respect of these deeds, from that which prevails in regard to deeds of land in the country. The reasons for that construction in country deeds, were based upon principles of great public convenience, which forbade that one should be the owner of the land, and another of a road or stream running through it. The practical inconveniences of a contrary rule, have led to this construction uniformily, unless where it expressly appears that the parties intended the contrary." Yet, it would seem, that in grants of city lands, where there are nice measurements and small and exact quantities, which are more definite in respect of intent; then, by clear inference, the soil of the street may be excluded.[1]

§ 318. The law, with respect to public highways, and to fresh-water rivers, is the same, and the analogy perfect as concerns the right of soil, and the presumptions from grants of land bounded thereon.[2] Such grants carry the grantee to the middle of the river, unless there are expressions in the terms of the grants, or something in the terms taken in connection with the situation and condition of the land granted, that clearly indicate an intention to stop at the edge or margin of the river. There must be a reservation or restriction, express or necessarily implied, which controls the operation of the general presumption, and makes the particular grant an exception.[3] In the elaborately-considered case of Child *v.* Starr,[4] in the Court for the Correction of Errors in New York, it was held, that lines running to a monument standing on the bank, and from thence running *by the river* or *along the river*, &c., do not re-

---

1 The Union Burial Ground *v.* Robinson, 5 Whart. (Penn.) R. 21; and see Tyler *v.* Hammond, *supra.*

2 *Ante*, § 54, *et seq.*

3 Per Nelson, J., in Howard, *et al.* *v.* Ingersoll, 13 How. (U. S.) R. 421.

4 Child *v.* Starr, 4 Hill, (N. Y.) R. 469, overruling Starr *v.* Child, 20 Wend. (N. Y.) R. 149.

strict the grant to the bank of the stream; for the monuments in such cases are only referred to as giving the lines to the river, and not as restricting the boundary on the river.[1] If the grantor, however, after giving the line *to the river*, bounds his land by the "bank," or upon the "margin," or describes the line as *running along* the bank or margin, he shows that he does not mean to consider the whole *alveus* a mere mathematical line, so as to carry this grant to the centre. And the construction is the same where the boundary is by *the shore* of the river.[2] In Dunlop *v.* Stetson,[3] a boundary described as running "upon the bank at high-water mark," was held by Story,

---

1 *Ex parte* Jennings, 6 Cowen, (N. Y.) R. 518, and the elaborate note of the reporter, p. 536; Claremont *v.* Carlton, 2 N. Hamp. R. 371; Hayes *v.* Bowman, 1 Randolph, (Va.) R. 420; Orendorff *v.* Steele, 2 Barb. (N. Y.) Sup. Ct. R. 126; Lunt *v.* Holland, 14 Mass. R. 151; Budd *v.* Burke, 3 Gill. (Md.) R. 198; Luce *v.* Charley, 24 Wend. (N. Y.) R. 451; Jackson *v.* Low, 12 Johns. (N. Y.) R. 252; Hooper *v.* Cummings, 20 Ib. 91; Arnold *v.* Mundy, 1 Halst. (N. J.) R. 1; Morrison *v.* Keen, 3 Greenl. (Maine) R. 474; King *v.* King, 7 Mass. 496; *Ex parte* Ipswich, 13 Pick. 431; Rix *v.* Johnson, 5 N. Hamp. R. 520; The State *v.* Gilmanton, 9 Ib. 461; Boscawen *v.* Canterbury, 3 Foster, (N. H.) R. 188; Canal Trustees *v.* Haven, 5 Ill. (Gilman,) R. 548; Norris *v.* Hill, 1 Mann, (Mich.) R. 202; McCullough *v.* Hall, 4 Rich. (So. Car.) R. 68; The Canal Appraisers *v.* The People, 19 Wend. (N. Y.) R. 571; Lowell *v.* Robinson, 4 Shep. (Maine) R. 357. The *filum aquæ* is ascertained by measurement across from ordinary low-water mark on one side, to the same on the other side, without regard to the channel or depth of water. McCullough *v.* Hall, 4 Rich. (So. Car.) R. 68. But land bounded on a lake or large pond, extends only to the margin. Hathem *v.* Stinson, 1 Fairf. (Maine) R. 183; Bradley *v.* Rice, 1 Shep. (Maine) R. 198; Wood *v.* Kelley, 30 Maine R. 47; Ib. 370; Canal Commissioners *v.* The People, 5 Wend. (N. Y.) R. 423.

2 Storer *v.* Freeman, 6 Mass. R. 435; Hatch *v.* Dwight, 17 Ib. 298; Nickerson *v.* Crawford, 4 Shep. (Maine) R. 245; Lapish *v.* Bangor Bank, 8 Greenl. (Maine) R. 85; Greenleaf *v.* Kelton, 1 N. Hamp. R. 531; Thomas *v.* Hatch, 3 Sumner, (Cir. Ct.) R. 170; Hopkins *v.* Kent, 9 Ham. (Ohio) R. 13. In Pennsylvania, North Carolina and Alabama, the great navigable rivers obey the law of tide-waters; the title of the riparian owner goes to low-water mark; beyond that the soil belongs to the Commonwealth, and the stream is a common fishery and a highway. Carsen *v.* Blazer, 2 Binney, (Penn.) R. 475; Shunk *v.* The Schuylkill Navigation Co. 14 Serg. & R. 71; Wilson *v.* Forbes, 2 Dev. (N. Car.) R. 30; Bullock *v.* Wilson, 2 Port. (Al.) R. 436; 2 Smith's L. Cases, 148.

3 Dunlop *v.* Stetson, 4 Mason, (Cir. Ct.) R. 349.

J., to exclude the flats between high and low-water mark, although, by a colonial ordinance, recognized as law, grants bounded generally upon tide-waters, carried the grantee to low-water mark. And by the Supreme Court of the United States, in a cession of lands from Georgia to the United States, one boundary of which was described as "beginning on the eastern bank of the Chattahoochee River, running thence up the said Chattahoochee River, and *along the western bank* thereof," it was held, that the entire river was excluded from the cession.[1] Indeed, it may be stated generally, that when the boundary given in a deed has physical extent, as a road, lane, street, fence, creek, or river, the grantee takes to the centre of the object so given, unless by some specific limitation of the grant the object is excluded.

### 4. *Actions by the Owner of the Fee.*

§ 319. It is now perfectly well-settled, that the owner of the fee is entitled to protect his rights in the soil by every species of action and remedy which would be open to him if his land were disencumbered of the way. In Goodtitle *v.* Alker,[2] which was ejectment for land subject to a highway, it was urged by the defendant, that in a case at the Summer Assizes at Exeter, it had been held by Lord Hardwicke, "that no possession could be delivered of the soil of the highway; and, therefore, no ejectment would lie of it; and if it was a nuisance, the defendant might be indicted." But Lord Mansfield, putting this case out of the way entirely, as being so loosely remembered and imperfectly reported, as to deserve no regard, nor be at all clear and intelligible, said: "There is no reason why the plaintiff should not have a right to *all* remedies for the freehold; subject still, indeed, to the servitude or easement. An assize would lie, if he should be disseized of it; an action of trespass

---

1 Howard, *et al.* *v.* Ingersoll, 13 How. (U S.) R. 381.

2 Goodtitle *v.* Alker, 1 Burr, 133.

would lie for an injury done to it."—"I see no ground why the owner of the soil may not bring ejectment, as well as *trespass*. It would be very inconvenient to say that in this case he should have no *specific* legal remedy; and that his only relief should be repeated actions of damages, for trees and mines, salt-springs and other profits under ground. 'Tis true, indeed, that he must recover the land subject to *the way;* but surely he ought to have a *specific* remedy, to recover *the land itself*, notwithstanding its being subject to an easement upon it." The point thus decided, has been repeatedly reaffirmed in subsequent decisions.[1] The correctness of Lord Mansfield's decision has, however, been questioned by no less an authority than the Supreme Court of the United States, and upon the very grounds which in that case were urged and overruled. The opinion in the case referred to, was delivered by Thompson, J. After alluding to the fact, that this doctrine of Lord Mansfield had crept into most of our elementary treatises, and been incidentally sanctioned by Judges, though never, to his knowledge, adopted in any case where it was the direct point in judgment, while it had been repudiated by the Supreme Court of Errors of Connecticut, he goes on to say, that the action cannot be sustained on principle, because the recovery of actual possession by the plaintiff would be wholly inconsistent with the admitted public right. "That right," he says, "consists in the uninterrupted enjoyment of the possession. The two rights are, therefore, incompatible with each other, and cannot stand together. The lessor of the plaintiff seeks specific relief,

---

1 Cooper *v.* Smith, 9 Serg. & R. (Penn.) R. 26; Alden *v.* Murdock, 13 Mass. R. 256; Bolling *v.* Mayor, &c. of Petersburg, 3 Rand. (Va.) R. 563; Thompson, *et al. v.* Proprietors of Androscoggin Bridge, 5 Greenl. (Maine) R. 62; 2 Selw. N. P. 728; 1 Saund. Pl. and Ev. 447; Dicta, S. P., per Sedgwick, J., in Commonwealth *v.* Peters, 2 Mass. R. 125; per Putnam, C. J., in Stackpole *v.* Healey, 16 Ib. 33; per Parsons, C. J., in Perley *v.* Chandler, 6 Id. 454; per Platt, J., in Jackson *v.* Hathaway, 15 Johns. (N. Y.) R. 447; 2 Smith's Leading Cases, (44 Law Lib.) 141.

and to be put into the actual possession of the land. The very fruit of his action, therefore, if he avails himself of it, will subject him to an indictment for a nuisance; the private right of possession being in direct hostility with the easement or use to which the public are entitled; and as to the plaintiff's taking possession subject to the easement, it is utterly impracticable."

§ 320. It has been well remarked that the action, in which this opinion was delivered, was brought to test the right of the public to an easement in the land and not to recover the land subject to the easement, and to the former point alone was the judgment of the Court invoked, and that, therefore, the remarks of Mr. Justice Thompson must be regarded as the extra-judicial dicta of an individual.[1] It is certainly manifest that the remarks were made upon a very imperfect review of the authorities, if not upon some misapprehension of principle. In regard to the compatibility of the public enjoyment with individual possession, the reasoning of Swift, J., in Peck *v.* Smith, would seem to be perfectly conclusive. An easement is a privilege, service, or convenience in the estate of another, by grant or prescription, and comprises no interest in the thing itself. It supposes that different rights in the use of the same thing may coexist in different persons; and nothing is more common than for one to have an easement in the land of another, who has an estate in fee and is in actual possession. A private right of way is such an easement. It is compatible with the right of the owner of the fee to depasture and mow it; take the trees and any thing growing on it; and hold it in possession for these purposes. If disseized by the grantee of the easement, he can recover possession in ejectment, there being no inconsistency in the recovery subject to the private right of way. The principle is precisely the same in regard to the right of the public in the soil of a highway; its right is but an easement, and, subject to that, it no more

[1] 2 Smith's Leading Cases, Wallace's note, (44 Law Library,) p. 141.

conflicts with the right of the public in a highway, than with that of an individual in a private way, for the owner of the fee to recover possession.[1]

### 5. *Abandonment and Reversion.*

§ 321. At common law, the doctrine of the earlier cases is, that there can be no loss of the public right by mere non-user. A highway once established must always remain such until changed or discontinued by process of law. In Rex *v.* Ward,[2] it was decided that an ancient highway cannot be changed or stopped up without the king's license first obtained upon the writ *ad quod damnum*, and on inquisition found thereon that such a change will not be prejudicial to the public; and that if any one change a highway without such authority, he may stop the new way whenever he pleases; that by the laying out the subjects have not such an interest therein as that they may justify their going there; nor is it any such way that the inhabitants are bound to repair or maintain it, or, under the ancient law, to watch there or to make amends if any robbery be there committed. And it is said, that in an action of trespass, brought by the owner of the land against those who shall go over such new way, the defendants ought to show specially, by way of excuse, how the old way was obstructed and the new one set out.[3] So, in Fowler *v.* Sanders,[4] it was held, that a right to narrow a highway by laying logs of wood thereon for fuel in front of an ancient house, being a nuisance,

---

1 Per Swift, J., in Peck *v.* Smith, 1 Conn. R. 135; and see Read *v.* Leeds, 19 Conn. R. 182.

2 Rex *v.* Ward, Cro. Car. 266, pl. 66; and see Payne *v.* Partridge, 1 Salk. 12, pl. 1, in which it was held, that the owner of a ferry cannot discontinue it and build a bridge in its stead, without license obtained under a writ of *ad quod damnum.*

3 Hawk. P. C. C. 76, § 4; and see Thomas *v.* Conell, Vaugh. 341.

4 Fowler *v.* Sanders, Cro. Jac. 446, recognized in Simmons *v.* Cornell, 1 R. I. Rep. 514.

could not be acquired by prescription. In Selwyn's Nisi Prius, it is said to have been the opinion of Gibbs, Justice, announced in an unreported case, that even if a highway has not been used, no length of time will be sufficient to prevent the king's subjects from using the way again if they think proper.[1]

§ 322. In regard to navigable rivers, the same principle has been frequently asserted. Thus, it has been expressly held, that twenty years' possession of the water of a public navigable river at a given level is not conclusive against the public. "An act of Parliament," said Holroyd, J., "is the only means by which such a right can be determined.[2] In Weld *v.* Hornby,[3] a party, who had been entitled for two centuries to a weir of brushwood for taking fish in a public river, in 1766 erected a stone weir instead thereof across two thirds of the stream, and, in 1784, carried it across the remaining part of the river. An action for obstruction having been brought between nineteen and twenty years from 1784, the jury, under the direction of the Court, that from the lapse of time they might infer a legal commencement of the right, returned a verdict for the defendant. Lord Ellenborough, in setting aside the verdict, remarked: "The right of the defendant to have a stone weir is plainly founded on encroachment. Weirs across rivers were from the earliest times considered nuisances; and however twenty years' acquiescence may bind parties whose private rights only are affected, yet the public have an interest in the suppression of public nuisances, though of longer standing." Again, in the case of Chad *v.* Tilsed,[4] it was considered that forty years usage, unsupported by other evidence, would not be sufficient to establish an exclusive right

---

1 2 Selwyn's N. P., by Wharton, (4th ed.) p. 503, citing Rex *v.* St. James.

2 Vooght *v.* Winch, 2 B. & Ald. 662.

3 Weld *v.* Hornby, 7 East, 195.

4 Chad *v.* Tilsed, 2 B. & B. 403; Best, on Presumptions of Law and Fact, p. 110.

over an arm of the sea; though, coupled with the general language of an ancient grant, it might be presumptive evidence of user previous to that time, and through it of an ancient right. But if water, which has been an ancient highway, by degrees change its course, and go over different ground from that whereon it used to run, the highway continues in the new channel as in the old.[1] In Rex *v.* Montague,[2] it was held, that a public right of navigation in a river or creek may be extinguished by natural causes, such as the recess of the sea or an accumulation of mud, &c. "Most probably," said Bailey, J., in that case, "the rights of the public, if they ever had any, arose from the flux and reflux of the tides of the sea, so as to make the channel navigable. If, then, the sea retreated, or the channel silted up, so as to be no longer navigable, why should not the public right cease? If they arose from natural causes, why should not natural causes also put an end to them?" Such obstructions, however, being the act of God, of course constitute no exception to the principle under discussion.

§ 323. But this doctrine of the ancient authorities has, however, been to some extent departed from in more modern decisions. In Beardslee *v.* French,[3] in which a right was claimed to maintain posts and bars across a highway, upon proof that such posts and bars had been there maintained ever since the laying out of said highway, a period of about ninety years, and were, together with the way, so maintained by the plaintiff, as the only protection from the highway to a large tract of land owned by him, it was said by Hosmer, Ch. J., speaking for the Court: "Evidence to prove a highway often consists in showing that the public have used and enjoyed the road; and the uninterrupted use of it, for a considerable space of time, affords a strong presumption of a grant. On the

---

[1] 1 Roll. Abr. 390; and Hawk. P. C. c. 76, § 4.

[2] Rex *v.* Montague, 4 B. & C. 604.

[3] Beardslee *v.* French, 7 Conn. R. 125.

other hand, the non-user of an easement of this kind, for many years, is *primâ facie* evidence of a release of the right to the person over whose land the highway once ran; and although the precise limit of time in respect of the public, in such cases, has not been established, there can be no doubt that the desertion of a public road for nearly a century is strong presumptive evidence that the right of way has been extinguished." In Commissioners *v.* Taylor,[1] certain lands were conveyed to the town of Georgetown for streets, but never used as such; but, on the other hand, enclosed and used as a farm for more than forty years; and it was held, that the doctrine of *non-user* would apply, which would forfeit a corporate right as well as *misuser*. The same principle has been established by the Supreme Court of Ohio, in the case of Fox *v.* Hart,[2] and in Kentucky, in the case of Rowan's Executors *v.* Portland.[3] In the latter case it would seem that the fee of the land dedicated was vested in town trustees for the public use. Marshall, Ch. J., in delivering the opinion of the Court said: "That the public right as growing out of the dedication in this case was subject to be divested and defeated by adverse possession and claim of individual right for twenty years, admits, as we think, of no doubt. The dedication was not to the Commonwealth as a corporate being and invested no title or interest in it. The maxim, *nullum tempus occurrit regi*, is therefore inapplicable. And there is nothing to exempt the right, which vested really in the town and its citizens, to be upheld by them for the public, from the operation of the statute of limitations, or from the presumptions arising from adverse claim and possession, as they would apply in ordinary cases of private right or public easements." And in Vermont, it was held, that the enclosure and occupation of land within the limits of a

---

[1] Commissioners *v.* Taylor, 2 Bay, (So. Car.) R. 282.

[2] Fox *v.* Hart, 11 Ohio, (Stanton,) R. 414.

[3] Rowan's Executors *v.* Portland, 8 B. Mon. (Ken.) R. 232, 259.

highway, for twenty years, under a claim of right, made a title by prescription to the land so enclosed and occupied as against the public.[1]

§ 324. So it has been very cogently observed by Lord Eldon:[2] "I have heard it stated that this (the presumption of abandonment from *non-user*) does not apply to the case of a public road. It applies more to that than to a private road. The reason given was, that there cannot be the same presumption of a surrender. If by matter of record the right appears vested in the public, it may be so; as there the right appears; and the surrender does not appear. But, if the right does not rest upon matter of record, and the public have not enjoyed, it is to be left to the jury to presume, and is almost conclusive not that it was surrendered, but that it never existed; and for this special reason; one man may surrender, or for many reasons may not enjoy his right; but the probability is, as to the public, that some instance of enjoyment would be shown. That is much stronger than the case of a private road, if for many years there has been no enjoyment; for what one man may relinquish, another may be disposed to assert." The rule laid down in the earlier cases, indeed, if not entirely superseded, is certainly to be considered as very much shaken by the good sense of the modern decisions and their greater conformity with the ideas of the age. But, where a street has been simply laid out and no steps taken towards its completion or preparation for public use, it has been held that a possession and occupancy of the land within the limits of such street for a period of more than twenty years, do not divest the rights of the public, because such a possession is not adverse, but perfectly consistent with the public rights.[3]

§ 325. The old common-law procedure for discontinuing or

---

1 Knight *v.* Heaton, 22 Vt. R. 480.

2 Hillary *v.* Walker, 12 Vesey, 139, 265.

3 Henshaw *v.* Hunting, 1 Gray, (Mass.) R. 203.

changing a highway, as we have seen, was by the writ of *ad quod damnum*. This is an original writ issuing out of and returnable into the Court of Chancery, directed to a sheriff to inquire, by a jury, whether the changing a highway will be detrimental to the public or not; the inquisition upon which, being a proceeding only *ex parte*, is traversable; and anciently the party aggrieved might have been heard against it before the Chancellor.[1] The change effected through this process must be as beneficial to the king and subjects as the old way was before. Therefore, such a writ having been obtained "to lay down timber, wood, and other materials for a wagon way," on an already existing way, it was quashed on motion before the Lord Chancellor, for the want of an equivalent to the public.[2] And the finding of a jury under a writ of *ad quod damnum* favorable to those at whose instance it has issued, is not a bar to an indictment for a nuisance. The jury by whom such an indictment is to be tried have a right to exercise their own judgment upon the matter, and may find that to be a public nuisance, which, under this writ, may have been found not to be to the prejudice of the public.[3] Where a new road is made in pursuance of such a writ, and inquisition thereupon found, after the person who sued out the writ has once made the said road, the parishioners ought to keep it in repair for the future; because, being discharged from the repairing of the old road, no new burden is laid upon them, but their labor is only transferred from one place to another. But if the new road lie in another parish, then the person who sued out the writ, or his heirs, ought not only to make the road, but to keep it in repair; otherwise, the parishioners of such other parish would have a new charge upon them, and no recompense

1 *Ex parte* Armitage, Ambl. 294; *Ex parte* Vennor, 3 Atk. 766.
2 *Ex parte* Armitage, *supra*.
3 Rex *v.* Russell, 6 B. & C. 600; 9 D. & R. 566.

by the former road being taken away.[1] In England, on account of the expense and difficulty attending a writ of *ad quod damnum*, and the more compendious and easy method of diverting highways provided by statutes,[2] that writ has fallen into almost complete disuse. In the United States, this process, although it doubtless exists, has seldom, if ever been resorted to, a more satisfactory remedy being attainable by special legislation in those States in which complete power over this subject has not been given to the authorities of the different towns and cities.

§ 326. From the principles already declared, it necessarily results, that whenever the public easement is relinquished or vacated, the owner of the soil is restored to his original dominion over the same. The land, it is said, *reverts* to the owner, disencumbered of the public use; but this does not precisely describe the fact. The land does not revert, because there has been no alienation. The public has only been entitled to a certain specific right, the enjoyment of which is incompatible with the exercise of certain private rights, which are, therefore, necessarily suspended. When, however, the public right is relinquished, this incompatibility vanishes, and, as an inevitable consequence, the private rights, thereby suspended, revive.[3]

---

1 *Ex parte* Vennor, 3 Atk. 771; Rex *v.* Flecknow, 1 Burr, 465, 523; 3 Burn's Jus. by Chitty, p. 550, (29th ed.)

2 13 Geo. III. c. 78, § 19; and 55 Geo. III. c. 68; 5 & 6 Will. IV. c. 50, § 85.

3 Fairfield *v.* Williams, 4 Mass. R. 427; Perley *v.* Chandler, 6 Mass. R. 457; Alden *v.* Murdock, 13 Mass. R. 256; Jackson *v.* Hathaway, 15 Johns. (N. Y.) R. 447; Barclay *v.* Howell, 6 Peters, (U. S.) R. 498, 513; Neville Road case, 8 Watts, (Penn.) R. 172; United States *v.* Harris, 1 Sumner, (Cir. Ct.) R. 21; John and Cherry Streets, 19 Wend. (N. Y.) R. 659, 666; 12 Ib. 371; Nicholson *v.* Stockett, 1 Walker, (Miss.) R. 67. By the 13 Geo. III. c. 78, § 17, where a new highway shall be made as thereinbefore directed, the old highway is directed to be stopped up, and the land and soil thereof sold by the surveyor to some person or persons whose lands adjoin thereto, if willing to purchase the same; if not, to some other person for the full value thereof; and after payment

of the purchase-money, it is declared that *the soil* shall become vested in such purchaser and his heirs; but all mines, minerals and fossils lying under the same shall continue to be the property of the persons who would have been entitled to the same if such old highway had continued. Upon this provision of the English statutes, the dissenting Judges in Peck *v.* Smith, 1 Conn. R. 156, based their argument, that the ultimate fee of highways was in the State. This provision has been commented upon by Mr. Wellbeloved, in his Treatise on Highways, as follows: "It seems evident from the wording of these acts, that a point was taken for granted, which admits of very great doubt; I mean the power to sell that of which a sale is directed. The surveyor of a highway can possess no greater interest in it than the public, whose servant he is; and if they have no title to the soil thereof, it is difficult to say how he can dispose of it; unless, indeed, we construe the act of parliament to have the effect, in the first place of divesting the freehold out of the owner, and then of granting the same to the surveyor, after which he is in with the power of sale. It may be admitted to be clearly the intention of the legislature, that the soil of all unnecessary highways should be sold. But, however the clause may be framed upon a false supposition as to the state of the law, yet it by no means appears to be so clearly worded as to alter that law. It will not, surely, be maintained that private property can be torn from the owner, and that, too, without any compensation, merely by *implication*. Individual rights ought not to be destroyed but by plain and express words; nothing less than an absolute enactment to that effect should suffice. Assuming, then, that this power of sale cannot embrace any greater estate or interest than such as the public were entitled to before its creation, the enactment seems to be defective as to the means of accomplishing such a sale. For, to omit any question which might arise as to the power of conveying this public easement, otherwise than by way of release to the owner of the soil, let us consider what interest would be obtained by the purchaser. Now, the sale must be made to one of three classes of purchasers—either first, to a mere stranger—secondly, to the owner of the land adjoining only on one side of the way—or, thirdly, to both the contiguous proprietors in equal moieties. First. If the purchase be made by a stranger, what will he acquire? The trees growing on the way cannot be his, for they already belong to the owners of the nearest adjoining land. For the same reason, all mines, minerals and other valuable property under ground would have been out of his power, even if the act itself had not deprived him of them. But, to proceed still further, this unfortunate purchaser, having obtained neither trees nor mines, will discover that it will not even be permitted him to grow grain upon his newly-acquired territory. For if he plough the land, he will render himself liable to be sued as a trespasser. To prove this, I need only refer to a case which is reported by Godbolt, p. 52, and the case of Lade *v.* Shepherd. And, to conclude the whole, he will not even acquire a right of pasturage. Stevens *v.* Whistler, 11 East, 51. Secondly. If the purchaser be the proprietor on only one side of the way, his right will be complete to no more than one moiety of the land: and as to all beyond the *medium filum viæ*, he must be considered as a stranger. Thirdly. We may conclude, then, that the third class of purchasers, viz., both the adjoining owners are those, and those only, who can safely buy what the legislature has directed to be sold. If they refuse to purchase, the land must remain unsold, since the act contains no provision to oblige them to a compliance; and, in such a case, it would seem that the highway cannot be stopped up, as the order of the Justices must be for the sale as well as the stopping up thereof." Wellbeloved on Highways, pp. 30, 31, 32. By the later statute, 5 & 6 Will. IV. c. 50, however, no power is given of selling the old highway when stopped up; it should therefore seem, when any way has been legally stopped up, that the owner of the soil in it will become entitled to the land discharged, from the right of the public. Shelford on Highways, 143.

# CHAPTER VIII.

## TRAVEL UPON HIGHWAYS.



§ 327. A HIGHWAY has been defined to be a road which every citizen has a right to use.[1] Its object is to facilitate communication among men, and the transportation of goods. But being open to the travel of the public generally, it is evident that this object would be liable to continual frustration, unless such travel were subject to some certain rules and regulations. The purpose of the following chapter is to explain and illustrate the rules and regulations of travel upon highways.

### 1. *Travel upon ordinary Roads and Streets.*

§ 328. *The Law of the Road.* One of the most usual incidents of travel upon highways is the meeting and passing of vehicles and teams. To prevent collision and to secure travel from interruption, it is necessary that there should be some certain rule in regard to their passing. This rule has been called the law of the road. In England, the customary rules of driving are: First, that, in meeting, each party shall bear or keep to the left, which is the reverse of the rule in this country; that is to say, in this country each party shall bear

---

[1] *Ante*, § 2.

or keep to the right. Secondly, that, in passing, the foremost person bearing to the left, the other shall pass on the off side. Thirdly, that in crossing, the driver coming transverse shall bear to the left hand, so as to pass behind the other carriage.[1] In England, these rules seem equally applicable to cases of persons on horseback, as well as to persons driving carriages.[2]

§ 329. The rule, however, that a driver is bound to keep on the left side of the road in England is not inflexible; although if he does not, he is bound to use more care and caution, and keep a better look-out to avoid collision than would be necessary if he were on that side.[3] In Wayde *v.* Carr,[4] the defendant's carriage was on the wrong side of the road, and the driver, in attempting to pass a hackney-coach which interposed between his mistress's carriage and the plaintiff's gig on the near instead of the off side, injured the plaintiff; and it was held that it was for the jury to decide the question of negligence, without regard to the law and usage of the road. "Whatever," said the Court, "might be the law of the road, it was not to be considered as inflexible and imperatively governing a case of this description. In the crowded streets of a metropolis, where this accident happened, situations and circumstances might frequently arise where a deviation from what is called the law of the road would not only be justifiable but absolutely necessary. Of this the jury were the best judges, and independently of the law of the road it was their province to determine whether the accident arose from the negligence of the defendant's servants. They had acquitted him of negligence, and having all the circum-

---

1 2 Steph. N. P. 984; Petersdorf, Abr. p. 55, note; Story on Bailments, § 599; Angell on Common Carriers, § 549; Wayde *v.* Carr, 2 Dow. & Ry. R. 255.

2 Turley *v.* Thomas, 8 Carr. & Payne, R. 103.

3 Pluckwell *v.* Wilson, 5 Carr. & Payne, R. 375.

4 Wayde *v.* Carr, 2 Dow. & Ry. 255.

stances of the case before them, had found their verdict for the defendant."

§ 330. That a deviation from what is called the law of the road may, at times, not only be justifiable but absolutely necessary, appears from the remarks of the Court in the case of Turley *v.* Thomas.[1] In that case it appeared that the plaintiff's servant was driving a gig on the proper side of the road, and that the defendant then was on horseback, riding at a great rate in the opposite direction, and was on his wrong side of the way, when he came into collision with the plaintiff's gig and broke it. And per Coleridge, J.: "The question in this case is whether the defendant is to blame, or whether the fault was wholly or in part in the plaintiff's servant. It has been suggested as a doubt by the learned counsel for the defendant, whether the rule of the road applies to saddle-horses or only to carriages. Now I have no doubt that it does. If a carriage and a horse are to pass, the carriage must keep its proper side and so must the horse. It has also been said to be doubtful whether, if a person driving a carriage is on his proper side, and sees a horse coming furiously on its wrong side, the driver of the carriage should give way and let the horse pass. Now, I think on this point that it is the duty of the person driving a carriage, under such circumstances, to give way if there be room, so as to let the horse pass and avoid an accident, although in so doing the carriage does go a little on what would otherwise be the wrong side of the road." In the above case, however, the jury returned a verdict for the defendant.

§ 331. In the United States, it has been decided that there is no law of the road requiring a man on horseback, when meeting a horse or vehicle, to turn out on the right or left side. The rider must govern himself in this respect according to his

---

1 Turley *v.* Thomas, 8 Carr. & Payne, R. 103.

notions of prudence at the time, under the circumstances.[1] But it has been said, in Vermont, that it is ordinarily a rule, sanctioned by common consent and immemorial usage, that a person on horseback should yield the travelled path to one who is travelling in a wagon or other vehicle.[2] In Pennsylvania, it was held, that although a footman or an equestrian has a right of way as well as the driver of a carriage, yet the enjoyment of that right is to be regulated by reason, and is not such that they can compel a teamster, who has a heavy draught, to leave the smooth beaten track of the road, if there is sufficient room to pass on either side. And where a road is narrow, or there is difficulty in passing, and it becomes impracticable or dangerous for the teamster to give part of the way, and the horseman can ride by, by passing out of the road, it is his duty to do so. If he refuses, and a collision ensues which occasions injury to his horse, it is attributable to his own negligence or obstinacy, and he is without remedy. And this rule was said to apply to a buggy laden with three men and drawn by a single horse.[3]

§ 332. If there is no other carriage to intercept the driver, he may pass on what part of the road he may think most convenient.[4] And, it has been held, if the street or road is very broad, he is not bound to observe the proper side of the road. In Wordsworth *v.* Willan,[5] which was an action on the case against the defendants, proprietors of a stage-coach, for the negligence of their servant, in driving so near the path on the wrong side of the road, that the plaintiff's horse becoming frightened, and, plunging, came in contact with the coach and broke his leg; it was said by Rook, J., that it could not be

---

1 Dudley *v.* Bolles, 24 Wend. (N. Y.) R. 465.

2 Washburn *v.* Tracey, 2 D. Ch. (Vt.) R. 128.

3 Beach *v.* Parmenter, 11 Harris, (Penn.) R. 196.

4 Aston *v.* Heaven, 2 Esp. R. 533; Palmer *v.* Barker, 11 Maine (Fairf.) R. 338; Johnson & Co. *v.* Small, 5 B. Mon. (Ky.) R. 25.

5 Angell on Carriers, § 552; Wordsworth *v.* Willan, 4 Esp. R. 273.

laid down as a certain rule, nor did public convenience require, that the driver is, under all circumstances, bound to keep on what is considered the proper side of the road; and that if there was no interruption of any other carriage, or the road was better, public convenience did not require that the driver should adhere to that law of the road. He took the rule to be, that if a carriage coming in any direction left sufficient room for any other carriage, horse, or passenger, on its proper side of the way, it was sufficient; but that it was evidence for the jury if the accident arose from want of that sufficient room; the driver was not to make experiments.

§ 333. The case cited in the preceding section was decided in England, where the "law of the road" is established by custom. In this country, where it is enacted by statute, the rule is probably a little more stringent. Thus it has been laid down that if a party, in travelling, voluntarily goes upon the prohibited side of the way, and from the size or character of his team or vehicle, or state of the road, should be unable to surrender to such as he might meet the portion of the way to which they were entitled, the fact that he could not yield the way might not, and probably would not, furnish a legal excuse, exonerating him from liability for an injury sustained by one passing, who was in nowise in fault. The wrong would consist in placing himself where he might be the occasion of the injury which has resulted; that is, on the prohibited side of the way. It would be legal fault in him to be found there occupying that part of the way belonging for the time to another, as against him. His inability to leave the part of the way, voluntarily occupied, would not form a valid excuse, exonerating him from liability for the injury sustained by another, by reason of such occupancy. But the traveller, whose part of the way is trenched upon by another, cannot for that reason, carelessly or imprudently rush upon the party or his team or vehicle, and if he sustain an injury recover damages therefor. He may probably attempt to pass, if such attempt would be reasonably safe and prudent. If otherwise, he must delay, and seek redress for the detention if damage result therefrom. But if, in a prudent attempt to pass, he sustain injury, there would seem to be no reason to doubt that the law would give redress. And where a traveller is delayed by such occupancy of the prohibited side of the road, damage arising from the detention would probably furnish a valid and substantial ground or cause of action.[1]

§ 334. In a prosecution for the penalty prescribed by the Massachusetts statute for not passing a carriage, which is met upon a road, "to the right of the middle of the travelled part of such road," it has been held to be no defence for the party so offending that he turned to the right of the middle of the *wrought* part of the road, even though in so doing he left sufficient room for travellers to pass with convenience and safety in the use of ordinary care and skill.[2] But this was a criminal proceeding. In civil suits it is not enough to entitle the plaintiff to recover for damages occasioned by a collision, for him to show that at the time of the collision the defendant was not complying with the statute; but he must also show that he himself exercised ordinary precautions to avoid the injury. The traveller on a highway, it has been said, is not with foolhardiness to rush into danger because his fellow traveller has wrongfully given him the opportunity to receive an injury. "A traveller may well occupy any part of the road, if no other person is occupying any portion of it. When, by reason of meeting another traveller, the occasion requires it, he must seasonably turn to the right. The law imposes this duty; but his disregard of that duty will not justify the traveller, who may be on the proper side of the road, in voluntarily or carelessly permitting himself to be injured, either in his person or property, and then seeking to recover damages

1 Per Woods, J., in Brooks *v.* Hart, 14 N. Hamp. R. 307.

2 Commonwealth *v.* Allen, 11 Met. (Mass.) R. 403.

therefor of his fellow traveller, who was wrongfully on the left of the centre of the road."[1]

§ 335. In Kentucky, under an act which prescribed that "all vehicles of every kind, meeting, shall give to each other *one half* of the *macadamized part of the road*, each *passing* to the right," it was held, that the plaintiff, whose team was injured in consequence of the carelessness of the defendant whilst it was *stopping* on the *left* of the road for him to pass, was entitled to recover damages therefor. "It appears," said the Court, "that the plaintiff's team, in ascending the hill, was occupying the left part of the road, when the stage, in turning a short bend of the road above him, hove in sight at the distance of fifty yards from him, and from the shortness of the distance between them, the rapidity of the stage's approach, and his then position on the road, had the plaintiff attempted to change the direction of his horses, with a view to *pass* to the right, that he could not have accomplished more than to have drawn his horses and wagon obliquely across the road by the time the stage arrived, thereby obstructing the entire road and necessarily producing a conflict. It was therefore impossible, from his position, to pass to the right, leaving the *one half* of the road to the stage, and, *lex neminem coget ad impossibilia*. Moreover, he did not attempt to *pass* to the right or left, but reined his team off the road to the left, in a corner of the fence adjoining, and halted there, leaving the greater part of the road for the stage to pass; and it is obvious, from the direction the stage-horses were taking just before, that they could have passed without a conflict, had it not been for their sudden turn to the right as they approached the plaintiff's team." And the Court refused a motion to set aside the verdict upon the ground that the plaintiff was guilty

---

1 Parker *v.* Adams, 12 Ib. 415.

of a violation of the road law, and a dereliction of duty, in failing to turn and pass the stage on the right.[1]

§ 336. In this country, a person may pass on the left side of the road, or across the same, for the purpose of turning up to a house, store, or other object on that side of the road; but in so doing, he must not interrupt or obstruct a man lawfully passing on that side, which would be in a direction, in a degree contrary to his; if he does, he acts at his peril, and must answer for the consequences of such violation of his duty. In such circumstances, he must pass before, or wait till after such person has passed on.[2] And in a case in which a carriage, in passing from one street into another, which was at right angles to it, and crossing the same, came accidentally into collision with another carriage, the Court held the driver liable for the damage which ensued. Before attempting to cross, it was observed, he ought to have seen that he could do it without interfering with persons who were in the proper exercise of their right of passing through the street.[3]

337. In cases where parties meet *on the sudden*, and an injury results, the party on the wrong side of the road should be held answerable, unless it clearly appears that the party on the proper side had ample means and opportunity to prevent it. "A man," says Chief Justice Best, "may not, *on a sudden*, be sufficiently self-possessed to know in what way to decide;

---

1 Johnson & Co. *v.* Small, 5 B. Mon. (Ky.) R. 25. In Maine, when persons meet and pass each other upon the public highway, it is, by the Rev. Stats. c. 26, the duty of each to pass "to the right of the middle of the travelled part of the road or bridge, when practicable." And when it is not practicable, that is, when it is difficult or unsafe for him to do so on account of his vehicle being heavily loaded, or for other cause, he should stop a reasonable time at a convenient part of the road, to enable the other person to pass, and without any request from him. Kennard *v.* Burton, 25 Maine R. 39.

2 Palmer *v.* Barker, 11 Maine (2 Fairf.) R. 338.

3 Fales *v.* Dearborn, 1 Pick. (Mass.) R. 345. But see per Dewey, J., in Parker *v.* Adams, 12 Met. (Mass.) R. 415, 420.

and, in such case, the wrongdoer is the party who is to be answerable for the mischief; though it might have been prevented by the other party's acting differently."[1]

§ 338. The Massachusetts act[2] prescribes, that "whenever any persons shall meet each other, on any bridge or road, travelling with carriages," &c., they shall turn to the right of the centre of the travelled part thereof. The term "road," used in the statute, has been construed to import any place set apart and appropriated, either *de jure* or *de facto*, to the purpose of passing with carriages, whether by public authority or by the general license and permission of the owners. All the reasons, it was said, which induced the legislature to prescribe the rule requiring travellers respectively to turn to the right, extend to all roads so used; and, therefore, it is no defence on a prosecution for the violation of the statute, to show that the place where the collision took place, was not a public way.[3] By the words, "the travelled part" of the road, used in this act, is intended that part which is usually wrought for travelling.[4] But when that part of the road which is wrought for travelling is hidden by snow, and a path is beaten and travelled on the side of the wrought part, persons meeting in such beaten and travelled path, are required to drive their vehicles to the right of the middle of such path.[5]

§ 339. In New York, under a statute which prescribes that carriages, in meeting, shall seasonably turn, drive, &c., "to the right of the centre of the road," it has been held, that it is not the centre of the smooth or most travelled part of the road which is the dividing line, but *the centre of the worked part*,

---

1 Chaplin *v.* Hawes, 3 Car. & Payne, R. 554; Angell on Carriers, § 555.

2 Revised Statutes, c. 51, § 1.

3 Commonwealth *v.* Gammons, 23 Pick. (Mass.) R. 201; Fales *v.* Dearborn, 1 Ib. 345.

4 Clark *v.* Commonwealth, 4 Pick. (Mass.) R. 125.

5 Jaquith *v.* Richardson, 8 Met. (Mass.) R. 213; Smith *v.* Dygert, 12 Barb. (N. Y.) Sup. Ct. R. 613.

although the whole of the smooth or most travelled path may be upon one side of that centre, unless the situation of the road is such that it is impracticable or extremely difficult for the party to turn out. The fact that the road is rough or rutty is no excuse.[1] By the terms, "seasonably turn, drive," &c., is meant that the travellers shall turn to the right in such season that neither shall be retarded in his progress by reason of the other occupying his half of the way, when he may have occasion to use it in passing.[2]

§ 340. It has been stated, that in England, the customary rule for travellers proceeding in the same direction is, that in passing, the foremost person bearing to the left, the other shall pass on the off side. In this country there is no such rule, and the law has been declared to be, that a traveller may use the middle or either side of the road at his pleasure, and without being bound to turn aside for another travelling in the same direction, provided there be sufficient room to pass on the one hand or on the other. If there be not sufficient room, it is the duty of the foremost traveller to afford it, on request made, by yielding an equal share of the road, if that be adequate and practicable; if not, the object must be deferred till the parties arrive at ground more favorable to its accomplishment. Should the leading traveller then refuse to comply, he would be answerable at law for it; but such refusal gives to the other no right to effect the passage by a forcible collision with him, redress being demandable only by due course of law. And it has been held, that evidence of a custom for the leading carriage to incline to the right, the other making the transit at the same time to the left, is not admissible. Neither is the principle of a statutory provision, made to regulate the deflection of those who are travelling in opposite directions, applicable to those who are travelling in the same direction; its object being

1 Earing *v.* Lansing, 7 Wend. (N. Y.) R. 185.

2 Per Woods, J., in Brooks *v.* Hart, 14 N. Hamp. R. 310.

to avoid, by a preconcerted movement, the collision which might otherwise ensue from the mutual misapprehension of intention, frequently observable between foot-passengers, and which could not occur to persons travelling in the same direction.[1]

§ 341. *Foot-Passengers.* All persons have a right to walk in a public highway, and are entitled to the exercise of reasonable care on the part of persons driving carriages along it. Thus, where it appeared that the plaintiff was walking in the carriage way in the neighborhood of Islington, about ten o'clock in the evening, when the defendant, who was driving a taxed cart, turned out from behind a postchaise and drove against him and knocked him down, it was held, that he was entitled to recover. It was proved by a policeman, that the footpath was in a bad state, and seldom used; and the counsel for the plaintiff was questioning another witness to the same point, when Denman, C. J., observed: "I do not think that any more evidence need be given on that subject. The policeman has proved the state of the path. A man has a right to walk in the road if he pleases. It is a way for foot-passengers as well as carriages. But he had better not, especially at night, when carriages are passing along."[2] But, however this may be, it is quite clear that a foot-passenger has a right to *cross* a highway, and that persons driving carriages are liable if they do not take care so as to avoid driving against the foot-passengers who are crossing the road; and if a person, driving along the road, cannot pull up because his reins break, that will be no ground of defence, because he is bound to have proper tackle.[3] This right of the foot-passenger, however, does not exempt him from due care on his own part. Thus, if a person in a

---

1 Bolton *v.* Colder, 1 Watts, (Penn.) R. 360.

2 Boss *v.* Litton, 5 Car. & Payne, R. 407; and see Leame *v.* Bray, 3 East, R. 593.

3 Cotterill *v.* Starkey, 8 Car. & Payne, R. 691; Wakeman *v.* Robinson, Bing. R. 213.

public street in a city, sees an omnibus coming, however furiously, and he will be headstrong enough to try to cross the street, and is run over, he cannot recover in an action against the proprietors of the omnibus, as no one has a right of action, if he meets with an accident which, by ordinary care, he might have avoided.[1] The rule, as to the proper side of the road, does not apply with respect to foot-passengers; but, as regards them, the carriages may go on whichever side of the road they may please.[2]

§ 342. *Rate of Speed.* Another duty which travellers are bound to observe, is to drive at a moderate rate of speed. To drive a carriage through a crowded or populous street, at such a rate or in such a manner as to endanger the safety of the inhabitants, is an indictable offence at common law, and amounts to a breach of the peace. In this country, driving faster than an ordinary travelling pace in the streets of populous cities, is very generally prohibited by statutes or municipal ordinances; and it is a well-settled principle, that a person, who is engaged in an illegal or prohibited course of conduct, is liable for all the consequences of his acts.[3] But, independently of this principle, driving at an immoderate rate of speed, is, in itself, a culpable negligence, from which, if an injury result, without fault of the person injured, the author is liable for it.[4] What is immoderate speed, is a question for the jury. Best, C. J., speaks of it as such speed that the horses cannot be stopped or properly directed; and Barbour, J., speaking for the Supreme Court of the United States, describes it as "rapid driving, which, under the circumstances of the case, amounts to rash-

---

1 Wolf *v.* Beard, 8 Car. & Payne, R. 373.

2 Cotterill *v.* Starkey, *supra.*

3 United States *v.* Hart, 1 Peters, (Cir. Ct.) R. 590. In this case, it was held, that the United States mail-coaches are subject to the same rule as other vehicles in this respect.

4 Per Best, C. J., in his charge to the Wilts Grand Jury, cited in note to 8 Car. & Payne, R. 694.

ness."[1] Thus it has been held, independently of any statute, that driving at the rate of fifteen miles an hour, or a mile in four minutes, on a public highway, is unlawful; and if death ensues from a collision thus produced, without fault of the injured party, the offence, in Pennsylvania, it seems, would be murder in the second degree, unless accompanied with such circumstances of passion as to reduce the offence to manslaughter.[2] But the reported cases, in which this point has been discussed, have related chiefly to the liability of the proprietors of stage-coaches to their passengers. In this class of cases, where there appears to have been manifest recklessness on the part of drivers, the books record the recovery of very exemplary damages. But as our purpose is simply to treat of the rights and duties of travellers in relation to each other, without regard to any relation depending upon contract, whether express or implied, these cases, though illustrative of the subject under consideration, need only be referred to without a full examination.[3]

§ 343. *Stopping by the Wayside.* It is the right of travellers to stop temporarily by the roadside for their own personal convenience, or for the purpose of lading or unlading their carriages; but this right must be strictly subordinated to the primary use of highways as thoroughfares for travel. Thus in a case, previously referred to,[4] it appeared, that one or two, and sometimes three large wagons of the defendant, were for several hours, both day and night, standing in a street thirty-seven feet wide before his warehouse, and usually occupied one half of the street, so that no carriage could pass on that side

---

1 Stokes *v.* Saltonstall, 13 Peters, (U. S.) R. 181.

2 Kennedy *v.* Way, 3 Law Reporter, (N. S.) 184.

3 Gough *v.* Bryan, 5 Dowl. P. C. 765; Mayor *v.* Humphries, 1 Car. & Payne, R. 251; McKinney *v.* Niel, 1 McLean, (Cir. Ct.) R. 540; Peck and Wife *v.* Niel, 3 McLean, (Cir. Co.) R. 22; Angell on Carriers, §§ 543–548.

4 Rex *v.* Russell, 6 East, R. 427; *Ante*, § 227.

next the warehouse, though two carriages might pass on the opposite side, the gutter being in the middle of the street; the wagons being loaded and unloaded in the streets, and the packages thrown down on the same side of the street, so as frequently, with the wagons, to obstruct even foot-passengers, and oblige them to cross the gutter to the other side. This was held to be an unreasonable interference with the free passage of the public, and to be indictable as a nuisance. So it is unlawful for stage-coaches or omnibuses to congregate by the sides of the streets of a populous city, and remain there an unreasonable length of time soliciting passengers.[1] And this right, when used within the bounds of reason, must be exercised with a proper regard to the safety of the public travel. Thus, if a horse and carriage are left standing in the street and without any person to watch them, the owner is liable for any damage done by them, although it is occasioned by the act of a passer-by in striking the horse; for if a man chooses to leave a horse and carriage standing in the street, he must take the risk of any mischief that may be done in consequence.[2] But in an action of trespass for an injury done to a horse by a pony and chaise running against it, where it appeared that the defendant's wife stood by the head of the pony, which was standing by the side of the street, holding it by the reins, when a Punch and Judy show coming by, frightened the pony, and he ran away, and almost pulled the defendant's wife down while she tried to hold him, and so obliged her to let go the reins; it was held, that the defendant's wife being a proper person to

1 Rex *v.* Cross, 3 Campb. R. 226.

2 Illige *v.* Goodwin, 5 Car. & Payne, R. 190. In this case, the plaintiff was a chinaman in St. Paul's Churchyard; and the cart of the defendant, (a scavenger,) backed against the window of the plaintiff's shop, and broke a quantity of china; the carman, not being present at the time, but came up soon after. There was, however, proof in this case, that the defendant had admitted that the horse was given to backing, and that it was very wrong in the man to leave it in the street.

have the care of the pony, the injury was the result of inevitable accident, and did not entitle the plaintiff to recover.[1]

§ 344. *Road-worthiness.* A traveller upon a highway is bound to have his harness and carriage in good road-worthy condition, and is liable for the damages occasioned by any insufficiency in this particular. Thus where the proof was that in going down hill, the chain-stay to the defendant's cart broke, and his horse became frightened in consequence and ran away; it was held that the defendant was bound to have good tackle, and was negligent if he did not.[2] In Johnson *v.* Small,[3] the injury resulted from a collision between a stage-coach and a wagon upon the declivity of a very precipitous hill. It appeared that one of the blocks or rubbers, which was necessary by the assistance of a lever, to one end of which it was fastened, to check the speed of the stage-coach, had become loose, and the driver when he received the team nine miles back had procured nails and attempted to fasten it, and said he thought it was fast. This block or rubber dropped off before or after he started down the hill, and in pressing upon the end of the lever without the block, the end under his foot was pressed down upon the off horse, who plunged and continued to plunge as often as it was pressed upon, which caused the other horses to take fright and press forward until they ceased to be under the control of the driver. The Court held that the jury might well have inferred that the stage driver was guilty of negligence in fastening the block or lever insecurely when he received the stage; and that if he was not guilty of negligence at that time, knowing that it had been loose and might not be well fastened, they might well have concluded that he was guilty of negligence, and the failure to exercise that care and vigilance, which a cautious and prudent man would have

---

1 Goodman *v.* Taylor, 5 Car. & Payne, R. 410.

2 Welsh *v.* Lawrence, 2 Chitty, R. 262; Smith *v.* Smith, 2 Pick. (Mass.) R. 621.

3 Johnson *v.* Small, 5 B. Mon. (Ky.) R. 25.

exercised, in not examining the rubbers before he commenced the descent of so dangerous a hill. The term negligence, it has been remarked, includes "not only careless driving, but exciting the horses to such a rate of speed that they cannot be stopped or properly directed, the knowingly driving unbroken or vicious horses, overloading a coach, or using one that has not sufficient strength or improper harness."[1]

§ 345. Whenever, in consequence of a violation of these rules or of the want of proper care and diligence in any other respect, a collision ensues, the party through whose fault it happens is liable for the injury, unless the injured party, through his own negligence or misconduct, contributed to the result. But if it appears that the damage was occasioned *partly* by the negligence of the plaintiff and *partly* by that of the defendant, an action cannot be maintained; for the rule is, that if the plaintiff's negligence in *any way concurred* in causing the damage, he is not entitled to recover.[2] "A party," said Lord Ellenborough, in Butterfield *v.* Forrester,[3] "is not

---

1 Per Lord Ch. J. Best, in his charge to the Wilts Grand Jury in 1827; cited in note to Cotterill *v.* Starkey, 8 Car. & Payne, R. 691; and see Christie *v.* Griggs, 2 Campb. R. 79; Hollister *v.* Nowlen, 19 Wend. (N. Y.) R. 234; Israel *v.* Clark, 4 Esp. R. 259; Ingalls *v.* Bills, 9 Met. (Mass.) R. 1; Bremner *v.* Williams, 1 Car. & Payne, R. 414; Sharp *v.* Grey, 9 Bing. R. 457; Angell on Carriers, §§ 534–539.

2 Flower *v.* Adam, 2 Taunt. R. 314; Pluckwell *v.* Wilson, 5 Car. & Payne, R. 358; Luxford *v.* Large, Ibid. 421; Williams *v.* Holland, 6 Ib. 23; Turley *v.* Thomas, 8 Ib. 104; Woolf *v.* Beard, 8 Ib. 373; Bridge *v.* Grand Junction Railway Co. 3 M. & W. R. 244; Vanderplank *v.* Miller, 1 Moo. & Malk. R. 169; Harlow *v.* Humiston, 6 Cow. (N. Y.) R. 191; Smith *v.* Smith, 2 Pick. (Mass.) R. 621; Lane *v.* Crumbie, 12 Pick. (Mass.) R. 177; Munroe *v.* Leach, 7 Met. (Mass.) R. 274; Churchill *v.* Rosebeck, 15 Conn. R. 359; Simpson *v.* Hand, 6 Whart. (Penn.) R. 311; Rathbun *v.* Payne, 19 Wend. (N. Y.) R. 399; Barnes *v.* Cole, 21 Ib. 188; Hartfield *v.* Roper, Ib. 615; Brownell *v.* Flagler, 5 Hill, (N. Y.) R. 282; Sills *v.* Brown, 9 Car. & Payne, R. 601; Lynch *v.* Nurdin, 1 Ad. & E. R. (N. S.) 29; Lack *v.* Seward, 4 Car. & Payne, R. 106; Davis *v.* Saunders, 2 Chitt. R. 639; Woolley *v.* Scobell, 3 M. & R. 105; Fitzsimmons *v.* Inglis, 5 Taunt. R. 534.

3 Butterfield *v.* Forrester, 11 East, R. 60.

to cast himself upon an obstruction which has been made by the fault of another, and avail himself of it, if he do not himself use common and ordinary caution to be in the right. In cases of persons riding upon what is considered to be the wrong side of the road, that would not authorize another to ride up against them. One person being in fault will not dispense with another's using ordinary care for himself. Two things must concur to support this action, an obstruction in the road by the fault of the defendant, and no want of ordinary care to avoid it on the part of the plaintiff." The rule of law thus laid down was entirely approved by Parke, B., in Bridge *v.* Grand Junction Railway Company,[1] who added, however, "that although there may have been negligence on the part of the plaintiff, yet unless he might, by the exercise of ordinary care, have avoided the consequences of the defendant's negligence he is entitled to recover; if by ordinary care he might have avoided them, he is the author of his own wrong." And in a subsequent case, where an ass was fettered and turned upon a highway to graze and there run over by the defendant in driving too fast, it was held that the mere fact of putting the ass upon the road would not bar the plaintiff of his action. "For," as was observed by the same Judge, "although the ass may have been wrongfully there, still the defendant was bound to go along the road at such pace as would be likely to prevent mischief. Were this not so, a man might justify driving over goods left on a public highway, or even over a man lying asleep there, or the purposely running against a carriage going on the wrong side of the road."[2] In both these cases, therefore, the rule in Butterfield *v.* Forrester, though approved by the Court, was not approved without qualification. From the first it would seem that the rule does not hold good

---

1 Bridge *v.* Grand Junction Railway Company, 3 M. & W. R. 246; and see Gough *v.* Bryan, 2 Ib. 770.

2 Davies *v.* Mann, 10 M. & W. R. 545; *Ante*, § 290.

where the plaintiff, though negligent, could not, by the exercise of ordinary care, have avoided the injury. From the second it would seem that though the fault of the plaintiff *concurred* with that of the defendant to produce the injury, yet the plaintiff may be entitled to recover under circumstances of peculiar negligence on the part of the defendant, though no precise criterion is indicated by the Court by which to determine when such circumstances exist. The rule has also been further qualified by an exception in favor of the plaintiff, in cases where, though there has been mutual neglect, the evidence shows an intentional wrong on the part of the defendant.[1]

§ 346. The first of these exceptions, suggested by Parke, B., is now unquestioned law; the second, though occasionally recognized in subsequent cases, does not seem to have shaped itself into any definite *formula* and has been frequently overlooked, if not intentionally disregarded.[2] Thus in Hartfield *v.* Roper,[3] the plaintiff who sued by his next friend, was a child of about two years of age, and was standing or sitting in the beaten track of a public highway, with no person near him. The defendant was driving a sleigh and horses upon the same road, and before the child was perceived the horses passed over him. The sleigh was at the time of the injury descending a hill, at the foot of which was a bridge, and the child was in the road six or eight rods from the bridge. The course of the road was such that in descending the hill there was a fair view of the road beyond the bridge. A daughter of one of the defendants, however, testified that she did not perceive the child, although she sat on the side of the sleigh which passed over the track in which was the child. The defendant had no sleigh-bells. The horses at the time of the injury were trot-

---

1 Brownell *v.* Flagler, 5 Hill, (N. Y.) R. 282; Clay *v.* Wood, 5 Esp. R. 44; Rathbun *v.* Payne, 19 Wend. (N. Y.) R. 399.

2 Rathbun *v.* Payne, 19 Wend. (N. Y.) R. 399; and see cases cited note 2, *supra.*

3 Hartfield *v.* Roper, 21 Wend. (N. Y.) R. 615.

ting, but not at great speed, and the parties in the sleigh were not conversing at the time of the accident. As soon as the child was discovered the horses were stopped, and the sleigh prevented from passing over him. The jury found a verdict for the plaintiff for five hundred dollars. Upon a motion for a new trial it was said by the Court, per Cowen J.: "Was the plaintiff guilty of negligence? His counsel seemed to think he made a complete exception to the general rule demanding care on his part, by reason of his extreme infancy. Is this indeed so? A snow path in the public highway, is among the last places in this country to which such a small child should be allowed to resort, unattended by any one of suitable age and discretion. The custody of such a child is confided by law to its parents, or to others standing in their place; and it is absurd to imagine that it could be exposed in the road as this child was, without gross carelessness. It is the extreme of folly even to turn domestic animals upon the common highway. To allow small children to resort there alone, is a criminal neglect. It is true that this confers upon travellers no right to commit a *voluntary injury* upon either; nor does it warrant *gross neglect;* but it seems to me that to make them liable for any thing short of that would be contrary to law. The child has a right to the road for the purposes of travel, attended by proper escort. But at the tender age of two or three years, and even more, the infant cannot personally exercise that degree of discretion, which becomes instinctive at an advanced age, and for which the law must make him responsible, through others, if the doctrine of mutual care between parties is to be enforced at all in his case. It is perfectly well settled that if a party, injured by a collision on the highway, has drawn the mischief on himself by his own neglect, he is not entitled to an action, even though he be lawfully in the highway pursuing his travels,[1] which can scarcely be said of a

---

1 Burcle *v.* N. Y. Dry Dock Company, 2 Hall, (N. Y.) R. 151.

toppling infant suffered by his guardians to be there, either as a traveller or for the purpose of pursuing his sports. The application may be harsh when made to small children, as they are known to have no personal discretion. Common humanity is alive to their protection, but they are not therefore exempt from the legal rule, when they bring an action for redress; and there is no other way of enforcing it, except by requiring due care at the hands of those to whom the law and the necessity of the case has delegated the exercise of discretion." "The illustration sought to be derived from the law in respect to the injury of animals turned or suffered to stray into the street, does not strike me as fortunate. If they be there without any one to attend and take care of them, that is a degree of carelessness in the owner which would preclude his recovery of damages arising from mere inattention on the side of the traveller. Indeed it could rarely be said that animals entirely unattended are lawfully in the roads or streets at all. They may be driven along the road by the owner or his servants; but if allowed to run at large for the purpose of grazing, or any other purpose, entirely unattended, and yet travellers are to be made accountable in all cases of collision, such a doctrine might supersede the use of the road, so far as comfort or expedition is concerned.[1] The mistake lies in supposing the injury to be wilful, to arise from some positive act, or to be grossly negligent. Such an injury is never tolerated, be the

1 As regards the application of this principle to cattle unlawfully upon a highway, see The Tonawanda Railroad Company *v.* Munger, 5 Denio, (N. Y.) R. 255, and Tower *v.* Providence and Worcester Railroad Co. 2 R. I. Rep. 404, in which it was held that a railroad company is not liable for negligently running an engine upon and killing the cattle of the plaintiff, which had unlawfully come upon the track of the railroad, though there was no physical obstacle to prevent their entry. The Court say the company are not liable for want of care towards such cattle, because they owe them no care; and that the incapacity of the cattle to exercise care on their part makes no difference, inasmuch as the care required is in the party and not in his property. In support of this doctrine the following cases are cited: Blythe *v.* Topham, Cro. Jac. 158; Bush *v.* Brainard, 1 Cowen, (N. Y.) R. 78; Sarck *v.* Blackburn, 4 Car. & Payne, R. 297; Blackman *v.* Simmons, Ib. 138; and see *post.*

negligence on the side of the party injured what it may.[1] But where it arises from mere inadvertence on the side of the traveller, he is always excused by the law, on showing that there was equal or greater neglect on the side of his accuser. It is impossible to say, then, that the accuser was not himself the author of the injury which he seeks to father on another."

§ 347. In the preceding case, however, the rule seems to have been pushed to a somewhat questionable extreme. In Lynch *v.* Nurdin,[2] at any rate, it was much less rigorously applied. In that case, the defendant's servant left a horse and cart unattended in a public street, and the plaintiff, a child under seven years of age, during the driver's absence, climbed on the wheel, and other children urged forward the horse, whereby the plaintiff was thrown to the ground and the wheel fractured his leg. The Court left it to the jury to say, first, whether it was negligence in the defendant's servant to leave the horse and cart for half an hour, in the manner described; and secondly, whether that negligence occasioned the accident. On a motion for a new trial for error in the instructions of the Court, Lord Denman, C. J., remarking upon Lord Ellenborough's doctrine in Butterfield *v.* Forrester, said, that ordinary care must mean that degree of care which may reasonably be expected from a person in the plaintiff's situation. Supposing, he proceeds to say, the plaintiff to have been in fault, "but to this extent, that he merely indulged the natural instinct of a child in amusing himself with the empty cart and deserted horse, then we think that the defendant cannot be permitted to avail himself of that fact. The most blamable carelessness of his servant having tempted the child, he ought not to reproach the child with yielding to that temptation. He has been the real cause of the mischief. He has been deficient in ordinary care; the child, acting without prudence or thought,

---

1 *Ante*, § 345.

2 Lynch *v.* Nurdin, 1 Ad. & El. R. (N. S.) 28; 41 Eng. C. L. R. 422.

has, however, shown these qualities in as great a degree as he could be expected to possess them. His misconduct bears no proportion to that of the defendant which produced it." And it was also held, that the coöperation of third parties to the injury was not a defence, if the means of injury were negligently left where it was extremely probable that they would be set in motion.[1]

§ 348. In the case of Robinson *v.* Cone,[2] Redfield, J., in adopting the rule as laid down in Lynch *v.* Nurdin, pronounced the case of Hartfield *v.* Roper altogether at variance with it, and far less sound in its principles, and infinitely less satisfactory to the instinctive sense of reason and justice. In that case, the plaintiff was a child more than three months below the age of four years, whose father sent him to school, about a fourth of a mile south of the foot of the hill where the accident occurred. At the time of the injury the plaintiff was sliding along down the hill, lying upon his face upon his hand-sled, his feet projecting back of the sled, and his left leg lopping off the sled, towards the east, his head being turned towards the west, and about two feet from the edge of the road, where was a bank rising abruptly about two feet or more. The defendant was coming into the village with a load of bark, on a sled drawn by two horses, and driving down the hill at a very rapid pace. He saw the plaintiff some distance before he reached him, but at first thought him a dog, as he said, and after he knew it was a boy, supposed that he would get out of the way; but when he perceived he would

---

1 In support of this decision the Court cited Ilott *v.* Wilkes, 3 B. & Ald. R. 304; 5 E. C. L. Rep. 295; Deane *v.* Clayton, 7 Taunt. 489; 2 E. C. L. R. 183; Bird *v.* Holbrook, 4 Bing. R. 628; 15 E. C. L. R. 91, relying particularly upon the latter case. See Marriott *v.* Stanley, 1 Man. & Gr. R. 568; 39 E. C. L. R. 559, note (*a*), p. 561, where the doctrine announced in Butterfield *v.* Foster is a good deal criticized; Jay *v.* Whitfield, 3 B. & Ald. 308, n.; Jordin *v.* Crump, 8 M. & W. R. 782.

2 Robinson *v.* Cone, 3 Law Reporter, (N. S.) 444.

not, attempted to stop his team, but found it impossible, and then made a desperate effort to pass the boy on the east side, where there was some twenty feet or more of clear space, smooth and well trod. The fore runners, there being two sets, passed the boy without injury; but the hinder runners, not following precisely in the track of the others, crossed the plaintiff's left leg, fracturing it so severely that amputation became necessary. A verdict given for the plaintiff with heavy damages, was, upon motion for new trial, affirmed.

§ 349. In Wynn *v.* Allard,[1] in Pennsylvania, it appeared that the plaintiff was walking in the middle of one of the most frequented streets of Wilkesbarre, in that State, where there were sidewalks for footmen, when the defendant, in driving his horses in a sleigh rapidly along ran against him and injured him, for which he brought an action of trespass. On the trial, the plaintiff offered to prove that at the time of the occurrence the defendant was intoxicated. The defendant objected to the evidence, and the Court rejected it and sealed a bill of exceptions at the instance of the plaintiff. The Court below instructed the jury, that if the injury done to the plaintiff was a consequence of the negligence of the defendant alone, he was entitled to recover damages; but if it was occasioned partly by the negligence and carelessness of both parties, the plaintiff was not entitled to recover. This direction and the rejection of the evidence mentioned, were the subjects of the errors assigned. Per Curiam:—"The direction was right; and if there was error it was on the part of the jury. The principle that there is no recourse by action for an injury, which is the consequence of negligence on both sides, was laid down by the Court in Simpson *v.* Hand,[2] which was a case of negligence in the case of ships. But the law of the particular case was laid down in this instance by the Court

1 Wynn *v.* Allard, 5 Watts & S. (Penn.) R. 544.
2 Simpson *v.* Hand, 6 Whart. (Penn.) R. 320.

below, in exact conformity to the direction of Mr. Justice Alderson in Pluckwell *v.* Wilson,[1] that a person who leaves the ordinary side of the road is bound to use more care and diligence, and to keep a better look-out to avoid concussion than would be requisite if he were to confine himself to the proper side. It was for the jury, therefore, to say, under all the circumstances, whether the plaintiff was chargeable with negligence, having left the sidewalk, in not looking behind as well as before, to avoid contact with persons riding or driving in the middle of the street. If he was, the defendant would be answerable only for negligence so *wanton* and *gross* as to be evidence of *voluntary injury.* But the evidence of intoxication ought to have been received; not because the legal consequences of a drunken man's acts are different from those of a sober man's acts, but because where the evidence of negligence is nearly balanced, the fact of drunkenness might turn the scale, inasmuch as a man partially bereft of his faculties would be less observant than if he were sober, and less regardful of the safety of others. For that purpose, but certainly not to inflame the damages, the evidence ought to have been admitted." Judgment was reversed, and a *venire de novo* awarded.

§ 350. From these cases, it is evident that the principle laid down in Butterfield *v.* Forrester, though generally applicable, is not of such an inflexible character that it will not yield in particular cases, where its application would amount to the encouragement of gross carelessness, or wanton and heedless negligence, or to impunity for intentional wrong. In Kennard *v.* Burton,[2] Shepley, J., after a somewhat extended review of the authorities, comes to the conclusion that the correct rule is, "that if the party by want of ordinary care *contributed* to produce the injury, he will not be entitled to recover; but if

---

[1] Pluckwell *v.* Wilson, 5 C. & Payne, R. 379.

[2] Kennard *v.* Burton, 25 Maine R. 39.

he did not exercise ordinary care, and yet did not by the want of it contribute to produce the injury, he will be entitled to recover." The latter clause of this statement is undoubtedly correct; but the preceding clause, though generally correct, is clearly not so without important exceptions. To ascertain the principle which governs these exceptional cases is by no means an easy task, inasmuch as the Courts themselves, while apparently coming to very just conclusions, have not always given the most satisfactory reasons for them. In some of the cases, undoubtedly, one party may have been more in fault than another, yet mere preponderance of negligence has never been recognized as the test of liability, and juries directed to return their verdicts in favor of the least guilty party; in other cases the danger and consequent injury on the one side from an equal degree of negligence may have greatly exceeded that upon the other, yet no Court has ever suggested that the magnitude of the danger would excuse any want of ordinary care in avoiding it. In either of the cases supposed, to give a verdict in favor of the injured party would be to proclaim a premium upon carelessness. But, in nearly all the cases of exceptions to the rule laid down in Butterfield *v.* Forrester, it appears from the facts stated, or from expressions casually dropped by the Judges, that there was present one element, which though not announced as the basis of the decisions, cannot have failed to have greatly, if not controllingly, influenced the judgments of the Courts, viz.: gross carelessness, (for, in the case of a fettered brute, or a child of tender years, not to be careful is little less than being grossly careless,) or inexcusable inattention on the part of the defendant. If this be the true explanation of these exceptional cases as is submitted, then the rule may be stated thus: If there be mutual negligence, and an injury ensues, the party injured will not be entitled to recover, except where he could not, by the exercise of ordinary care have avoided the injury, or where the injury is the result of an intentional wrong on the part of the defendant, or of such gross negligence and want of care as in law is equally culpable.[1]

§ 351. Whether, by the operation of this rule, the injured party shall be barred of his action, is a question of fact to be determined in each particular case by the jury under the direction of the Court. Negligence, however, to have this effect, must be negligence existing at the time of the injury, not such as the plaintiff may have been guilty of at some previous period. In Munroe *v.* Leach,[2] it appeared that the parties were the drivers of two coaches, belonging to rival lines, running from Roxbury to Boston. In the course of the trip, on which the collision occurred, they had mutually attempted, several times, to intercept each other's progress by cutting each other off, as they had before been in the habit of doing. Just previous to the collision, the plaintiff's driver attempted to pass the defendant, who thereupon pressed upon him, and the plaintiff's driver, though he tried to avoid the danger all he could, was driven into a snow-drift, and one of his horses lamed. It was contended that the action could not be maintained, as the plaintiff's driver was himself in fault, as he and the defendant were mutually running and cutting each other off, to prevent each other going ahead. This view was adopted by the presiding Judge, who thereupon directed the jury to give a verdict for the defendant. On a motion for a new trial, the Court were of the opinion, that this direction assumed a fact as proved, which should have been left to the jury on the evidence, and for this consideration adjudged that the plaintiff was entitled to a new trial. All that is proved, it was remarked, is that the plaintiff's driver had been in fault *previously* to the transaction complained of. But this was no justification of the defendant in the commission of the like

---

1 *Ante*, § 290.

2 Munroe *v.* Leach, 7 Met. (Mass.) R. 274.

fault. And it appears by the evidence reported, that the injury complained of was solely caused by the misconduct of the defendant, the plaintiff's driver trying all he could to avoid it.[1]

§ 352. Where the plaintiff, in an action of trespass, for driving the defendant's carriage against the plaintiff's and oversetting it, thereby wounding the plaintiff, claimed that the injury occurred entirely through the negligence of the defendant, without any negligence on the plaintiff's part; and also, that if the plaintiff was guilty of negligence, the defendant drove his carriage against the plaintiff's by design or gross negligence, and thereby caused the injury; and that in either of these events, the plaintiff was entitled to recover; and the defendant did not claim to justify himself, on the ground that the plaintiff was guilty of any negligence, at the time when the collision took place, but by a course of misconduct pursued by the plaintiff on the road, *previous* to the collision, and at some distance from the place where it happened; which misconduct of the plaintiff could not possibly have concurred in directly producing the injury complained of; it was held, that the Court might properly omit to charge the jury as to the effect of negligence on the part of the plaintiff.[2] So in an action against a railway company for so negligently managing and lighting their station that the plaintiff, being a passenger by the railway, was thrown down while on his way to the carriages; where the defendant's counsel, at the trial, rested his defence on the ground that the accident was entirely owing to the want of ordinary care on the part of the plaintiff, and that there was no negligence on the part of the defendant; the Judge having left it to the jury to say whether the accident occurred from the alleged negligence of the defendants, or whether it was entirely the plaintiff's own negligence which caused it, it

---

[1] As regards the application of this rule to injuries occasioned by defects and obstructions in highways, see *ante*, Chap. VI. § 290, *et seq.*

[2] Churchill *v.* Roseback, 15 Conn. R. 359.

was held, on motion for a new trial for misdirection, on the ground that the Judge ought to have told the jury that if the plaintiff contributed to the injury the defendants were entitled to the verdict, although they might have been guilty of negligence; that the defendants were not entitled to a new trial, the issue on which they rested their defence having been left to the jury.[1]

§ 353. *The right to go upon adjoining Lands where the Highway is impassable.* In England, the rule of law is well settled, that where a highway becomes obstructed and impassable from temporary causes, a traveller has a right to go *extra viam* upon adjoining land, without being guilty of trespass.[2] In this country the same principle has often been incidentally recognized and treated as well-settled law,[3] and in the case of Campbell *v.* Race, has been directly affirmed.[4] Highways being established for public service, and for the use and benefit of the whole community, a due regard for the welfare of all requires, that when temporarily obstructed, the right of travel should not be interrupted. And this right, therefore, rests upon the maxim of the common law, that where public convenience and necessity come in conflict with private right, the latter must yield to the former. Its exercise may also be justified upon the familiar doctrine that inevitable necessity or accident may be shown in excuse for an alleged trespass. If a traveller in a highway, by unexpected and unforeseen occurrences, such as a sudden flood, heavy drifts of snow, or the falling of a tree, is shut out from the travelled paths, so that he cannot reach

---

1 Martin *v.* The Great Northern Railway Co. 30 Eng. L. & Eq. R. 473.

2 Henn's case, W. Jones, 296; 3 Salk. 182; 1 Saund. 323, note 3; Absor *v.* French, 2 Show. 28; Young *v.* ———, 1 Ld. Raymond, 725; Taylor *v.* Whitehead, 2 Douglas, 745; Bullard *v.* Harrison, 4 M. & S. 387, 393; 2 Bl. Com. 36.

3 Holmes *v.* Seeley, 19 Wend. (N. Y.) R. 507; Williams *v.* Safford, 7 Barb. (N. Y.) Sup. Ct. R. 309; Newkirk *v.* Saller, 9 Ib. 652; 3 Kent. Com. 424, *ante*, § 5.

4 Campbell *v.* Race, 7 Cush. (Mass.) R. 408.

his destination without passing upon adjacent lands, he is under a necessity so to do; that is to say, the act to be done can only be accomplished in that way. Such a temporary and unavoidable use of private property, must be regarded as one of those incidental burdens to which all property in a civilized community is subject.[1]

§ 354. In the case above referred to,[2] it was urged in argument that the effect of establishing this rule of law would be to appropriate private property to public use without providing any means of compensation to the owner. But it was remarked by the Court in reply: "If such an accidental, occasional, and temporary use of land can be regarded as an appropriation of private property to public use, entitling the owner to compensation, which may well be doubted, still the decisive answer to this objection is quite obvious. The right to go *extra viam*, in case of temporary and impassable obstructions, being one of the legal incidents or consequences which attaches to a highway through private property, it must be assumed that the right to the use of land adjoining the road was taken into consideration and proper allowance made therefor, when the land was originally appropriated for the highway, and that the damages were then estimated and fixed, for the private injury which might thereby be occasioned." And it was also held, that this right was not impaired by the duty imposed upon towns, in this country, to keep their highways in suitable repair, and to be liable for the damages occasioned by the want of such repair.

§ 355. Having its origin in necessity, this right, it has been said, must be limited by that necessity; *cessante ratione, cessat ipsa lex.* "Such a right is not to be exercised from convenience merely, nor when, by the exercise of due care, after notice of obstructions, other ways may be selected and the obstructions avoided. But it is to be confined to those cases

---

1 Ibid. 411, 412.

2 Campbell *v.* Race, *supra.*

of inevitable necessity or unavoidable accident, arising from sudden and recent causes which have occasioned temporary and impassable obstructions in the highway. What shall constitute such inevitable necessity or unavoidable accident, must depend upon the various circumstances attending each particular case. The nature of the obstruction in the road, the length of time during which it has existed, the vicinity or distance of other public ways, the exigencies of the traveller, are some of the many considerations which would enter into the inquiry, and upon which it is the exclusive province of the jury to pass, in order to determine whether any necessity really existed, which would justify or excuse the traveller."[1]

### 2. *Travel upon Turnpike Roads.*

§ 356. Travel upon turnpike roads is regulated by the same rules and principles as travel upon ordinary roads and streets. It is chiefly distinguished from the latter kind of travel by the fact that it is burdened with tolls. Toll, in the restricted sense in which it is here used, is the price of the privilege of travel upon this particular species of highway. At common-law, there are two sorts of toll, viz.: *toll thorough* and *toll-traverse.* Toll-traverse is the price paid for passing over the private soil of another, and may be claimed by prescription, the license to pass being the implied consideration for the claim.[2] Toll thorough is the price for passing upon a public highway, and rests upon the principle which governs every grant, viz.: that he who receives it, does, or did something as an equivalent to him who pays it. It is strictly a *quid pro quo;* and, to support a prescription for this species of toll, it is not enough to prove an immemorial usage to take the toll,

---

[1] Per Bigelow, J., in Campbell *v.* Race, *supra.*

[2] 7 Com. Dig. 478, Toll, (D., a.) ; Cro. El. 711 ; James *v.* Johnson, 2 Mod. R. 143; Pelham *v.* Pickersgill, 1 Term R. 660.

without also showing the consideration upon which it rests.[1] In Truman *v.* Walgam,[2] the defendant pleaded, to an action of trespass, for stopping the plaintiff's wagon on the highway in Gainsborough, prescription for toll through the streets of Gainsborough, in consideration of repairing *divers* streets there; and the plea was adjudged bad, because it did not say that the defendant repaired *all* the streets; and, for any thing that appeared, the plaintiff might have been passing through a street which the defendant did not repair. "Courts," it was observed, "are exceeding careful and jealous of these claims of right to levy money upon the subject; these tolls began and were established by the power of great men." But if a person, claiming a toll for passing over an highway, can show that the liberty of passing over the soil, and the taking of toll for such passage, are both immemorial, and that the soil and the tolls were, before the time of legal memory, in the same hands, though severed since, it will be presumed that the soil was originally granted to the public in consideration of the tolls, and such original grant is a good consideration to support the demand.[3]

§ 357. In this country, it has been held in Vermont, that the enjoyment for more than twenty years, without molestation, of a right to take toll upon a public highway, is equivalent to an express grant so to do. "Indeed," said the Court, "under special circumstances, the dedication of private property to public use, or the abandonment of a right to use such property by the public, and its surrender to private use, will be presumed in a much less time than the usual term of prescription."[4] In

---

1 7 Com. Dig. 477, Toll, (C.); Haspurt *v.* Wills, 1 Mod. R. 47; Warren *v.* Prideux, Ib. 104; Smith *v.* Shepherd, Cro. El. 710; 3 Dane, Abr. 178, ch. 76, art. 11; 15 Petersdorf, Abr. 62.

2 Truman *v.* Walgam, 2 Wils. R. 296.

3 Pelham *v.* Pickersgill, 1 Term R. 660; Yarmouth *v.* Eaton, 3 Burr, R. 1402.

4 Barton Turnpike Co. *v.* Bishop, 11 Vt. R. 198.

Massachusetts, however, it has been held, that if a turnpike road has not been lawfully laid out, the allowance of it by the Common Pleas, and the existence of it as a turnpike road, *de facto*, for nearly twenty years, gives no right to demand toll, "if," say the Court, "such a right can, by any length of time, be established."[1] But in this country, and, indeed, in England, this right is almost universally granted by statutory enactments, and can be exercised only in strict compliance with the terms of the grant.[2] If there be any ambiguity in the language of such grant, it will be construed rather in favor of the public than of the grantee.[3] And, inasmuch as this right depends upon the varying provisions of special statutes, each statute being encumbered with multitudinous qualifications designed to subserve the wants and the policy of particular localities, the cases on this subject necessarily relate rather to the construction of these statutes than to an exposition of principles, and are not, therefore, of sufficient general interest to justify more than a merely cursory consideration.

§ 358. Tolls are not demandable for travelling on turnpike roads between two gates, without passing a gate, or unless the gate be shunned and the road travelled again;[4] though it has been held, that even if travellers travel the road until they come near the gate, and then turn aside into another road, they are

---

1 Fales *v.* Whiting, 7 Pick. (Mass.) R. 225.

2 "The imposition of toll," says Wellbeloved, "to be applied to the maintenance of a road, is the revival of an old principle, but with some difference in its adaptation to practice. Under the ancient system of tenures, the lord of the soil frequently claimed the privilege of receiving tolls from all who travelled along his highway; nor was this esteemed a mere bounty, for he was liable, in consideration of such toll, to keep the way in good order, and, in some countries, even to defend the passengers from depredations. There was an instance in France, where the lord was fined for permitting a merchant to be robbed upon his highway." Wellbeloved on Highways, p. 252.

3 *Post*, § 368.

4 Lexington and Georgetown Turnpike Co. *v.* Redd, 2 B. Mon. (Ky.) R. 31; per Williams, C. J., in Fowler *v.* Pratt, 11 Vt. R. 381; Centre Turnpike Co. *v.* Vandusen, 10 Ib. 197.

liable to pay the toll.[1] In New York, it is enacted, that "every person who, to avoid the payment of the legal toll, shall, with his team, carriage or horse, turn out of a turnpike road, or pass any gate thereon, on ground adjacent thereto, and again enter on such road, shall, for each offence, forfeit the sum of five dollars to the corporation injured." Under this act, if a traveller turns off at a place little more than half a mile from the gate, it will be held a turning off on "ground adjacent to the gate," within the meaning of the act. And it makes no difference that the person, after turning off, travels upon an old highway for the distance of six or seven miles before again entering the turnpike road, nor that other persons have been in the habit of doing so; the question being, whether he turned off, *bonâ fide*, or with a view to avoid paying toll.[2] But if, in such a case, the party does not again reënter the turnpike road, he is exempt from toll, though his purpose in turning off was to evade its payment.[3]

§ 359. *Exemptions from the Payment of Toll.* Clauses in statutes, conferring an exemption from the payment of toll, are construed most liberally in favor of the immunity. Thus, where the toll prescribed in the charter of a turnpike company was twenty-five cents for a four-wheeled pleasure-carriage, and for a wagon ten cents, it was held, that a vehicle, which was a four-wheeled pleasure-carriage and a wagon, was subject to

---

1 Fitch *v.* Lothrop, 2 Root, (Conn.) R. 524.

2 Carrier *v.* Schoharie Turnpike Co. 18 Johns. (N. Y.) R. 56; The Watervliet Turnpike Co. *v.* M'Kean, 6 Hill, (N. Y.) R. 616; 1 Rev. Stat. 588, § 55.

3 Centre Turnpike Co. *v.* Vandusen, 10 Vt. R. 197. In New Hampshire, it has been held, that case lies against the selectmen of a town for laying out a highway, merely for the purpose of enabling travellers to evade the payment of toll at a turnpike gate. But if the public convenience should require that a road be laid out to a turnpike, it may lawfully be done, although it may enable passengers to evade the payment of toll. Proprietors of the Third Turnpike Road *v.* Champney, 2 N. Hamp. R. 199; Cheshire Turnpike *v.* Stevens, 10 N. Hamp. R. 133.

the toll of ten cents only.[1] So it has been held, that an act, exempting carts, &c., loaded with manure, from toll, exempts them from toll if they are *going empty* to fetch manure.[2] Exemptions in favor of husbandry are to be beneficially construed.[3] An exemption in favor of persons going to and from mills, comprehends saw-mills as well as grist-mills.[4] But an exemption in favor of persons going to and from a blacksmith's shop, has been held to embrace only persons going with the express purpose of having work done in the shop.[5] And an exemption in favor of the inhabitants of a particular town, going to market with the produce of their farms, and returning from market, is personal, and is waived if the person carries, or brings back from the place of market, the goods of others, even though such goods constitute but a portion of his load.[6] Individuals, or the inhabitants of a particular district, who have for more than twenty years been permitted to pass a turnpike gate toll free, may, it has been held, prescribe for a right so to pass, and an individual so exempted, if denied permission to pass, would, it seems, be justified in passing forcibly, using, however, no more force than would be necessary for such purpose.[7] Contractors carrying the mails for the United States,

---

1 Turnpike Co. *v.* Freeman, 14 Conn. R. 85.

2 Harrison *v.* James, 2 Chitty, R. 547.

3 Hickinbotham *v.* Perkins, 3 Moore, R. 185.

4 Hearsey *v.* Pruyn, 7 Johns. (N. Y.) R. 179.

5 Stratton *v.* Herrick, 9 Johns. (N. Y.) R. 356; Stratton *v.* Hubbell, Ib. 357.

6 Hearsey *v.* Boyd, 7 Johns. (N. Y.) R. 183; and see Passumpsic Turnpike Co. *v.* Langdon, 6 Vt. R. 546.

7 Panton Turnpike Co. *v.* Bishop, 11 Vt. R. 198. For other American cases, as to exemptions in favor of persons going "*on the ordinary domestic business of family concerns,*" see Green Mountain Turnpike Co. *v.* Hemenway, 2 Vt. R. 512; Centre Turnpike Co. *v.* Smith, 12 Vt. R. 212; Kent *v.* Newburyport Turnpike, 4 Pick. (Mass.) R. 388; Medford Turnpike *v.* Torrey, 2 Pick. (Mass.) R. 538; Proprietors of the Second Turnpike *v.* Taylor, 6 N. Hamp. R. 499; Newburgh and Cochecton Turnpike Co. *v.* Belknap, 17 Johns. (N. Y.) R. 33. *In favor of particular kinds of vehicles,* Pardee *v.* Blanchard, 19 Johns. (N. Y.) R. 442; Moss *v.* Moore, 18 Ib. 128; Merrick *v.* Phelps, 5 Conn. R. 465; Talcott Mountain Turnpike Co. *v.* Marshall, 11 Ib. 185; Turnpike Co. *v.* Freeman, 14

are not, for that reason, exempt from tolls;[1] but the keeper of a toll-gate has no authority to stop the carriage in which the mail is carried, for a refusal to pay; his only remedy for such refusal being by an action at law.[2]

§ 360. *The Establishment of Toll-Gates.* A turnpike company can collect its tolls only at the legally established gates. And it has been held, that, where a power given to a turnpike company to erect toll-gates within certain limits, at their discretion, has been once exercised, the power is at an end; and the company cannot, without some strong and manifest necessity, change the local situation of the gates which have been once erected, merely to suit their own convenience;[3] and, if they do make such change, they have no right to collect tolls

---

Ib. 457; Housatonic Turnpike *v.* Frink, 15 Pick. (Mass.) R. 443; Turnpike Co. *v.* Newland, 4 Dev. (N. Car.) R. 463; Cincinnati, &c. Turnpike *v.* Neil, 9 Ham. (Ohio) R. 11. *Going to and from mill*, Chestney *v.* Coon, 8 Johns. (N. Y.) R. 150; Bates *v.* Sutherland, 15 Ib. 510; *supra*, notes 3 & 4. For English cases in favor of persons *passing several times in one day*, Loaring *v.* Stone, 3 D. & R. R. 797; 2 B. & C. R. 575; Norris *v.* Prate, 10 Moore, R. 293; 3 Bingh. R. 41; Waterhouse *v.* Keen, 4 B. & C. R. 200; Fearnley *v.* Mosley, 5 B. & C. R. 25; Fenton *v.* Swallow, 4 Ad. & El. R. 723; Jackson *v.* Curwen, 7 D. & R. R. 838; 5 B. & C. R. 31; Gray *v.* Shilling, 4 Moore, R. 371; Chambers *v.* William, 7 D. & R. R. 842; Williams *v.* Sanger, 10 East, R. 66; Hopkins *v.* Thorogood, 2 B. & Ad. R. 916; Niblet *v.* Pottow, 1 Bing. R. (N. C.) 81. *In favor of husbandry*, Rex *v.* Adams, 6 M. & S. R. 52; Harrison *v.* James, 2 Chit. R. 547; Pratt *v.* Brown, 8 C. & Pay. R. 244; King *v.* Gough, 2 Chit. R. 655; Chambers *v.* Eaves, 2 Campb. R. 393; Hickinbotham *v.* Perkins, 3 Moore, R. 185; Harrison *v.* Brough, 6 T. Rep. 706; Stevens *v.* Duffts, 4 Burr. R. 2258. *Carriage of road materials*, Ormond *v.* Widdicombe, 2 B. & Ald. R. 49. *Going to church*, Lewis *v.* Hammond, 2 B. & Ald. R. 206. *Merely crossing*, Phillips *v.* Harper, 2 Chit. R. 412; Mayor *v.* Oxenham, 5 Taunt. R. 340; Pope *v.* Langworthy, 1 Nev. & M. R. 647; 5 B. & Ad. R. 464; Bussey *v.* Storey, 4 B. & Adol. R. 98. *Stage-wagon*, The Queen *v.* Ruscoe, 8 Ad. & Ell. R. 386.

1 Dickey *v.* Maysville and Lexington Turnpike Co. 7 Dana, (Ky.) R. 113; Proctor *v.* Crozier and Marshall, 6 B. Mon. (Ky.) R. 269; Turnpike Co. *v.* Newland, 4 Dev. (N. Car.) R. 463; Newland *v.* Buncombe Turnpike Co. 4 Ired. (N. Car.) R. 372; The Derby Turnpike Co. *v.* Parks, 10 Conn. R. 522.

2 Hopkins *v.* Stockton, 2 W. & Serg. (Penn.) R. 163.

3 Griffin *v.* House, 18 Johns. (N. Y.) R. 397; Hartford and Dedham Turnpike Corp. *v.* Baker, 17 Pick. (Mass.) R. 432; State *v.* The Norwalk and Danbury Turnpike Co. 10 Conn. R. 157. But see Fowler *v.* Pratt, 11 Vt. R. 369.

at the removed gates.[1] Nor can the power to make such changes be acquired by repeated removals during a period of nearly forty years, and the acquiescence of the public.[2] But a company, having by its charter authority to erect "so many gates or turnpikes as may be necessary to collect their tolls," may increase the number of gates originally established, and change their situation from time to time, provided the gates are not placed in any situation prohibited by the charter.[3] And they may be so erected as to intersect and stop an old highway, provided they are erected as prescribed by the act, which is to be considered as so far controlling the use of the old road.[4] A company, authorized to erect gates at such places as they see fit, and to demand tolls at certain rates, for every ten miles, and in the same proportion for a shorter distance, may demand tolls according to the distances between the gates or turnpikes on the road; and are not limited to the distance travelled by the persons from whom tolls are demanded.[5]

§ 361. By a statute in New York, it is provided, that the location of a toll-gate may be changed, by a certain course of proceeding therein prescribed, whenever the commissioners of the town in which the toll-gate may be located, or a majority of them "shall be of the opinion that the *location of such gate is unjust to the public interest by reason of the proximity of*

---

1 Turnpike Co. *v.* Hosmer, 12 Conn. R. 361.

2 State *v.* Norwalk and Danbury Turnpike Co. 10 Conn. R. 157.

3 The Cheshire Turnpike *v.* Stevens, 10 N. Hamp. R. 133.

4 Farmers' Turnpike Road *v.* Coventry, 10 Johns. (N. Y.) R. 389.

5 Mallory *v.* Austin, 7 Barb. (N. Y.) Sup. Ct. R. 626; Stewart *v.* Rich, 1 Caines, (N. Y.) R. 182; The People *v.* Kingston Turnpike Co. 23 Wend. (N. Y.) R. 193. As to the construction of statutory provisions imposing penalties upon toll-collectors for an abuse of their office, by shutting the gates after they have been commanded by the proper authorities to be thrown open, or by exacting toll from persons who are exempt from the payment of toll, see Trowbridge *v.* Baker, 1 Cow. (N. Y.) R. 251; Williams *v.* Smith, 6 Ib. 166; Jones *v.* Estis, 2 Johns. (N. Y.) R. 379; Conklin *v.* Elting, Ib. 410; Norval *v.* Cornell, 16 Johns. (N. Y.) R. 73.

*diverging roads*, or for other reasons." In a proceeding under this statute, to change the location of a toll-gate, it was held, that there is no propriety or justice in allowing a company to make a plank-road or turnpike road on a main thoroughfare leading to a large village, for the distance of seven-eighths of a mile, and to collect tolls for that distance of all persons travelling on such thoroughfare; where the place selected for such road is that part of the thoroughfare most contiguous to the village, with which a large number of roads have united and added their travel to the piece of road over which the plank or turnpike road has been constructed.[1]

§ 362. In Connecticut, a turnpike company, incorporated in 1799, were authorized, by their charter, to erect and keep up turnpike gates on their road. In 1818, the company erected a gate on their road, with upright posts, and a cross-beam over the gate, supporting a roof twelve feet six inches above the travelled path. When the charter was granted, and the gate established, it was usual to erect turnpike gates with cross-beams of this height. In June, 1833, a traveller came to the gate in question, with a load of clocks, placed upright in three tiers, the greatest height of the load being thirteen feet above the travelled path, and higher than such loads usually are. He paid the toll, and the gate-keeper opened the gate in the usual way; but the height of the load being greater than the cross-beam and roof, it could not pass under them, and he thereupon forcibly removed them. In an action of trespass, brought by the turnpike company, for this injury to their property, it was held, that this was a reasonable exercise of their right, and, consequently, that the defendant was liable.

§ 363. For the recovery of tolls due for travelling upon a turnpike road, the proper action is assumpsit.[2] In actions of this

---

1 McAllister *v.* Albion Plank-road Co. 11 Barb. (N. Y.) Sup. Ct. R. 610.

2 Proprietors of the Second Turnpike *v.* Taylor, 6 N. Hamp. R. 499; Seward *v.* Baker, 1 Tenn. R. 616; Peacock *v.* Harris, 10 East, R. 104; Ayers *v.* The

nature, the declaration must show the plaintiff's right to demand the toll; if by statute, setting forth the statute, or parts thereof, by virtue of which the right is claimed; if by prescription, alleging the prescription, and also the consideration or equivalent for the demand.[1] If the corporation are authorized to stop and detain travellers until the tolls shall be paid, this is merely a cumulative remedy, and does not preclude the maintenance of an action for such tolls.[2] It is no defence to such an action, that the company have neglected to comply with their charter, by not exposing to view the rates of toll as therein prescribed; nor, on account stated, and acknowledged by the creditor, that the collector was irregularly appointed.[3] Neither can a defendant, in such a suit, show a forfeiture of the franchise by way of defence, though he might, it seems, show that the franchise has expired by its own limitation, or has been surrendered, or that the act conferring it has been repealed.[4] And, where one claims to pass a toll-gate, toll free, by reason of any privilege or exemption, and is permitted to pass under such claim, he is not liable, in an action of assumpsit, for the toll, even when his claim of privilege is not well founded. There being no express promise to pay, in any event, the law will not, under such a state of facts, imply a promise.[5]

§ 364. In addition to the common-law remedy, turnpike companies are often further protected by penalties imposed upon

---

Turnpike Co. 4 Halst. (N. J.) R. 33; Chelsey *v.* Smith, 1 New Hamp. R. 22.

[1] 3 Dane, Abr. 181, ch. 76, A. 11; § 27. For precedent of declaration, see 2 Chit. Plead. (9th Amer. ed.) p. 51.

[2] Chelsey *v.* Smith, 1 N. Hamp. R. 22.

[3] Centre Turnpike Co *v.* Smith, 12 Vt. R. 212; Peacock *v.* Harris, 10 East, R. 104. Erecting a toll-board, with the rates of toll in small Roman characters, but of a large size, was held to be a compliance with the Massachusetts statute, which required them to be in large or capital letters. Nichols *v.* Bertram, 3 Pick. (Mass.) R. 342.

[4] Adams *v.* Beach, 6 Hill, (N. Y.) R. 271.

[5] Centre Turnpike Co. *v.* Smith, 12 Vt. R. 212.

such as forcibly pass their gates. Where such penalties are prescribed, the mere *passing* a turnpike gate, and refusing to pay toll when demanded, is a *forcible* passing, if the person so passing be liable to pay toll; [1] but simply riding through, without payment, and without any force or violence, or refusal to pay, will not expose a traveller to the penalty.[2] And a person, who is exempted, in respect of his business at the time of passing, from the payment of toll, does not incur the penalty, though he shall refuse to pay toll, and forcibly pass the gate without making known his business, or notifying the toll-gatherer of his exemption.[3]

### 3. *Travel upon Canals.*

§ 365. The doctrine of the common-law, that neither party can recover for damage which has resulted from mutual negligence, has, in this country, been applied to canal boats. The "Canal Regulations," in New York, have adopted, for the regulation of canal navigation, what is essentially the American law of the road; that is, when boats meet on the canals, it is the duty of the master of each to turn out to the right, so as to be wholly on the right side of the centre of the canal.[4] If, at the time of the collision, both boats, either through negligence or design, are near the centre of the canal, neither having turned sufficiently to the right, whatever injury results, is the common fault of both parties, and the owners of each boat must submit to the injury done to them, in consequence of the mutual default. Every boat navigating the New York canals in the night-time, is also required to carry conspicuous lights on its bow; and a want of lights on the bow, when it is so

---

1 Pingry *v.* Washburn, 1 Aik. (Vt.) R. 264; Nichols *v.* Bertram, 3 Pick. (Mass.) R. 342.

2 Columbia Turnpike Co. *v.* Woodworth, 2 Caines, (N. Y.) R. 97.

3 Green Mountain Turnpike Co. *v.* Hemmenway, 2 Vt. R. 512; Pingry *v.* Washburn, 1 Aik. (Vt.) R. 264.

4 1 New York Rev. Stat. 248, § 154; Ib. 695, § 1.

dark as to require them, is negligence.[1] In Dygert *v.* Bradley, the defendant's boat, in navigating the canal, came violently into collision with that of the plaintiff, while lying-to, near one of the locks, waiting her turn to pass. It was held, that it was not enough, that the defendant managed his boat in a prudent and skilful manner, but that he was also bound to know, whether, from the state of the water in the canal at the time, and from the size of his boat and her being heavily laden, he could pass the plaintiff's boat without hazard; and, if there were hazard, either not to have made the attempt to pass, or, having the control of the speed of his boat, to have proceeded so slowly and cautiously, that no injury could have been produced from the collision.[2]

§ 366. In the construction of a State law in New York,[3] it has been held, that, in passing the Erie and Champlain canals, freight-boats are bound to afford every facility for the passage of packet-boats, as well through the locks, as elsewhere on the canal. And where a freight-boat, passing on the Erie canal, was waiting for the emptying of a lock, when a packet-boat overtook her, it was held, that the packet-boat should pass first. On request, the master of the freight-boat, refusing to consent to this, the master of the packet may use all necessary means to obtain the preference due to him, short of a breach of the peace; as, by pulling back the freight-boat, and forcing his own forward, doing no unnecessary damage to the freight-boat. Should the freight-boat be detained or injured, through the obstinate resistance of the master to the exercise of the right of preference of the packet, this is the fault of the former, for which he cannot recover damages against the master of the latter.[4]

---

1 Rathburn *v.* Payne, 19 Wend. (N. Y.) R. 399; Ang. on Carriers, § 637.

2 Dygert *v.* Bradley, 8 Wend. (N. Y.) R. 469.

3 Passed April 13th, 1820, sess. 43, ch. 202, § 4 and 10.

4 Farnsworth *v.* Groot, 6 Cowen, (N. Y.) R. 698.

§ 367. Under the laws of Pennsylvania,[1] where an ascending and descending boat have to pass each other, near to, or at a narrow place in the canal, constructed for the purposes of inland navigation, it is the duty, as between themselves, of the ascending boat to wait at such distance from such narrow place, as to permit the descending boat to pass with safety; and if any injury be sustained by the descending, through a non-compliance of the law on the part of the ascending boat, the latter is liable in damages for such injury. It is, however, the right of persons plying on the canal, to stop their boats for a reasonable time to unlade, taking care to select an eligible place to do this,—that is, a place so wide that other boats can pass with safety, and to have their boat thrown close to the beam-side of the canal at both ends. And, it has been held, that where the boat of a third party, thus properly moored to the bank of the canal, is concerned, and the ascending boat will not comply with the act of the assembly aforesaid, it is the duty of the persons having charge of the descending boat, to keep her at a proper distance, and under their control, so as to insure safety; and if, through culpable negligence, or a want of due caution in passing each other, a collision takes place, through, and by which, the descending boat is driven against and staves in such third boat, the owners, or persons in charge of the descending boat, are answerable in damages for the injury sustained by such third boat. The dereliction of duty on the part of the ascending boat, will not authorize the master of the descending boat to abandon his duty to a third person, and thereby subject him to loss; though, it seems, in the event of loss under such circumstances, the injured party is entitled to look for indemnity to the owners of both boats.[2]

§ 368. Where a canal is made, pursuant to an act of the legislature, the right of the proprietors to take toll is derived

---

1 Act of April 10, 1826, § 7.

2 Sheerer *et al.* *v.* Kissinger *et al.* 1 Penn. (Barr,) R. 44.

entirely from the act, and is to be considered as if there was a bargain between them and the public, the terms of which are expressed in the statute; and the rule of construction is, that any ambiguity of the terms of the contract, must operate against the company of adventurers, and in favor of the public. The proprietors, therefore, can claim nothing which is not clearly given them by the act.[1]

§ 369. By the ninth section of the charter of the Chesapeake and Delaware Canal Company, the company are empowered to demand and receive certain tolls upon articles therein enumerated, and upon all other articles, not enumerated, in the same proportion; and the charter proceeds: "Every boat or vessel which has not commodities on board to pay the sum of four dollars, shall pay so much as, with the commodities on board, will yield the sum aforesaid; and every empty boat or vessel, four dollars, except an empty boat or vessel returning, whose load has already paid the tolls affixed, in which case, she shall pass toll-free." And, by the eleventh section of the charter, it is declared, that "the canal and works to be erected thereon, in virtue of the charter, when completed, shall forever thereafter be esteemed, and taken to be navigable, as a public highway, free for the transportation of all goods, com-

---

1 The Proprietors of the Stourbridge Canal *v.* Wheeling and others, 2 B. & Adol. R. 792; Gildart *v.* Gladstone, 1 East, R. 675; The Dock Company of Kingston-upon-Hull *v.* Browne, 2 B. & Ad. R. 58; Barrett *v.* Stockton Railway Co. 2 Man. & Gr. 134; 2 Scott, N. R. 339. For other English decisions upon the right of canal companies to demand and receive tolls, see Leeds and Liverpool Navigation Co. *v.* Hustler, 1 B. & C. R. 424; 8 E. C. L. R. 118, overruling the case of Hollingshead *v.* Liverpool and Leeds Canal Co. 2 B. & Ald. R. 66; Frazer *v.* Swansea Canal Co. 3 Nev. & M. R. 391; Jenkins *v.* Cooke, 1 Ad. & El. R. 372; Staffordshire and Worcestershire Canal Co. *v.* Trent and Mersey Canal Co. 6 Taunt. R. 151; Monmouthshire Canal Co. *v.* Kendall, 4 B. & Ald. R. 453; Brittain *v.* Cromford Canal Co. 3 B. & Ald. R. 139; Lees *v.* Manchester Canal Navigation, 11 East, R. 645; Rex *v.* Tone Conservators, 1 B. & Adol. R. 561; Regina *v.* Leicestershire and Northampton Union Canal Co. 3 Railway Cases, 1; Hall *v.* Grantham Canal Navigation, 13 Law J. (N. S.) 583; Hall *v.* Grantham Canal Co. 13 Mees. & W. R. 114.

modities, or produce whatsoever, on payment of the toll imposed by this act; and no tax whatsoever, for the use of the water of the said canal, or the works thereon erected, shall at any time hereafter be imposed by all, or either of the said States." In a case before the Supreme Court of the United States, the following questions occurred upon the construction of this charter: First, is the canal company entitled to charge compensation or toll for passengers on board a boat passing through the canal? Second, has any one a right to navigate the canal, without leave of the company, for the transportation of passengers, with passenger-boats, paying, or offering to pay, toll upon the boats, as empty boats, or upon commodities on board, but without toll or compensation for passengers? The Court held, as to the first question, that the charter conferred upon the company no right to demand or receive toll for passengers. "The articles upon which the company is authorized to take toll," was the language of Taney, Ch. J., "are particularly enumerated, and the amount specified. The toll is imposed on commodities on board of a vessel passing through the canal. No toll is given on the vessels themselves, except only when they have no commodities on board, or not sufficient to yield a toll of four dollars. Passengers are not mentioned in the enumeration, nor is any toll given upon a vessel on account of the persons or passengers it may have on board. Now, it is the well-settled doctrine of this Court, that a corporation created by statute is a mere creature of the law, and can exercise no powers except those which the law confers upon it, or which are incident to its existence.[1] And as no power is given to this corporation to demand toll from passengers on board, it is very clear that no such power can be exercised, and no such

---

1 Head and Amory *v.* The Providence Ins. Co. 2 Cranch, (U. S.) R. 127; Dartmouth College *v.* Woodward, 4 Wheat. (U. S.) R. 636; Bank of the United States *v.* Dandridge, 12 Ib. 64; Charles River Bridge *v.* Warren, 11 Pet. (U. S.) R. 544; Bank of Augusta *v.* Earle, 11 Ib. 587.

toll lawfully taken." The canal company, it was further remarked, is not the absolute owner of the works; it has no rights of property except those derived from the provisions of the charter, and holds its property only for the purposes for which it was created. And, in answer to the second question, it was held, that the company had not a right to refuse permission for passengers to pass through the canal. On the contrary, any one had a right to navigate the canal for the transportation of passengers, with passenger-boats, without paying any toll on the passengers on board, upon his paying, or offering to pay, the toll prescribed by law upon the commodities on board, or the toll prescribed by law upon a vessel or boat, when it was empty of commodities. For the word "empty," it was said, as used in the charter, must be interpreted in the light of its context; and, as the law was speaking of cargo, and of cargo only, and not of persons or passengers, looking at its connections, that word evidently meant without cargo. And inasmuch as by the charter every vessel suited to the navigation of the canal, was authorized to pass through, upon the payment of the toll *imposed by law*, and there being none imposed by law on persons or passengers, nor any distinction in the charter between vessels with or without passengers, there was no reason why the canal, contrary to usage, should be limited to a highway solely for the transportation of merchandise.[1]

### 4. *Travel upon Railroads.*

§ 370. Public railroads, like turnpike roads and canals, are

---

1 Perrine *v.* Chesapeake and Delaware Canal Co. 9 How. (U. S.) R. 172. Though a canal company is forbidden by its act of incorporation from charging a higher rate of tolls than is specified in the act, this does not prevent it from entering into a special agreement to charge *a less rate*. Delaware and Hudson Canal Co. *v.* The Pennsylvania Coal Co. 21 Penn. (9 Harris,) R. 131. When a boat is induced by the canal company to enter the canal, in the expectation that, for a fair compensation, it shall have a passage through, the law implies an agreement on the part of the company, that the boat shall get through in a reasonable time. Muir *v.* Canal Co. 8 Dana, (Ky.) R. 161.

the creatures of statutes; and, as with turnpike roads and canals, the rights and duties of their proprietors and of the public, flow directly from these statutes, and from the mutual relations thereby created between them. They are open to the travel of the entire public, upon the payment of the prescribed rate or toll;[1] and, as in the case of turnpike roads and canals, if there be any ambiguity in the language of the acts, by which the right to the rate or toll is granted, that construction is to be adopted which is most favorable to the public, as against the grantee.[2] The public, however, while entitled without distinction to travel upon railroads, are entitled to do so only in a particular manner, in vehicles controlled and managed by the company, and of the control and management of which, it would seem, the company are not allowed to divest themselves, even for the purpose of giving them up to another company.[3]

§ 371. *The Power of Railroad Corporations to adopt Rules and Regulations.* The relation which a railroad company holds to the public, is that of a common carrier; and, as such, independently of express statute authority, they are entitled and

---

1 *Ante*, § 18. With reference to the legal obligation of railway companies to transport upon their roads property and passengers at a reasonable expense, Chancellor Walworth, in Beekman *v.* Saratoga and Schenectady Railroad Co. 3 Paige, Ch. Rep. 45, says: "The privilege of making a road and taking tolls thereon, is a franchise as much as the establishment of a ferry or a public wharf, and taking tolls for the use of the same. The public have an interest in the use of the railroad, and the owners may be prosecuted for the damage sustained, if they should refuse to transport an individual, or his property, without any reasonable excuse, upon being paid the usual rate of fare. The legislature may, from time to time, regulate the use of the franchise of railway companies, and limit the amount of toll which they may take, in the same manner as they may regulate the toll to be taken at a ferry, or for grinding at a mill, unless a legislative contract with the company intervenes." Beekman *v.* Saratoga and Schenectady Railroad Co. 3 Paige, Ch. Rep. 45.

2 Barrett *v.* Stockton and Darlington Railway Co. 2 M. & Gr. R. 134; 2 Scott, N. R. 337, affirmed in Exchequer Chamber, 3 Scott, N. R. 803; 2 Railway Cases, 467, affirming judgment of C. P. 2 Ib. 443; Parker *v.* Great Western Railway Co. 7 Scott, N. R. 835; *ante*, § 368.

3 Beman *v.* Rufford, 6 Eng. Law and Eq. R. 106.

bound to adopt and enforce reasonable and suitable regulations in reference to the use of their road, as well for the good of the public as their own; and this right and duty extend not only to the regulation of their cars and of the passengers in transit, but likewise to the use of the houses and buildings connected with the road. This authority, it has been remarked, is incident to the ownership of such houses and buildings, and to the employment of the company as passenger-carriers; "and all such regulations will be deemed reasonable, which are suitable to enable them to perform the duties they undertake, and to secure their own just rights in such employment; and also such as are necessary and proper to ensure the safety and promote the comfort of passengers. The reasonableness of such regulations, must in some measure be judged of with reference to the particular depot at which they are adopted. Regulations may be proper and necessary at one of the termini of the road, where there is usually a great throng of passengers and other persons connected with the business of the road, which would not be required at a way-station, where few persons enter or leave the cars, and where they stop but a few moments."[1] The duty of a railroad company has been compared, in this respect, to that of an inn-keeper, whose premises are open to all guests, and who is not only empowered, but bound, so to regulate his house, as well with regard to the peace and comfort of his guests, who there seek repose, as to the peace and quiet of the vicinity, as to repress and prohibit all disorderly conduct therein; and who, of course, has a right, and is bound to exclude from his premises, all disorderly persons, and all persons not conforming to regulations necessary and proper to secure such quiet and good order.[2] These regulations, being such as the company have the power to make, in virtue of their ownership of the depot

---

1 Per Shaw, Ch. J., in Commonwealth *v.* Power, 7 Met. (Mass.) R. 596.
2 Markham *v.* Brown, 8 N. Hamp. R. 523.

buildings, and of their employment as carriers of passengers, are not necessary to be made in the form of by-laws, to be carried into effect by penalties and prosecutions. They may make them as an individual carrier might make them, and may delegate to their superintendent authority to make them, and, by himself and his assistants, to enforce their observance. Accordingly, it has been held, where the entrance of innkeepers or their servants into a railroad depot, to solicit passengers to go to their inns, is an annoyance to passengers, or a hindrance and interruption to the railroad officers in the performance of their duties, the superintendent of the depot may make a regulation to prevent persons from going into the depot for such purpose; and if, after notice of the regulation, they refuse to comply with it, he and his assistants may forcibly remove them, using no more force than is necessary for that purpose. And, even if such a person has a ticket, and enters with the *bonâ fide* intention of taking passage in the cars, unless he exhibits his ticket, or discloses his intention, he may be justifiably removed by the superintendent.[1] But the mere opinion of the superintendent, that a person has violated the regulations of the road, without proof of the fact, or the fact that he has conducted himself offensively towards the superintendent, will not alone justify his forcible removal.[2]

---

1 Commonwealth *v.* Power, *supra.*

2 Hull *v.* Power, 12 Met. (Mass.) R. 482; and see Barker *v.* The Midland Railway Co. 18 Com. B. R. 46, and 5 Am. Law Reg. 57. This was an action by the plaintiff, an omnibus proprietor, who carried passengers and their luggage for hire, to and from a railway station of the defendants, for a refusal by the defendants' servant to allow him to drive his vehicle into the station-yard. There were demurrers and cross-demurrers raised by the pleadings, and the Court decided in favor of the defendants, on the ground, that no duty was shown on the defendants' part, to permit the plaintiff to come upon their land. Where the superintendent exceeds his power, in such case, it seems that he alone is liable, and that the company will not be held responsible, unless it authorizes or commands the acts complained of, or subsequently ratifies them. The Eastern Counties Railroad Co. *v.* Broom, 3 Eng. Law and Eq. R. 406; Roe *v.* The Birkenhead, &c. Railroad Co. 7 Ib. 546.

§ 372. The rules and regulations which the proprietors of railroads may adopt, it has been said, in another case, "have no limits, except that they must be reasonable, lawful, and within the limits of the charter. And these regulations may be adopted by the board of directors, in the form of by-laws or resolutions, under their corporate seals, or by any officer or agent having charge of any particular branch of their business, in relation to the business committed to his charge. In this manner, the company, or its officers, may regulate the number of trains to be run daily, the time of departure, the rate of speed, the quantity and kind of loading for each car, the mode and time of receiving freight, giving receipts, issuing tickets, taking fare, &c. And they may, in like manner, establish trains exclusively for passengers, and exclusively for freight, or mix and divide them as they see fit." And, in this case, it was held, that the railroad company were justified in refusing to carry a passenger, who tendered a proper pass, if his object, in using the road, was to violate one of the rules of the road, which excluded freight or "express matter" from the passenger train, or if they had good reason to believe that he was going out with that purpose, and he did not disclaim it.[1]

§ 373. The law, as laid down by Mr. Justice Story, in Jencks *v.* Coleman,[2] in reference to *steamboats*, is, without doubt, equally applicable to railroads, unless it be varied by statute. "The right of passengers," he remarked, "to a passage on board of a steamboat, is not an unlimited right, but is subject to such reasonable regulations as the proprietors may prescribe, for the due accommodation of passengers, and for the arrangements of their business. The proprietors have not only this right, but the further right to consult and provide for their own interests in the management of such boats, as a common incident to their right of property. They are not bound to admit pas-

---

1 Menihew *v.* The Milwaukie and Mississippi Railroad Co. 5 Am. Law Reg. 364.

2 Jencks *v.* Coleman, 2 Sum. (Cir. Ct.) R. 221.

sengers on board, who refuse to obey the reasonable regulations of the boat, or who are guilty of gross and vulgar habits of conduct, or who make disturbances on board, or whose characters are doubtful, or dissolute, or suspicious; and, *à fortiori*, whose characters are unequivocally bad.[1] Nor are they bound to admit passengers on board, whose object it is to interfere with the interests or patronage of the proprietors, so as to make the business less lucrative to them. While, therefore, I agree, that steamboat proprietors, holding themselves out as common-carriers, are bound to receive passengers on board under ordinary circumstances, I at the same time insist, that they may refuse to receive them, if there be a reasonable objection. And, as passengers are bound to obey the orders and regulations of the proprietors, unless they are oppressive and grossly unreasonable, whoever goes on board, under ordinary circumstances, impliedly contracts to obey such regulations; and may justly be refused a passage, if he wilfully resists or violates them."

§ 374. In Cheney *v.* The Boston and Maine Railroad Company,[2] the purchasers of tickets for a passage on the road, from one place to another, were required, by the rules of the company, to go through in the same train; and passengers who were to stop on the road, and afterwards finish their passage in another train, were required to pay more than when they were to go through in the same train. The plaintiff, not knowing these rules, purchased a ticket from Durham to Boston, and entered the cars, with an intention to stop at Exeter,

---

1 But although carriers of passengers are not obliged to admit persons who are notoriously and unequivocally bad, yet, supposing a person to be of infamous character, if he has paid his fare, and has been admitted as a passenger, it furnishes no excuse for turning him out, so long as he has not been guilty, during the journey, of any impropriety of conduct; and none for treating him in so scandalous and disgraceful a manner, as to compel him to leave the conveyance. Coppin *v.* Braithwaite, 8 Jur. 875, Exch., cited in Angell on Carriers, § 532.

2 Cheney *v.* The Boston and Maine Railroad Co. 11 Met. (Mass.) R. 121.

31 *

an intermediate place, and to go to Boston in the next train. When he took his ticket, he was informed of the rule that required him to go through in the same train, and a check was given him, on which were the words, "good for this trip only." The conductor then offered to give back to the plaintiff the money which he had paid, deducting the amount of his passage from Durham to Exeter, which the plaintiff refused to accept, but demanded the ticket in exchange for the check. He stopped at Exeter, and went on to Boston on the same day, in the next train, and he offered his check, which was refused, and he was obliged to pay $1.50 for a ticket, from Exeter to Boston. In an action against the defendants, for a breach of contract, in not carrying the plaintiff from Durham to Boston, it was held, that the action could not be maintained. And Dewey, J., said: "The question, as to the right of the plaintiff to be transported as a passenger, does not depend upon his knowledge, at the time of the purchase of his ticket, of the difference of the price to be paid for a passage through the whole distance by one train, or that of a passage by different trains. The plaintiff might have inquired and informed himself as to that. If he did not, he took the mode of conveyance, the price of the ticket and the superscription thereon secured to him under the rules and regulations of the company. It appears, however, that before reaching Exeter, the plaintiff was fully apprised of the different rates of fare, and the rules applicable to way-passengers, and that the agent of the defendants, the conductor of the train, offered to refund to him the money that he had paid for his ticket, deducting the usual fare from Durham to Exeter, which the plaintiff refused to accept. In the opinion of the Court, this was all that the defendants were required to do; and as the plaintiff declined this offer, and thereupon left the train, stopping at Exeter, he voluntarily relinquished his passage through by a continuous train, for which he held a ticket; and whatever loss he has sustained, was occasioned by his own act, and occurred under such circumstances as preclude him from all claim for damages for any default of the company in the matter. Nor can he sustain any legal claim to recover back the sum paid for his first ticket, or any part thereof."[1]

§ 375. So, in the Northern Railroad Company *v.* Paige,[2]

---

1 The following case was reported for The Boston Daily Advertiser, January 22, 1849. Court of Common Pleas, Essex County:—Isaac G. Loring *v.* Joseph W. Aborn. "This was an action of trespass against a railroad conductor, for ejecting the plaintiff from the cars of the Boston and Maine Railroad, under the following circumstances: The plaintiff got into the cars at Lawrence, with a ticket for North Andover. It is a rule of the railroad, that passengers must, immediately after starting, surrender their tickets, or pay their fares if they have no tickets, or be turned out of the cars by the conductor. The plaintiff, when asked for his ticket by the defendant, showed it, but refused to give it up at that time, (alleging that, on a former occasion, he had been put out of the cars, after giving up his ticket,) but promising to give it up when near the end of his route. There was no stopping-place between Lawrence and North Andover. The conductor then stopped the train, and on the plaintiff's persisting in his refusal, put him out by force. Mellen, J., ruled, that the regulation of the road was reasonable, and that the plaintiff had no right to retain his ticket till he had got near the end of his route, even if he had not previously known of the rule, and that on his refusal to give it up, the conductor was justified in ejecting him with a reasonable degree of force; and that, under the circumstances, (it being evident that the plaintiff meant to try his right,) it made no difference that the conductor did not demand payment of the fare before ejecting the plaintiff; that the only question for the jury was, whether unnecessary force was used; and the Judge observed, that the jury, on this point, would not be very nice in scanning the acts of the conductor in the line of his duty, but would make allowance for any little irritation on his part, produced by the conduct of the plaintiff; that the burden of proof, on the question of the degree of force, was on the plaintiff; and that, unless the jury were satisfied that too much force was used, the defendant was entitled to a verdict." Verdict for the defendant. Angell on Carriers, § 590, note; 1 Law Reporter, (N. S.) 461. But a by-law, declaring that a railroad company will not be responsible for the care of a passenger's luggage, unless booked and paid for, is unreasonable and void. Williams *v.* The Great Western Railway Co. 28 Eng. Law and Eq. R. 439. But see Angell on Carriers, § 571.

2 The Northern Railroad Co. *v.* Paige, 22 Barb. (N. Y.) Sup. Ct. R. 130. The Court also stated, as an additional reason for this decision, the fact, that an agreement had previously been made between the plaintiffs and the Hudson River Railroad Company, that each might sell tickets on the other's line, which should be paid for to the company carrying the passenger, when returned to the company issuing them; and that, consequently, the surrender of the ticket was necessary to enable the plaintiffs to demand from the Hudson River Railroad Company the price of the ticket.

where the defendant claimed a right to retain his ticket to the end of his journey, in defiance of a rule or custom, which was previously known to him, requiring passengers, soon after starting, to surrender their passage-tickets to the conductor, and receive his check in the place of them; the Court, recognizing the principles established in the preceding case, held the following language: "The law will imply, under the circumstances of this case, that the contract, on the part of the plaintiff, was to convey the defendant over their road, provided he surrendered his ticket to the conductor, when it was demanded, as required by the custom of the road. Under this contract, the defendant would not be entitled to his passage in the plaintiffs cars, without the surrender of the ticket; and his refusal to deliver up his ticket to the conductor, when demanded, would justify the latter in exacting from him his fare in cash; and on his refusal to pay his fare, putting him out of the cars. The custom in question was a reasonable custom. The ticket purchased by the defendant, if not surrendered, could be used to secure a second, or any number of rides over the road, without the payment of fare. Its surrender, therefore, was necessary to the protection of the company from fraud. The form of the ticket entitled the *bearer*, whoever he might be, to one passage over the plaintiffs' road. The purchaser, after riding himself, upon the ticket, could sell or hand it to another, who, with the ticket, could also secure a passage over the road, without the payment of fare."

§ 376. A railroad corporation in Connecticut, established, and gave public notice of a regulation, that the fare in their cars, from Norwich to New London, would be fifty cents, if it was paid, and a ticket procured by the passenger, before entering their cars; otherwise it would be fifty-five cents. The plaintiff, without a ticket, took a seat in one of their cars at Norwich, and, when called upon by the conductor, after the cars had left for New London, offered to pay fifty cents for his passage from Norwich to New London, and refused to pay any more; whereupon the conductor, with the aid of persons in the employment of the defendants, forcibly removed him from the car. Upon the trial of an action of trespass, brought to recover damages for the injury sustained by the plaintiff, he claimed to have proved, that he went to the defendants' office, where the tickets were usually sold, at a reasonable time before the train left for New London, to procure a ticket; that said office was closed, and there was no one of whom a ticket could be procured, then or afterwards, until after the departure of the cars, and that he informed the conductor of these facts at the time his fare was demanded. It was admitted, that the regulation of the defendants was a reasonable and legal one; but the plaintiff claimed that, having applied for a ticket at a reasonable time, and not having been able to obtain one by the default of the defendants, who were bound by their notice to furnish all reasonable facilities to enable parties to obtain tickets, he was not to be injured by a regulation with which it was impossible for him to conform. But it was held, that the published rule was a proffered contract, which might be closed by a mere acceptance, but which, until accepted, might be withdrawn at pleasure; that closing the office was, for the time, at any rate, a most effective withdrawal, and necessarily communicated notice of such withdrawal to the plaintiff; that the proposition being withdrawn, the parties were in the same condition as before it was made; the defendants continuing common carriers, and, as such, bound to carry the plaintiff for fifty-five cents, but not otherwise; and that the plaintiff refusing that sum, the conductor had a right to remove him from the cars, using no unnecessary force for that purpose; and that, for such removal, the defendants were not liable in an action of trespass.[1]

1 Crocker *v.* The New London, Willimantic and Palmer Railroad Co. 24 Conn. R. 249. But see dissenting opinions by Hinman and Storrs, JJ., Ib. 266, 267.

§ 377. In England, railroad cômpanies are sometimes authorized to enforce their rules and regulations, by imposing forfeitures or penalties for the breach thereof, and to recover the same by summary proceedings. In such a case, to justify the resort to such a proceeding, the party proceeded against must have been guilty of a breach of some rule or regulation punishable by *penalty* or *forfeiture*. Thus, a railway company were empowered to make orders for regulating the travelling upon, and use of the railway, and for, or relating to passengers passing thereon; such orders or regulations to be binding upon such travellers on pain of forfeiting and paying a sum not exceeding £5, which the company should attach to a default; recoverable in a summary way by adjudication of Justices, one half the penalty to go to the informer, and the other half to the company. And any officer, or agent of a company, was authorized to seize and detain any person whose name and residence should be unknown to such officer or agent, who should commit any offence against the act, and to convey him, &c. before a Justice, without any warrant or other authority than that act. The company made a by-law under their common seal, by which each passenger, not producing or delivering up his ticket on leaving the company's premises, was required to pay the fare from *the place whence the train originally started*. In an action for seizure and detention under this by-law, it was held, that though it might be reasonable to insist that the passenger who does not produce his ticket at the end of his journey shall pay the fare charged from the most remote terminus, since no other might be ascertainable by the company, yet, inasmuch as the violation of the by-law, under which the fare was claimed, was not punishable by forfeiture or penalty, the arrest of the plaintiff was unauthorized.[1]

1 Chilton *v.* The London and Croydon Railway Co. 16 M. & W. R. 212. In this case, it was also very strongly intimated, that the only power to apprehend, given by the act, was for such offences as were made punishable by forfeiture

§ 378. *Their Duty to receive Persons as Passengers.* Subject to such rules and regulations as may be properly made, it is the duty of railroad companies, as common carriers, to receive all persons who apply for seats by their conveyance, provided there is room for them, and a tender of, or offer to pay, the fare, is made at the time.[1] And this duty, it has been observed, is imposed by the common law, and a breach of this duty is a breach of the law, for which an action lies, founded on the common law, and requiring not the aid of a contract to support it.[2] And it is not a lawful excuse, for refusing to receive passengers, that the company run their cars in connection with a coach or another train of cars, which extends the line to a certain place, and have agreed not to receive passengers who come from that place, on certain days, unless they come in such coach or other train of cars. Neither have the company, by a notice brought home to the individual, the right to limit their general duty in this manner.[3] This duty, moreover, involves the obligation, that the passengers, after they have paid their fare and taken their seats, shall not be over-crowded, and be thereby, as it were, expelled.[4] The company must also carry

---

and penalty by the *act* itself, and not simple violations of the by-laws and regulations of the company.

1 Angell on Carriers, § 524; Bretherton *v.* Wood, (Exch.) 3 Bro. & Bing. R. 524; Messiter *v.* Cooper, 4 Esp. R. 260; Bennett *v.* Dutton, 10 N. Hamp. R. 481. Where a railroad company issue excursion tickets to passengers, to go to a certain place, and back by some return train, it would seem that the company are not excused from carrying such passengers, according to their contract, upon the ground that there is no room for them in the train; but, in order to avail themselves of this answer, they should make their contract conditional upon there being room. Hawcroft *v.* The Great Northern Railway Co. 8 Eng. Law and Eq. R. 362.

2 Bretherton *v.* Wood, *ub. sup.*

3 Bennett *v.* Dutton, 10 N. Hamp. R. 481.

4 Per Scates, J., in Galena and Chicago Railroad Co. *v.* Yarwood, 15 Ill. R. 472. And see Long *v.* Horne, 1 C. & Payne, R. 610, in which it was held, that if coach proprietors take more than the legal number on the coach, a passenger may refuse to occupy his seat, and sue for expenses incurred, for the contract

the passenger the entire distance they engage to carry him; they cannot refuse to proceed at any intermediate stage, for their undertaking is absolute, and hence, in case of accident, they would be bound to provide another conveyance.[1] In Weed *v.* The Saratoga and Schenectady Railroad Company,[2] it was held, that if a railroad company contracts to carry passengers and their baggage *beyond the limits of their own road*, their duty, as carriers, extends through the whole route, in respect to which the contract is made. The defendants, in this case, having undertaken to carry from Saratoga Springs to Albany, were, in the opinion of the Court, estopped from saying, that their duty as carriers continued no further than Schenectady, the termination of their own road. In order to limit their liability to a part of the route, they should, at least, have given notice that, after the car struck the tract beyond Schenectady, the traveller must look to another company, if in fact there was another.

§ 379. So, also, it is the duty of the company to afford, in the progress of the journey, the accommodations they profess to afford. Thus, if there is a general usage to allow certain intervals for refreshment, the company cannot, at their pleasure, vary such usage; for it may be that such usage is the very reason for preferring that particular conveyance to the less accommodating arrangement of another line of convey-

---

entered into by them must be performed in terms. And, also, if places be taken for several persons to go inside a coach *together*, it is a breach of the contract, if the owner only provides distinct seats for them. Ibid; Deevort *v.* Loomer, 21 Conn. R. 245. The circumstance that a passenger is a "steamboat-man," and, as such, is carried gratuitously, does not deprive him of the right of redress enjoyed by other passengers. Steamboat New World *v.* King, 16 How. (U. S.) R. 469.

1 Dudley *v.* Smith, 1 Campb. R. 167; Ker *v.* Mountain, 1 Esp. R. 27; Messiter *v.* Cooper, 4 Esp. R. 260; Jeremy on Carriers, 23; Story on Bailments, § 600.

2 Weed *v.* The Saratoga and Schenectady Railroad Co. 19 Wend. (N. Y.) R. 534.

ance. In other words, every passenger is understood to contract for the usual reasonable accommodations.[1]

§ 380. *Their Liability for the Baggage of Passengers.*— The duty of railroad companies as regards the transportation of the personal baggage of passengers, and of goods and merchandise generally, is, unless their responsibility be expressly limited by notice to the passenger, precisely the same as that of the proprietors of stage-coaches, steamboats, or any other class of common carriers; that is, they insure the same against all losses, whether proceeding from the negligence or misconduct of themselves, their servants, or even all third persons, with the exception of the owner.[2] The charge for the transportation of baggage is included in the fare of the passenger and is a sufficient consideration for the liability assumed.[3] And in Pennsylvania, in a suit against stage owners for loss of baggage, it was held, that payment of the fare need not be expressly proved; for it may be inferred without violent implication, inasmuch as the payment of fare is seldom or never neglected. And even if the fare is not paid, the passenger is liable to pay it; and this obliges the owners of a public conveyance to the exercise of diligence.[4] The proprietors of a

1 Angell on Carriers, § 533; Story on Bailm. § 597; Jeremy on Carr. 23.

2 Angell on Carriers, § 571. Respecting the power of common carriers to limit their common-law liability as to the safety of a passenger's baggage by notice; and their power by notice to require the owner to state the nature or value of the property, see Angell on Carr. § 292 *et seq.* Mr. Angell remarks: "It would appear, that where the company take care to embody the notice in the tickets delivered to every passenger on taking his place, as part of the terms on which they are willing to accept him, this would constitute a special contract on the subject, so that the company would not be liable for negligence." Ang. on Carr. § 571 *a;* citing Palmer *v.* Grand Junction Railway Co. 4 M. & Welsb. R. 752.

3 Hawkins *v.* Hoffman, 6 Hill, (N. Y.) R. 586; Bennett *v.* Dutton, 10 N. Hamp. R. 481; Logan *v.* Ponchartrain Railroad Co. 11 Rob. (Louis.) R. 24; Powell *v.* Myers, 26 Wend. (N. Y.) R. 591; Brook *v.* Pickwicke, 4 Bing. R. 218; Peixotti *v.* M'Laughlin, 1 Strob. S. C. R. 468; Jones *v.* Voorhees, 6 Ohio R. 358.

4 McGill *v.* Rowand, 3 Barr, (Penn.) R. 451; and see Bingham *v.* Rogers, 6 Watts & S. (Penn.) R. 451; Whitesell *v.* Crane, 8 Ibid. 369.

railroad, who receive passengers and commence their carriage at the station of another road, are bound to have a servant there to take charge of baggage until it is placed in their cars; and if it is the custom of the baggage-master of the station, in the absence of such servant, to receive and take charge of the baggage in his stead, the proprietors will be responsible for baggage so delivered to him.[1] Our present purpose, however, does not involve any particular discussion of the liabilities of railroad companies as common carriers; we, therefore, refer the reader, who wishes to pursue this subject further, to the books which are more expressly devoted to that branch of the law.

§ 381. But though it is settled, that passenger carriers are responsible for baggage, yet there is still a very wide field for controversy remaining, in determining what is properly included in the term baggage. In Jordan *v.* The Fall River Railroad Company,[2] Fletcher, J., in delivering the opinion of the Court, remarked upon this subject as follows: "It is quite impossible for the Court to restrict, within certain and prescribed limits, the quantity or value or kind of articles, which may be embraced in the term baggage of the travelling world. The most that can be done is, to prescribe some general rules as to the character, description and purposes of articles which may be taken as baggage. It may be said, in general terms, that baggage includes such articles as are of necessity or convenience for personal use, and such as it is usual for persons travelling to take with them. It has been said, that articles for instruction or amusement, as books, or a gun, or fishing tackle, fall within the term baggage. In the case of Brooke *v.* Pickwick,[3] the carrier was held responsible for a lady's trunk containing apparel and jewels. So, in the

1 Jordan *v.* The Fall River Railroad Company, 5 Cush. (Mass.) R. 69.

2 *Supra.*

3 Brooke *v.* Pickwick, 4 Bing. R. 218.

case of M'Gill *v*. Rowand,[1] which was for apparel and jewelry. In Jones *v*. Voorhees,[2] the carrier was held responsible for a watch which was lost in a trunk, as being an appendage to the traveller. But a carrier is not liable for merchandise as baggage. In Pardre *v*. Drew,[3] the passenger carrier was held not responsible for a trunk of silk goods as baggage. So in Hawkins *v*. Hoffman,[4] the carrier was held not liable for samples used for effecting sales of goods. So carriers are not liable for large sums of money as baggage taken for the purpose of transportation. In the case of the Orange County Bank *v*. Brown,[5] it was held, that the owner of a steamboat used for carrying passengers was not liable for a trunk, containing a large sum of money, brought on board by a passenger as baggage, the object being the transportation of the money. In the case of Weed *v*. Saratoga and Schenectady Railroad Co.[6] it was held, that a railroad company was liable for money in a trunk, to a reasonable amount for travelling expenses, as baggage. In that case, the sum was $285, in the trunk of a passenger from Saratoga to New York. In the case of Orange County Bank *v*. Brown, above cited, it was also supposed, though not expressly adjudged, that money for travelling expenses might be carried as baggage at the risk of the carrier. But in the case of Hawkins *v*. Hoffman, a doubt was expressed, whether any money could be considered as baggage. Upon consideration of the whole subject, and refer-

---

1 M'Gill *v*. Rowand, 3 Barr, (Penn.) R. 451.

2 Jones *v*. Voorhees, 10 Ohio R. 145, 150.

3 Pardre *v*. Drew, 25 Wend. (N. Y.) R. 459.

4 Hawkins *v*. Hoffman, 6 Hill, (N. Y.) R. 586.

5 Orange County Bank *v*. Brown, 9 Wend. (N. Y.) R. 85.

6 Weed *v*. Saratoga and Schenectady Railroad Co. 19 Wend. (N. Y.) R. 534; but see Bomer *v*. Maxwell, 9 Humph. (Tenn.) R. 621, in which the word baggage was held to include only such articles as are necessary for the personal convenience of the passenger, and not to embrace money (in this case $160) nor a watch, handcuffs, locks, &c.

ing to the cases, the Court have come to the conclusion, that money *bonâ fide* taken for travelling expenses and personal use may properly be regarded as forming a part of a traveller's baggage."[1]

§ 382. But where merchandise, carried by a passenger as baggage, is exposed to view, and the company choose to take it without making any bargain for its carriage, the company will be responsible for its loss.[2] And in any case where articles are received into the custody of the company, whether they may be properly considered as baggage or not, the company, upon common and familiar principles, and wholly irrespective of their liability as common carriers, will be responsible for a loss occasioned by gross negligence.

§ 383. The delivery of the baggage to the carrier and the loss of it by his negligence having been established by proof *aliunde*, the current of authority in this country is to the effect, that it is competent for the party by his own evidence, there being no other known to him, to prove the contents of his trunk, and the value of the baggage that was taken from it.[3]

---

[1] In England, by sect. 169, of 5 and 6 Will. IV. c. 107, every passenger travelling upon the Great Western Railway, may take with him, without extra charge, his articles of clothing, not exceeding certain weight and dimensions; and the company are not to be liable for the safe carriage of any article carried with a passenger, except his articles of clothing, not exceeding the given weight and dimensions. In the case of Williams *v.* The Great Western Railway Co. 28 Eng. Law & Eq. R. 439, tried in the Court of Exchequer, it was observed by Pollock, C. B., "the term 'articles of clothing' ought to include all things necessary to the toilet."

[2] Great Northern Railway Company *v.* Shepherd, 9 Eng. Law & Eq. R. 479; in that case the liability of the company for baggage was limited by statute to 56 lbs. weight for each passenger, travelling by the train in which the defendant went; and it was held, that this permitted a husband and wife, travelling together, to take 112 lbs. weight of luggage between them.

[3] Herman *v.* Drinkwater, 1 Greenl. (Maine) R. 27; Sneider *v.* Geiss, 1 Yeates, (Penn.) R. 34; Clarke *v.* Spence, 10 Watts, (Penn.) R. 335; Openheimer *v.* Edney, 9 Humph. (Tenn.) R. 385; Johnson *v.* Stone, 11 Humph.

The admission of this testimony rests upon the principle of necessity, which applies, it has been held, not only to the party himself but also to his wife. "The wife," said Rogers, J., in McGill *v.* Rowand, "usually packs her husband's trunk, and always her own, and therefore to say that she cannot in a proper case be a witness, will amount almost to a repeal of the rule and in most cases to a denial of justice. We, therefore, see no reasonable objection to the admission of the husband or wife, or both, to testify to the amount of their wearing apparel, and to its value, belonging to each, including in the catalogue the wife's jewelry, and every other article pertaining to her wardrobe, that may be necessary or convenient to either in travelling."[1] But as the rule is admitted upon a principle of necessity, it can have no application to other goods than those which come under the general name of baggage; because, as to other goods, it is the duty of the owner, and in accordance with common usage, to provide himself with bills of lading or other evidences of the delivery to the carriers; and if he do not, he is himself guilty of negligence.[2]

§ 384. But in Massachusetts, in the case of Snow *v.* The Eastern Railroad Company,[3] the rule was altogether repudiated. In that case, the testimony of the plaintiff was offered to prove the contents of his trunk, containing wearing apparel,

---

(Tenn.) R. 419; Whitsell *v.* Krane, 8 Watts & Ser. (Penn.) R. 389; Fulton *v.* Railroad Company, 20 Ohio R. 319.

1 McGill *v.* Rowand, 3 Barr, (Penn.) R. 451.

2 Johnson *et als.* *v.* Stone, 11 Humph. (Tenn.) R. 419; Clarke *v.* Spence, 10 Watts, (Penn.) R. 335; Pudor *v.* Boston and Maine Railroad, 26 Maine R. 458; S. C. 10 Law Reporter, 117. In the latter case the declaration having alleged, that the box, delivered to the defendants and lost, contained medical books medicines, surgical instruments and chemical apparatus, and articles of clothing, the testimony of the plaintiff was held to be inadmissible, the Court remarking that the admission of such testimony should be limited to clothing and personal ornaments. And see Bingham *v.* Rogers, 6 Watts & S. (Penn.) R. 495.

3 Snow *v.* The Eastern Railroad Co. 12 Met. (Mass.) R. 44.

several books, and twenty-five dollars of money, and which was lost while he was travelling, as a passenger, on the defendants' road. The Court, after admitting the rule as applicable to carriers who have criminally despoiled their passengers, observed: "The present case does not fall within the principle. Here was no robbery, no tortious taking away by the defendants, no fraud committed. It is simply a case of negligence on the part of carriers. The case is not brought within any exception to the common rule, and is a case of defective proof on the part of the plaintiff, not arising from necessity, but from want of caution. To admit the plaintiff's oath, in cases of this nature, would lead, we think, to much greater mischiefs, in the temptation to frauds and perjuries, than can arise from excluding it. If the party about to travel, places valuable articles in his trunk, he should put them under the special charge of the carrier, with a statement of what they are, and of their value, or provide other evidence, beforehand, of the articles taken by him. If he omits to do this, he then takes the chance of loss, as to the value of the articles, and is guilty, in a degree, of negligence,—the very thing with which he attempts to charge the carrier."

§ 385. In South Carolina, likewise, the Court have refused to adopt this rule. But in that State, it has been decided, that a check in the possession of a passenger, is evidence that his baggage was delivered to the company; and, as a trunk is the usual means by which a passenger conveys his baggage, it is evidence that a trunk, with its contents, was delivered. These facts having been thus proved, it has been further decided that, in the absence of proof as to the contents of the trunk and their value, the jury may give damages proportioned to the value of the articles which they, in their judgment, think the trunk did and might fairly contain; and if the company choose to leave the jury to the chances of mere vague conjecture, and suffer them to go beyond the plaintiff's own valuation, by withholding his affidavit, it will be their own folly, and they will have no right to complain.[1]

§ 386. *Their Liability in regard to the Road and its Equipment.* The proprietors of a railroad, as passenger carriers, are bound to the most exact care and diligence, not only in the management of their trains and cars, but also in the structure and care of their track, and in all the subsidiary arrangements necessary to the safety of passengers.[2] Their duty to keep their road in sufficient order and repair, so that persons and property may at all times pass in safety, is, as in the case of a turnpike corporation, an implied one, resulting from their ownership and the receipt of tolls. And, it has been said, if a distinction in practice were permitted, the rule of liability for neglect ought to be most stringently enforced against railroad corporations, whose slightest inattention to the duties they assume, may be, and frequently is, attended with the most frightful results.[3] The same rule exacts from them the utmost care in equipping their roads with proper cars, and in proportioning the speed of their trains to the strength of the road, and the number of passengers, and the amount and kind of freight, which they are transporting.[4]

§ 387. In Hegeman *v.* The Western Railroad Corporation,[5]

---

1 Dill *v.* The South Carolina Railroad Co. 7 Rich. (So. Car.) R. 158; citing Butler *v.* Basing, 2 Carr. & Payne, 613, to the point, that in the absence of proof, the jury might infer the value of the baggage.

2 McElroy *v.* Nashua and Lowell Railroad Corp. 4 Cush. (Mass.) R. 400. And see Palmer *v.* Grand Junction Railway Co. 4 M. & Welsb. R. 749; Bridge *v.* Grand Junction Railway Co. 3 Ib. 244; Angell on Carriers, § 538.

3 The Cumberland Valley Railroad Co. *v.* Hughes, 11 Penn. (1 Jones) R. 141. And see Peters *v.* Ryland, 20 Penn. (8 Harris) R. 497.

4 Carpue *v.* London and Brighton Railway Co. 5 Ad. & El. R. (N. S.) 447. And see Oliver *v.* New York and Erie Railroad Co., referred to in Angell on Carriers, § 538.

5 Hegeman *v.* The Western Railroad Corp. 16 Barb. (N. Y.) Sup. Ct. R. 353.

the plaintiff brought an action to recover damages, for a personal injury received by him while a passenger upon the defendants' railroad. The injury was occasioned by the breaking of the axle of the car in which he was seated. The defendants gave evidence, tending to show, that the axle which broke was made of the best quality of iron, and well made; that it had been examined from time to time, and that no external defect could be discovered. But, upon examining the iron where it was broken, a *fire-crack* appeared, and the iron did not appear to be good. It also appeared upon the trial, that an article called a *safety-beam* was in extensive use upon railroads in this country, the object of which was, in case an axle should break, to hold the wheel and axle in their place. The car was not constructed with this *safety-beam*, and it was insisted, on the part of the plaintiff, that the omission was evidence of negligence. The Judge charged the jury, that the defendants were responsible for all defects in the axle, which might have been discovered and remedied, to the same extent as if they had manufactured the axle in their own workshop and by their immediate agents. He also left it to the jury to say, whether or not the defendants were guilty of negligence, in not informing themselves of the utility of a *safety-beam*, and furnishing their cars with them. The jury returned a verdict for the plaintiff for $9,900, which, upon a motion for a new trial, was affirmed. "From the very necessity of the case," said Harris, J., in delivering the opinion of the Court, "the defendants are obliged to carry on their business through the instrumentality of agents. Some are employed to construct or keep in repair their road-way; others to construct or repair their engines and cars; and others, again, to operate such engines and cars upon the road. For neglect, or want of skill in any of these, the defendants, as principals, are answerable to third persons. Whether the engine or car which they place upon the road for the purpose of carrying passengers, has been manufactured in their own workshops, by agents employed directly for that purpose, or by a manufacturer engaged in the business of supplying such articles for sale, they are alike bound to see that, in the construction, no care or skill has been omitted for the purpose of making such engine or car as safe as care and skill can make it. When such care and skill has been exercised, the defendants' duty, in this respect, has been discharged. If, on the other hand, a defect exists in the construction, which might have been detected and remedied, they are answerable for the consequences."[1] And, as to the duty of the defendants, to provide their cars with *safety-beams*, he also remarked: "But the plaintiff, without regard to the question arising upon the defect in the axle, had insisted, that the defendants were liable by reason of their omission to provide the car with a *safety-beam*. Evidence had been given to show, that this improvement had been extensively known and used prior to the time when the accident happened; and, also, to show its *utility* as a safeguard against accidents. The evidence, though objected to, was properly received. The defendants were bound to use every precaution which human skill and foresight could suggest to insure the safety of their passengers. If, then, it could be shown, that the safety-beam was an article of such established utility, and so extensively known, that it ought to have been used by the defendants upon their cars, they might justly be

---

[1] To this point, he cited Sharp *v.* Gray, 9 Bing. R. 457, and Ingalls *v.* Bills, 9 Met. (Mass.) R. 1, in the latter of which, the cases bearing upon this question, both English and American, have been examined with great clearness and ability; and the doctrine stated by Mr. Justice Hubbard, who pronounced the judgment of the Court, as the result of his examination, is, that "if an accident happens from a defect in the coach, which might have been discovered and remedied upon the most careful and thorough examination of the coach, such accident must be ascribed to negligence. On the other hand, if the accident arises from a hidden and internal defect, which a careful and thorough examination would not disclose, and which could not be guarded against by the exercise of a sound judgment, and the most vigilant oversight, then the proprietor is not liable."

charged with negligence in not adopting it. The Judge was right, therefore, not only in receiving the evidence, but in submitting it to the jury, to say whether, taking into consideration the vigilance required of carriers of passengers, and the publicity of the invention, and of its use prior to the time of the injury, the defendants were, or were not, *negligent* in not informing themselves of the utility and necessity of the invention, and availing themselves of it."[1]

§ 388. *Their Liability for the Conduct of their Servants or Agents.* So it is the duty of the proprietors of railroads to see that all the agents and servants employed in the management of the road, are careful, competent, and not addicted to intemperate habits.[2] Their responsibility to passengers for injuries resulting from the default of their agents or servants, extends to all acts done by them in the course of their employment, even though done in disobedience of orders. Thus, where a suit was brought against a railroad company, by a person who was injured by a collision, it was held, that if the plaintiff was lawfully on the road, at the time of the collision, and the collision and consequent injury to him were caused by the gross negligence of one of the servants of the company, then and there employed on the road, he was entitled to re-

---

[1] It has been held, that it is the duty of the proprietor of a stage-coach to examine it previous to the commencement of every journey; and, it has been said, where the vehicle is crowded with passengers, if no inspection of it takes place previous to each journey, the proprietor or master is guilty of gross negligence. Bremmer *v.* Williams, 1 C. & Payne, R. 414; Ware *v.* Gay, 11 Pick. (Mass.) R. 106; Ingalls *v.* Bills, 9 Met. (Mass.) R. 1. And see Israel *v.* Clark, 4 Esp. R. 259; Camden and Amboy Railroad Co. *v.* Burke, 13 Wend. (N. Y.) R. 611; Cole *v.* Goodwin, 19 Wend. 251; Story on Bailments, § 592; Angell on Carriers, § 533 *et seq.* In New Jersey Railroad Co. *v.* Kennard, 21 Penn. (9 Harris) R. 203, it was held, that an instruction to the jury, that "no car is good if the windows are not so constructed as to prevent the passengers from putting their limbs through them," is not erroneous, when applied to a car run on a railroad, which, in some places, is so narrow as to endanger projecting limbs. And see Miller *v.* Canal Commissioners, 21 Penn. (9 Harris) R. 23.

[2] Angell on Carriers, § 541.

cover, notwithstanding the circumstances, that the plaintiff was a stockholder of the company, riding by invitation of the president, paying no fare, and not in the usual passenger cars. And, also, that the fact that the engineer having control of the colliding locomotive, was forbidden to run on that track at the time, and had acted in disobedience of such orders, was no defence to the action.[1] And even if a part of their road be entrusted to the management of servants or agents, employed and paid by another company, yet, it being within the scope of their duty to see that such part of their road is rightly constructed, attended and managed, before they are justified in carrying passengers over it, they will be responsible for the negligence of such servants or agents.[2] In Pennsylvania, it has been held, that the owners of passenger cars used upon a railroad belonging to the State, are liable as common carriers for an injury sustained by a passenger occasioned by a collision of their trains, though the motive-power of the road was furnished by the State, and under the control of its agents, through whose negligence the accident happened.[3]

---

1 Philadelphia Railroad Co. *v.* Derby, 14 How. (U. S.) R. 468; 20 Curtis, (U. S.) S. C. Decis. 291. And see Sleath *v.* Wilson, 9 Car. & Payne, R. 607; Williams *v.* The Madison and Indianapolis Railroad Co. 5 Ind. (Port.) R. 340. But where a railroad company, by its printed rules and regulations, prohibited its engineers from allowing any one, not in its employ, to ride upon the engines; and the plaintiff applied to an engineer for permission to ride upon the engine, and was informed that it was against the rules of the company to carry him in that place, but the engineer finally consented that the plaintiff might ride with him, and he did so, without the knowledge of the conductor, and paying no fare; it was held, that the consent of the engineer conferred no legal right, and that the plaintiff, not being lawfully upon the engine, was a wrongdoer, and could not recover damages of the company for an injury sustained while riding in that place. And it was also held, that the *onus* was on the plaintiff to show, that the engineer had authority from the company to permit him to ride upon the engine; the presumption being, that he had no right to be there, whether he paid fare or not. Robertson *v.* The New York and Erie Railroad Co. 22 Barb. (N. Y.) Sup. Ct. R. 91.

2 McElroy *v.* The Nashua and Lowell Railroad Corp. 4 Cush. (Mass.) R. 400.

3 Peters *v.* Ryland, 20 Penn. (8 Harris) R. 497.

§ 389. In a case of injury to a railroad passenger by collision, it appeared that the train had been hired of the company by a society for an excursion, the tickets for which were sold and distributed by the treasurer of the latter body, from whom the plaintiff purchased his, and that the accident was occasioned by the running, in the dark, against another train, which was standing still at an intermediate station on the line; yet it was held that the company were liable for the accident, although the plaintiff's ticket was purchased of the treasurer of the society, they having constituted him their agent to contract with those who took the tickets, by giving him such tickets to distribute.[1]

§ 390. The agents or servants of a railroad company cannot, however, commit the company to a liability which they have no power under their charter to contract. The agent of the defendants, who were a railroad corporation, running their cars from New Haven to Plainville, sold the plaintiff a ticket for the fare from New Haven to Collinsville, which was five miles beyond Plainville. The plaintiff, for injuries which he received in a stage running between Plainville and Collinsville, brought his action, upon a special contract to carry safely by railroad and stage from New Haven to Collinsville. The defendants had never, by any corporate vote, expressly authorized or sanctioned contracts similar to that upon which the plaintiff declared, nor had their directors, by any vote, directed any such contract to be made, nor did their charter confer upon them any power to enter into the same. But the plaintiff claimed to have proved that the defendants, for more than six months before, and at the time of the sale of his ticket, had been and were in the daily usage of entering into and fulfilling contracts identically like that alleged in the declaration; that, during that entire period, they had publicly represented and

1 Skinner *v.* The London, Brighton and South Coast Railway Co. 2 Eng. Law and Eq. R. 360.

held themselves out to the community, through their duly authorized agents, and knowingly permitted their agents to represent them, as vested with powers requisite to enter into and fulfil such contracts; that he, the plaintiff, had purchased his ticket upon the faith of such representations; and that, therefore, the defendants should be estopped from denying the obligations which their contract with him purported to create. But the Court held, that the company were not estopped by a contract which neither they nor their agents had any power to make, from showing their incapacity, under their charter, to incur the liability which was sought to be charged upon them.[1]

§ 391. *Their Responsibility for Injuries to Passengers.* And not only has the law taken measures for the security of travellers, by requiring of railroad companies the exercise of the utmost care and skill in the performance of their undertaking; so that the most inconsiderable departure from their duties will render them liable for the consequences; but in its scrupulous care to guard the public from all but the inevitable accidents of travel, it has gone still further, and imposed upon the carrier the *onus* of proving, in case of accident resulting in damage to his passengers, that the damage has resulted from a cause which human skill and foresight could not prevent.[2] Thus, in a case where an accident happened to a passenger on a *railroad*, Lord Denman, Ch. J., instructed the jury, that it having been shown that the exclusive management of the machinery and the railway was in the hands of the defendants, it was presumable that the accident arose from their want of care, unless they gave some explanation of the cause by which it was produced; which explanation the plaintiff, not having the same means of knowledge, could not reasonably be ex-

[1] Hood *v.* The New York and New Haven Railroad Co. 22 Conn. R. 502; S. C. Ib. 1.

[2] Ang. on Carr. § 568.

pected to give.[1] And the same doctrine was recognized in a subsequent English case of injury by collision, in which it was remarked, " This is not the case of two vehicles belonging to different persons running against each other, where no negligence can be inferred against either party in the absence of evidence as to which of them was to blame. But here all the trains belong to one company, and whether the accident arose from the trains running at too short intervals, or from the mismanagement by their servants of any of the trains, or of their officers at the station, in not sending to stop the train that was coming on, they are equally liable. It was not necessary for the plaintiff to trace more specifically where the negligence lay; and if the accident arose from some inevitable fatality, it lay on the company to show it."[2] This presumption of negligence, however, exists only in favor of passengers, injured while lawfully in the course of conveyance by the proprietors of the road as common carriers.[3]

§ 392. The responsibility of the proprietors of railroads for the safety of their passengers, forms, however, no exception to the rule previously noticed,[4] that where the injured party has contributed to the injury by his own carelessness or unauthorized conduct, he shall not recover damages except in case of gross negligence, and wanton or wilful wrong on the part of the proprietors of the road. Thus, where a passenger was taken on the train of a railroad company, to be transported for

---

1 Carpue *v.* The London and Brighton Railway Co. 5 Ad. & Ell. R. (N. S.) 747.

2 Skinner *v.* The London, Brighton and South Coast Railway Co. 2 Eng. Law and Eq. R. 360; and see Holbrook *v.* The Utica and Schenectady Railroad Co. 16 Barb. (N. Y.) Sup. Ct. R. 113; McKinney *v.* Niel, 1 McLean, (Cir. Ct.) R. 540; Stokes *v.* Saltonstall, 13 Peters, (U. S.) R. 181; 13 Curtis, (U. S.) S. C. Decis. 114; Christie *v.* Griggs, 2 Campb. R. 79.

3 Terry *v.* The New York Central Railroad Co. 22 Barb. (N. Y.) Sup. Ct. R. 574.

4 *Ante*, § 345.

a short distance, and was told that the passenger cars were full, and that he must ride in the baggage car, and having entered the baggage car, there commenced playing and scuffling with two fellow-passengers, and in the course thereof ran from the baggage car into the passenger car, and, the train being thrown from the track, rushed out at the forward end of the latter car, and jumped from the platform, by which his leg was broken; it was held, that it was culpable negligence in him to put himself in that position, contrary to the terms upon which he was received as a passenger, which made the leap necessary to escape the peril, and that, consequently, he was not entitled to recover.[1] So a man who should choose to ride on a railroad with his head and arms out of the car window, or who, in passing a dangerous place on the road, should disregard an audible warning by the conductor of the danger of putting his head or limbs outside the car, would not ride like a prudent man, and would have to bear the consequences of his foolhardiness.[2]

---

1 Galena and Chicago Union Railroad Co. *v.* Yearwood, 15 Ill. R. 468.

2 New Jersey Railroad Co. *v.* Kennard, 21 Penn. (9 Harris) R. 203. But it was said in that case, to be the duty of the proprietors of railroads so to construct the windows of their cars, where designed for a road so narrow in places as to be dangerous to projecting limbs, as to prevent passengers from putting their limbs through. And if the car is not so constructed it was said to be the duty of the conductor to give information of the danger at each particular place where there was any exposure to it. A general verbal warning would not be sufficient. "It would be of no service," said the Judge in his charge to the jury, afterwards adopted by the full Court, "to a foreigner ignorant of the language, or to a sleeping passenger, or to a child incapable of reason. The utmost care of a parent or nurse, is insufficient to restrain a child's curiosity to look at things outside. Should either of these be injured by the want of a proper construction of the car, an action would lie for it. Nor would written notice stuck up be any better. There may be passengers who cannot read, and they would of course not be affected by it. Others may get into the car at night, and some might not observe it even in daytime, and neither of these would be chargeable with negligence. At best, however, such notice is too general to be of service. It gives no more than general information, known to everybody without, that injury may result from putting heads or limbs through the windows; and would seldom be recollected at the critical moment."

§ 393. A lunatic was travelling in the cars, upon a railroad, in company with his father, who had paid the fare for both and taken tickets. The father got out at a stopping place, to procure refreshments, leaving his son in the cars, without giving notice to any one of his situation; and while absent the train started. On regaining the cars the father did not find his son where he had left him, the latter having changed his seat. The conductor, in the absence of the father, applied to the lunatic for his ticket, not knowing him to be insane, or that his fare had been paid. The lunatic refusing to deliver his ticket, the conductor caused the train to be stopped, and the lunatic to be put off the cars; in consequence of which the lunatic was run over by another train of cars and killed. The evidence not showing any negligence or want of care on the part of the conductor, but showing great negligence and imprudence in the conduct of the lunatic and his father; it was held, that an action could not be maintained by the personal representative of the lunatic, against the railroad company, under the New York statute, authorizing the recovery of damages in case of death by the wrongful act, neglect or default of another.[1]

§ 394. Where, however, there is a choice of positions upon a railroad, either of which a passenger may lawfully take, the application of this rule does not oblige him to select that which is the least dangerous. In Carroll *v.* The New York and New Haven Railroad Company,[2] the plaintiff was injured by a collision of two trains running in opposite directions. The plaintiff was, at the time of the collision, in the post-office apartment of the baggage car, being lawfully there and with the acquiescence of the conductor. It was a much more danger-

---

[1] Willetts *v.* The Buffalo and Rochester Railroad Company, 14 Barb. (N. Y.) Sup. Ct. R. 585.

[2] Carroll *v.* The New York and New Haven Railroad Company, 1 Duer, (N. Y.) R. 571.

ous location, on the happening of such a collision as took place, than a seat in the passenger cars, and he knew this fact; and had he been in a passenger car, he would not have been injured, unless the collision had been productive of consequences to him not suffered by any one in a passenger car. It was held, that negligence is the violation of the obligation which enjoins care and caution in what we do, and that the plaintiff, not being under an obligation to be more prudent and careful than he was, in contemplation of there possibly being such culpable conduct on the part of the defendants as would endanger his life, if he remained where he was, and his personal safety on any part of the train, and, not being a trespasser, was not to be precluded from his action because he might have selected a position of comparative safety.

§ 395. And though a passenger may have been upon the cars in violation of the rules of the railroad company, yet, if it appears to the jury that these rules have been waived or revoked in his favor, he will nevertheless be entitled to his action for injuries suffered from any want of care on the part of the company. In an action of this description, the evidence tended to show that the reporters for "Bell's Life in London," of whom the plaintiff was one, when going to the races in that capacity, were accustomed to travel free. The plaintiff, acting *bonâ fide* as such reporter, was supplied with a ticket, which bore the name of a person connected with the paper, but not the plaintiff's, and on it were the words, not transferable, and a memorandum that any other person using it than the person named in it would be liable to a penalty, as if he was a passenger who had not paid his fare. Having showed this pass to one of the servants of the defendants at the station, who said it was all right, and opened the door of the carriage for him to enter; it was held, that there was evidence to go to the jury that the plaintiff was lawfully in the carriage, and if the jury were of the opinion that this irregular use of the tickets, however worded, was with the knowledge and permission of the superintendents of the station, who were placed there to regulate such matters, this would be such proof of license as would make it wrong to say the plaintiff was a trespasser in the carriage.[1]

§ 396. *Their Responsibility for Injuries to Persons other than Passengers.* The responsibility of the proprietors of railroads for injuries, occasioned to persons and property not in the course of transportation on their road, is precisely the same as that of the proprietors of any other vehicle upon the common highway; that is, they are liable for the want of ordinary care, skill and diligence on the part of themselves or their servants or agents, unless the party injured has contributed to the injury by the want of ordinary care on his own part; in which case they will not be liable except for gross negligence or intentional wrong.[2] Thus, where a person, while walking upon the track of a railroad, in one of the streets of a city, was struck down and run over by a locomotive and tender, it was held, the proprietors of the road were responsible for no more than ordinary care, and that a charge to the jury that they were bound to exercise the utmost care and diligence was erroneous.[3] Where the law requires that a bell or whistle shall be sounded before crossing any other road, the omission so to do is *primâ facie* proof of negligence, yet, even in such case, it is incumbent on the plaintiff to give some proof tending to show that the injury complained of resulted from the want of a signal, and that he himself was in the exercise of ordinary care, in order to entitle him to recover.[4] And

---

1 The Great Northern Railway Company *v.* Harrison, 26 Eng. Law & Eq. R. 443; and see Collett *v.* The London and North Western Railway Company, 6 Eng. Law & Eq. R. 305.

2 Ante, § 345 *et seq.*

3 Brand *v.* The Schenectady and Troy Railroad Company, 8 Barb. (N. Y.) R. 368; Spencer *v.* The Utica and Schenectady Railroad Company, 5 Ibid. 337; Burton *v.* Railroad Company, 4 Har. (Del.) R. 252.

4 Galena, &c. Railroad Co. *v.* Loomis, 13 Ill. R. 548; and see Wilson *v.* Rochester and Syracuse Railroad Company, 16 Barb. (N. Y.) Sup. Ct. R. 167; Bradley *v.* The Boston and Maine Railroad, 2 Cush. (Mass.) R. 539.

where it appears from the plaintiff's testimony, which is clear, explicit and undisputed, that the negligence and imprudence of the party injured contributed to the injury, the Court may properly nonsuit the plaintiff, instead of submitting the question of negligence to the jury.[1]

§ 397. In an action against a railroad company for running over and killing a slave, where it appeared that the slave was asleep on the track, that the cars were going at their usual speed and at the usual hour, and the engineer, when within a short distance of the slave, attempted to stop the cars by letting off the steam and reversing the wheels, but the impetus which they had received carried them on about seventy yards before they stopped; it was held, that this was not a case of negligence to subject the company to damages. The negroes being reasonable beings, endowed with intelligence, as well as the instinct of self-preservation and the power of locomotion, it was natural and reasonable to suppose, that they would get out of the way, and the engineer was not guilty of negligence because he did not act upon the presumption that they had lost their faculties by being drunk or asleep. If, it was added, the cars are to be stopped, whenever a man is seen walking on the track, lest perchance he may be a deaf mute, and whenever negroes are seen lying on the track, lest they may be drunk or asleep, a knowledge of this impunity would be an inducement to obstruct the highway and render it impossible for the company to discharge their duty to the public, as common carriers. The proximate cause of the slave's death being his own voluntary imprudence, the company were not liable.[2]

---

1 Haring *v.* New York and Erie Railroad Company, 13 Barb. (N. Y.) Sup. Ct. R. 9; and see The Aurora Branch Railroad Company *v.* Grimes, 13 Ill. R. 585; New York and Erie Railroad Company *v.* Skinner, 19 Penn. (7 Harris) R. 298.

2 Herring *v.* The Wilmington and Raleigh Railroad Company, 10 Ired. (N. Car.) R. 402; Richardson *v.* Railroad Company, 8 Rich. (So. Car.) R. 120; Felder *v.* Railroad Company, 2 McMullen, (So. Car.) R. 403; and see Macon and Western Railroad *v.* Davis, 13 Geo. (Cobb) R. 68.

§ 398. *Injuries to Cattle astray upon the Road.* Closely allied to this modification of liability, by the negligence of the party injured, is the principle by which trespassers, injured in the act of trespassing, are denied redress, except where the proprietors of the railroad have been guilty of gross negligence or intentional wrong. This principle has been oftenest applied to cases of cattle injured or killed while straying upon the track of the road. It is well settled, that the proprietors of a railroad are not under obligation to fence their road, to prevent cattle from straying upon it, unless they are required so to do; and, though unfenced, the entry of cattle thereon is a trespass. And, being unlawfully upon the road, the proprietors of the road owe them no duty of care and diligence, and, consequently, their owners are entitled to no remedy, if they fail to receive it. The trespass of the cattle is, in the eye of the law, the trespass of their owners, and subjects them to the rule, which precludes the recovery of damages for injuries occasioned, in the whole or in part, by the plaintiff's wrong.[1]

---

[1] The Tonawanda Railroad Co. *v.* Munger, 5 Denio, (N. Y.) R. 255; S. C. 4 Comst. (N. Y.) R. 349; Tower *v.* Providence and Worcester Railroad Co. 2 R. I. R. 404; Perkins *v.* The Eastern, &c. Railroad Co. 29 Maine R. 307; Vandegrift *v.* Rediker, 2 New Jer. R. 185; Ricketts *v.* Junction Railway Co. 12 Eng. Law and Eq. R. 521, and note; Vanderkar *v.* The Rensselaer and Saratoga Railroad Co. 13 Barb. (N. Y.) Sup. Ct. R. 390; Towns, &c. *v.* Cheshire Railroad Co. 1 Fost. (N. H.) R. 363; Parker *v.* The Rensselaer and Saratoga Railroad Co. 16 Barb. (N. Y.) Sup. Ct. R. 315; Williams *v.* Michigan Central Railroad Co. 2 Mich. R. 259; Great Western Railroad Co. *v.* Thompson, 17 Ill. R. 131; Central Military Tract Railroad Co. *v.* Rockafellow, Ib. 541; Illinois Central Railroad Co. *v.* Reedy, Ib. 580; Langlois *v.* Buffalo and Rochester Railroad Co. 19 Barb. (N. Y.) Sup. Ct. R. 364; The New York and Erie Railroad Co. *v.* Skinner, 19 Penn. (7 Harris) R. 298; Manchester Railway Co. *v.* Wallis, 25 Eng. Law and Eq. R. 373. But see, to the contrary of this rule, Danner *v.* South Carolina Railroad Co. 4 Rich. (So. Car.) R. 329; Kerwhacker *v.* C. C. & C. Railroad Co. 3 Ward & Smith, (Ohio) R. 172. In the latter case, it was held, that the rule of the Common Law of England, requiring the owners of cattle to keep them on their own lands, had never been in force in Ohio, being inapplicable to the circumstances, condition and usages of the people, and also inconsistent with the legislation of the State. That the right of a railroad company to the free, exclusive and unmolested use of its railroad tract, is nothing

And though cattle are lawfully put, or suffered to be upon the public highways, and from thence stray upon the track of

---

more than the right of every land proprietor, in the actual use and occupancy of his lands; and, having left its railroad unenclosed through a country where domestic animals are allowed to be at large, they take the risk of intrusions upon their roads by such animals, and are bound to use, at least, ordinary and reasonable care and diligence to avoid unnecessary injury to them. And where railroad companies are required by statute, or by the terms of their charters, to fence their roads, the rule laid down in the text is inapplicable. See *ante*, § 21. It is the duty, by law, of the Vermont Central Railroad Company, to erect and maintain such fences and cattle-guards upon their road, as will prevent horses and other animals from passing them. Quimby *v.* Vermont Central Railroad Co. 23 Vt. R. 393. Yet, the degree of negligence, of which the corporation will be held guilty, in the omission to discharge this duty, will depend on the locality of their road, and of the particular place, in respect to which the omission occurs; and, it has been held, that it is the duty of the owner of cattle, knowing the exposed situation of the railroad track, to exercise as much care and prudence in keeping his property from exposure, as is required of the company in guarding against injuring them; and if he permits his cattle to run in the highway, knowing that there is no obstruction to their passing from thence upon the railroad track, he is guilty of the same degree of negligence as that with which the company are chargeable, in permitting their road to remain thus exposed. Trow *v.* The Vermont Central Railroad Co. 24 Vt. R. 487; Jackson *v.* Rutland and Burlington Railroad Co. 25 Vt. R. 150. But see Hurd *v.* The Same, Ib. 116. For the rule, in New York, where the proprietors of the railroad are required to fence, see *ante*, § 21. The failure of a railroad company to erect cattle-guards and fences, as required by statute, does not make the company liable for damages to cattle which have entered on the railroad from the owner's land, through the want of a fence, which the owner was bound by agreement to build, and keep in repair. Talmadge *v.* The Rensselaer and Saratoga Railroad Co. 13 Barb. (N. Y.) Sup. Ct. R. 493. And see Clark *v.* Syracuse and Utica Railroad Co. 11 Ib. 112. But see Norris *v.* Androscoggin Railroad Co. 39 Maine R. 273. And so, where the cattle of a stranger are on the lands of another, and pass upon a railroad through a gate left open by the proprietor of such lands, and are killed, the company are not liable. Brooks *v.* The New York and Erie Railroad Co. 13 Ib. 594. But see Nashville, &c. Railroad Co. *v.* Peacock, 25 Ala. R. 299. Neither is a railroad company, by omitting to fence its road, made responsible for injuries done by their locomotive to cattle straying upon their track, through the negligence and carelessness of their owner; and it is held to be gross negligence for a person to suffer his cattle to go at large on the highways, in the immediate vicinity of a railroad, whether the railroad be fenced or not. Marsh *v.* The New York and Erie Railroad Co. 14 Barb. R. 364. And see Perkins *v.* Eastern Railway Co. 29 Maine R. 307. Where a railroad company run their cars, by arrangement, over the road of another com-a railroad, and are there injured or killed by the passage of the cars, they are, nevertheless, trespassers, and their owners will not, under the above rule, be entitled to recover, unless the proprietors of the road have rendered themselves liable by the omission of some duty or precaution required by statute, or have been guilty of gross negligence or intentional wrong.[1]

§ 399. *Injuries to Servants by the Negligence of Fellow-Servants.* Another qualification of the liability of railroad companies is, that they are not answerable to their agents or servants, for injuries received, in consequence of the misfeasance or negligence of other agents or servants, while engaged in the same common service. The earliest reported case, in which this principle was asserted, is that of Priestley *v.* Fowler,[2] determined in the Court of Exchequer, in 1837. The action was brought by a servant against his master, for the

---

pany, who have omitted to comply with the statutes in regard to cattle-guards and fences, the former company is not liable to an injury to cattle straying on the road, in consequence of such omission. Parker *v.* The Rensselaer and Saratoga Railroad Co. 16 Barb. R. 315. In Indiana, under their statutes, railroad companies must fence in their roads, or pay for all animals, straying from adjoining lands without fault of the owner, killed or injured, in running the road, without regard to the question of negligence, misconduct, or inevitable accident. Williams *v.* The New Albany, &c. Railroad Co. 5 Ind. (Porter) R. 111. In Fawcett *v.* North Midland Railway Co. 2 Eng. Law and Eq. R., where the act required the defendants to keep gates constantly closed at road-crossings, and the plaintiff's horse leaped out of his enclosure into the highway, and passed on to the railroad, because the gate was open, it was held, that the horse, as to the defendants, was lawfully on the highway, and, therefore, the plaintiff was entitled to recover. And see Towns *v.* Cheshire Railroad Co. 1 Fost. (N. H.) R. 363; Cornwall *v.* Sullivan Railroad Co. 8 Fost. (N. H.) R. 161; Jones *v.* Waltham, 4 Cush. (Mass.) R. 499; Waldron *v.* Rensselaer, &c. Railroad Co. 8 Barb. (N. Y.) Sup. Ct. R. 390; Terry *v.* New York Central Railroad Co. 22 Ib. 574; Angell on Carriers, § 567 *c*, and note; Gristman *v.* Railroad Co. 1 Kelly, (Geor.) R. 173.

1 The Tonawanda Railroad Co. *v.* Munger, 5 Denio, (N. Y.) R. 255; Clark *v.* Syracuse and Utica Railroad Co. 11 Barb. (N. Y.) Sup. Ct. R. 112.

2 Priestley *v.* Fowler, 3 Mee. & Welsb. R. 1, affirmed in Wigmore *v.* Jay, 5 Exch. Rep. 354; Hutchinson *v.* The York, Newcastle, &c. Railway Co. Ibid. 343.

negligence of another servant, in overloading a *van*, by which the plaintiff was injured. Chief Baron Abinger, in delivering the opinion, remarked, that there was no precedent for such an action, and he rested his opinion, that the master was not liable to such an action, upon the broad ground, that from the mere relation of master and servant, no contract, and, therefore, no duty can be implied on the part of the master, to cause the servant to be safely and securely carried, or to make the master liable for damage to the servant, arising from any vice or imperfection, unknown to the master, in the carriage, or in the mode of loading or conducting it. "The servant," he observed, "is not bound to risk his safety in the service of his master, and may, if he thinks fit, decline any service in which he reasonably apprehends injury to himself; and in most of the cases in which danger may be incurred, if not in all, he is just as likely to be acquainted with the probability and extent of it, as his master. In that sort of employment, especially, which is described in the declaration in this case, the plaintiff must have known as well as his master, and probably better, whether the van was sufficient, whether it was overloaded, and whether it was likely to carry him safely. In fact, to allow this sort of action to prevail, would be an encouragement to the servant to omit that diligence and caution which he is in duty bound to exercise on the behalf of his master, to protect him against the misconduct or negligence of others who serve him, and which diligence and caution, while they protect the master, are a much better security against any injury the servant may sustain by the negligence of others engaged under the same master, than any recourse against his master for damages could possibly afford."[1]

---

1 Chief Baron Abinger also exposed the absurdity of the action, by tracing the alarming consequences of admitting the principle upon which it was sought to be maintained. "He who is responsible by his general duty," was his language, "or, by the terms of his contract, for all the consequences of negligence

§ 400. The rule, thus laid down, was recognized in the case of Skip *v.* The Eastern Counties Railway Company.[1] The plaintiff was a guard in the service of the defendants, a railway company, and his duty was to attach certain carriages to the engine of a goods train, and to dispatch the same within a certain time, so as to avoid collision with a passenger train. In consequence of the plaintiff's not having had another person to assist him, the engine started, threw him upon the rails, and a truck passed over his arm. The plaintiff, for three months previously, had done the same work without any assistance, and without making any objection. It was held, in an action for compensation for the injury, that the plaintiff, having voluntarily undertaken the duty, was not entitled to recover. And, in that case, it was said, that, although the defendants were bound to see that their servants were persons of proper care and skill, yet that they, and not the jury, were judges of the sufficiency of their number; and if the plaintiff thought the duties were more than he could perform, he ought to have left the service, or not to have originally accepted it.

§ 401. In this country, in the States of South Carolina,

---

in a matter in which he is the principal, is responsible for the negligence of all his inferior agents. If the owner of the carriage is therefore responsible for the sufficiency of his carriage, to his servant, he is responsible for the negligence of his coach-maker, or his harness-maker, or his coachman. The footman, therefore, who rides behind the carriage, may have an action against his master, for a defect in the carriage, owing to the negligence of the coach-maker, or for a defect in the harness, arising from the negligence of the harness-maker, or for drunkenness, neglect, or want of skill in the coachman; nor is there any reason why the principle should not, if applicable to this class of cases, extend to many others. The master, for example, would be liable to the servant for the negligence of the chambermaid, for putting him into a damp bed; for that of the upholsterer, in sending in a crazy bedstead, whereby he was made to fall down while asleep, and injure himself; for the negligence of the cook, in not properly cleaning the copper vessels used in the kitchen; of the butcher, in supplying the family with meat of a quality injurious to the health; of the builder, for a defect in the foundation of the house, whereby it fell, and injured both the master and the servant by the ruins."

[1] Skip *v.* Eastern Counties Railway Co. 24 Eng. Law and Eq. R. 396.

Massachusetts, and New York, the same principle has been recognized and affirmed.[1] In Farwell *v.* The Boston and Worcester Railroad Company,[2] the plaintiff, an engineer on the road of the defendants, brought his action for injuries sustained in consequence of the negligence of a switch-tender upon that road. Shaw, C. J., pronounced the action "one of new impression in our Courts," and he considered it an argument against such an action, (though not a decisive one,) that no such action had before been maintained. He held, that the general considerations of policy and security, which render the master responsible to strangers, for the negligence of the servant while in the course of his master's service, do not apply to the case of a servant bringing his action against his own employer, for injuries arising in the course of that employment, "where all such risks and perils, as the employer and the servant respectively intend to assume and bear, may be regulated by the express or implied contract between them, and which, in contemplation of law, must be presumed to be thus regulated." The liability, therefore, if maintained at all, must be maintained on the ground of contract; and, the learned Judge contended, there being no express contract between the parties applicable to this point, the contract must be an implied contract of indemnity, arising out of the relation of master and servant. And, he was of the opinion, that there was nothing in that relation from which such a contract could be inferred; the general rule, resulting from considerations as well of justice as of policy, being, that he who engages in the employment of another for the performance of specified duties and

---

1 Murray *v.* South Carolina Railroad Co. 1 McMullen, (So. Car.) R. 385; Coon *v.* The Syracuse and Utica Railroad Co. 6 Barb. (N. Y.) Sup. Ct. R. 231; S. C. 1 Seld. (N. Y.) Court of Appeals, R. 574; Sherman *v.* The Rochester and Syracuse Railroad Co. 15 Barb. (N. Y.) Sup. Ct. R. 574; Brown *v.* Maxwell, 6 Hill, (N. Y.) R. 592.

2 Farwell *v.* The Boston and Worcester Railroad Co. 4 Met. (Mass.) R. 49, affirmed in Hayes *v.* Western Railroad Co. 3 Cush. (Mass.) R. 270.

services, for compensation, takes upon himself the natural ordinary risks and perils incident to the performance of such services, and, in legal presumption, the compensation is adjusted accordingly. And, he also thought, while from the nature of the relation no such contract can be inferred, there are no grounds of policy or general expediency which should dispose Courts to establish a responsibility aside from what is necessarily implied. For each servant, in a common employment, being an observer of the conduct of the others, can give notice of any misconduct, incapacity or neglect of duty, and leave the service, if the common employer omits such remedy as the safety of all requires; and, by these means, more effectually secure the safety of each, than he could by a resort to the employer for indemnity in every case of loss by the negligence of a fellow-servant. Regarding the case in this light, he considered it the ordinary case of one sustaining an injury in the course of his own employment, in which he must bear the loss himself. And it was accordingly held, that the defendants, having used due diligence in the selection of competent and trusty servants and furnished them with suitable means to perform the service in which they employed them, were not answerable to one of these servants for an injury received by him, in consequence of the carelessness of another.

§ 402. In Ryan *v.* The Cumberland Valley Railroad Company,[1] the plaintiff was a common laborer, employed in digging and filling cars with dirt and such like work, for the purpose of repairing the road, and the work was carried on partly by means of a train of gravel cars, made to dump to either side, and moved by locomotive power. As the hands boarded about four miles distant from their work, it was usual for them to ride to and fro in the gravel cars. While the plain-

---

1 Ryan *v.* The Cumberland Valley Railroad Company, Am. Law Register, August, 1855, p. 598; and see Mitchell *v.* The Pennsylvania Railroad Comny, 1 Am. Law Reg. 717; Strange *v.* McCormick, 10 Am. Law Journal, 398.

tiff and others were thus going to their work, at railroad speed, the accident complained of happened, by the dumping of one of the cars, which seems not to have been hooked, and throwing the plaintiff out upon the road. The Court held, that the accident, having resulted from the carelessness of a fellow-servant, fell within those ordinary risks of the plaintiff's employment, against which the law furnished no protection but by an action against the actual wrongdoer. And they remarked, that a different rule would have very little application to great corporations, for they would immediately act on the maxim, *conventio vincit legem*, and provide against it in their contracts. But it would live to embarrass the more private and customary relations, and be the source of abundant litigation.

§ 403. In Ohio, however, this exemption of the master from liability to his servant for injuries resulting from the carelessness of a fellow-servant, has been limited to the case where both servants stand as equals to each other, and no power or control is given to the one over the other. This limitation is based upon the reason, that the case of an injury to a subordinate by his superior is not the case of an injury by a fellow-servant, but that the superior stands to the subordinate in the place of the master himself, and that, therefore, the master is responsible to him for the negligence and misfeasance of the superior in the same manner that he would be for his own. In Railroad Company *v.* Keary, (Keary the plaintiff below,) a brakeman on one of the trains of the company, brought his action to recover damages for injuries occasioned without his fault, by the conductor of the train, or the superintendent of the road; the plaintiff at the time, by the rules and regulations of the company, being subject to the orders of said conductor and superintendent. The Court held, that he was entitled to recover. And their language was: "This conclusion rests wholly upon the idea that the company, from the very nature of the contract of service, is under obligations to them, as well as they to the company; and that amongst their obligations is that of superintending and controlling, with skill and care, the dangerous force employed, upon which their safety so essentially depends. For this purpose, the conductor is employed, and in this he directly represents the company. They contract for and engage his care and skill. They commission him to exercise that dominion over the operations of the train which essentially pertains to the prerogatives of the owner, and he is in the discharge of a duty which the owner, as a man and a party to the contract of service, owes to those placed under him, and whose lives may depend on his fidelity. His will alone controls every thing, and it is the will of the owner that his intelligence alone should be trusted for this purpose. This service is not common to him and the hands placed under him. They have nothing to do with it. His duties and their duties are entirely separate and distinct, although both necessary to produce the result. It is his to command and theirs to obey and execute. No service is common that does not admit a common participation; and no servants are fellow-servants, when one is placed in control over the other. The servants employed to execute cannot recover for injuries arising from a failure in that part of the business committed to them, because it is their failure and not that of their employer; and although it should happen from the negligence of but one of them, yet each one entered the common service with a knowledge that others must be engaged, and that they were jointly bound to perform what was jointly entrusted to them, and public policy may be concerned in their keeping a supervision over each other for the purpose. But how this can be made to extend to the conductor, over whose acts they have no supervision or control, and are not presumed to be possessed of the requisite intelligence for the purpose, we are wholly unable to see; and equally so, how the safety of travellers is likely to be jeoparded by adding to the responsibility of the conductor for his carelessness, that of the company that places him in power."[1]

§ 404. In Farwell *v.* The Boston and Worcester Railroad Corporation, it was urged upon the Court that the rule, though applicable when two or more servants are in the same department of duty, could not apply where two or more are employed in different departments of duty, at a distance from each other, and where one could in no degree control or influence the conduct of another. But the Court overruled the distinction, with the remark, that "when the object to be accomplished is one and the same, when the employers are

---

1 The Cleveland, Columbus and Cincinnati Railroad Company *v.* Keary, 3 Ohio (Warden & Smith) R., N. S. 201; affirming Stevens *v.* Little Miami Railroad Company, 20 Ohio R. 415. The Court, in the above cases, were evidently inclined to repudiate the rule of Priestley *v.* Fowler altogether, and, in the former case, they referred to Dixon *v.* Ranken, 1 Am. Railway Cases, 569, determined by the highest Court in Scotland, in 1852, in which the English doctrine was rejected, as contrary to the law recognized in that tribunal. In that case, Lord Cockburn, after alluding to the English cases and to the fact that the rule had been pressed upon the Court, not only on account of the weight of the English authority, but for its own inherent justice, remarked: "This last recommendation fails with me, because I think that the justice of the thing is exactly in the opposite direction. I have rarely come upon any principle that seems less reconcilable to legal reason. I can conceive some reasons for exempting the employer from liability altogether, but not one for exempting him only when those who act for him injure one of themselves. It rather seems to me that these are the very persons who have the strongest claim upon him for reparation, because they incur danger on his account, and certainly are not understood, by our law, to come under any engagement to take those risks on themselves." And see Hayes *v.* The Western Railroad Company, 3 Cush. (Mass.) R. 270, where the point decided in the Ohio cases was raised but not passed upon by the Court; also Sherman *v.* The Rochester and Syracuse Railroad Company, *supra*, in which a brakeman brought his action for damages for injuries occasioned by the negligence of the conductor and was held entitled to recover, though it does not appear that the distinction made in the Ohio cases was there directly pressed upon the Court. And see Coon *v.* Syracuse and Utica Railroad Company, 6 Barb. (N. Y.) Sup. Ct. R. 231, where also the distinction was suggested, but not admitted. In Georgia it has been decided that the rule does not apply to a case where the servant who is injured is a *hired* slave. Scudder *v.* Woodbridge, 1 Kelly (Geo.) R. 195.

the same, and the several persons employed derive their authority and their compensation from the same source, it would be extremely difficult to distinguish what constitutes one department and what a distinct department of duty." And they further said, that the rule did not rest upon the opportunity which servants enjoy to provide for their safety or to supervise the conduct of their fellow-servants, as taken for granted in the distinction pressed upon the Court, but upon the absence of any implied contract or obligation of indemnity on the part of the master. And it may be stated as the settled doctrine of the law, that where servants acting in different spheres of employment under the same employer, yet contribute necessary portions of labor or service to the carrying out of one primary object; as, for instance, in the case of a railroad, to the safe and speedy transportation of passengers and freight, they are to be accounted fellow-servants and are subject to the rule above discussed.[1]

§ 405. In Priestley *v.* Fowler, it did not appear that the defendant knew of any vice or imperfection in the carriage, or in the mode of loading or conducting it, by which the accident was alleged to have happened; and the Court refrained from expressing any opinion as to what would have been his liability provided such knowledge had appeared. They, however, remarked, that the master was, without doubt, bound to provide for the safety of his servant in the course of his employment, to the best of his judgment, information and belief. From this and from the dicta and observations scattered through the cases, in which this subject has been considered, it is evident that where the principal is wilfully negligent of his duty to provide suitable vehicles and to employ servants of proper skill and habits, he will be responsible to his servants for the consequences of such negligence. And it has been

---

[1] Coon *v.* Syracuse and Utica Railroad Company, 6 Barb. (N. Y.) Sup. Ct. R. 231.

held, that a railroad company, which, having had notice that one of its locomotive engines was defective and dangerous, yet continued to run it, was responsible to a servant of the company, employed to use it, for an injury sustained by him, without fault on his part, in consequence of such defects.[1]

§ 406. In Tarrant *v.* Webb, the plaintiff, who was at work for the defendant upon a scaffolding, erected by another servant of the defendant, was injured by the falling thereof. The learned Judge, in summing up, told the jury that the defendant would be liable, if he employed incompetent persons to erect the scaffolding, and the jury thereupon returned a verdict for the plaintiff. It did not appear that the defendant knew his servant to be incompetent. A rule *nisi* for a new trial was obtained on the ground of misdirection, for that the employment by the defendant of incompetent persons simply would not make him liable, and at all events would not do so unless he knew of the incompetency, and the plaintiff did not. But *per* Jarvis, C. J.: "It may not be necessary for the other servants to make out that the master *knew* of the incompetency of his servant, but it may be enough to say that he was bound *to use ordinary care to employ competent persons.*" And the Court granted a new trial, because, under the charge of the Judge at *Nisi Prius*, the jury might have been of the opinion that the defendant had taken great care in the selection of the person who erected the scaffolding, and yet that he was incompetent for the work, and so have returned the verdict which they did. The master, it was remarked, cannot *warrant* the competency of his servants.[2]

§ 407. *Injuries resulting in Death.* At common law, an injury resulting in the immediate death of the party injured, fur-

---

1 Keegan *v.* The Western Railroad Company, 4 Seld. (N. Y.) R. 175; Noyes *v.* Smith, 5 Am. Law Reg. 615.

2 Tarrant *v.* Webb, 5 Am. Law Register, 306.

nishes no ground for an action for damages.[1] But recently, by statutes, both in England and in many of the States of this country, the common law, in this respect, has been modified. In England, it is enacted by statute 9 & 10 Vict. c. 93, § 1, that "whensoever the death of a person shall be caused by wrongful act, neglect, or default, and the act, neglect or default is such as would (if death had not ensued) have entitled the party injured to maintain an action, and recover damages in respect thereof, then and in every such case the person who would have been liable if death had not ensued, shall be liable to an action for damages, notwithstanding the death of the person injured, and although the death shall have been caused under such circumstances as amount in law to felony." By section 2, it is further enacted, "That every such action shall be for the benefit of the wife, husband, parent, and child of the person whose death shall have been so caused, and shall be brought by and in the name of the executor or administrator of the person deceased; and in every such action the jury may give such damages as they may think proportioned to the injury resulting from such death to the parties respectively, for whose benefit such action shall be brought; and the amount so recovered, after deducting the costs not recovered from the defendant, shall be divided amongst the before-mentioned parties, in such shares as the jury by their verdict shall find and direct." By section 3, the action for damages must be brought within twelve calendar months after the death of such deceased person. In a case involving the construction of this statute, the question was whether the jury, in giving damages apportioned to the injury resulting from the death of the deceased, to the parties for

---

1 Baker *v.* Bolton, 1 Camp. R. 493; Carey and Wife *v.* The Berkshire Railroad Co.; Skinner *v.* The Housatonic Railroad Corp. 1 Cush. (Mass.) R. 475. In Ford *v.* Monroe, 20 Wend. (N. Y.) R. 210, the plaintiff was allowed to recover for the loss of the service of a child, who was run over and killed; but see the remarks of Metcalf, J., upon this case in Carey and Wife, &c. 1 Cush. (Mass.) R. 478, 479.

whose benefit the action was brought, were confined to injuries of which a pecuniary estimate may be made, or may add a *solatium* to those parties in respect of the mental suffering occasioned by such death; and it was held by the Court of Queen's Bench, that the latter could not be taken into consideration.[1]

§ 408. In an action under a similar statute, in Pennsylvania,[2] the Court allowed the jury to find the damages according to the value of the life lost; and suggested that, in estimating them, they might compute them by the probable accumulations of a man of such age, habits, health and pursuits, as the deceased, during what would probably have been his lifetime; and then added: "I think this would be a fair measure of damages in this case; but if the jury can find a better rule than the one suggested, they are at liberty to adopt it." On a motion for a new trial for misdirection, the charge of the Court was approved, and Lowrie, J., in delivering the opinion of the Court above, remarked: "From our present experience and observation, we are unable to discover any substantial error in the instructions complained of. It would be wrong to limit the value of a man's life by his probable accumulations, for many men make none in a lifetime, and many have arrived at an age when they no longer attempt to make any, and many women never make any; and yet every one is entitled to his life, and we have as yet discovered no standard for its valuation. It is not human possessions that are destroyed, but humanity itself; and as this has no market value, it must necessarily be very much a matter of human feeling. Hard, then, as the task may be, and however uncertain its results, it is to be performed by the jury, aided by the cautions and counsels of the Judge, who has been trained in the consideration of juridical questions. Looking, on the one hand, to

1 Blake *v.* The Midland Railway Company, 10 Eng. Law and Eq. R. 437.

2 Pennsylvania Railroad Co. *v.* McCloskey's Adm'r. 23 Penn. (11 Harris) R. 526.

the dignity of human nature, as it has been assailed, and on the other to the position and rights of the defendant, and considering the dignity of their positions as judges of most sacred right, and their own dignity and responsibility as individuals, and loving mercy even while doing justice, the jury must place a money value upon the life of a fellow-being, very much as they would upon his health or reputation. The law can furnish no definite measure for damages which are essentially indefinite."

§ 409. The act of the State of New York, of December 13, 1847, providing for compensation for wrongful act, neglect or default, limits the damages to be recovered to a just and fair compensation with respect to the pecuniary injury resulting to the wife and next of kin of the deceased; if there is no wife and next of kin of the deceased, there can be no such pecuniary damages to be recovered as the act contemplates.[1]

§ 410. In Massachusetts, the statute is as follows: "If the life of any person, being a passenger, is lost by reason of the negligence or carelessness of the proprietor or proprietors of any railroad, steamboat, stage-coach, or of common carriers of passengers, or by the unfitness or gross negligence or carelessness of their servants or agents in this commonwealth, such proprietor or proprietors, and common carriers, shall be liable to a fine not exceeding five thousand dollars, nor less than five hundred dollars, to be recovered by indictment, to the use of the executor or administrator of the deceased person, for the benefit of his widow and heirs; one moiety thereof to go to the widow, and the other to the children of the deceased; but if there shall be no children, the whole to the widow, and, if no widow, to heirs according to the law regulating the distribution of intestate personal estate among heirs." Of this statute, it has been observed, that it is confined to the death of passengers carried by certain enumerated modes of conveyance.

---

[1] Laws of 1847, p. 575.

A limited penalty is imposed as *a punishment* of carelessness in common carriers. And as this penalty is to be recovered by indictment, it is doubtless to be greater or smaller within the prescribed maximum and minimum, according to the degree of blame which attaches to defendants, and not according to the loss sustained by the widow and heirs of the deceased. The penalty, when thus recovered, is conferred on the widow and heirs, not as damages for their loss, but as a gratuity from the State.[1] In New Hampshire, it has been held, that an indictment to recover the fine imposed by a statute, almost identical with the Massachusetts statute, where the life of a person was lost by carelessness on a railroad, must be against the corporation, and not against the individual stockholders, and must show that there is a surviving relative of the deceased entitled to the fine.[2]

§ 411. *Injuries to Property on the Line of the Road.* The use of fire to generate the motive-power of railroad cars, being an authorized use of that element, any injury which results from its *careful* employment, unless by statute otherwise provided, is *damnum absque injuria*, and does not afford ground for an action. This results from the principle, already discussed, that no person is answerable in damages for the exercise of a lawful authority, unless such damages are the consequence of malice, unskilfulness, or negligence.[3] The authority to use a steam-engine, for the purpose of propelling cars upon a railroad, it has been said, is an authority to emit sparks therefrom; and, if the approved means which science and skill

---

1 Per Metcalf, J., in Carey and Wife *v.* Berkshire Railroad Co., and Skinner *v.* Housatonic Railroad Co. 1 Cush. (Mass.) R. 475.

2 The State *v.* Gilmore, 4 Fost. (N. H.) R. 461; and see Kearney *v.* The Boston and Worcester Railroad Corp. 9 Cush. (Mass.) R. 108. For an application of the rule in case of mutual negligence to actions of this description, see *ante*, § 393; for an application of the rule of Priestley *v.* Fowler, see Sherman *v.* The Rochester and Syracuse Railroad Co. 15 Barb. (N. Y.) Sup. Ct. R. 574.

3 *Ante*, Chap. V.

have invented, are applied to prevent sparks from causing injuries, the proprietors of the road are free from responsibility.[1] Their right to use fire in this way, is as unquestionable as the right of a blacksmith to use it in his business, or the right of any individual to use it in his own house for domestic purposes; and the liability for damages resulting therefrom, is the same in the one case as in the other. The exercise of reasonable or ordinary care and diligence, is all that is required; and, if that requirement be not fulfilled, the proprietors of the road are responsible for the consequences. The question of liability, therefore, is a question of fact, to be determined by the jury, by the application of this test to the circumstances of each particular case.[2] What is reasonable care, must depend, in a great measure, upon the state of things at the time of the accident, taking into the account the force and direction of the wind, the dryness of the weather, and the proximity of combustible materials.[3] In one case, it was said, by reasonable care and diligence, is meant, having engines properly constructed, in good order, with suitable fixtures for preventing injuries by fire; the spark-catchers, such as are known to the company to have been used and approved of, and best calculated to prevent the emission of sparks, while allowing sufficient draft to create steam enough to propel the engine at proper speed; and such care and diligence in using the locomotive

---

[1] Rood *v.* New York and Erie Railroad Co. 18 Barb. (N. Y.) Sup. Ct. R. 80; Moshier *v.* The Utica and Schenectady Railroad Co. 8 Ib. 427.

[2] Boroughs *v.* The Housatonic Railroad Co. 15 Conn. R. 124; Philadelphia and Reading Railroad Co. *v.* Yeiser, 8 Barr. (Penn.) 366; McCready *v.* South Carolina Railroad Co. 2 Strobh. (So. Car.) R. 356; Cook *v.* Champlain Transportation Co. 1 Denio, (N. Y.) R. 91; Ellis *v.* Ports. and Roan. Railroad Co. 2 Ired. (N. Car.) R. 138; Baltimore and Susquehannah Railroad Co. *v.* Woodruff, 4 Md. R. 242; Piggott *v.* Great Western Railway Co. 3 Man. Gr. & Scott, 229; 54 E. C. L. 229; Aldridge *v.* Great Western Railway Co. 3 Man. & Gr. 515; 42 E. C. L. 272.

[3] Per Willard, J., in charging the jury, in Cook *v.* The Champlain Transportation Co. 1 Denio, (N. Y.) R. 97.

upon the road, as would be exercised by skilful, prudent, and discreet persons, having control of the engine, regarding their duty to the company, and having a proper desire to avoid injuring property along the road.[1] In order to entitle the plaintiff to recover for injuries of this kind, it is incumbent upon him to prove the negligence alleged; the *onus* not being upon the defendant to prove the exercise of proper care upon proof of damage by fire.[2]

§ 412. By statute, in Massachusetts, "where any injury is done to a building or other property of any person or corporation, by fire *communicated* by a locomotive engine of any railroad corporation, the said railroad corporation shall be held responsible, in damages, to the person or corporation so injured." In an action under this statute, where a shop, adjoining a railroad track, was destroyed by fire, communicated by a locomotive engine, and, while the shop was burning, the wind wafted sparks from it across a street, sixty feet, upon a house, and set it on fire, whereby it was injured; it was held, that the owner of the house was entitled to recover of the railroad corporation the damages caused by the fire.[3] The statute liability is, however, limited to property of a permanent nature, and creates in the proprietors of the road such an interest as entitles them to effect an insurance thereon in their own behalf.[4]

---

1 Baltimore and Susquehannah Railroad Co. *v.* Woodruff, 4 Md. R. 242.

2 Philadelphia and Reading Railroad Co. *v.* Yeiser, 8 Barr, (Penn.) R. 366; Rood *v.* New York and Erie Railroad Co. 18 Barb. (N. Y.) Sup. Ct. R. 80; Aldridge *v.* Great Western Railway Co. 3 Man. & Gr. 515. But see McCready *v.* South Carolina Railroad Co. 2 Strobh. (So. Car.) R. 356.

3 Hart *v.* Western Railroad Corp. 13 Met. (Mass.) R. 99. And see Lyman *v.* Boston and Worcester Railroad Corp. 4 Cush. (Mass.) R. 288. In the latter case, it was held, that the statute in question, applies to railroads established before as well as since its passage; and extends as well to estates, a part of which is conveyed by the owner, as to those of which a part is taken by authority of law, for the purposes of a railroad.

4 Chapman *v.* Atlantic and St. Lawrence Railroad Co. 37 Maine R. 92.

§ 413. But railroad corporations, being subject to the same rules of law in the conduct of their business, as an individual would be in the same business, any act which, though lawful in itself, would, on account of the time, place, or manner of performing it, amount to a nuisance, if done by an individual, will also be a nuisance when done under the same circumstances by such corporation. Accordingly, where a railroad corporation, by the ringing of their bells, and blowing off steam, and other noises, in the neighborhood of a meeting-house, on the Sabbath, and during the period of public worship, so annoyed and molested the congregation worshipping there, as greatly to depreciate the value of the house, and render the same entirely unfit for a house of religious worship; it was held, that the corporation, in creating that disturbance, were engaged in an unlawful business, and were responsible to the society of the church for the damages which they had thereby occasioned.[1]

§ 414. *The Power of Cities to Regulate the use of Railroads in Streets.* Where the tracks of a railroad are laid, under lawful authority, in the streets of a city, the proprietors, unless legally prohibited, may use thereon locomotive engines propelled by steam; and, consequently, are not liable for mere accidents caused by the fright of horses, occasioned by the smoke and noise arising from the escape of steam, the ringing of signal bells, and the movements of the cars, these being the indispensable accompaniments of this species of motive-power. In the exercise of this right, however, they are bound to use all due precaution to avoid danger to others, and to travel at a rate of speed prudent under the circumstances.[2] The dangers incident to this mode of using the streets of populous cities, make it preëminently fit that such use should be subjected to

---

1 The First Baptist Church, &c. *v.* The Schenectady and Troy Railroad Co. 5 Barb. (N. Y.) Sup. Ct. R. 79.

2 Burton *v.* Railroad Co. 4 Harring. (Del.) R. 252.

strict control and regulation by the cities authorities; and where, therefore, a statute gives such authorities power to *regulate the running of railroad cars* within the corporate limits, this will be held to authorize the entire prohibition of the use of locomotive engines propelled by steam, in any part of the city.[1] Indeed, the language of the High Court of Errors and Appeals in Mississippi, though not called upon to decide that point, was, that the corporation of a city has the power to regulate the mode of propelling cars within its limits, to say whether steam or horse-power shall be employed, and to prescribe the rate at which they may move. "This results," it was said, "from the same principle which authorizes it to control the speed of carriages and of horsemen,—the principle of necessary protection to the safety of its citizens and their property."[2]

§ 415. *Sale of the Road.* Where the interest, which the proprietors of a railroad have in the soil over which it passes, is merely an easement or right of passing and transporting persons or things over the land of another, it cannot be sold, assigned, or taken on execution.[3] But the tangible property and estate of the corporation is alienable like the property of an individual; and where, by the act of incorporation, the land, taken for a railroad, is itself vested in the corporation in fee simple, such land may be transferred, assigned, or sold upon execution.[4] But even in such a case, though the lands and tangible effects of the corporation have been disposed of, the franchise or right of transporting persons and property

---

1 Buffalo and Niagara Falls Railroad Co. *v.* The City of Buffalo, 5 Hill, (N. Y.) R. 209.

2 Donnaher *v.* The State, 8 Sm. & Marsh. (Miss.) R. 649. And see The New Orleans and Carrollton Railroad Co. *v.* The Second Municipality of New Orleans, 1 Robinson, (La. Ann.) R. 128.

3 Ammant *v.* Pittsburgh Turnpike Company, 13 Serg. & R. (Penn.) R. 210.

4 State *v.* Rives, 5 Ired. (N. C.) R. 297; Arthur *v.* The Commercial and Railroad Bank of Vicksburgh, 9 Sm. & Mar. (Miss.) R. 394.

over the road for toll still remains in the corporation, and cannot be sold or assigned without the consent of the power which granted it. And, though the loss of the real estate may be a good cause for the forfeiture of the franchise and the dissolution of the corporation, yet it will not of itself work a forfeiture and dissolution, without prosecution for that purpose on the part of the State.[1]

### 5. *Travel upon Ferries.*

§ 416. A ferry, as we have already seen, forms a part of the public highway, wherever rivers or waters are to be passed in boats; and, therefore, having once been legally established, it becomes the duty of the proprietor to maintain it in a proper manner, and to have suitable ferry-ways, boats and attendants, at all seasonable times, for the accommodation of travellers. As an equivalent for this obligation the proprietor is authorized to exact a toll from those who make use of his ferry; and to the exclusive right of ferriage at the particular place to which this obligation attaches, undisturbed by the competition of rival establishments.[2] Being a part of the highway, any obstruction of the use thereof is a nuisance, and as such renders

---

1 State *v.* Rives, 5 Ired. (N. C.) R. 297; Arthur *v.* The Commercial and Railroad Bank of Vicksburgh, 9 Sm. & Mar. (Miss.) R. 394.

2 Charles River Bridge *v.* Warren Bridge, 7 Pick. (Mass.) R. 344; Fay, petitioner, 15 Ib. 243; Almy *v.* Harris, 5 Johns. (N. Y.) R. 175; Johnson *v.* Hitchcock, 15 Ib. 185; Day *v.* Stetson, 8 Greenl. (Maine) R. 365; Chadwick *v.* Proprietors of Haverhill Bridge, 2 Dane's Abr. ch. 67, art. 4; Blessett *v.* Hart, 2 Willes, R. 512; Tripp *v.* Frank, 4 Term R. 666. In the latter case, however, it was held, that if there be an exclusive ferry from A. to B., this does not prevent persons from going in another boat from A. directly to C., though it lie near to B., provided it be not done fraudulently, as a pretence for avoiding the regular ferry. It is no answer to an action by the owner of a ferry for the disturbance of his right, that the ferryman has neglected his duty, for such a default does not, *ipso facto*, destroy the right to the franchise, which must be impeached by *scire facias*, or *quo warranto*. Peter *v.* Kendal, 6 B. & Cr. 703; and see Cotton *v.* Houston, 4 Monr. (Ky.) R. 288.

the author of it liable to an indictment, and also to an action on the case for damages in favor of any individual who has sustained a special injury by reason of the obstruction.[1]

§ 417. Ferrymen are common carriers and liable as such for the carriage of the goods and persons they receive upon their boats; although whether they are bound either by express contract, or by a contract implied from usage, to receive carriages with their contents on board, and land them at the end of the transit across the river, is, in the absence of any provision in the act creating the ferry, a question for the jury to determine. And for the loss of articles not usually carried across the ferry, and to carry which is not within the ordinary employment of the owners of the ferry, the owners would not be liable; and more especially if the owners had no knowledge thereof, and the compensation was only for the personal emolument of the boatman.[2] But the fact that the State exacts a bond and surety of the ferryman and stipulates for the rates of ferriage, does not in the least impair the common law liability which attaches to the carriage of goods for

---

1 Payne *v.* Patrick, 3 Mod. R. 289; S. C. 1 Salk. R. 12. The discontinuance of a ferry is not, in Virginia, an indictable offence. Carter *v.* Commonwealth, 2 Virg. Cas. 354. An action on the case does not lie for a simple refusal to carry a passenger over a ferry; unless the toll has been paid or tendered, Payne *v.* Patrick, *supra*; in which case the action is maintainable even though the plaintiff has likewise a right by statute to sue for and recover a penalty for such refusal. Wallen *v.* M'Henry, 3 Humph. (Tenn.) R. 245.

2 Story on Bailm. § 496; Angell on Carr. § 82; Smith *v.* Seward, 3 Barr, (Penn.) R. 342; Pomeroy *v.* Donaldson, 5 Missouri R. 36; Cohen *v.* Hume, 1 M'Cord, (S. C.) R. 444; Gardner *v.* Greene, 8 Ala. R. 96; Spivy *v.* Farmer's Adm'r, 1 Mur. (N. C.) R. 339; Fisher *v.* Clisbee, 12 Ill. R. 344; Rutherford *v.* M'Gowen, 1 N. & M. (S. C.) R. 17; Peixotti *v.* M'Laughlin, 1 Strob. (S. C.) R. 468. The owners of a private ferry may so use it, (although on a road not opened by public authority, or repaired by public labor,) as to subject himself to the liability of a common carrier; and he does do so, if he notoriously undertakes, for hire, to convey across the river all persons indifferently, with their carriages and goods. Littlejohn *v.* Jones, 2 M'Mul. (S. C.) R. 365.

him; the bond being intended as only an additional security afforded by the State, because of the public nature of the ferryman's employment.[1]

§ 418. The keeper or owner of a public ferry is bound to transport goods across the stream after nightfall, and a failure to do so, will, in Alabama, subject him to an action, under the statute, without suit upon the bond; but yet, in such actions, the defendant may show the prevalence of high winds, rendering it dangerous; or, that the application was after the usual bedtime, and that the residence was at some distance from the ferry.[2]

§ 419. A ferryman is liable as a common carrier for the safety of a carriage as soon as it is fairly on the slip or drop of the flat, though driven by the servant or owner of the carriage; as it is then, with the horses, in the ferryman's possession, and he must have his flats so made that all drivers, with horses and carriages, may safely enter thereon; and if in making the attempt to enter, the property is lost or injured, the ferryman is liable.[3] It is likewise the duty of the ferrymen to have their boats properly constructed and furnished so as to secure horses and other animals from getting overboard, and, if through the neglect of any suitable precaution such animal is lost, the ferryman is liable, even though he may have committed it to the charge of its owner or his servant, whose mismanagement or unskilfulness contributed to the loss. In such a case the owner or servant is regarded as the agent of the ferryman. But it would seem, that, where the animal is of such a disposition that he cannot be safely transported in a

---

[1] Babcock *v.* Herbert, 3 Ala. R. 392; and see Judge of Wilcox County Court *v.* Pharr, 4 Stew. & Port. (Ala.) R. 332.

[2] Pate *v.* Henry, 5 Stew. & Porter, (Ala.) R. 101; and see Phillips *v.* Bloomington, 1 Iowa R. 498.

[3] Cohen *v.* Hume, 1 McCord, (S. C.) R. 439.

boat, and such that no prudent man would intrust him there, the loss may be attributed to the misconduct of the owner, in improperly putting such an animal on board a boat.[1]

§ 420. The defendant kept a ferry across the Missouri River, and the plaintiff applied to cross the river. The boat was brought up to the bank, and fastened by a chain to a stake driven into the bank, and the driver of the wagon was directed to drive into the boat. The horses entered and drew in the fore wheels of the wagon; but when the hind wheels struck the boat, the stake was broken, and the boat receded from the shore, the hind wheels of the wagon being out over the end of the boat. The driver, being urged thereto by several persons on the shore, dismounted, and cut his fore horses loose from the wagon, and backed the wagon out of the boat into the river. One of the hind horses was drowned, and it was held, that the loss was not occasioned by the act of God. In this case, the jury found, that, by the negligence of the ferryman, he had caused the accident to happen, and thereby produced the state of alarm in which the driver imprudently backed his wagon into the river. The Court said, that neither the plaintiff, nor the driver of his wagon, could be supposed to have the same presence of mind, on such an occasion, as the ferryman.[2]

§ 421. If the ferry be rented, and in the possession of the ferryman as tenant, the owner is not liable for the loss of the goods, in crossing it, delivered to the ferryman. The remedy is against the tenant, because he is, *pro hac vice*, the owner.[3] But if the owner employs one to act as ferryman for a year, and agrees to pay him one third of the profits, as his hire, the

1 Fisher *v.* Clisbee, 12 Ill. R. 344. Ferrymen would not, however, be liable for the loss of slaves under such circumstances. Boyce *v.* Anderson, 2 Peters, (U. S.) R. 154.

2 Pomeroy *v.* Donaldson, 5 Missouri R. 36.

3 Ladd *v.* Chotard, 1 Miner, (Ala.) R. 366; Biggs *v.* Ferrell, 12 Ired. (N. C.) R. 1.

ferryman does not become *the owner;* and if loss is suffered by a third person, he has a right of action against the owner, because the ferryman is his servant, and is doing the work for him.[1]

§ 422. It is sometimes difficult to determine, whether the ferryman is the lessee or agent of the owner, or a partner with him. The defendant, being the owner of a farm and ferry, leased them, by parol, to one H., for the term of one year; the profits and proceeds of the farm to be divided equally between them. H. was to keep and manage the ferry at his own expense of labor, the defendant having put the boat in good repair, and the expense of subsequent repairs to be borne equally between them. It was agreed, that H. should pay the defendant one half the receipts of the ferry weekly, and every week during the continuance of the lease, and should manage the said farm and premises in a careful, prudent and husband-like manner, and allow no one, but a suitable man, to attend the ferry, and be responsible to the defendant for "damages occasioned by wilful misconduct, or neglect in the management of the said farm and premises, and in the management of the said ferry, and the scow and boat." It was held, that by this agreement, H. became tenant of the defendant, both of the farm and ferry, and that the defendant was not responsible for the negligence of H. in so managing the ferry that damage had accrued to the person and property of a passenger in the boat.[2]

§ 423. A custom, that the inhabitants of a certain vill should pass over a ferry toll-free, has been holden good. Such a custom may have a reasonable commencement, as that the inhabitants of the town might have been at the charge of procuring the grant, and, in consideration of that, that one man

---

1 Biggs *v.* Ferrell, *supra.*

2 Felton *v.* Deall, 22 Vt. R. 170. And see Boyce *v.* Anderson, 2 Leigh, (Va.) R. 550; Angell on Carriers, § 588.

should find the boats and enjoy the tolls, but that the inhabitants should be exempt from payment. The interest of the ferryman would be encumbered with this discharge. If toll were extorted from an inhabitant under such circumstances, he might have an action on the case, because there would be a special damage. But in the particular instance which gave rise to these resolutions, judgment was given for the ferryman, the defendant, because he was charged, in an action on the case, for not keeping a boat, which being a general, and not merely a particular damage, was held to be punishable only by indictment.[1] In North Carolina, it has been held, that a power of distress, given in case of refusal to pay toll, is constitutional, and replevin lies for its abuse.[2]

§ 424. Ferry franchises are partly of a public and partly of a private nature. So far as the accommodation of passengers are concerned, they are *publici juris*, and subject to the legislation of the State. Thus laws may be passed to punish neglect or misconduct in conducting the ferries, and to secure the safety of passengers from danger and imposition. But so far as they require capital and produce revenues, they are *privati juris*; and the State cannot take them away, nor deprive their owners of their legitimate rents and profits. The franchise, however, may be forfeited by nonuser or misuser, judicially ascertained; and the government, in the exercise of the sovereign power of eminent domain, may resume the property for public use, on making a just compensation, but not otherwise.[3]

---

1 Payne *v.* Patrick, 3 Mod. R. 289; S. C. 1 Show. R. 257, and 1 Salk. R. 12.

2 The State *v.* Patrick, 3 Dev. (N. Car.) R. 478. Where the defendant has been in the habit of crossing a ferry without paying the toll, the jury may presume that he knows the rates and contracted to pay them, although they were not posted up as they were required to be by the statute. Addison *v.* Hard, 1 Bailey, (S. Car.) R. 431.

3 Benson *v.* Mayor, &c. of New York, 10 Barb. (N. Y.) Sup. Ct. R. 223.

## 6. *Travel upon Navigable Rivers.*

§ 425. Under this head it is proposed to state the rules which vessels are bound to observe towards each other, in traversing the great natural highways of rivers and the ocean. Ships at sea, manifestly require a rule as well as carriages on land. But from the complex character of their evolutions it is impossible to lay one down approaching the simplicity of that which has been treated of as "the law of the road." The combination of circumstances in which two meeting vessels find themselves, may be extensively varied by the state and direction of the wind, and the relative position of the ships towards the wind, and towards each other; and it hence arises that a rule of clearly advantageous operation in one case, becomes useless, or even positively mischievous in another. The rules to be followed by vessels moved by sails are, in England, usually called the "Trinity Rules," as though deriving their force from the Trinity Board; but they are not really enacted by that corporation, being of date older far than its charter.[1]

---

And see The State *v.* The Freeholders of Hudson County, 3 Zabriskie, (N. J.) R. 206.

[1] West. Rev. 61. Prior to the reign of Henry VIII. the Trinity House was a kind of college at Deptford, belonging to a society of seamen, with authority by charter, "to take knowledge of those that destroyed sea-marks." This monarch granted the society a charter to erect themselves into a corporate body, "To consist of all the seamen of the realm;" and the charter recites, "That the brethren of the guild or fraternity, and their successors, shall and may be able, every year, of themselves, to elect, ordain, and successively constitute one master, four wardens, and eight assistants, to govern and oversee the same." And also, "That they may have power and authority forever of granting and making laws and ordinances among themselves, for the relief, increase and augmentation of the shipping of this our realm of England." Shortly before the demise of Charles II. the corporation of the Trinity House, in imitation of many other corporations, and in proof of their loyalty to their sovereign, surrendered into his hands their charter, which was regranted to them by his successor, James II., in the year 1685; and this last is the charter under which the corporation at present enjoys and exercises its several rights. Instead of a master, four wardens, and eight assistants, chosen annually by general election,

They are framed with a view to prevent collision, and, at the same time, to effect this object with the least possible hindrance of the vessels to which they are applied. Being a means

---

James II. ordained that there should be one master, four wardens, eight assistants, and eighteen elder brethren, all of whom, in the first instance, were to be named by himself, and future vacancies were to be filled up by the elder brethren themselves, from among younger brethren, a name given by James I. to brethren of the guild generally, who were also to be selected, and approved of by the elder brethren. The Trinity rules, as recited by the Trinity Board, on the occasion of its promulgating a regulation for steam-vessels, are contained in the following notice: viz.:

NAVIGATION OF STEAM VESSELS.

" *Trinity House, London*, 30*th Oct.* 1840.

" The attention of this corporation having been directed to the numerous severe, and in some instances, fatal accidents which have resulted from the collision of vessels navigated by steam; and it appearing to be indispensably necessary, in order to guard against the recurrence of similar calamities, that a regulation should be established for the guidance and government of persons with the charge of such vessels; and whereas the recognized rule for sailing vessels is,—

" 1. That those having the wind fair shall give way to those on a wind;

" 2. That when both are going by the wind, the vessel on the starboard tack shall keep her wind, and the one on the larboard tack bear up, thereby passing each other on the larboard hand;

" 3. That when both vessels have the wind large, or a-beam, and meet, they shall pass each other in the same way on the larboard hand; to effect which two last-mentioned objects the helm must be put to port; and as steam vessels may be considered in the light of vessels navigating with a fair wind, and should give way to sailing vessels on a wind on either tack, it becomes only necessary to provide a rule for their observance when meeting other steamers or sailing vessels going large;

" Under these considerations, and with the object before stated, this board has deemed it right to frame and promulgate the following rule, which, on communication with the Lords Commissioners of the Admiralty, the elder brethren find has been already adopted in respect of steam vessels in her majesty's service, and they desire earnestly to impress on the minds of all persons having charge of steam vessels the propriety and urgent necessity of a strict adherence thereto; viz.:

" RULE.

" When steam vessels on different courses must unavoidably or necessarily cross so near, that by continuing their respective courses there would be a risk

simply to that end, it follows that they may be at any time violated, when that end would not be subserved by their observance; and cases may, and often do occur, which not only excuse such violation, but which render an adherance to them a fault. There is no law, it has been said, either of the sea or the road, by which a person is justified in adhering to a particular course, when it will be productive of mischief.[1]

§ 426. A vessel that has the wind free, or is sailing before or with the wind, must get out of the way of the vessel that is closehauled, or sailing by or against it.[2] When two vessels approach each other, both having a free or fair wind, the one with her starboard tacks aboard keeps on her course, or, if any change is made, she luffs so as to pass to the windward of the other; or, in other words, each vessel passes to the right.[3] When both vessels are beating to windward, closehauled, on opposite tacks, the vessel on the larboard tack ports her helm and bears away.[4] If the vessels are sailing in opposite courses, both having the wind free, the vessel on the larboard tack ports

---

of coming in collision, each vessel shall put her helm to port, so as always to pass on the larboard side of each other.

"A steam vessel passing another in a narrow channel must always leave the vessel she is passing on the larboard hand.

"By order,

"J. Herbert, Secretary."

1 Handayside *v.* Wilson, 3 Carr. & Payne, R. 538.

2 The Woodrop Sims, 2 Dod. R. 85; The Chester, 3 Hagg. R. 318; Sills *v.* Brown, 9 Carr. & Payne, R. 601; Vennal *v.* Gardner, 1 Crompt. & Mees. R. 21; Jameson *v.* Dunkeld, 12 Moore, R. 148; The Leopard, Davies, 193; Schooner Catherine *v.* Dickinson, 17 How. (U. S.) R. 170; St. John *v.* Paine *et al.* 10 Ib. 557; The Rose, 7 Jurist, 381; The Ann and Mary, Ib. 999; The Harriet, 1 Rob. Jun. R. 182. These rules are binding on fishing vessels, while engaged on their fishing grounds, The Summit, 2 Curtis, (Cir. Ct.) R. 150; and upon pilot boats and other vessels, and in bays and harbors, as well as on the high seas. The Clement, Ib. 363.

3 Lowry *v.* Steamboat Portland, 1 Law Rep. 315. St. John *v.* Paine *et al.* *supra.*

4 Story on Bailm. 383; 42 West. Rev. 65; The Lady Anne, 1 Eng. Law and Eq. R. 670; and see second Trinity Rule, *supra.*

her helm and bears away. The one on the starboard tack holds her course, or slightly puts her helm to port.[1] This rule should govern vessels, too, sailing on the wind and approaching each other, when it is doubtful which is to windward; but if the vessel on the larboard tack is so far to windward that if both persist in their course the other will strike her on the leeward side, abaft the beam, or near the stern, in such case the vessel on the starboard tack must give way, as she can do so with greater facility, and less loss of time and distance than the other.[2] If a vessel closehauled on the starboard tack, and one with a free wind on the larboard tack are coming in an angular direction, and the latter is on the windward side of the track of the former, the helm of the vessel sailing free is starboarded, and she passes to windward, going astern of the other.[3] If, in such case, the one with the wind free is on the leeward side of the track of the other, the helm of the vessel sailing free is ported, and she passes to the leeward, going astern of the other. If the vessels are approaching in a *straight* direction, the vessel sailing free ports her helm and goes before the wind, passing to leeward of the other.[4] The vessel to the windward is to keep away when both vessels are going the same course in a narrow channel, and there is danger of running foul of each other.[5] A vessel with a free course must give way to a vessel beating up to windward, and tacking. If a collision occurs between such vessels, the *onus* of proof lies on the vessel having free course, to show that all

1 Ibid; Third Trinity Rule, *supra;* 3 Kent's Com. 230.

2 Lowry *v.* The Steamer Portland, 1 Law Rep. 318; The Brig Cynosure, 7 Law Rep. 222; Dana's Seaman's Manual, 71; St. John *v.* Paine *et al.* 10 How. (U. S.) R. 557.

3 42 West. Rev. 65.

4 West. Rev. 65; Cases No. 4 and No. 5.

5 Marsh *v.* Blythe, 1 McCord, R. 360.

possible skill was used on her part, and that the collision arose from the fault of the other vessel, or was unavoidable.[1]

§ 427. It was declared in The Harriet, and The Hope,[2] that it was not merely the right, but also, in a certain sense, the duty of a vessel closehauled meeting another free, or of a vessel closehauled on the starboard tack, meeting another also on a wind, to hold her course without deviation. It would be a deviation either to bear up or to throw herself in stays; but if the vessel, though sailing on a bow-line, happened just at the moment to be a little off the wind, it does not appear to be considered any deviation to make such slight change of helm as will enable her to stand on closehauled.[3]

§ 428. These rules have their exceptions in extreme cases, depending upon the special circumstances of the case, and in respect to which no general rule can be laid down or applied. Either vessel may find herself in a position at the time when it would be impossible to conform to them without certain peril to herself, or a collision with the approaching vessel. Under such circumstances, the master must necessarily be thrown upon the resources of his own judgment and skill in extricating his own vessel, as well as the vessel approaching, from the impending peril.[4] Thus a vessel is justified in deviating from the strict rule of navigation in cases of reasonable alarm, especially where the opposing vessel is neglecting her own duty of giving way, in a proper manner.[5] Nor is the privilege conferred upon the vessel closehauled, when meeting with a vessel that has the wind free, to be insisted upon when the existence of the right to exercise it admits of the slightest

---

1 The Baron Holberg, 3 Hagg. R. 215; Moore *v.* Moss, 14 Ill. R. 106; The Gazelle, 10 Jurist, 1065; The Clement, 2 Curtis, (Cir. Ct.) R. 363.

2 1 Rob. Jun. 154, 182; see also The Jupiter, 3 Hagg. R. 320.

3 42 West. Rev. 64.

4 St. John *v.* Paine *et al.* 10 How. (U. S.) R. 557.

5 42 West. Rev. 64; The Friends, 1 Rob. Jun. R. 478; The Rose, 7 Jurist, 381; The Athol, 1 Notes of Cases, 586.

doubt. It was decided in the case of The Traveller,[1] that as *at night* a vessel closehauled on the larboard tack can never be quite sure whether a sail seen approaching her lee bow is close up to the wind or a little from it, it is the duty of the former to port her helm and bear away, even though the other may have the wind quite free. And it seems that it would, *à fortiori*, go hard with a vessel sailing free on the starboard tack, and meeting another with a fair wind also, were a collision to occur which might have been avoided, had not the former pertinaciously clung to her privilege.[2]

§ 429. Indeed, it is no excuse for running into a vessel, that she is out of her place, and that the colliding vessel is in hers, unless it be in the obscurity of a dark night or a dense fog.[3] At other times, circumstances may render it expedient and proper to depart from the rules, for, as has been well remarked, they are all subordinate to the rule prescribed by common sense, and applicable to all cases, under any circumstances, which is, that every vessel shall keep clear of every other vessel, when she has the power to do so, notwithstanding such other may have taken a course not conformable to established usage.[4] In the case of a vessel going so near to a rock or shoal of sand that if she followed the rule she would inevitably become a wreck; the observance of the rule must yield to the still higher consideration of the preservation of property or of human life.[5] Where there has been any departure from the rules, the *onus* of proving its necessity will rest with the party making such departure. Thus, an action for damage brought by the suffering ship, which being closehauled and on the starboard tack, was run foul of by the Celt,

---

1 The Traveller, 7 Jurist, 1094.

2 42 West. Rev. 64.

3 Handayside *v.* Wilson, 3 Carr. & Payne, R. 538; The Hope, 1 W. Rob. R. 157; Hawkins *v.* Dutchess of Orange Steamboat Co. 2 Wend. (N. Y.) R. 452; Moore *v.* Moss, 14 Ill. R. 106; Cummins *v.* Spruance, 4 Harr. (Del.) R. 315.

4 Lowry *v.* Steamboat Portland, 1 Law Rep. 313; The Lady Anne, 1 Eng. L. & Eq. R. 670.

5 The Friends, 1 Rob. R. 469.

which had the wind free, was dismissed, the damaged vessel having, with a view to avoid the collision, worn round and gone to leeward. The Trinity Masters were of the opinion, that, being closehauled, she ought to have continued her course, and that the collision was occasioned by her not having done so.[1] In all cases of doubt, according to a belief traditionary among mariners, the helm is to be ported.[2]

§ 430. If a vessel chooses to avail herself of a particular mode of going down a river, at a particular time, which renders it difficult to escape a collision, she must bear the consequences of a contingency to which she has exposed herself. Thus, a plea in the Admiralty, in a cause of damage, that the ship causing the collision was being warped down the river at the time, and in consequence could not get out of the way, was overruled.[3]

§ 431. Steam-vessels, possessing a propelling power equal to a favorable wind, having it always at command and capable of modification in any direction, must give way to sailing vessels on a wind on either tack, and, therefore, must never cross their bows.[4] Where a flatboat and steamboat were both descending the Mississippi River, and the flatboat was caught in an eddy of the river, which impelled it towards the steamboat, and so produced a collision, it was held, that the latter should have kept further away. It was the duty of her pilot to have foreseen the effect of the eddy upon the flatboat and have avoided it.[5] The rule, however, presupposes that the steamer discovered, or ought to have discovered, the sailing vessel when at a sufficient distance to avoid her, by changing

---

1 The Celt, 3 Hagg. R. 321.

2 42 West. Rev. 64.

3 The Hope, 2 Rob. R. 8; and see *ante*, § 229.

4 The Shannon, 2 Hagg. R. 174; 42 West. Rev. 64; Hawkins *v.* Dutchess of Orange Steamboat Co. 2 Wend. (N. Y.) R. 452; The Columbine, 2 W. Rob. R. 272; St. John *v.* Paine, 10 How. (U. S.) R. 567; Steamboat Co. *v.* Whildin, 4 Harr. (Del.) R. 228; The Leopard, Davies, 193.

5 Fretz *v.* Bull, 12 How. (U. S.) R. 466.

her own course. But where, in the night or in a dense fog, they are brought suddenly and unexpectedly close to each other, and the ordinary rules of navigation will not prevent a collision, it is the duty of each to act according to the emergency, and to take any measure that will be most likely to attain the object.[1] Nor does the rule, under any circumstances, exempt the sailing vessel from the exercise of ordinary care. A sailing vessel having the wind free, and meeting a steam-vessel in an opposite direction, kept on her course, but the steamer ported her helm. A claim for damages, preferred by the sailing vessel, against the steamer in respect of such collision, on the ground, that had the steamer kept on her course the collision would have been avoided, was dismissed with costs. The Court held, that the established principle of navigation, that vessels having the wind free, and meeting each other in opposite directions, rendering a collision probable, should port their respective helms, was applicable in this case, and that the sailing vessel was therefore to blame in not having ported her helm.[2] But it is to be observed that these rules do not apply to changes of course made when the vessels are at a distance and there is no probability of collision.[3]

§ 432. When hailed in a fog, a steamer must back her engines immediately;[4] and when coming down a river in a dark night, a steamer meets a sailing vessel beating up the river, it is the duty of the master to ease her engines and to slacken her speed, until he ascertains the course of the sailing vessel; and in case of collision in the absence of these precautions, the defence that the master of the steamer immediately put her helm to port, in compliance with the Trinity rules,

---

1 Peck *et al.* *v.* Sanderson, 17 How. (U. S.) R. 178, 182.

2 The City of London, 4 Notes of Cases, 40; Flanders on Mar. Law, § 373; but see Newton *v.* Stebbins, 10 How. (U. S.) R. 586.

3 The Propeller Monticello *v.* Mollison, 17 How. (U. S.) R. 152.

4 The Pearth, 3 Hagg. R. 414; see, also, The Rose, 1 W. Rob. R. 274.

will not be sustained.[1] "On the approach of danger," says Mr. Justice McLean, "every officer should be called to the deck, and the master, to whom the vessel is chiefly entrusted, should take the command. I am aware that this has not been required; and I am also aware that the destruction of human life has become so common from collisions of steamboats, that the country look upon them as ordinary occurrences. A vessel cannot be held faultless, when the measures dictated by prudence and necessity are not taken to avoid the collision."[2]

§ 433. If two steamers are meeting on opposite courses, so near each other that there is risk of collision, it is the duty of each vessel to put the helm a-port so as to pass to the right.[3] A steam-vessel passing another in a narrow channel, must always leave the vessel she is passing on the larboard hand.[4] Where the vessels are approaching near each other at an angle, and whether they will meet at the angle depends upon the relative distances and speed of the boats, which no one can calculate or determine, it is their duty to stop and reverse their engines.[5] A custom, among navigators of steamboats on a river, to observe particular situations in ascending and descending, it has been held, will bind such navigators to its observance, and a failure to do so will be at the peril of the owners.[6] Where one steamer is struggling in a narrow and dangerous channel, it is the duty of another not to attempt to pass her if in so doing there is danger of collision.[7]

---

1 The James Watts, 2 Rob. R. 270.

2 Ward *v.* Chamberlain, 5 Am. Law Reg. 330, 342.

3 St. John *v.* Paine, 10 How. (U. S.) R. 557; The Duke of Sussex, 1 W. Rob. R. 274; 42 West. Rev. 66; Lowry *v.* Steamboat Portland, 1 Law Rep. 313; Lockwood *v.* Lashell, 19 Penn. R. 344; Ward *v.* Chamberlain, 5 Am. Law Reg. 330.

4 The Gazelle, 1 W. Rob. R. 274; Trinity Rules, *supra*, note.

5 Ward *v.* Chamberlain, 5 Am. Law Reg. 330.

6 Jones *v.* Pitcher, 3 Stew. & Port. (Ala.) R. 135; Drew *v.* Chesapeake, 2 Doug. (Mich.) R. 33; Myers *v.* Perry, La. Ann. R. 372; Williamson *v.* Barrett, 13 How. (U. S.) R. 101; Moore *v.* Moss, 14 Ill. R. 106.

7 The Rhode Island, 1 Blatch. (Cir. Ct.) R. 363.

§ 434. It is the duty of every steamboat to keep a trustworthy person employed as a look-out; and if there be none such, additional to the helmsman, or if he was not stationed in a proper place, or not vigilantly employed in his duty, it must be regarded as *primâ facie* evidence that the collision was the fault of the steamboat.[1] A steamer, however, is not bound to be furnished with unusual and extraordinary means to discover vessels, which, from their own carelessness in not providing sufficient and proper lights, could not be seen except by the use of such extraordinary precautions. A sailing vessel, it has been said, has no right to neglect proper precautions on her own part, and then throw the responsibility of accident upon the steamer because she has not adopted extraordinary measures to avoid it.[2]

§ 435. By the English Admiralty sailing regulations, made pursuant to the 14 and 15 Vict. c. 79, steam and sailing vessels are required, between sunset and sunrise, to exhibit lights of a certain character, and in particular positions; and, it is enacted, "that if in any case of collision between two or more vessels, it appear, that such collision was occasioned by the non-observance of these regulations, the owner of the vessel, by which any such rule has been infringed, shall not be entitled to recover any recompense whatsoever for any damage sustained by such vessel in such collision, unless it appears to the Court, before which the case is tried, that the circumstances of the case were such as to justify a departure from the rule."[3] In a case, involving a construction of these rules, it was determined, that the statute was imperative, and the

1 The Propeller Genesee Chief *et al.* *v.* Fitzhugh *et al.* 12 How. (U. S.) R. 443; St. John *v.* Paine, 10 Ib. 557; The Emily, 1 Blatch. (Cir. Ct.) R. 236; Ward *v.* Armstrong, 14 Ill. R. 283.

2 Ward *v.* Armstrong, *supra.*

3 The General Steam Navigation Co. *v.* Morrison, 20 Eng. Law and Eq. R. 267; S. C. Ib. 455; The Aliwal, 25 Ib. 602; The General Steam Navigation Co. *v.* Mann, 26 Ib. 339.

regulation must be literally complied with at the peril of the party. It was the case of a sailing vessel at anchor, which, by the regulation, was required to exhibit, between sunset and sunrise, a constant bright light at the masthead. She exhibited a light in the larboard mizzen rigging, but none at the masthead; and, it was held, as it appeared that the collision arose out of the non-observance of the regulation, that she could not recover.[1] Parties navigating vessels are, however, bound to keep a look-out in the same manner as before that statute. And if a collision takes place between two vessels, and the vessel injured is without the light required by the rules made under the act, the vessel inflicting the injury is liable, if the injury could have been prevented by proper care on her part.[2]

§ 436. Previous to the adoption of these regulations, there were, in many English ports, Trinity-House regulations, requiring vessels at anchor, in a navigable river, or port of much commerce, to have a light hung out conspicuously in dark nights;[3] and the New York canal boats are subject to a like regulation.[4] By the act of Congress, also, providing for the better security of the lives of passengers, on board of vessels propelled by steam, it is made the duty of the master and owner of every steamboat, running between sunset and sunrise, to carry one or more signal lights, that may be seen by other boats navigating the same waters, under the penalty of two hundred dollars.[5]

§ 437. The fact, that such statutes and rules exist, shows very plainly that the exhibition of signal lights is to be looked upon as a prudent and proper precaution, the absence of which argues a want of ordinary care. There is, however, no general

---

1 Valentine *v.* Cleugh, 29 Eng. Law and Eq. R. 49.

2 The General Steam Navigation Co. *v.* Morrison, 20 Eng. Law and Eq. R. 267.

3 3 Kent's Com. 230.

4 Rathbun *v.* Payne, 19 Wend. (N. Y.) R. 399.

5 Act of 1838, ch. 191, § 10.

and absolute usage upon this subject. In Carsley *v.* White, the collision occurred after dark, and there was no light burning on the deck of the damaged vessel. Morton, J., who delivered the opinion of the Court, said: "Whether common care and prudence required of the plaintiffs to have a light, and the omission to have it amounted to negligence, must depend upon the darkness of the night, the number and situation of the vessels in the harbor, and all the other circumstances connected with the transaction. This is a question of fact within the province of the jury."[1] And in St. John *v.* Paine,[2] it was held, that a schooner sailing in waters much frequented by other vessels, on a bright starlight night, was not precluded, by her omission to exhibit signal lights, from recovering in an action against a steamer for collision. But in Simpson *v.* Hand, it was held, that the hoisting of a *light* in a river or harbor at night, *amid an active commerce*, was a precaution imperiously demanded by common prudence, and the omission of it was not to be considered otherwise than as negligence, *per se.*[3] So it has been held, that although the Court cannot establish a rule to bind vessels, navigating the high seas, to carry signal lights, yet, where one vessel does so, and another does not, the Court, in case of a collision, will go some way to treat the dark boat as the wrongdoer.[4]

§ 438. A vessel lying in the channel of a port, from necessity, which alone justifies her lying there, is bound, in the night time, to show a light. "Whatever may be the custom," remarks Mr. Justice Ware, in a case of this description, "it appears to me hardly to admit a question, that a vessel, lying in a channel, at the entrance of a harbor, where vessels are often passing and repassing, ought, in the night time, in com-

---

1 Carsley *v.* White, 21 Pick. (Mass.) R. 254.

2 St. John *v.* Paine, 10 How. (U. S.) R. 557.

3 Simpson *v.* Hand, 6 Whart. (Penn.) R. 311.

4 Bark Delaware *v.* Osprey, 2 Wallace, Jr. (Cir. Ct.) R. 268.

mon prudence, to show a light. When she lies out of the channel way, where vessels pass, it may not, perhaps, be required; but if she places herself in the common passage way, though she may have a right to lay there in a case of necessity, certainly it is not demanding too much to require her, while she is occupying the common highway, to give notice, by a light, of her position to others who are passing, and who are entitled, of common right, to a free and unobstructed passage."[1]

§ 439. Where a collision occurred between two steam-vessels, the Ocean and the Santa Claus, on the Hudson River, the former going up and the latter down; and it appeared that the Ocean had but one light, that the night was dark, and the weather thick and cloudy, and that, under these circumstances, a vessel carrying but one light, though moving, appears to an approaching vessel as if at anchor, and her course can be determined only when very near; it was held, that even though the Santa Claus mistook the position of the Ocean, yet, as the want of two lights on the Ocean was calculated to, and probably did mislead, the Santa Claus was not wholly in fault.[2]

§ 440. The rate of sailing is not regulated by any fixed rule, but depends upon the locality and other circumstances. In a dark night or in a dense fog, it is the duty of a vessel to proceed with diminished speed and a vigilant look-out. It would seem, however, that a vessel may be justified in sailing at full speed, even under such circumstances, for the purpose of avoiding the possibility of being run into by reason of the large number of vessels following in her wake.[3] In the case of The Itinerant, the Court said: "It is unquestionably the

---

1 The Scioto, Davies's R. 359, citing Hay *v.* Le Neve, Abbott on Shipping, 230; Jacobson's Sea Laws, 340. And see Kelly *v.* Cunningham, 1 Cal. R. 365; Innis *v.* The Steamer Senator, Ib. 459; Blue Wing *v.* Buckner, 12 B. Mon. (Ky.) R. 246.

2 The Santa Claus, 1 Blatch. (Cir. Ct.) R. 370.

3 The Ebenezer, 2 W. Rob. R. 206.

duty of every master of a ship, whether in an intense fog or great darkness, to exercise the utmost vigilance, and to put his vessel under command, so as to secure the best chance of avoiding all accidents, even though such precautions may occasion some delay in the prosecution of the voyage. It may be, that, for such a purpose, it would be his duty to take in his studding-sails ; but such is the constantly varying combination of circumstances, arising from locality, wind, tide, number of vessels in the track, and other considerations, that the Court cannot venture to lay down any general rule, which would absolutely apply in all cases."[1] In the case of The Europa, it was held, that a steamship going at the rate of twelve and a half knots an hour, in a dense fog, in the track of steamers between England and America, could not, whether such speed was proper or not, avail herself of the plea of inevitable accident, unless she had taken every possible precaution against collision.[2] A neglect, at any time, of due means to check a vessel entering a river or harbor, where there are others lying at anchor, or the omission, on the part of a steamer, to slacken her speed, in ascending a narrow channel thronged with river-craft, is such a fault as will create a case of responsibility for the damages which ensue.[3]

§ 441. Where a steamboat is navigating the waters of a river or harbor, with another vessel in tow, and a collision ensues between the tow and a third vessel, the question may arise, whether the steamboat or the tow is responsible for the damages. In all cases, where the tug is under the direction and control of the master and hands on board of the tow, there is no difficulty in assigning to the latter a responsibility for all

1 The Itinerant, 2 W. Rob. R. 236.

2 The Europa, 2 Eng. Law and Eq. R. 557. And see The Virgil, 2 W. Rob. R. 201 ; The Rose, Ib. 1 ; The Perth, 3 Hagg. R. 414 ; The Iron Duke, 9 Jurist, 476.

3 The Neptune, 1 Dod. R. 467 ; Newton v. Stebbins, 10 How. (U. S.) R. 586.

the damage that may happen through the fault of either vessel. The converse of the proposition will hold equally good, where the tow is under the exclusive direction and control of the tug. But where there is a divided command and direction in the navigation of the vessels, there must necessarily be, in some measure, a divided responsibility assigned to each. What that measure shall be, is a question of some difficulty.[1] In the case of The Express,[2] a steamboat was towing a canal boat in New York Bay, the latter being attached to the former by a hawser from her stern. The vessels were respectively under the direction and control of their own masters and crews. The captain of the tug was warned, before he lashed the canal boat astern, that she steered badly, and ought to be taken alongside. The canal boat took a sheer, and came into collision with, and damaged a third vessel, which was lying at anchor in the bay. It was held, that after the captain of the tug had been warned that the tow steered badly, and requested for that reason to take her alongside, it was his duty in going around among the vessels lying at anchor in the bay, to have kept the strictest watch over the tow, and to have seized the first moment of apparent danger, for the purpose of arresting the sheer, and preventing the collision; and that, not having been in the exercise of this degree of care, he was responsible for the damages, and this, although the master of the tow may likewise have been in fault, and, therefore, properly responsible for the collision.[3]

§ 442. In Sprowl *v.* Hemmingway,[4] a brig, which was towed at the stern of a steamboat, employed in the business of towing vessels in the River Mississippi, below New Orleans, was through the negligence of the master and crew of the steam-

---

1 Per Nelson, J., in The Express, 1 Blatch. (Cir. Ct.) R. 365.

2 Ibid.

3 And see Reeves *v.* The Ship Constitution, Gilpin, (D. C.) R. 579; The Carolus, 2 Curtis, (Cir. Ct.) R. 69.

4 Sprowl *v.* Hemningway, 14 Pick. (Mass.) R. 1.

boat, over whom those in the charge of the brig had no control, brought into collision with a schooner lying at anchor. It was held, that the owner of the brig was not responsible for the damage sustained by the schooner. In this case, the decision turned upon the question, whether the master and crew of the towing steamboat did not stand in such relation to the defendant, as would render him liable for their acts, as being his servants, or in respect of their being engaged in his business or employment. And the Court said, per Shaw, Ch. J.: "Tried by either of these principles, we think that the defendant is not responsible for damages, attributable to the carelessness or want of skill of the master and crew of the towing vessel. They were not the servants of the defendant; were not appointed by him; did not receive their wages or salaries from him; the defendant had no power to remove them; had no power to order or control them in their movements; had no contract with them, but only through them, with the owners of the steamboat, for a participation in the power, derived from the public use and employment of that vessel, by her owners. After making such contract, it was perfectly in the power of the owners of the steamboat, to appoint another master, pilot and crew, and the defendant would have had no cause of complaint."

§ 443. The owners of a ship are not relieved from responsibility in a case of collision, from the circumstance of having a pilot on board, who is appointed by public authority, if the pilot was received on board not under the compulsion of any statute.[1] But where a pilot has been received in obedience to a statutory injunction, enforced by a penalty, the owners are not to be liable for the misconduct or mismanagement of the

[1] The Carolus, 2 Curtis, (Cir. Ct.) R. 69; Yates *v.* Brown, 8 Pick. (Mass.) R. 23; Snell *v.* Rich, 1 Johns. (N. Y.) R. 305; Burry *v.* Donaldson, 4 Dallas, (Penn.) R. 206; The Neptune, 1 Dod. R. 467.

pilot.[1] "If the master cannot navigate without a pilot, except under a penalty, is he not, under the compulsion of law, to take a pilot? And, if so, is it just that he should be answerable for the misconduct of a person, whose appointment the provisions of the law have taken out of his hands, placing the ship in the hands and under the conduct of the pilot? The consequence is, that there is no privity between them."[2] Even in the tribunals of another country, the rights of parties are to be determined by the law of the port where the collision occurs; and if such collision results from the mismanagement of pilots, compulsorily received, the owners of the vessels will not be responsible.[3]

§ 444. Where a pilot has been compulsorily received on board a vessel, all the responsibility attaches to him under all the circumstances, while within his pilot grounds; and it is no part of the duty of the master to interfere with the management, except in the extreme case of the utter incapacity of the pilot, and for the preservation of life and the property under his care.[4] If, however, there is an interference on the part of the master and his crew, and the collision occurs by reason thereof, or partly by reason thereof, the owners will be responsible for the damages, provided the master or his crew were at fault. And an interference, as distinguished from a suggestion, is the doing that which the pilot alone ought to have done. It has, therefore, been held, that a hail from any of the crew on the look-out to alter the helm, if such advice be

---

1 Smith *v.* Condry, 1 How. (U. S.) R. 28; The Maria, 1 Rob. R. 95; The Protector, Ib. 45; The Diana, Ib. 131; The Agricola, 2 Ib. 10; The Creole, Legal Intelligencer of May 7, 1852; The Christiana, 2 Hagg. R. 183.

2 Carruthers *v.* Sydebotham, 4 M. & S. R. 77. But see Attorney-General *v.* Case, 3 Price, R. 302.

3 Smith *v.* Condry, 1 How. (U. S.) R. 28.

4 The Lochlibo, 1 Eng. Law and Eq. R. 651. And see Cook *v.* Parhan, 24 Ala. R. 21.

adopted by the pilot as a proper measure in his own judgment, will exonerate the owners; otherwise, if the advice be adopted by the pilot, unthinkingly, and on the mere report of the look-out.[1] So, if the collision results partly from the defect of the vessel or its anchor, the owner will be responsible.[2]

§ 445. It is a general principle of maritime law, that a vessel under sail must avoid one at anchor, provided the anchorage be properly taken up. But if the place of anchorage be an improper place, the owners of the vessel which is injured must abide the consequences of a collision, unless other circumstances alter the equity of the case. An anchorage in the channel or thoroughfare of a river, is an improper place, and can only be justified by absolute necessity. Where a steamer, by user, has acquired the right to pass upon a particular passage way to a wharf, it is for the jury to decide whether other navigators, under the circumstances, are bound to know that there is such a passage way, and where it is. The fact, however, that a vessel is anchored in an improper place, does not excuse other vessels from the observance of ordinary care and skill, and if, through want of such care and skill, a collision occurs, the colliding vessel will be responsible for the damages.[3] An anchored vessel is also bound to be securely anchored. A commander of a ship was condemned in Admiralty, in a cause of damage, the collision having been occasioned by his anchoring too near the damaged vessel, and with only one anchor, when, in consequence of the weather being squally and tempestuous, she should have been anchored with more than one.[4] The owners of a vessel, disabled by the

1 Ibid. And see Snell *v.* Rich, 1 Johns. (N. Y.) R. 304; The Montreal, 24 Eng. Law and Eq. R. 580; The Diana, 1 W. Rob. R. 131.

2 The Massachusetts, 1 W. Rob. R. 371; The Creole, Legal Intelligencer of May 7, 1852.

3 Strout *v.* Foster, 1 How. (U. S.) R. 89; Knowlton *v.* Sanford, 32 Maine R. 148; Steamboat United States *v.* The Mayor, 5 Missouri R. 230.

4 The Massachusetts, 1 W. Rob. R. 71; The Volcano, 2 Ib. 337; Vantine *v.* The Lake, 2 Wallace, Jr. (Cir. Ct.) R. 52.

negligence of its crew, are answerable for damage done by its accidentally drifting against another vessel.[1]

§ 446. Where a collision takes place between two vessels at sea, which is the result of inevitable accident, without the negligence or fault of either party, each vessel must bear its own loss.[2] In answer to the question, "What is inevitable accident?" Dr. Lushington uses the following language: "Inevitable accident, in the absolute and strict sense of the term, very seldom takes place. 'Inevitable' must be considered as a relative term, and must be construed not absolutely, but reasonably, with regard to the circumstances of each particular case. In the strict sense of the term, there are very few cases of collision that can be said to be inevitable; for it is almost always possible, the bare possibility considered, to avoid such an occurrence. But the import of the words 'inevitable accident,' in my view, is this,—where a man is pursuing his lawful avocation in a lawful manner, and something occurs which no ordinary skill or caution could prevent, and, as the consequence of that occurrence, an accident takes place."[3]

§ 447. Where a collision occurs between two vessels from the negligence or fault of both parties, neither party can, at common law, recover for damages sustained.[4] The principle is applicable to collisions between ships at sea, to the same extent and under the same qualifications, as to collisions between carriages upon the common highway.[5] In Admiralty, in cases of

---

1 Secombe *v.* Wood, 2 M. & Rob. R. 290.

2 Steinback *v.* Rae, 14 How. (U. S.) R. 532; The Woodrop Sims, 2 Dod. R. 83; Broadwell *v.* Swigert, 7 B. Mon. (Ky.) R. 39; 3 Kent's Com. 231.

3 The Europa, 2 Eng. Law and Eq. R. 557.

4 Kent *v.* Elstob, 3 East, R. 18; Vanderplank *v.* Miller, 1 Moo. & Malk. R. 21; Lock *v.* Seward, 4 C. & Payne, R. 106; Vennall *v.* Gardner, 1 Crompt. & Mees. R. 21; Simpson *v.* Hand, 6 Whart. (Penn.) R. 311; Barnes *v.* Cole, 21 Wend. (N. Y.) R. 188; Halderman *v.* Beckwith, 4 McLean, (Cir. Ct.) R. 286; Barrett *v.* Williamson, Ib. 589; S. C. 13 How. (U. S.) R. 101; The Brig Verruna *v.* Clark, 1 Texas R. 30; Kelly *v.* Cunningham, 1 Cal. R. 365.

5 *Ante*, § 345 *et seq.*

collision where the fault is mutual, the damages are equally divided between the colliding vessels.[1] The rule applies, however, only where they are both in fault, at the time, and in the acts, which produced the injuries.[2] And, it has been said, that the rule is subject to modification, where the faults are egregiously unequal; "for a slight fault on one side would not justify a destructive retaliation on the other, even at the same time."[3] Whether this be so or not, where both vessels are to blame, a Court of Admiralty will order the vessel most to blame to pay all the costs. That was the decree in the case of Rogers *v.* Brig Rival. "Upon the facts of this case," said Sprague, J., "and the answers of the experts, it appears that both vessels were to blame. In such case, it is the settled doctrine of the Admiralty, that the whole damage should be equally divided between the two vessels. I think the Rival was most in fault, and that she ought, therefore, to bear all the costs."[4]

§ 448. When collision occurs, the suffering ship should receive from the other colliding vessel every assistance in its power to render. It is held to be a suspicious circumstance, when effort has not been made to help the damaged vessel; and the owners of the Celt, though not otherwise in fault, were condemned in all costs and expenses of the suit, because the master made no attempt to save the ship run down.[5]

§ 449. Causes of collision are *communis juris.* Hence a Court of Admiralty has jurisdiction to entertain a suit between two foreign vessels, where the collision occurred within the territorial waters of the sovereign under whose commission it sits.

---

1 The Woodrop Sims, 2 Dod. R. 85; Hay *v.* Le Neve, 1 Bell's Com. 579–582; 2 Shaw's Scotch Appeal Cases; Jacobson's Sea Laws, 328; Ward *v.* Chamberlain, 5 Am. Law Reg. 330; The Scioto, Davies's R. 359.

2 Ralston *v.* The State Rights, 1 Crabbe, (Cir. Ct.) R. 22.

3 Ibid.

4 Rogers *v.* Brig Rival, 9 Law Rep. 28.

5 The Celt, 3 Hagg. R. 321.

In the case of The Johann Friederich, a protest against the jurisdiction of the Court, on the ground, that both the vessels were the property of foreign owners, and that the collision occurred whilst they were in the prosecution of their respective voyages on the high seas, was overruled, it appearing that the place of collision was on the English coast, within the jurisdiction of the Court of Admiralty,—causes of collision being *communis juris.*[1] In these causes of collision between foreign vessels, the judgment of the *forum rei sitæ*, where the proceeding is *in rem*, is of universal obligation, and absolutely conclusive.[2] The same principle applies in such cases equally to movable property as to immovable. *Immobilia ejus jurisdictionis esse reputantur, ubi sita sunt.* Whatever the Court having jurisdiction of the subject-matter determines, will be held valid in every country where the same question comes directly or indirectly in judgment before any foreign tribunal.[3]

---

1 The Johann Friederich, 1 W. Rob. R. 35; Abbott on Shipping, (5th Am. ed.) 314.

2 Story's Conflict of Laws, p. 495.

3 Flanders on Maritime Law, § 385; Angell on Carriers, § 610. The author takes this occasion to acknowledge his indebtedness to the books above cited, in the entire preparation of the preceding sections, and to refer the reader to them for a more extended examination of this subject than a work on the Law of Highways seemed to call for. The following explanation of sea-phrases used in the preceding sections, is taken from "The Seaman's Manual," by Davis, as quoted in 42 West. Rev. 69:—

*Bear-up*, or *bear-away*—To put the helm *up*, (or to the windward or weather side,) and keep a vessel away to leeward.

*Closehauled*—*On a bow line*—*On a wind*—Applied to a vessel which is sailing with her yards braced up, so as to get as much as possible to the windward.

*Free*—*Large*—Applied to a vessel sailing with a fair wind.

*Larboard*—The left side of a vessel looking forward.

*Lee*—The side opposite to that from which the wind blows. *A-lee*—The situation of the helm when the tiller is put to the lee side.

*Leeway*—What a vessel loses by drifting to leeward.

*Luff*—To put the helm down, (or to the lee side,) so as to bring the ship nearer to the wind.

*Port*—Used instead of larboard. To port the helm, is to put the tiller to the larboard side.

*Starboard*—The right side of a vessel looking forward. To starboard the helm, is to put the tiller to the starboard side.

*Stays*—*In stays*—The situation of a vessel when she is staying, or going from one tack to the other.

*Tack*—To put a ship about, so that from having the wind on one side, you bring it round on the other by the way of her head; the opposite of wearing. A vessel is on the *starboard tack*, when she has the wind on her starboard side; and, on the *larboard tack*, when she has the wind on her larboard side.

*Wear*—To turn a vessel round, so that from having the wind on one side, you bring it upon the other, carrying her *stern* round by the wind. In tacking, the same result is produced by carrying a vessel's *head* round by the wind.

# INDEX.

[References are to the Sections.]

A.

## D.

E.

F.